BLACKBIRD™

BOOK 1 | THE GREAT BEAST

WRITER SAM HUMPHRIES

ARTIST JEN BARTEL

LAYOUT ARTIST PAUL REINWAND

COLORIST TRIONA FARRELL

CHAPTER 1 COLORS BY JEN BARTEL AND NAYOUNG WILSON

LETTERER JODI WYNNE

DESIGNER DYLAN TODD

EDITOR JIM GIBBONS

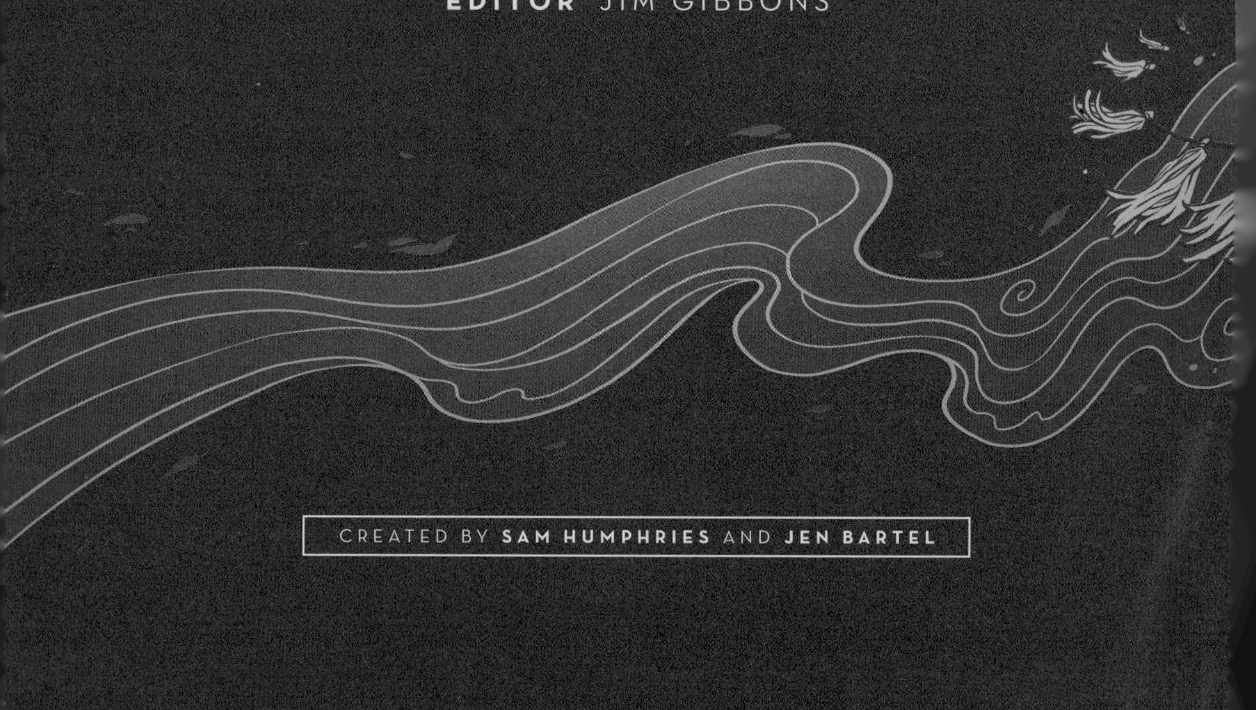

CREATED BY **SAM HUMPHRIES** AND **JEN BARTEL**

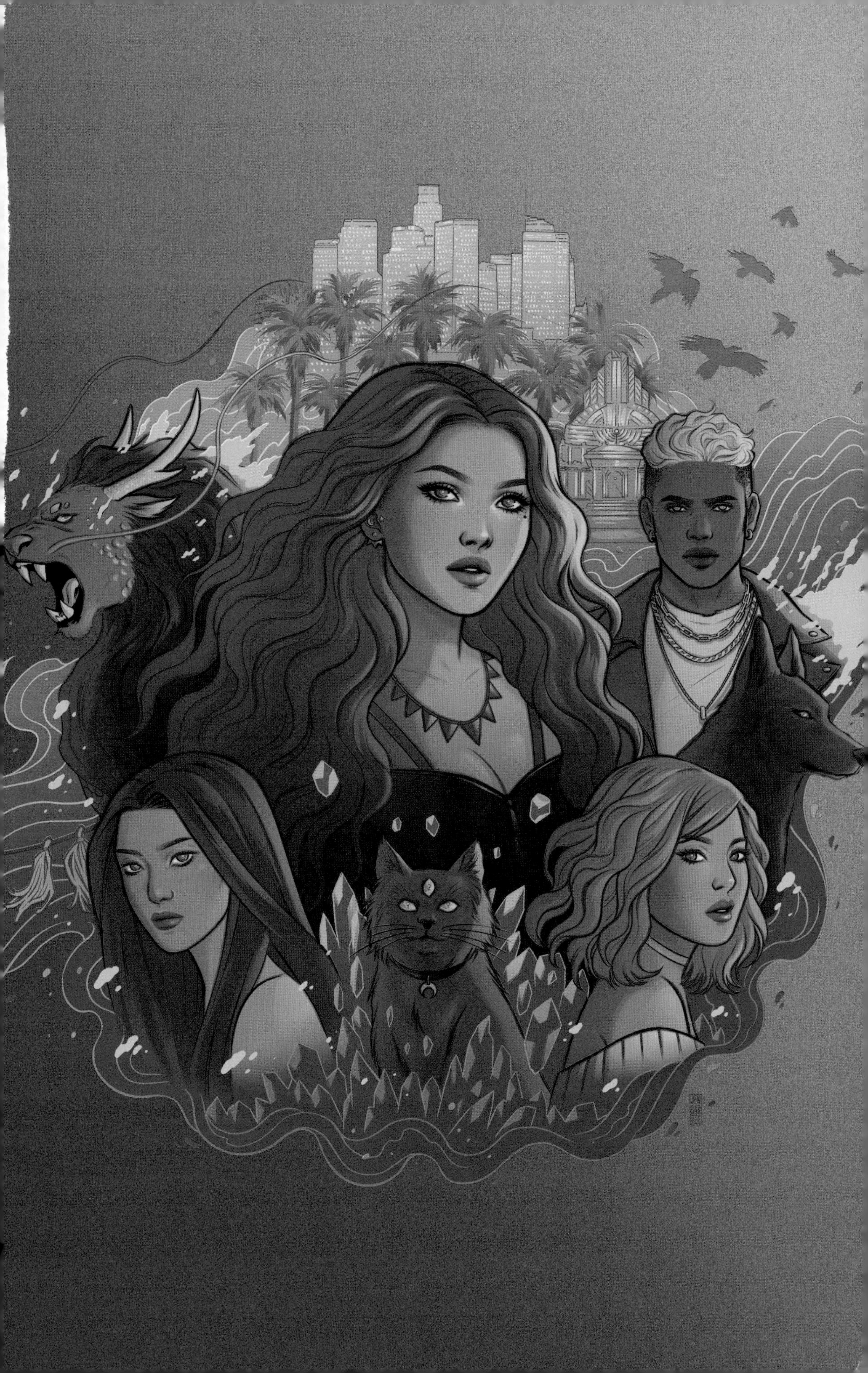

To Hopey, the original crazy baby.
— Sam

To Tyler, Frejya, Eden, and most of all, Stella.
— Jen

SPECIAL THANKS:
Kris Anka, Alisa Bendis, Brian Bendis, Marguerite Bennett,
Andy Khouri, Irene Koh, Bryan Lee O'Malley, Jeanine Schaefer,
and the incredible team that brought this book to life.

ROBERT KIRKMAN
CHIEF OPERATING OFFICER

ERIK LARSEN
CHIEF FINANCIAL OFFICER

TODD McFARLANE
PRESIDENT

MARC SILVESTRI
CHIEF EXECUTIVE OFFICER

JIM VALENTINO
VICE PRESIDENT

ERIC STEPHENSON
PUBLISHER

COREY HART
DIRECTOR OF SALES

JEFF BOISON
DIRECTOR OF PUBLISHING PLANNING
& BOOK TRADE SALES

CHRIS ROSS
DIRECTOR OF DIGITAL SALES

JEFF STANG
DIRECTOR OF SPECIALTY SALES

KAT SALAZAR
DIRECTOR OF PR & MARKETING

DREW GILL
ART DIRECTOR

HEATHER DOORNINK
PRODUCTION DIRECTOR

NICOLE LAPALME
CONTROLLER

IMAGECOMICS.COM

BLACKBIRD, VOLUME 1. MAY 2019.

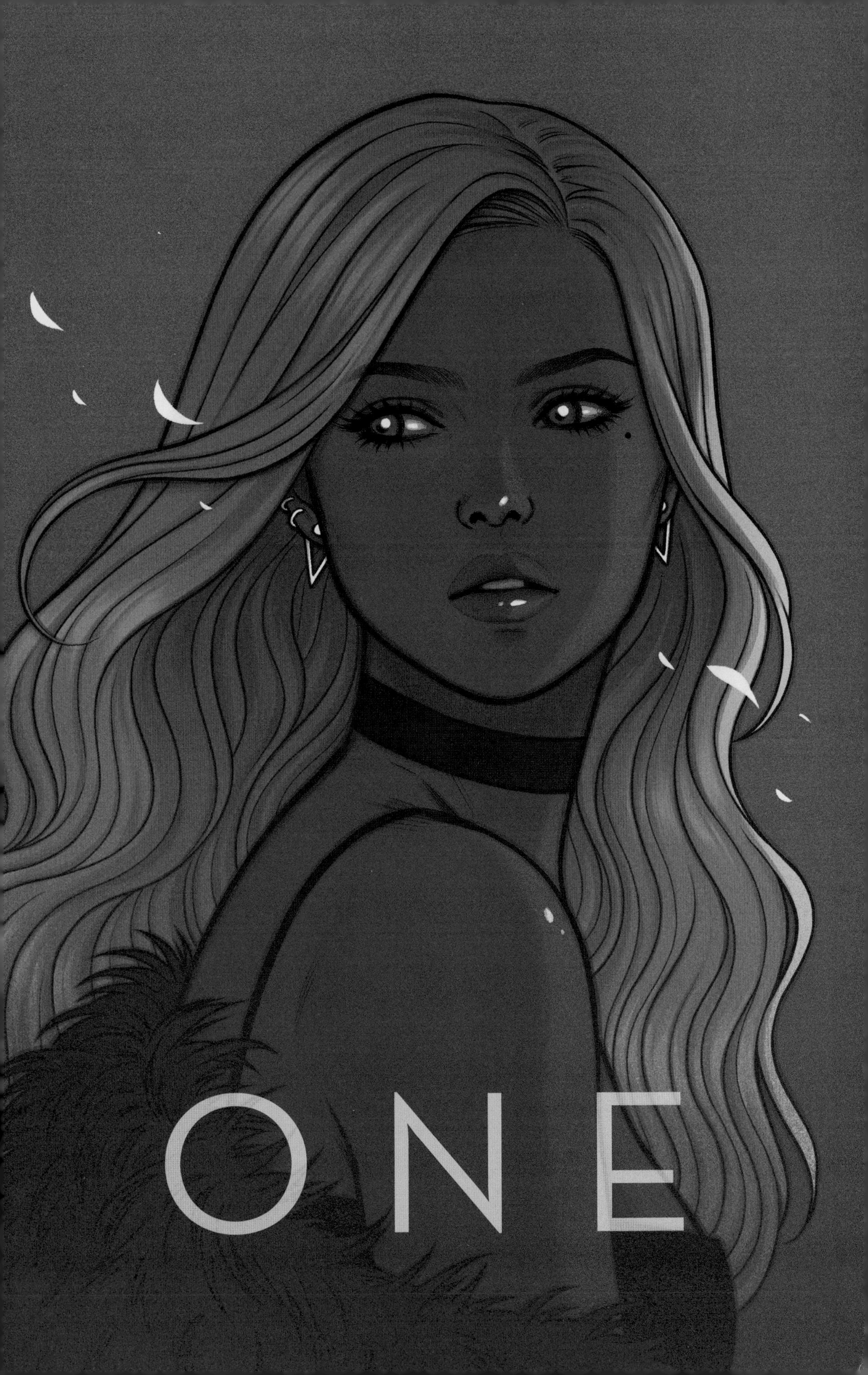
ONE

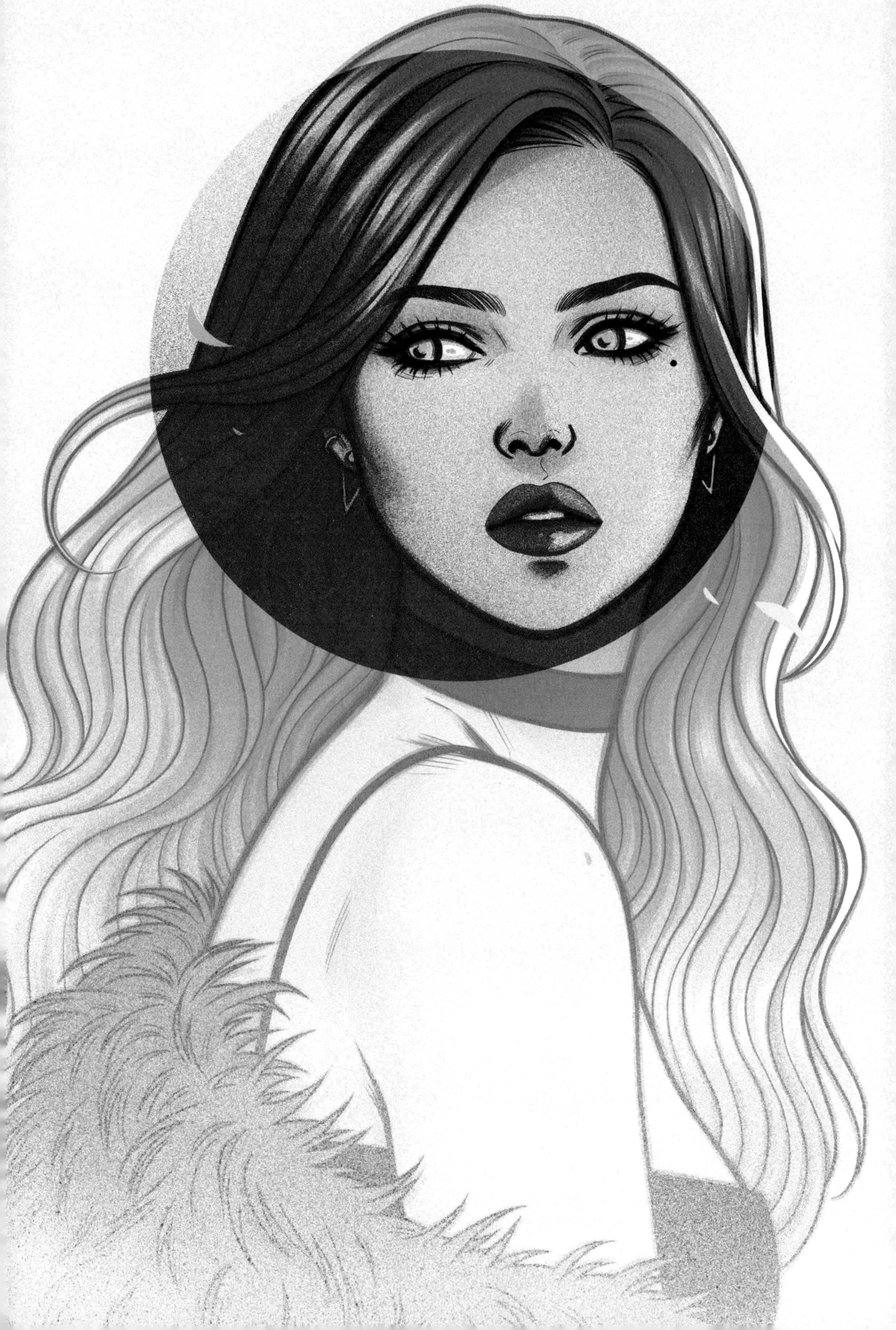

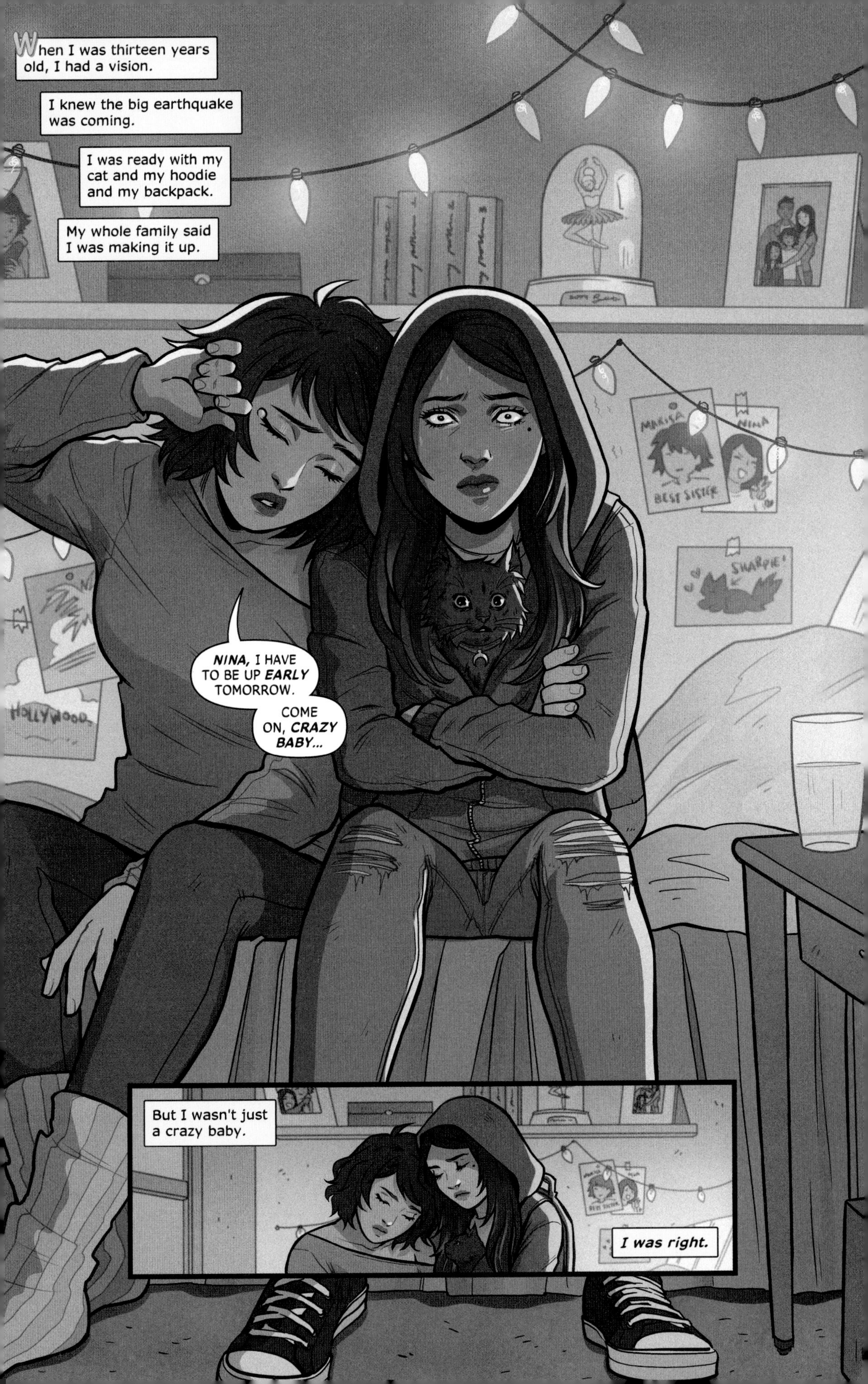
When I was thirteen years old, I had a vision.
I knew the big earthquake was coming.
I was ready with my cat and my hoodie and my backpack.
My whole family said I was making it up.
MARISA
NINA
BEST SISTER
SHARPIE!
HOLLYWOOD
NINA, I HAVE TO BE UP EARLY TOMORROW.
COME ON, CRAZY BABY...
But I wasn't just a crazy baby.
I was right.

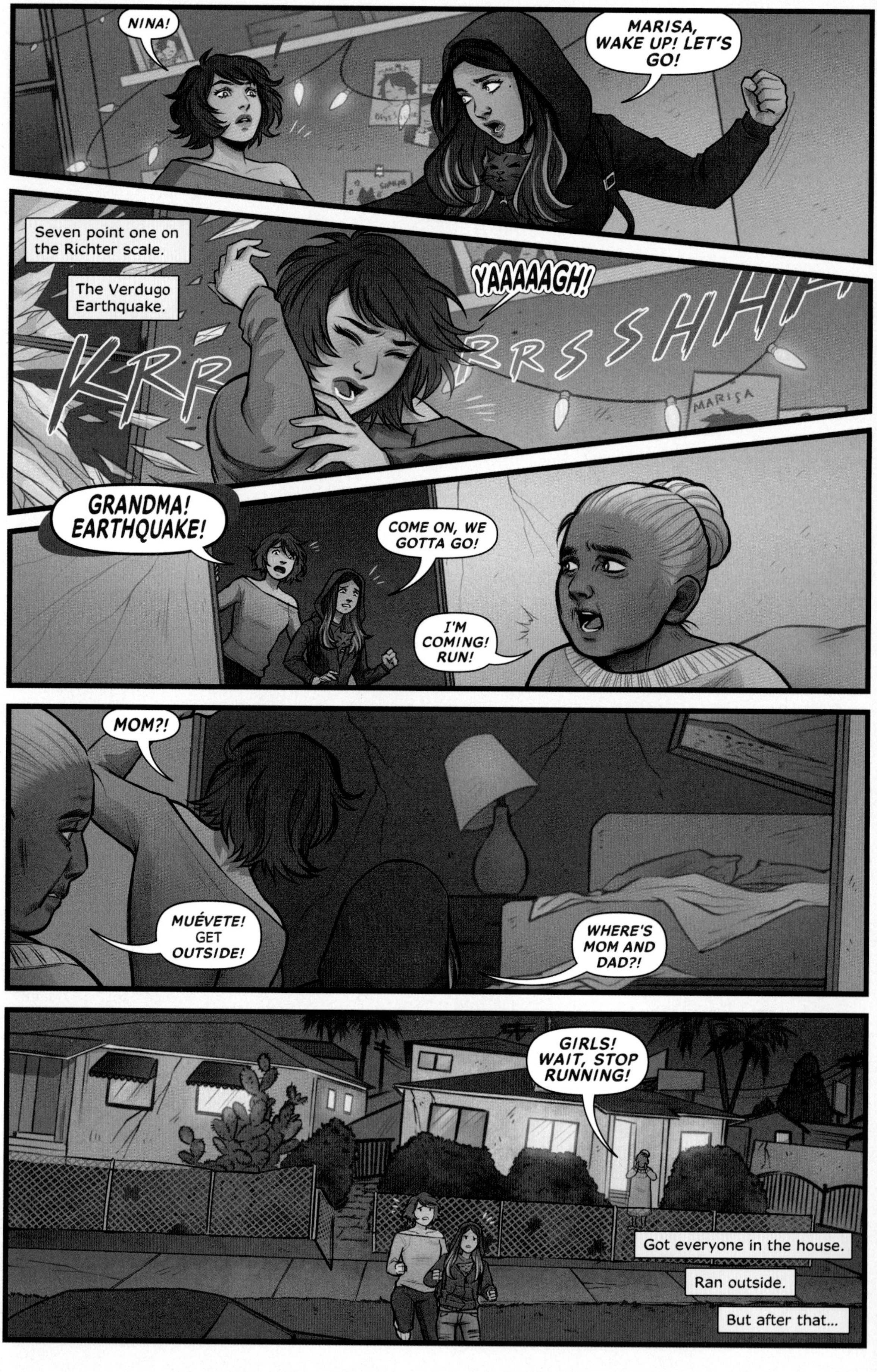
NINA!
MARISA, WAKE UP! LET'S GO!
Seven point one on the Richter scale.
The Verdugo Earthquake.
YAAAAAGH!
KRRRRSSHHH
MARISA
GRANDMA! EARTHQUAKE!
COME ON, WE GOTTA GO!
I'M COMING! RUN!
MOM?!
MUÉVETE! GET OUTSIDE!
WHERE'S MOM AND DAD?!
GIRLS! WAIT, STOP RUNNING!
Got everyone in the house.
Ran outside.
But after that...

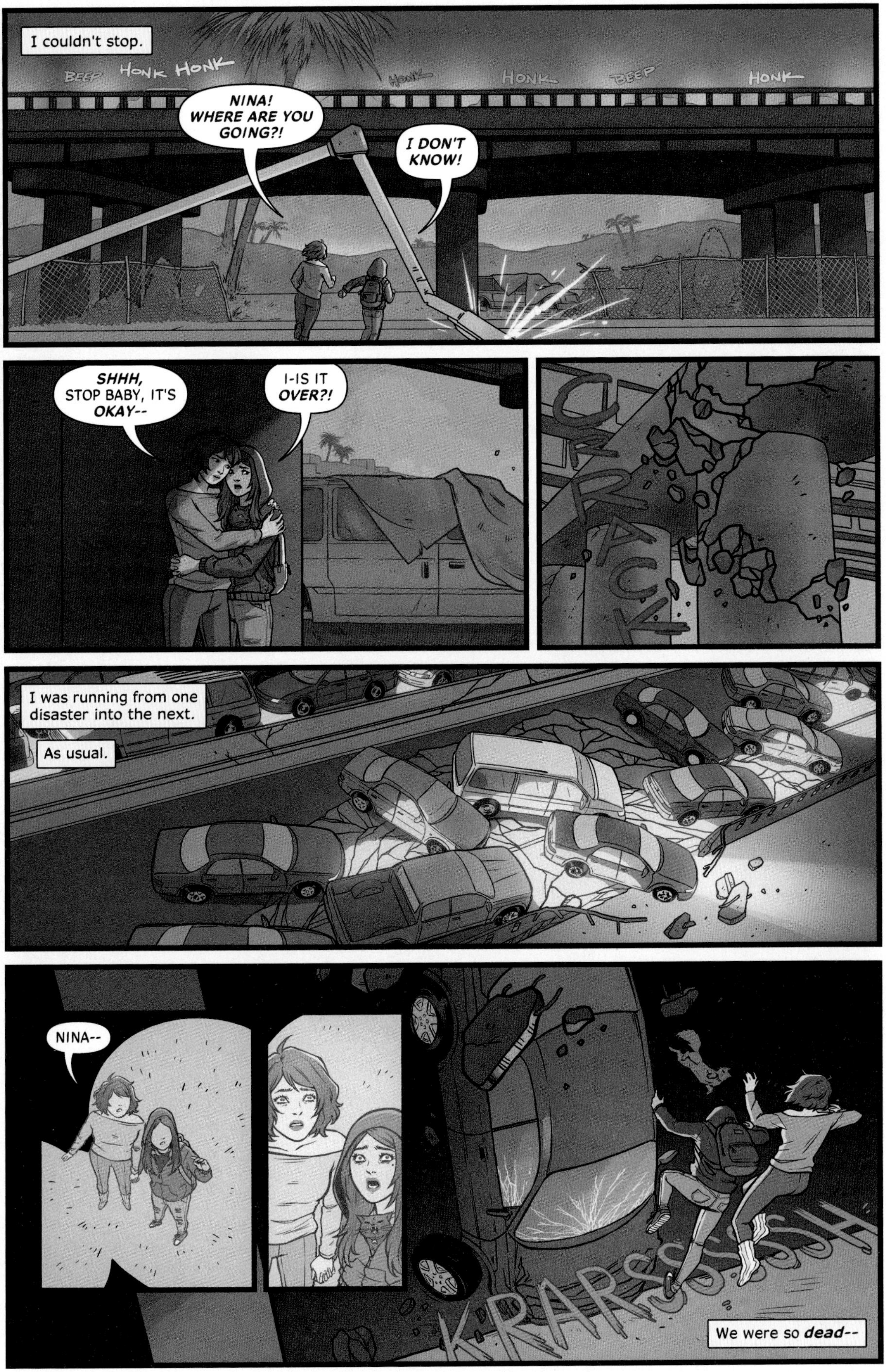
I couldn't stop.
BEEP HONK HONK
HONK HONK BEEP HONK
NINA! WHERE ARE YOU GOING?!
I DON'T KNOW!
SHHH, STOP BABY, IT'S OKAY--
I-IS IT OVER?!
CRRACK
I was running from one disaster into the next.
As usual.
NINA--
KRARSSSSSH
We were so dead--

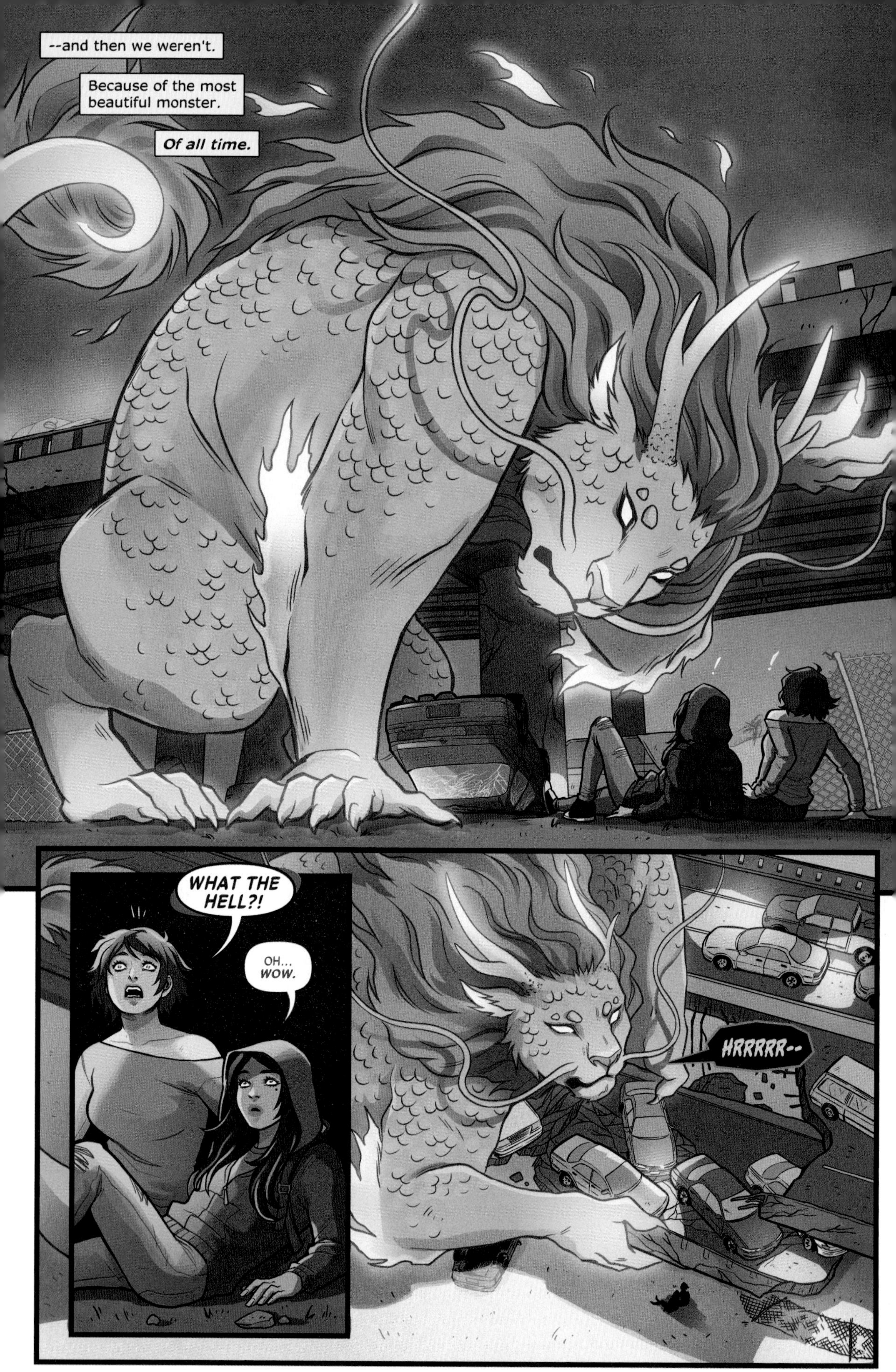
--and then we weren't.
Because of the most beautiful monster.
Of all time.
WHAT THE HELL?!
OH... WOW.
HRRRRR--

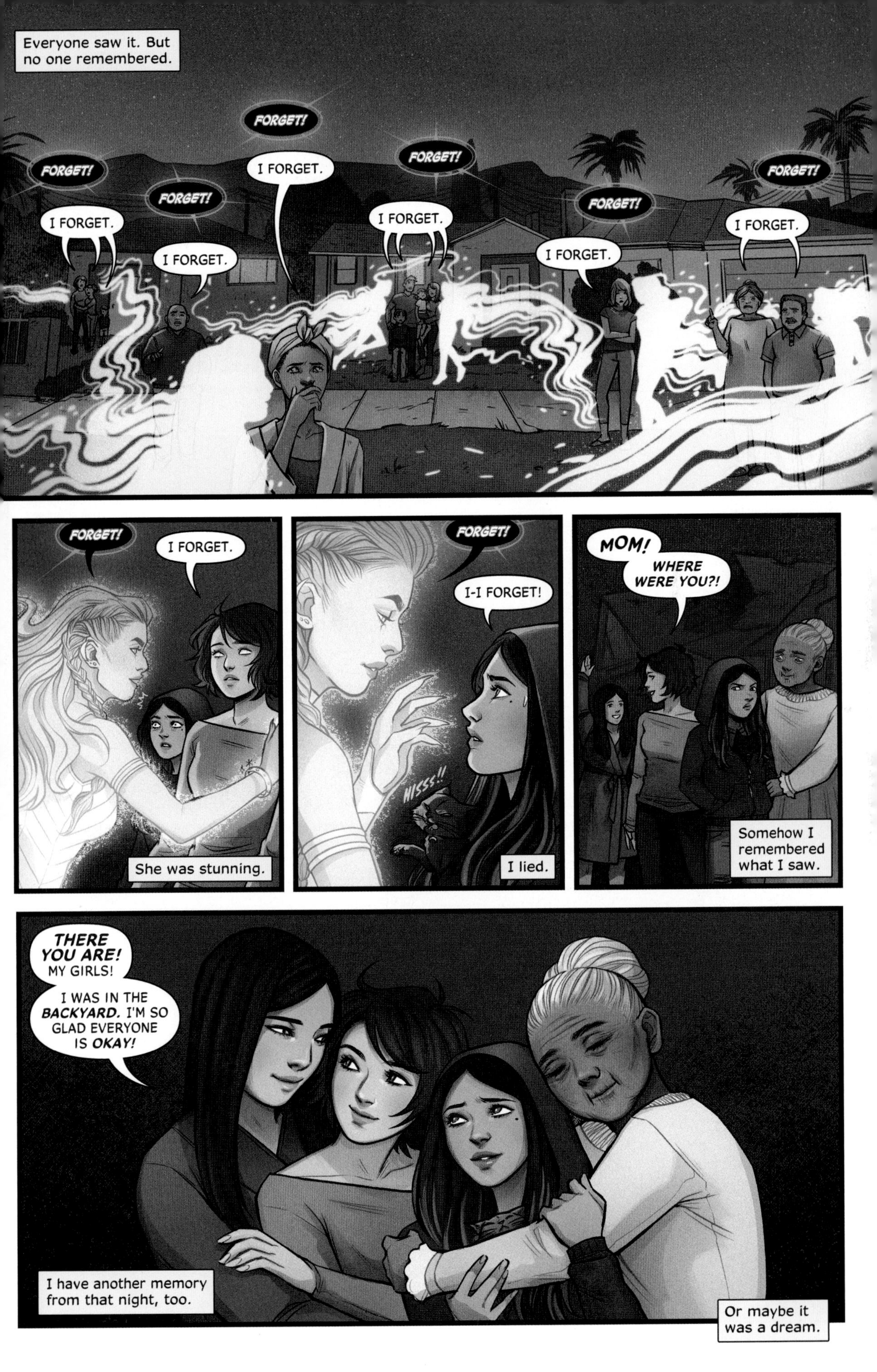

Everyone saw it. But no one remembered.
FORGET!
I FORGET.
FORGET!
I FORGET.
FORGET!
I FORGET.
FORGET!
I FORGET.
FORGET!
I FORGET.
FORGET!
I FORGET.
FORGET!
I FORGET.
She was stunning.
FORGET!
I-I FORGET!
HISSS!!
I lied.
MOM!
WHERE WERE YOU?!
Somehow I remembered what I saw.
THERE YOU ARE! MY GIRLS!
I WAS IN THE BACKYARD. I'M SO GLAD EVERYONE IS OKAY!
I have another memory from that night, too.
Or maybe it was a dream.

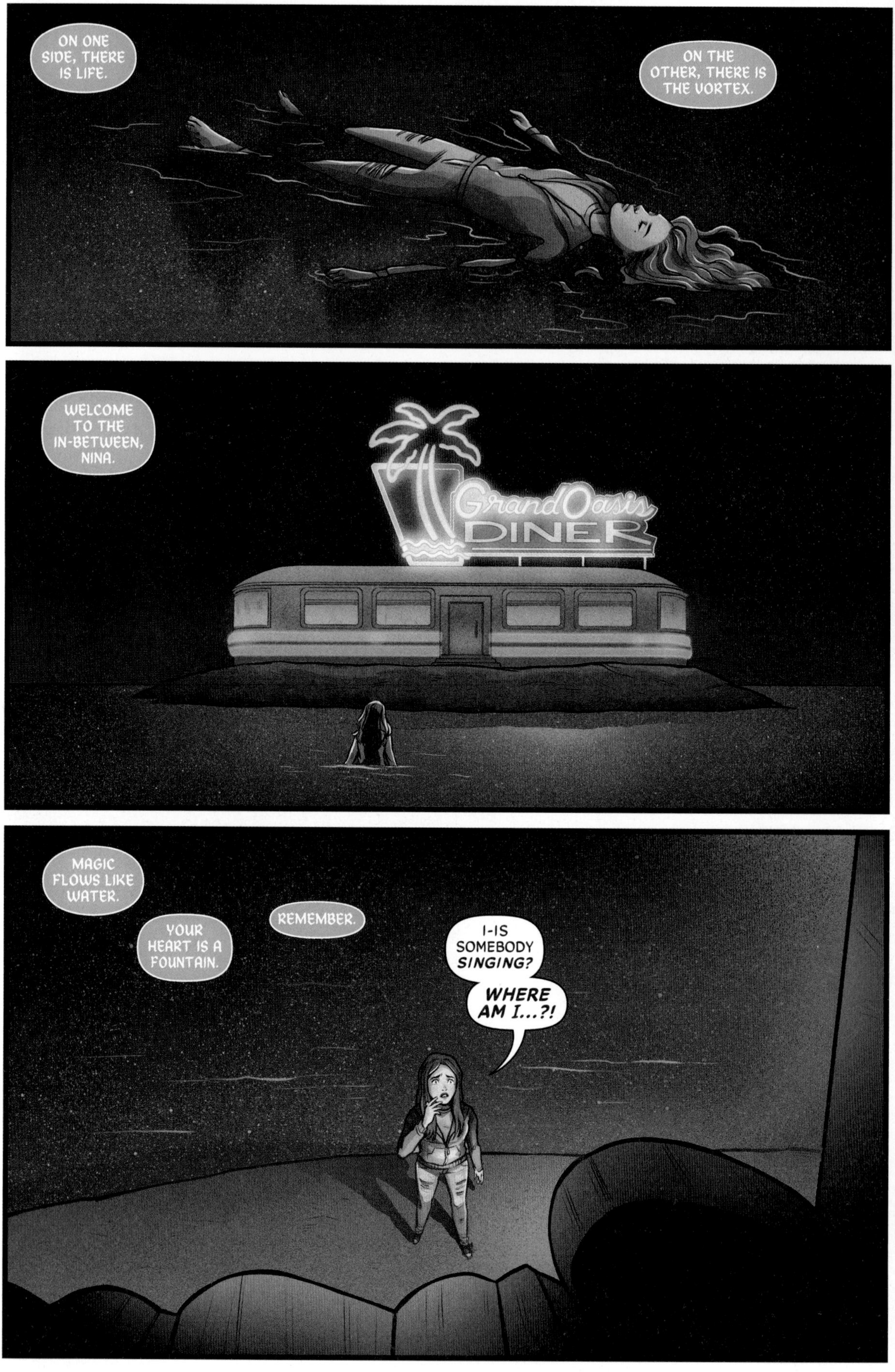
ON ONE SIDE, THERE IS LIFE.
ON THE OTHER, THERE IS THE VORTEX.
WELCOME TO THE IN-BETWEEN, NINA.
Grand Oasis
DINER
MAGIC FLOWS LIKE WATER.
YOUR HEART IS A FOUNTAIN.
REMEMBER.
I-IS SOMEBODY *SINGING?*
WHERE AM I...?!

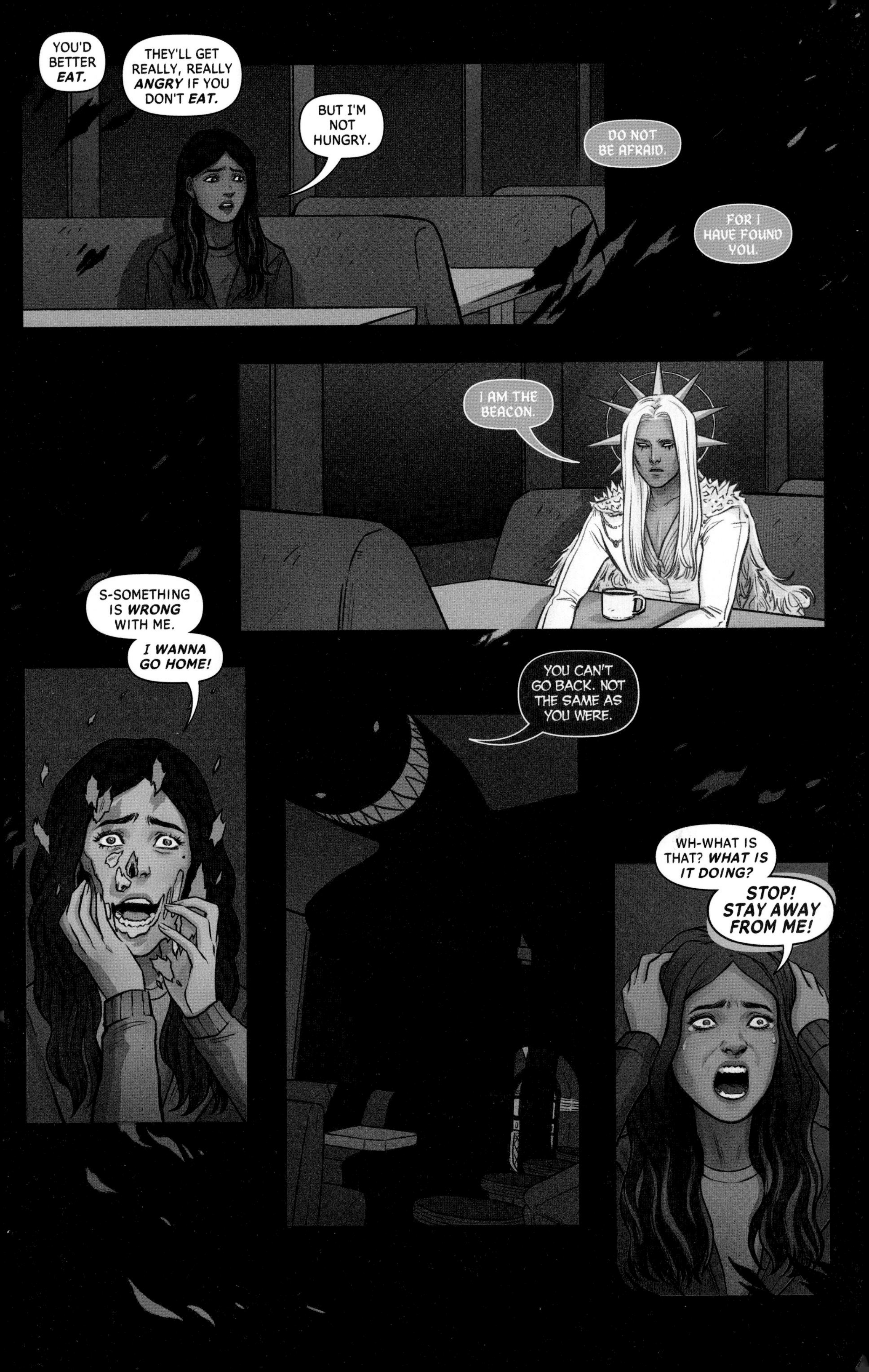
YOU'D BETTER *EAT.*
THEY'LL GET REALLY, REALLY *ANGRY* IF YOU DON'T *EAT.*
BUT I'M NOT HUNGRY.
DO NOT BE AFRAID.
FOR I HAVE FOUND YOU.
I AM THE BEACON.
S-SOMETHING IS *WRONG* WITH ME.
I WANNA GO HOME!
YOU CAN'T GO BACK. NOT THE SAME AS YOU WERE.
WH-WHAT IS THAT? *WHAT IS IT DOING?*
STOP! STAY AWAY FROM ME!

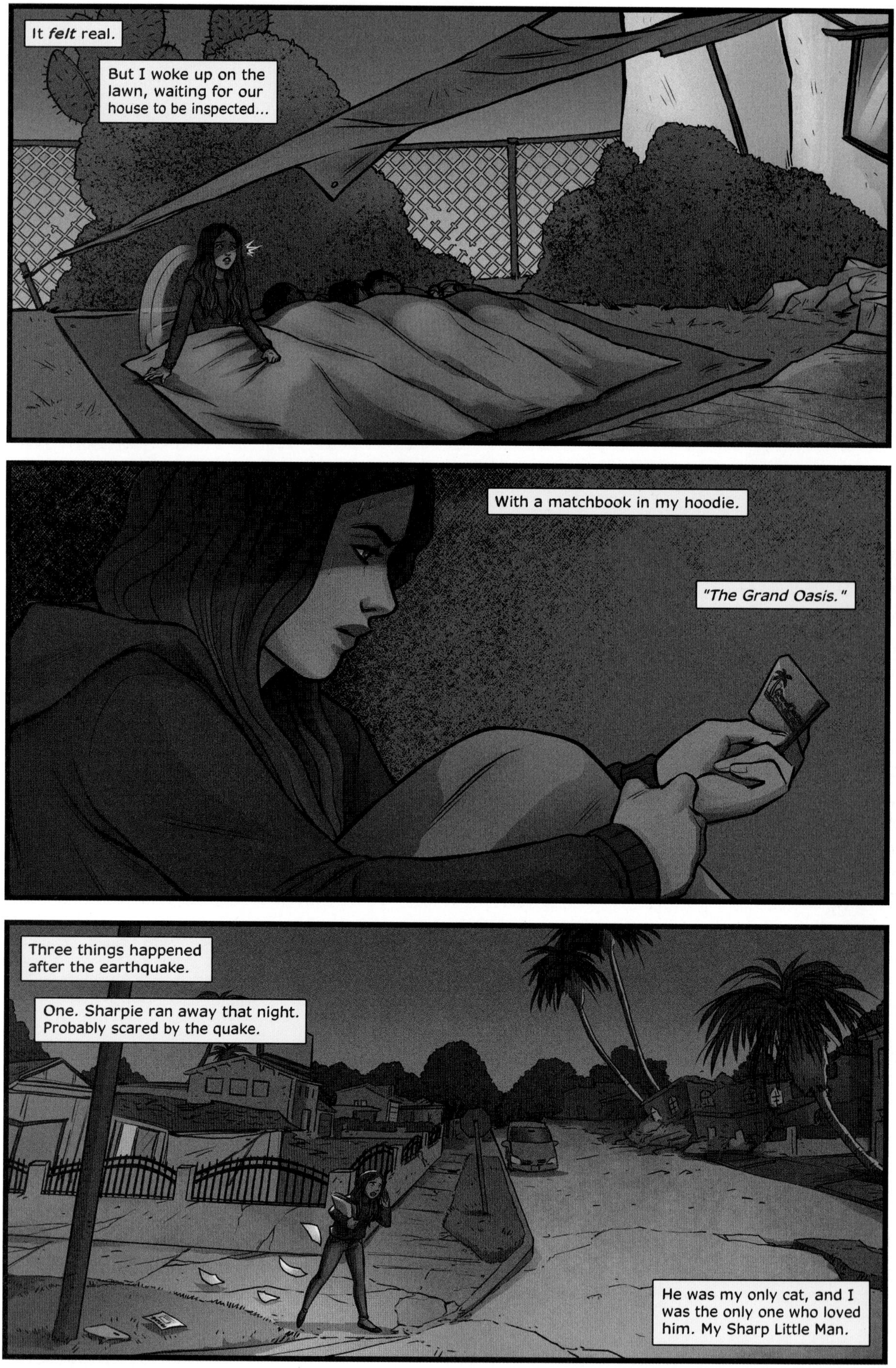
It *felt* real.
But I woke up on the lawn, waiting for our house to be inspected...
With a matchbook in my hoodie.
"The Grand Oasis."
Three things happened after the earthquake.
One. Sharpie ran away that night. Probably scared by the quake.
He was my only cat, and I was the only one who loved him. My Sharp Little Man.

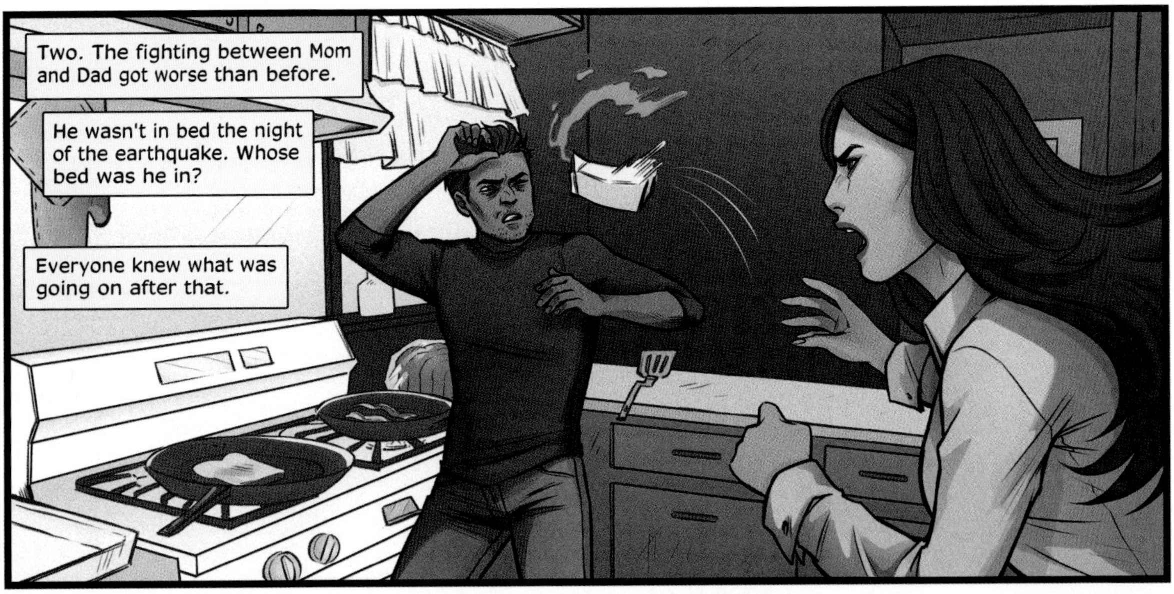
Two. The fighting between Mom and Dad got worse than before.
He wasn't in bed the night of the earthquake. Whose bed was he in?
Everyone knew what was going on after that.

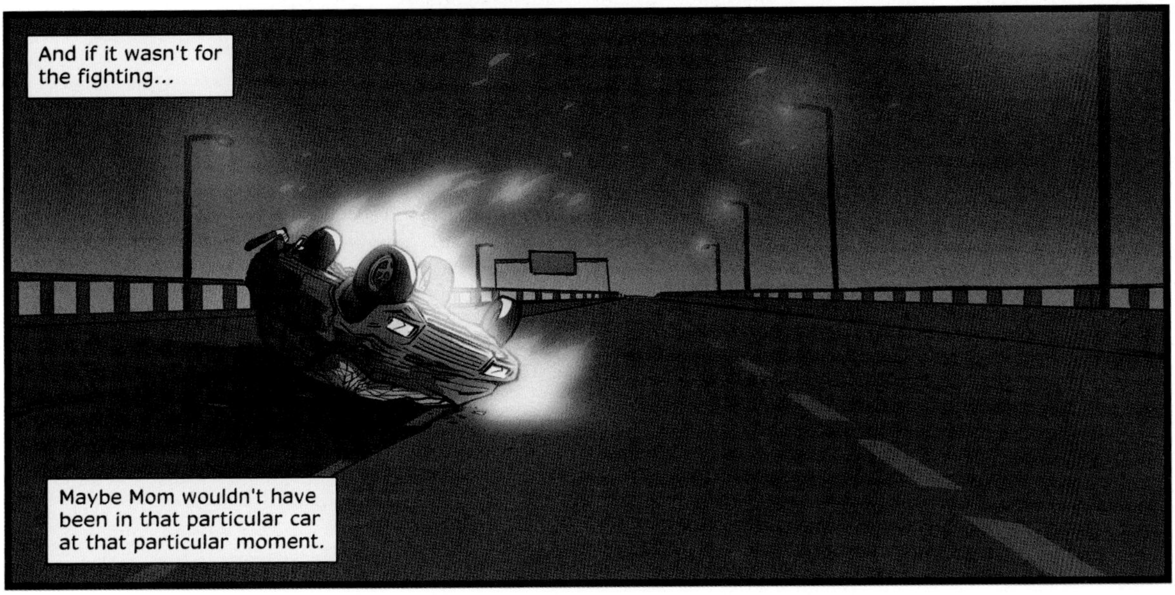
And if it wasn't for the fighting...
Maybe Mom wouldn't have been in that particular car at that particular moment.

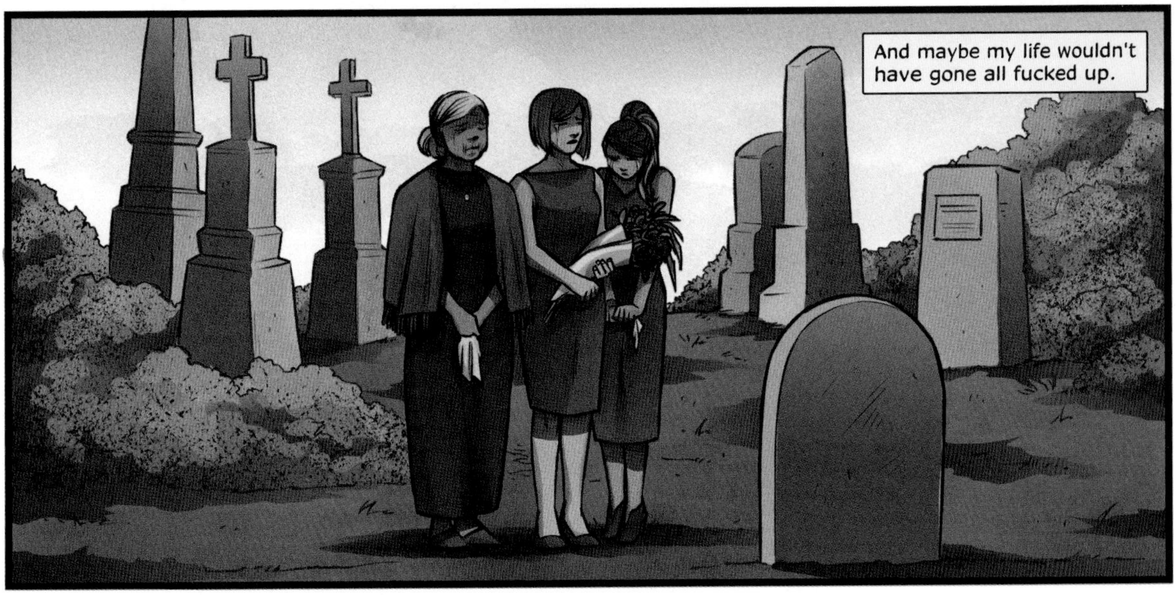
And maybe my life wouldn't have gone all fucked up.

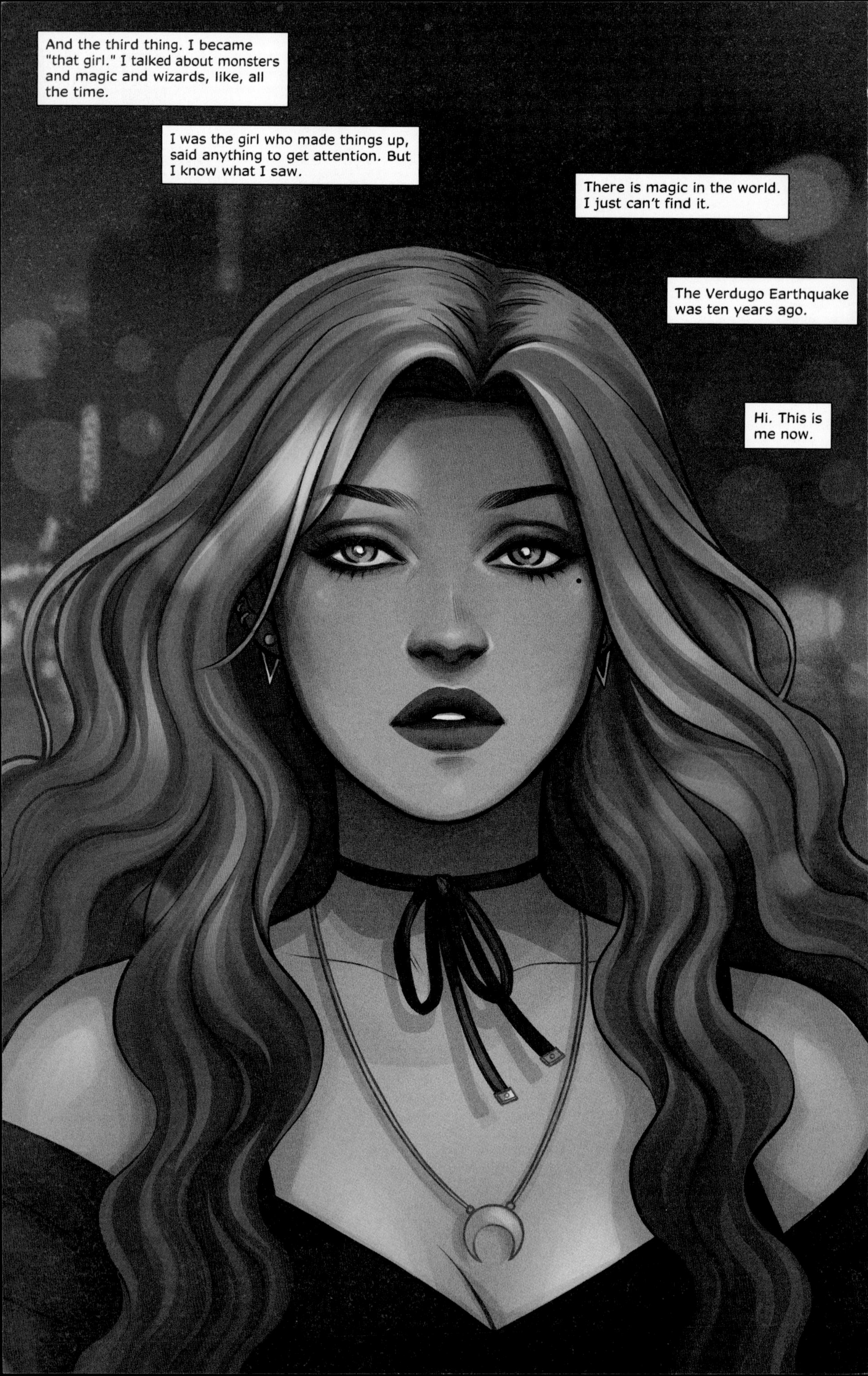
And the third thing. I became "that girl." I talked about monsters and magic and wizards, like, all the time.
I was the girl who made things up, said anything to get attention. But I know what I saw.
There is magic in the world. I just can't find it.
The Verdugo Earthquake was ten years ago.
Hi. This is me now.

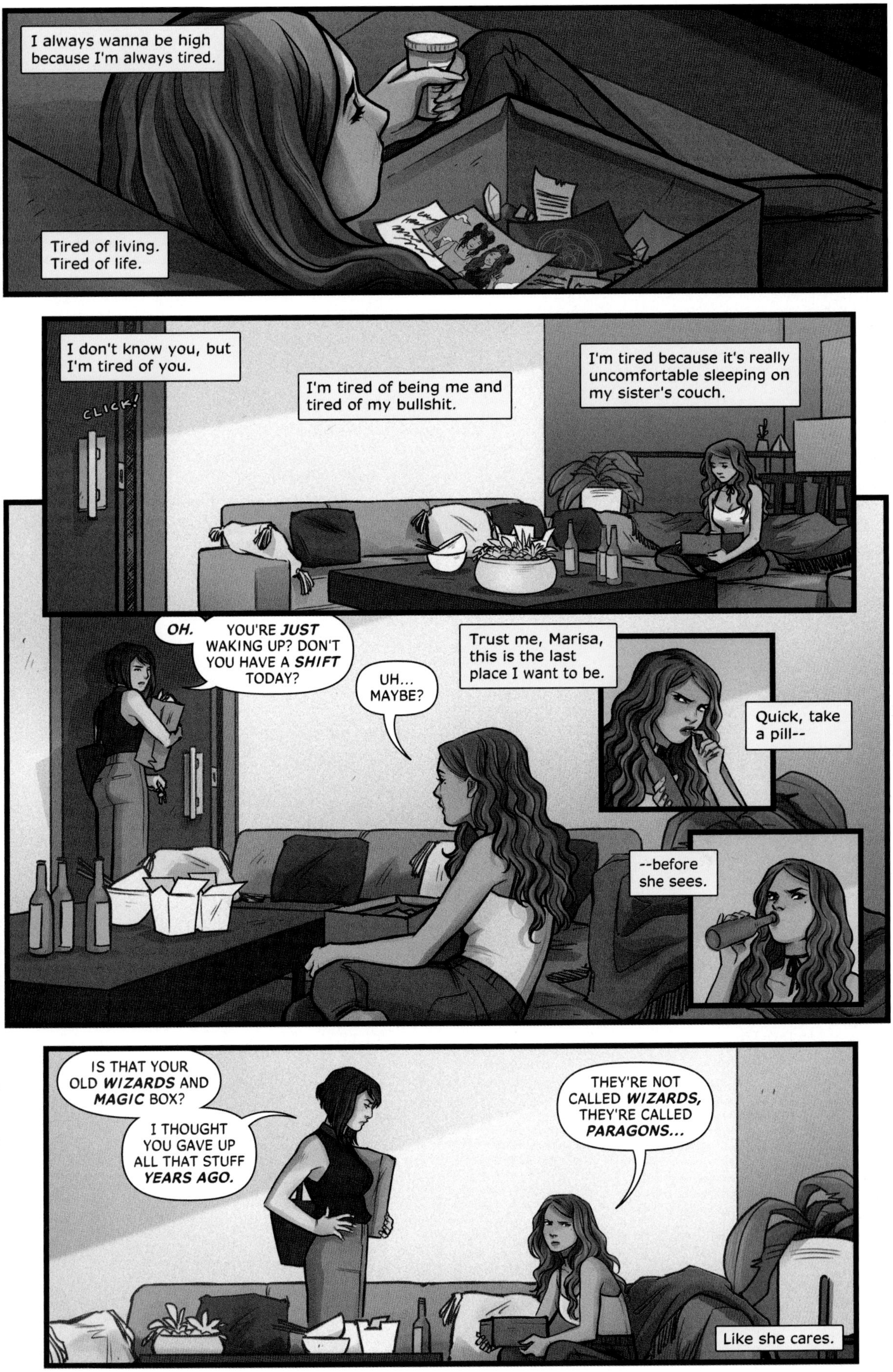
I always wanna be high because I'm always tired.
Tired of living. Tired of life.
I don't know you, but I'm tired of you.
CLICK!
I'm tired of being me and tired of my bullshit.
I'm tired because it's really uncomfortable sleeping on my sister's couch.
OH.
YOU'RE JUST WAKING UP? DON'T YOU HAVE A SHIFT TODAY?
UH... MAYBE?
Trust me, Marisa, this is the last place I want to be.
Quick, take a pill--
--before she sees.
IS THAT YOUR OLD WIZARDS AND MAGIC BOX?
I THOUGHT YOU GAVE UP ALL THAT STUFF YEARS AGO.
THEY'RE NOT CALLED WIZARDS, THEY'RE CALLED PARAGONS...
Like she cares.

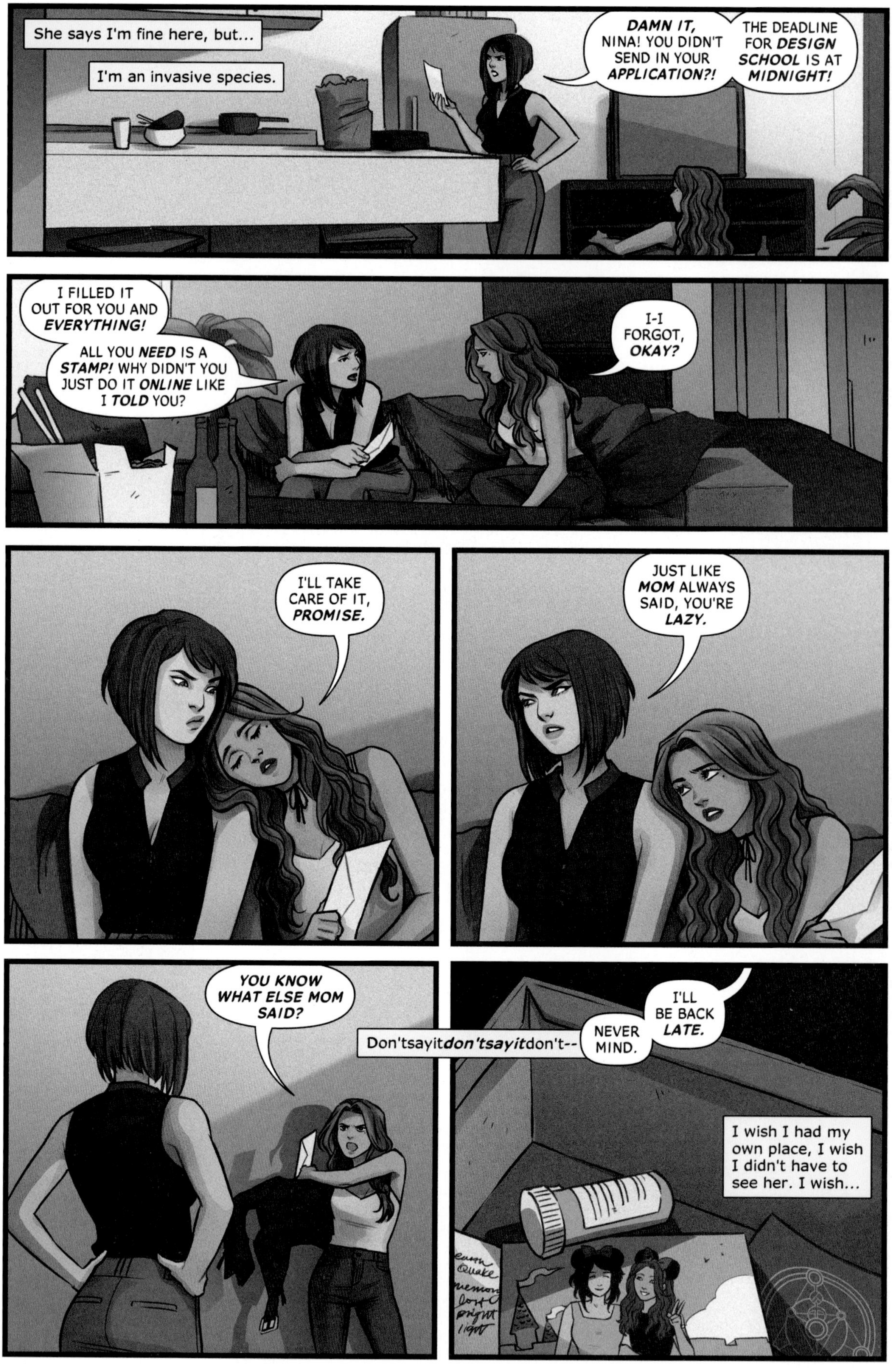
She says I'm fine here, but...
I'm an invasive species.
DAMN IT, NINA! YOU DIDN'T SEND IN YOUR *APPLICATION?!*
THE DEADLINE FOR *DESIGN SCHOOL* IS AT *MIDNIGHT!*
I FILLED IT OUT FOR YOU AND *EVERYTHING!*
ALL YOU *NEED* IS A *STAMP!* WHY DIDN'T YOU JUST DO IT *ONLINE* LIKE I *TOLD* YOU?
I-I FORGOT, *OKAY?*
I'LL TAKE CARE OF IT, *PROMISE.*
JUST LIKE *MOM* ALWAYS SAID, YOU'RE *LAZY.*
YOU KNOW WHAT ELSE MOM SAID?
Don'tsayit*don'tsayit*don't--
NEVER MIND.
I'LL BE BACK *LATE.*
I wish I had my own place, I wish I didn't have to see her. I wish...

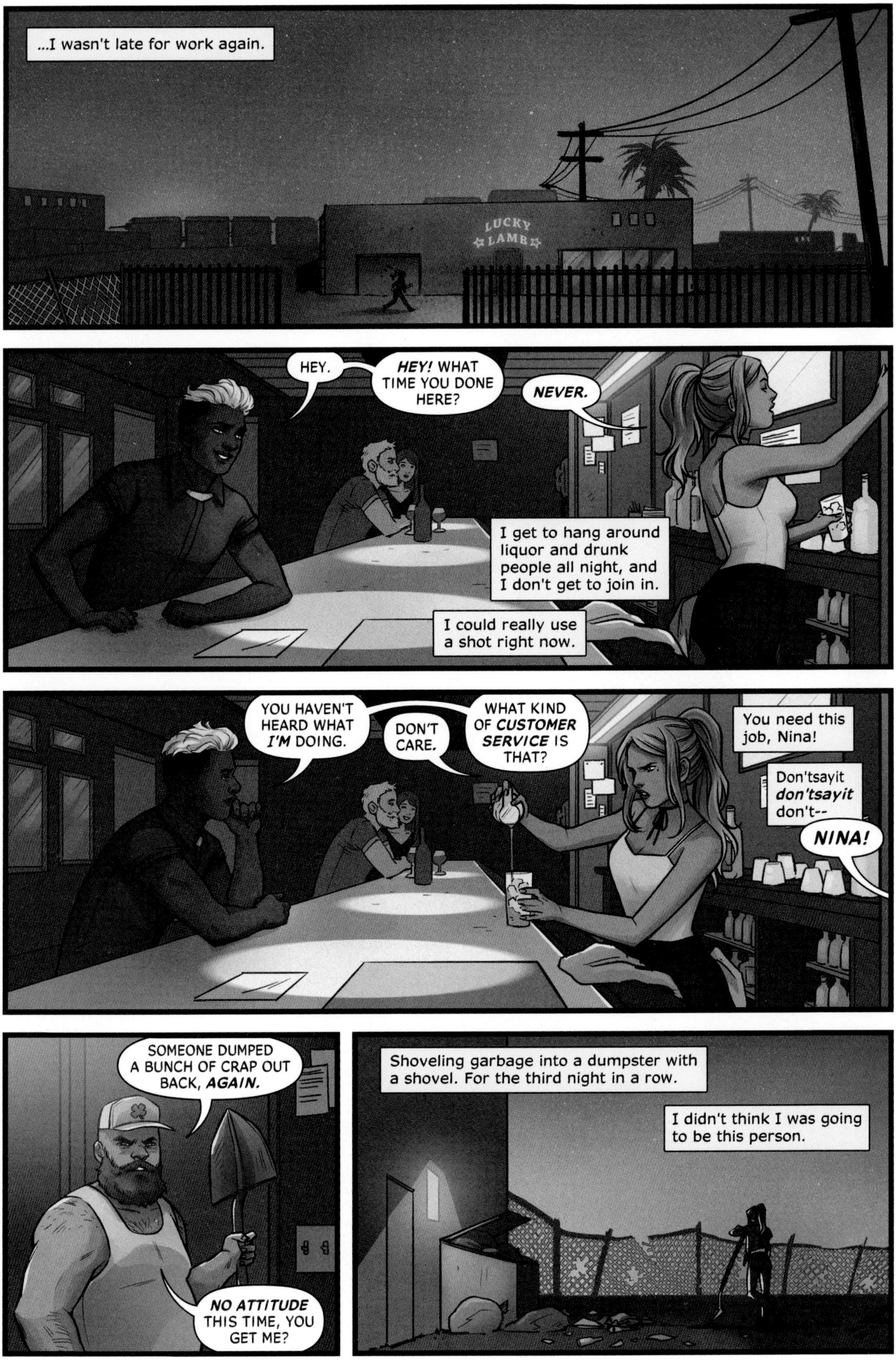

...I wasn't late for work again.
LUCKY LAMB
HEY.
HEY! WHAT TIME YOU DONE HERE?
NEVER.
I get to hang around liquor and drunk people all night, and I don't get to join in.
I could really use a shot right now.
YOU HAVEN'T HEARD WHAT I'M DOING.
DON'T CARE.
WHAT KIND OF CUSTOMER SERVICE IS THAT?
You need this job, Nina!
Don'tsayit don'tsayit don't--
NINA!
SOMEONE DUMPED A BUNCH OF CRAP OUT BACK, AGAIN.
NO ATTITUDE THIS TIME, YOU GET ME?
Shoveling garbage into a dumpster with a shovel. For the third night in a row.
I didn't think I was going to be this person.

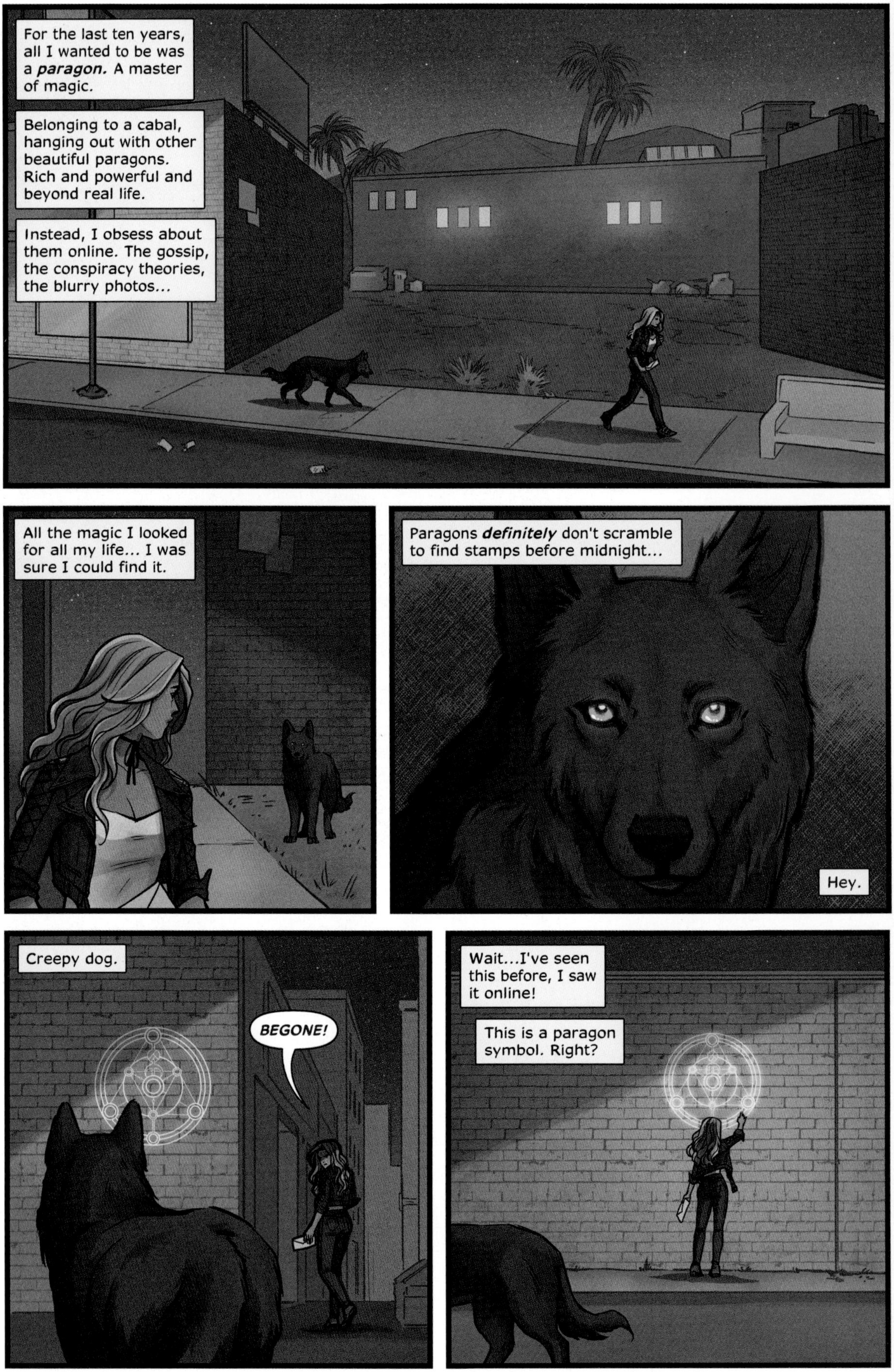
For the last ten years, all I wanted to be was a *paragon.* A master of magic.
Belonging to a cabal, hanging out with other beautiful paragons. Rich and powerful and beyond real life.
Instead, I obsess about them online. The gossip, the conspiracy theories, the blurry photos...
All the magic I looked for all my life... I was sure I could find it.
Paragons *definitely* don't scramble to find stamps before midnight...
Hey.
Creepy dog.
BEGONE!
Wait...I've seen this before, I saw it online!
This is a paragon symbol. Right?

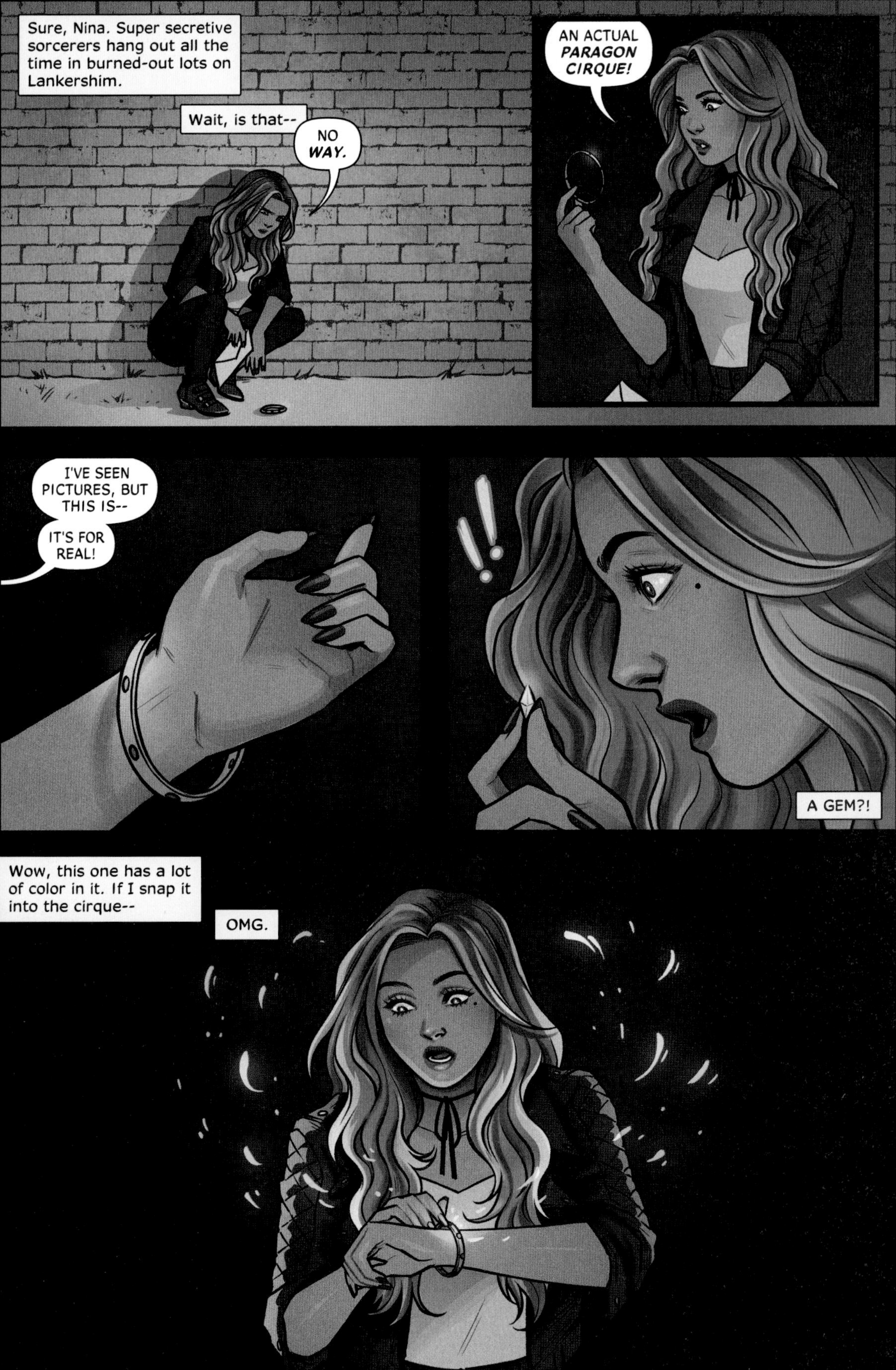
Sure, Nina. Super secretive sorcerers hang out all the time in burned-out lots on Lankershim.
Wait, is that--
NO *WAY.*
AN ACTUAL *PARAGON CIRQUE!*
I'VE SEEN PICTURES, BUT THIS IS--
IT'S FOR REAL!
A GEM?!
Wow, this one has a lot of color in it. If I snap it into the cirque--
OMG.

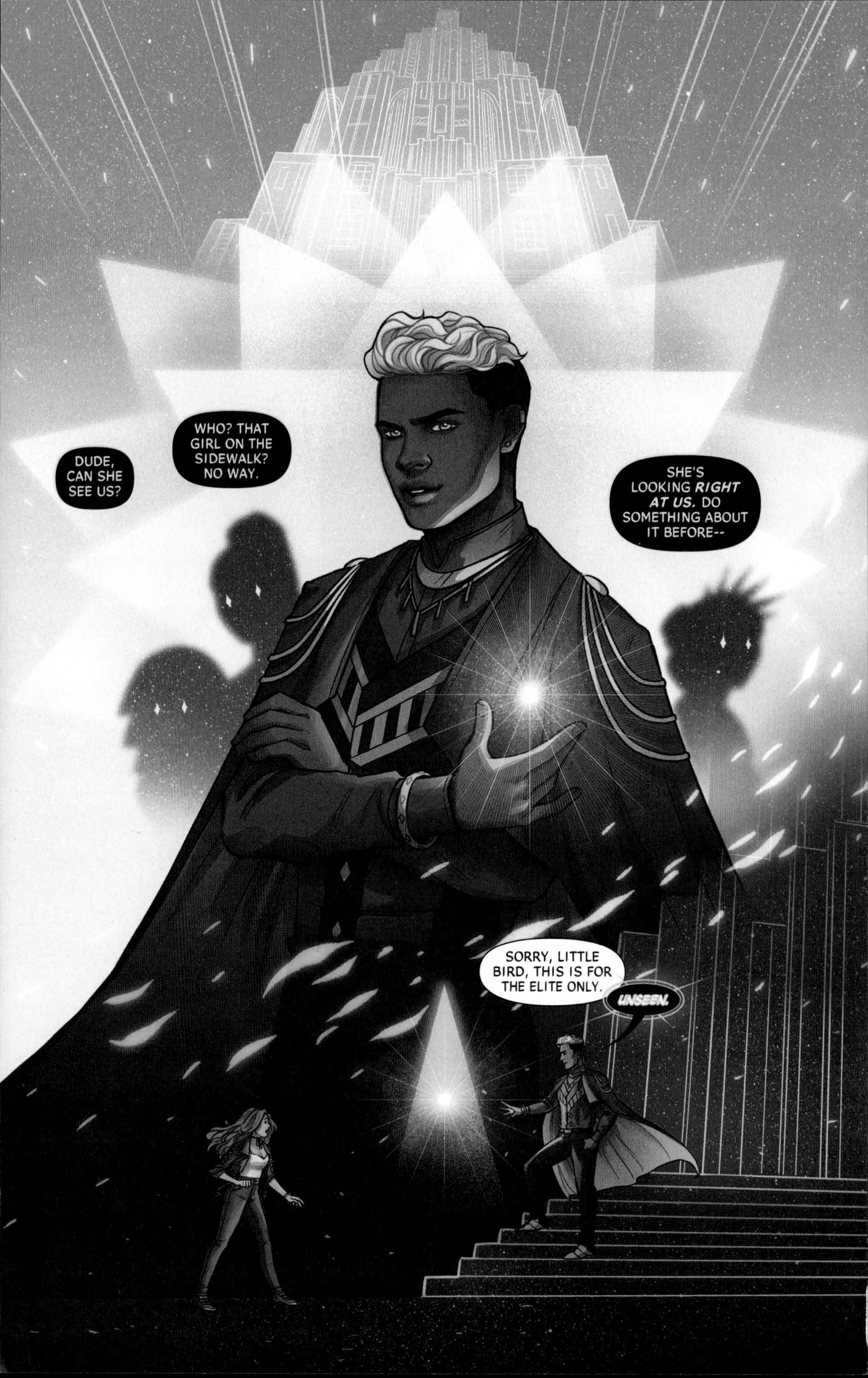
DUDE, CAN SHE SEE US?
WHO? THAT GIRL ON THE SIDEWALK? NO WAY.
SHE'S LOOKING **RIGHT AT US.** DO SOMETHING ABOUT IT BEFORE--
SORRY, LITTLE BIRD, THIS IS FOR THE ELITE ONLY.
UNSEEN.

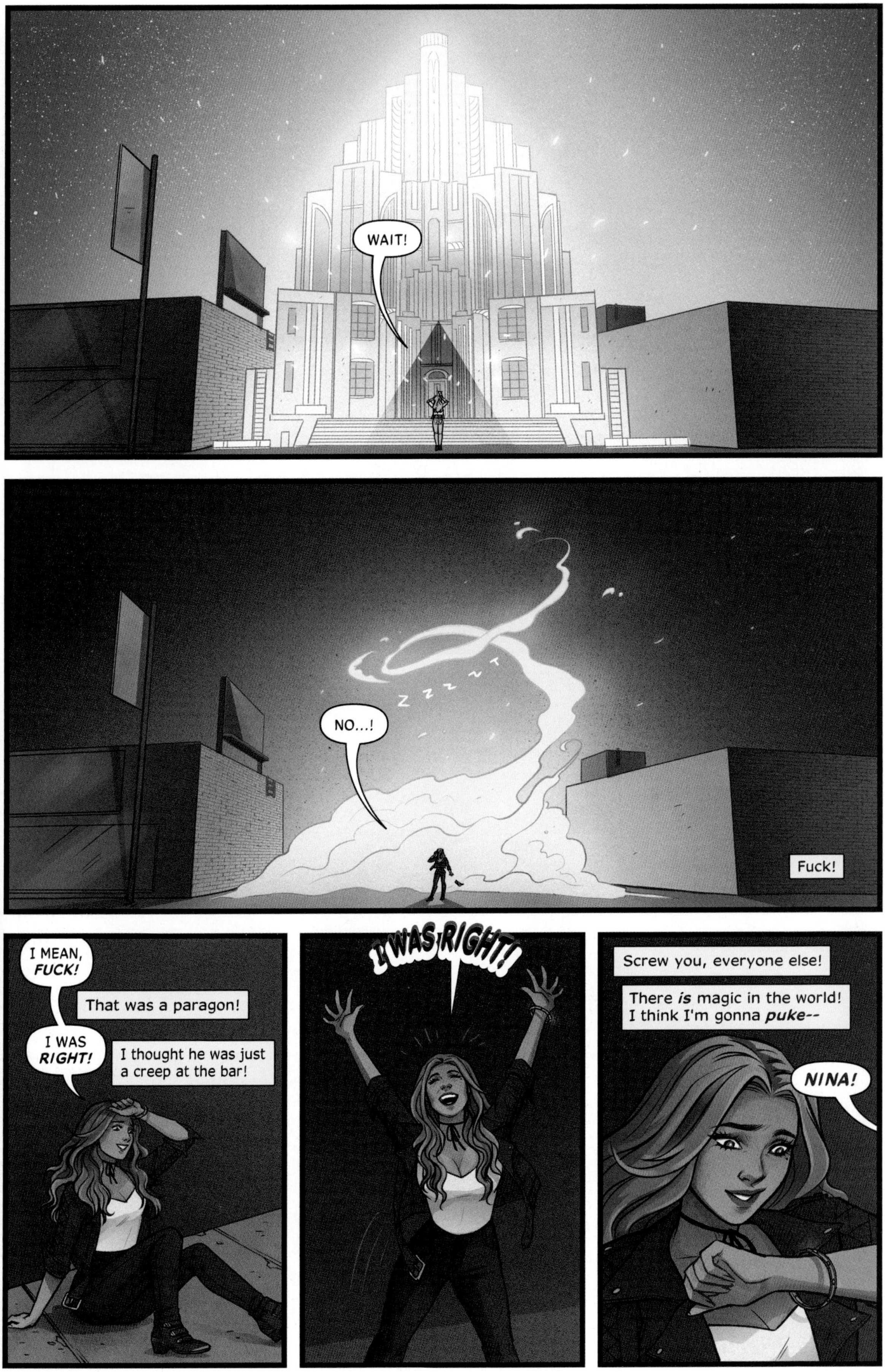
WAIT!
Z Z Z Z
NO...!
Fuck!
I MEAN, *FUCK!*
That was a paragon!
I WAS *RIGHT!*
I thought he was just a creep at the bar!
I WAS RIGHT!
Screw you, everyone else!
There *is* magic in the world! I think I'm gonna *puke--*
NINA!

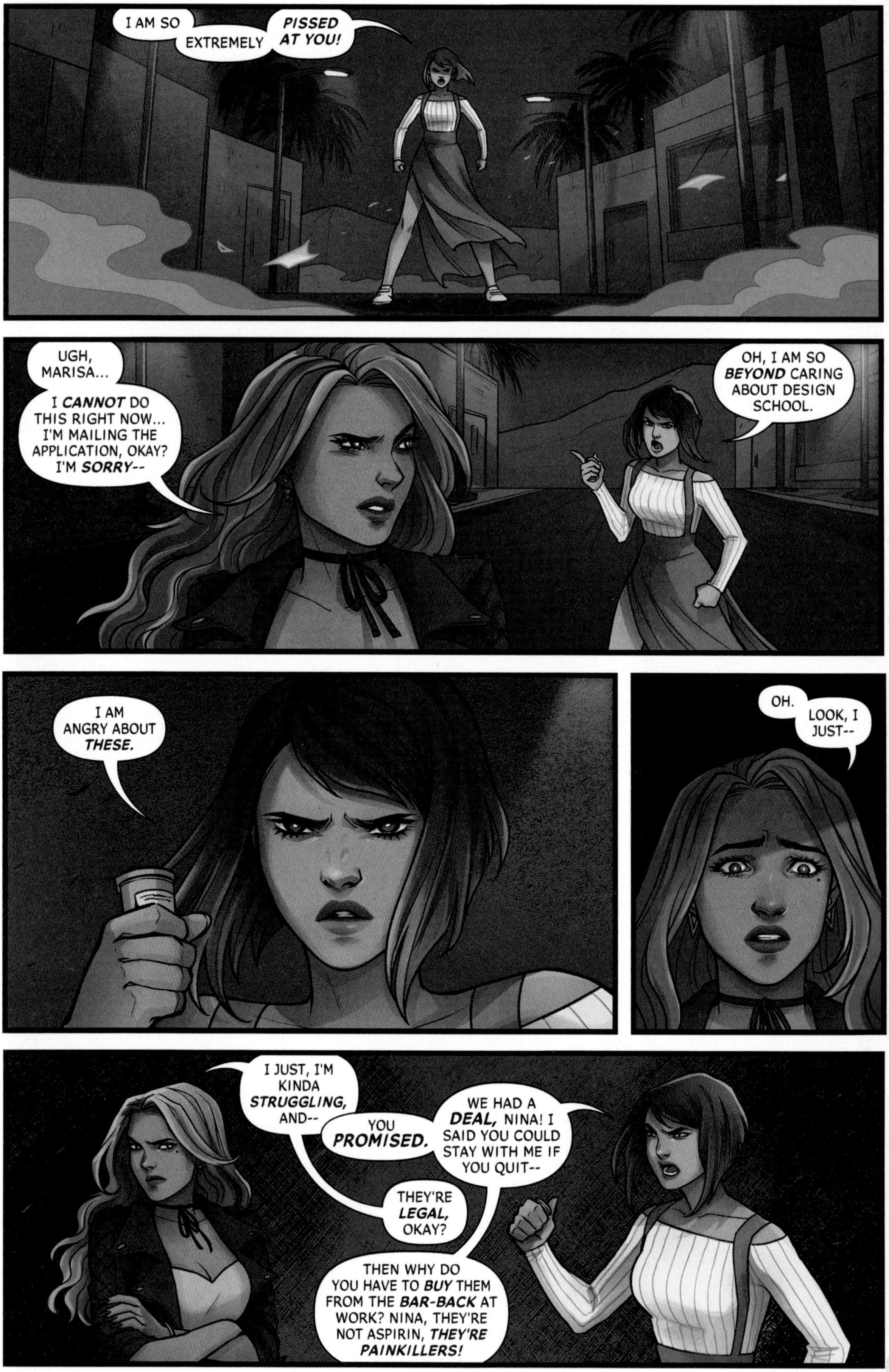
I AM SO
EXTREMELY
PISSED AT YOU!
UGH, MARISA...
I CANNOT DO THIS RIGHT NOW... I'M MAILING THE APPLICATION, OKAY? I'M SORRY--
OH, I AM SO BEYOND CARING ABOUT DESIGN SCHOOL.
I AM ANGRY ABOUT THESE.
OH.
LOOK, I JUST--
I JUST, I'M KINDA STRUGGLING, AND--
YOU PROMISED.
WE HAD A DEAL, NINA! I SAID YOU COULD STAY WITH ME IF YOU QUIT--
THEY'RE LEGAL, OKAY?
THEN WHY DO YOU HAVE TO BUY THEM FROM THE BAR-BACK AT WORK? NINA, THEY'RE NOT ASPIRIN, THEY'RE PAINKILLERS!

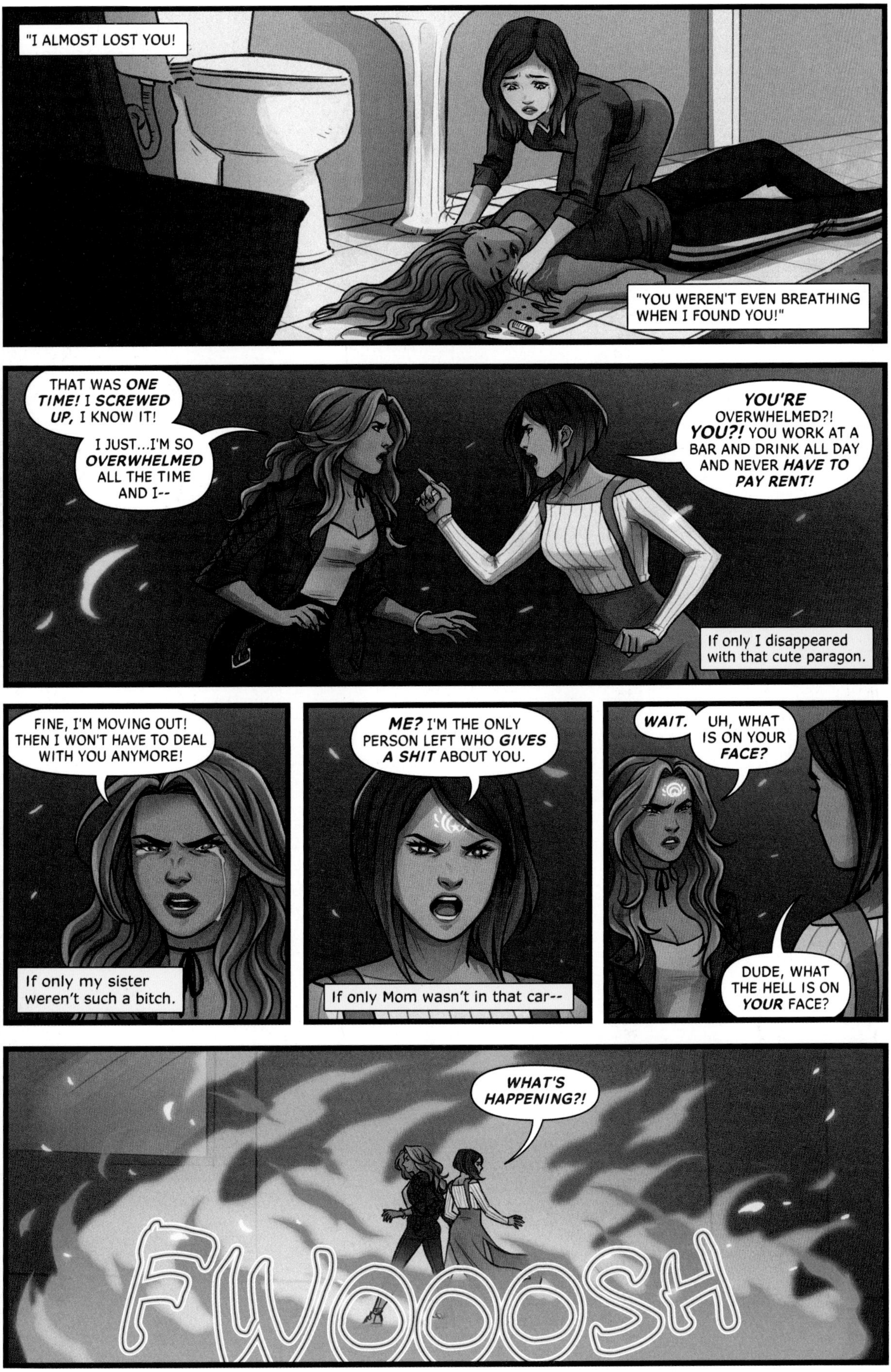
"I ALMOST LOST YOU!
"YOU WEREN'T EVEN BREATHING WHEN I FOUND YOU!"
THAT WAS ONE TIME! I SCREWED UP, I KNOW IT!
I JUST...I'M SO OVERWHELMED ALL THE TIME AND I--
YOU'RE OVERWHELMED?! YOU?! YOU WORK AT A BAR AND DRINK ALL DAY AND NEVER HAVE TO PAY RENT!
If only I disappeared with that cute paragon.
FINE, I'M MOVING OUT! THEN I WON'T HAVE TO DEAL WITH YOU ANYMORE!
If only my sister weren't such a bitch.
ME? I'M THE ONLY PERSON LEFT WHO GIVES A SHIT ABOUT YOU.
If only Mom wasn't in that car--
WAIT.
UH, WHAT IS ON YOUR FACE?
DUDE, WHAT THE HELL IS ON YOUR FACE?
WHAT'S HAPPENING?!
FWOOOSH

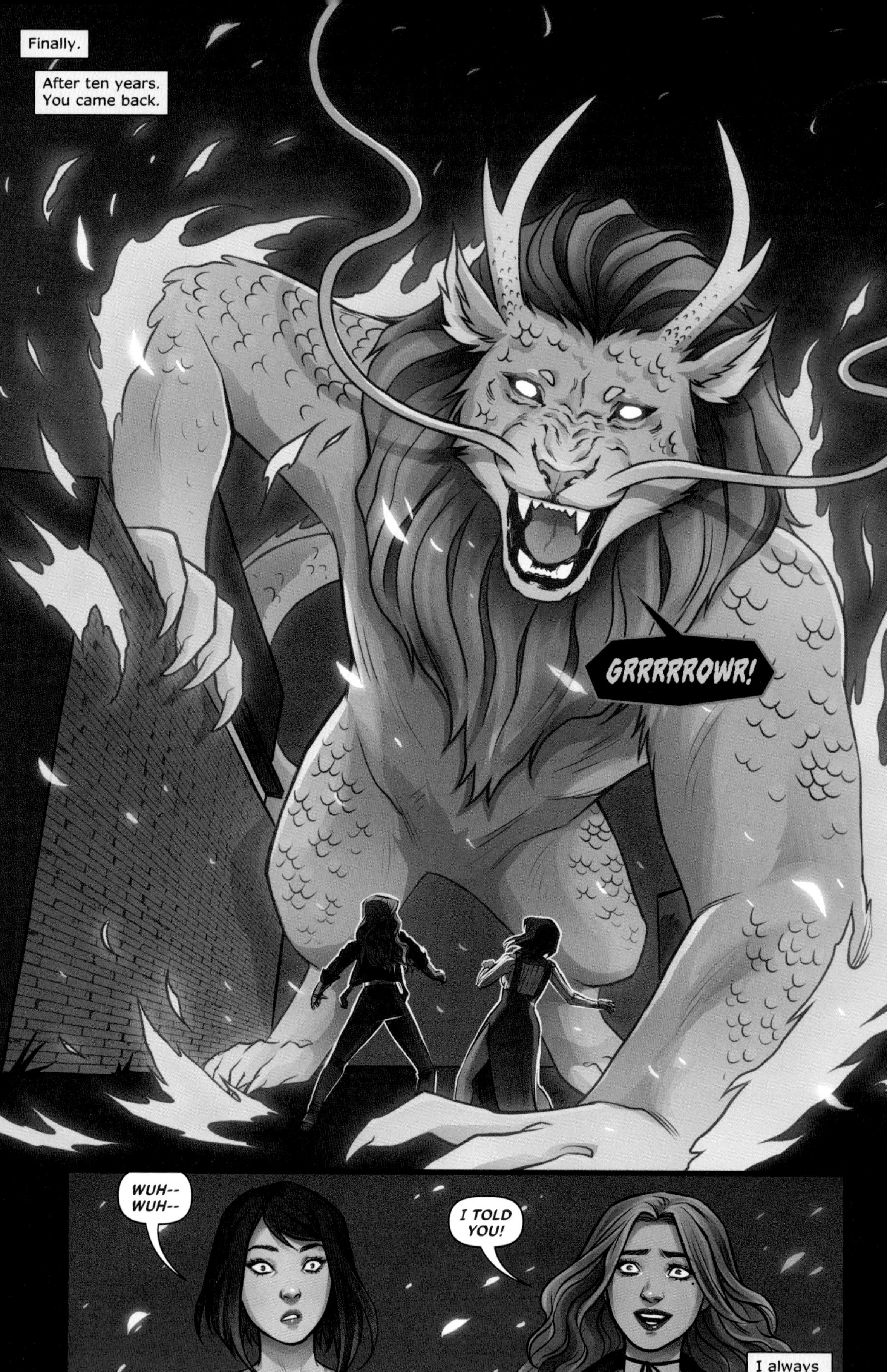
Finally.
After ten years. You came back.
GRRRRROWR!
WUH-- WUH--
I TOLD YOU!
I always believed.

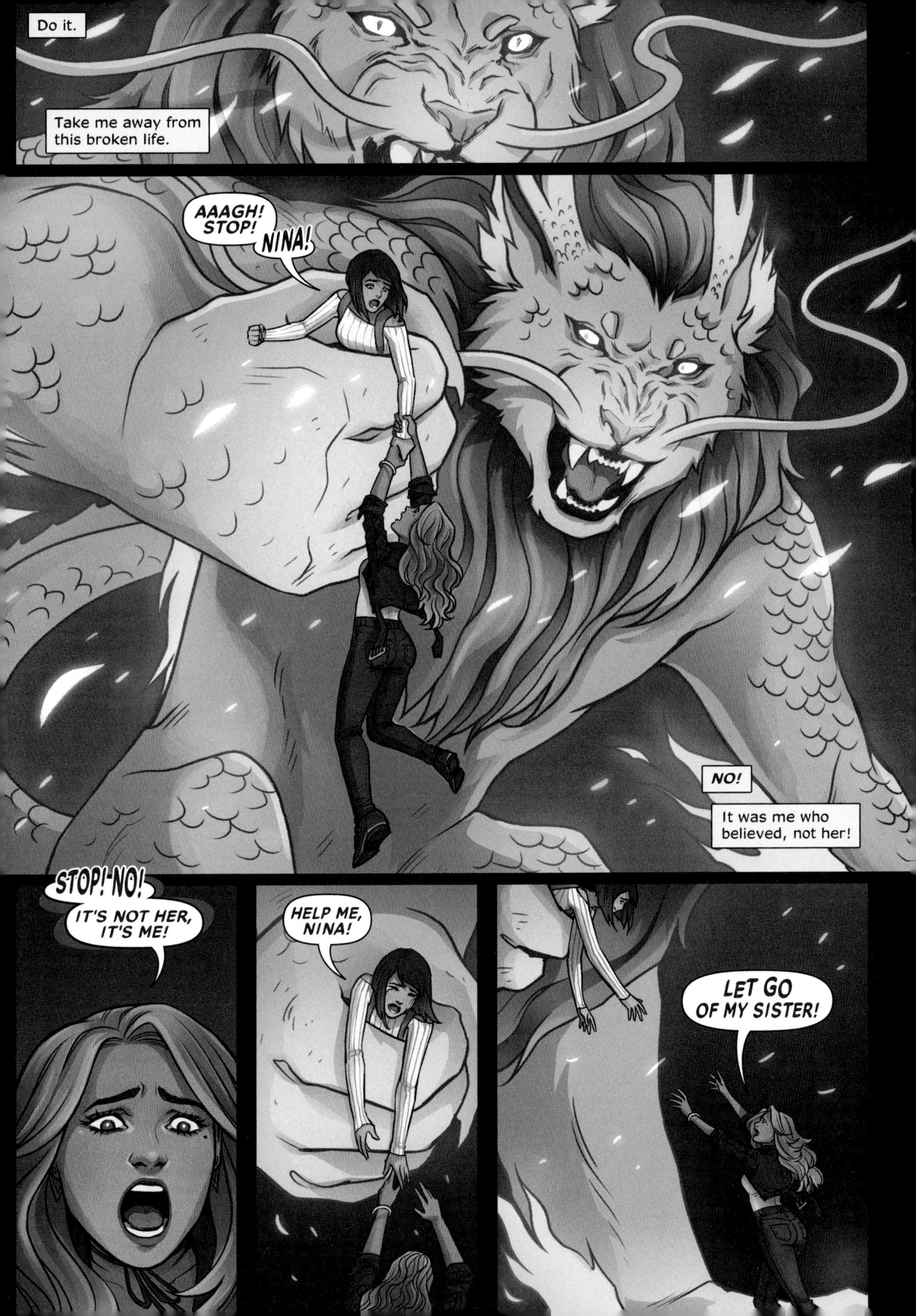

Do it.
Take me away from this broken life.
AAAGH! STOP!
NINA!
NO!
It was me who believed, not her!
STOP! NO!
IT'S NOT HER, IT'S ME!
HELP ME, NINA!
LET GO OF MY SISTER!

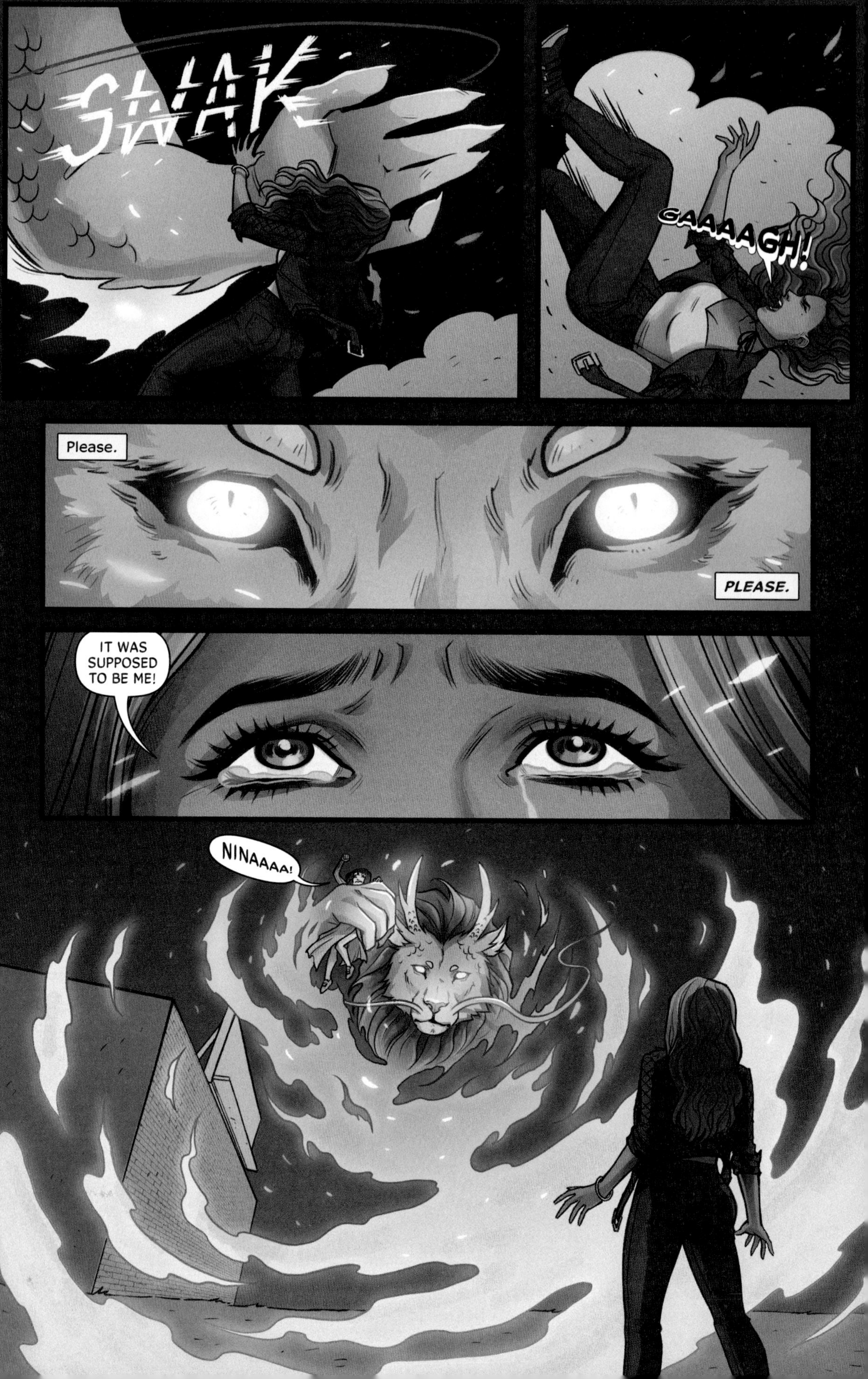
SHAK
GAAAAGH!
Please.
PLEASE.
IT WAS SUPPOSED TO BE ME!
NINAAAA!

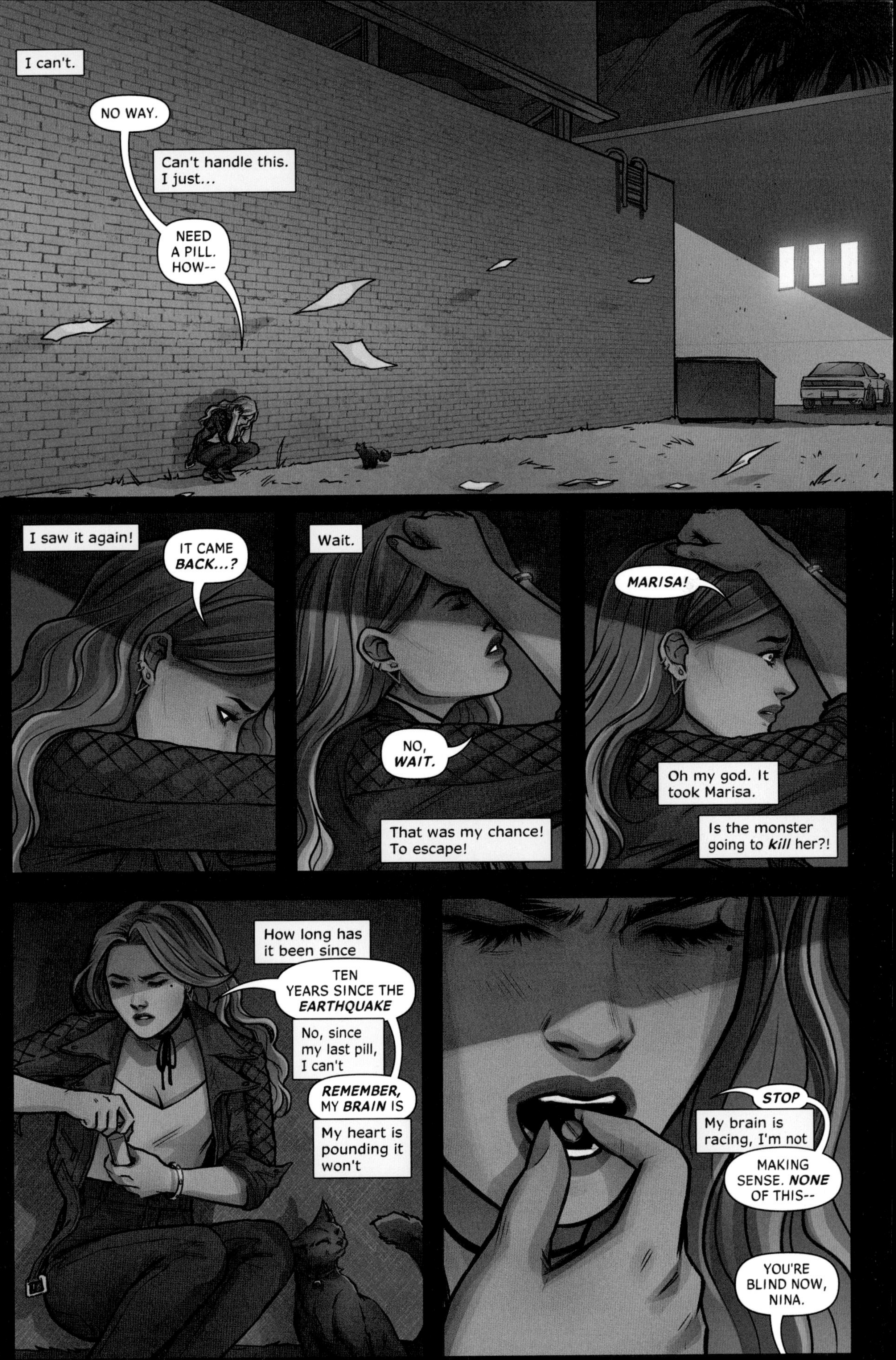
I can't.
NO WAY.
Can't handle this. I just...
NEED A PILL. HOW--
I saw it again!
IT CAME BACK...?
Wait.
NO, WAIT.
That was my chance! To escape!
MARISA!
Oh my god. It took Marisa.
Is the monster going to kill her?!
How long has it been since
TEN YEARS SINCE THE EARTHQUAKE
No, since my last pill, I can't
REMEMBER, MY BRAIN IS
My heart is pounding it won't
STOP
My brain is racing, I'm not
MAKING SENSE. NONE OF THIS--
YOU'RE BLIND NOW, NINA.

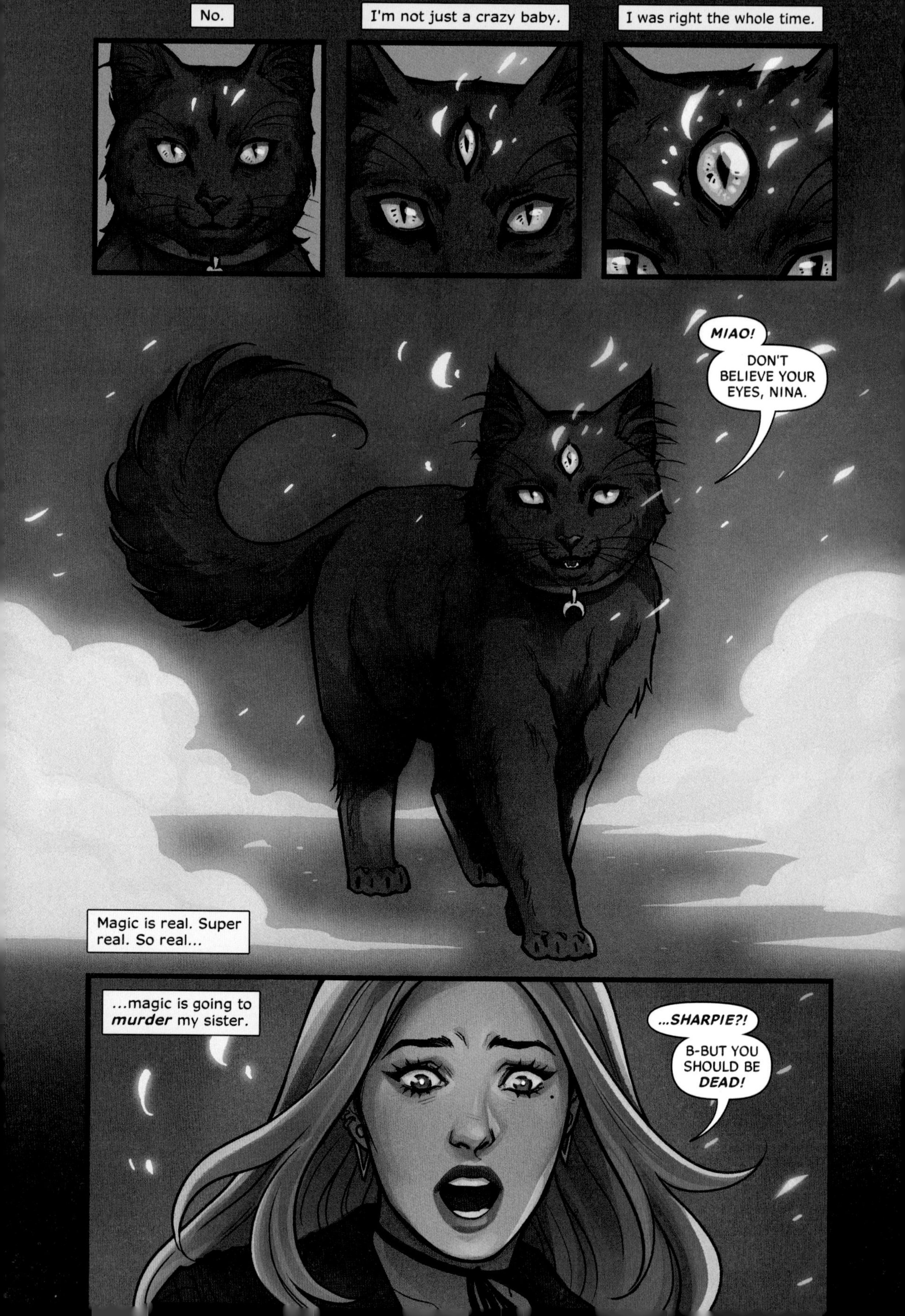
No.
I'm not just a crazy baby.
I was right the whole time.
MIAO! DON'T BELIEVE YOUR EYES, NINA.
Magic is real. Super real. So real...
...magic is going to *murder* my sister.
...SHARPIE?!
B-BUT YOU SHOULD BE *DEAD!*

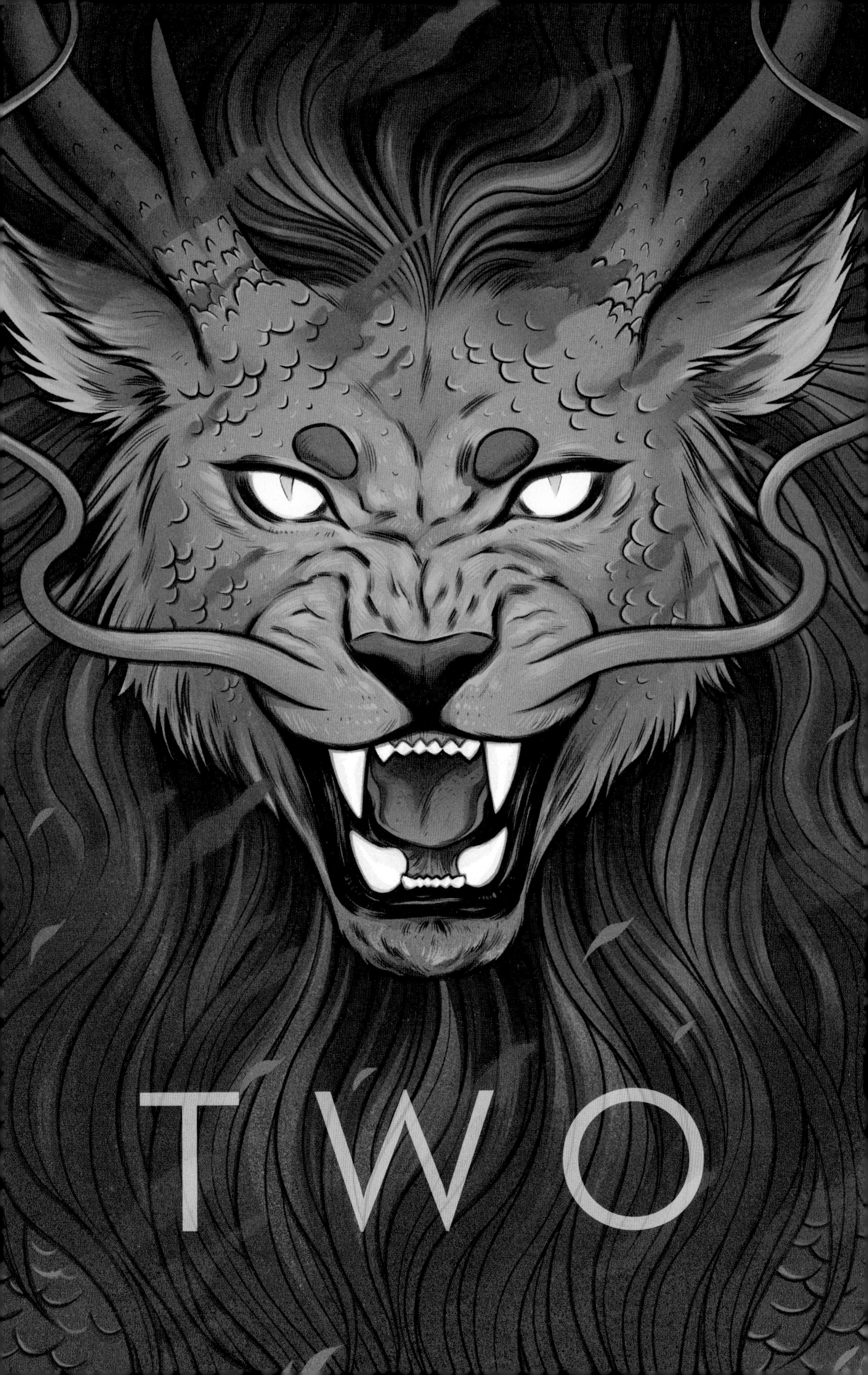
TWO

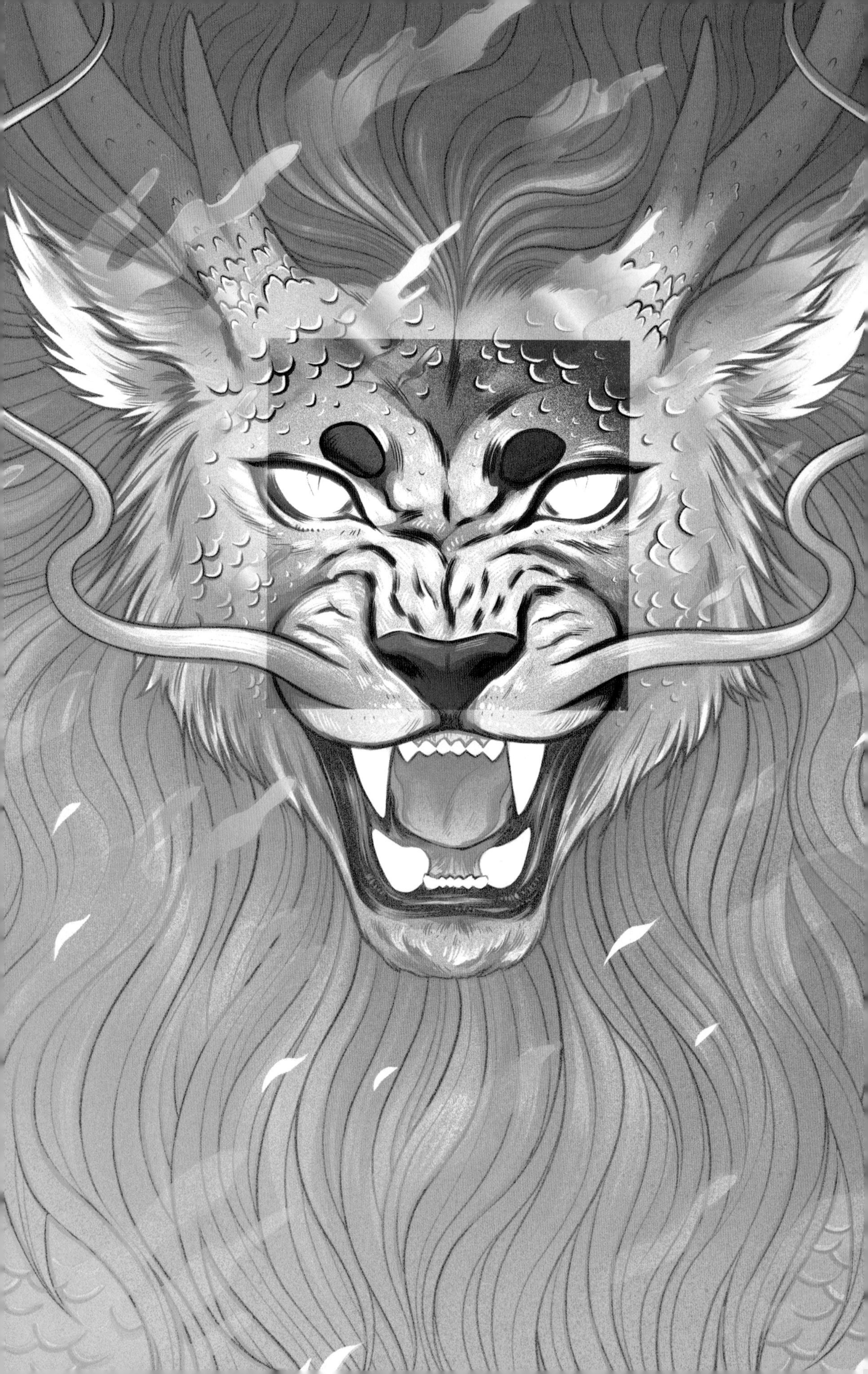

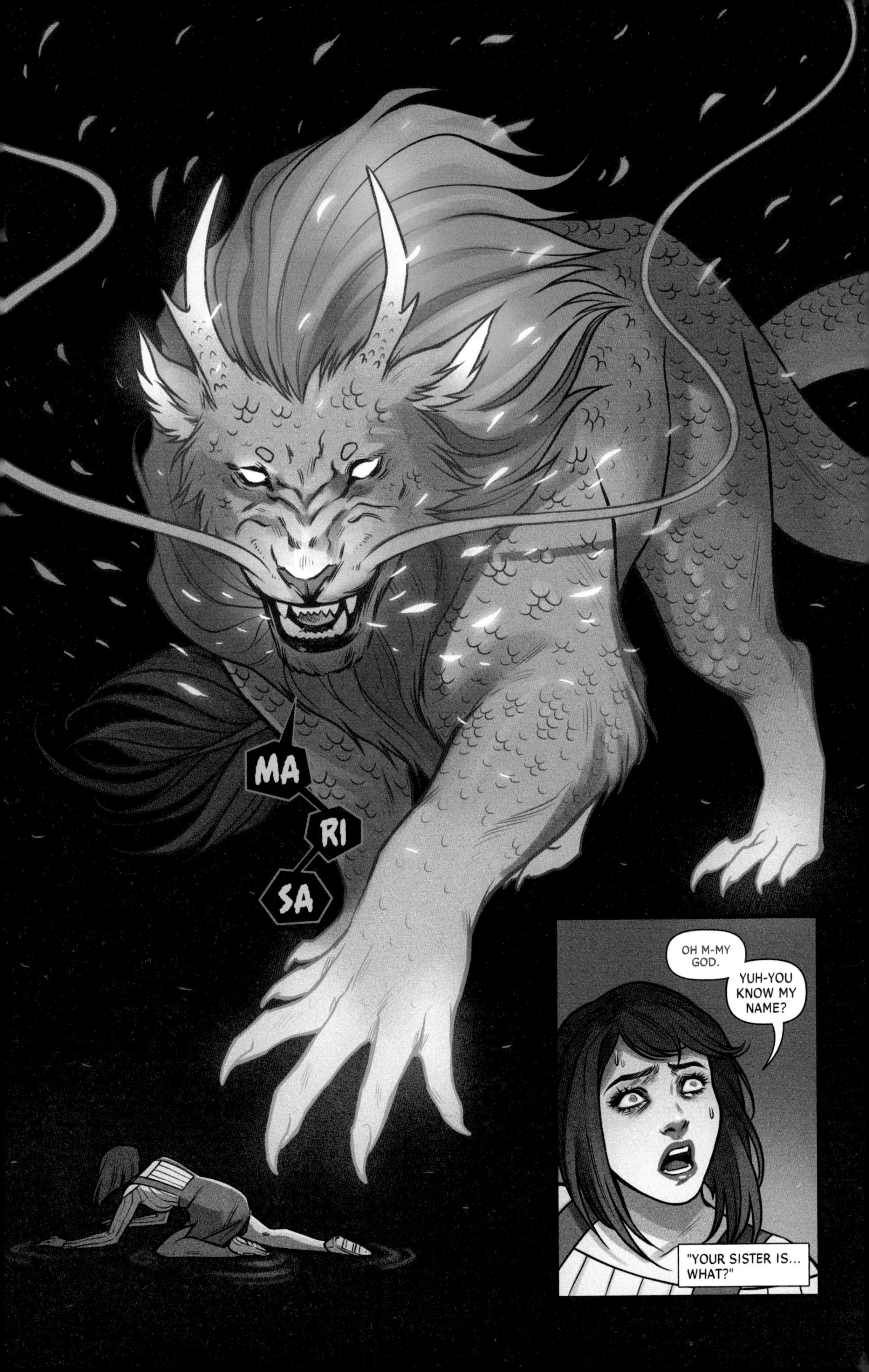
MA
RI
SA
OH M-MY GOD.
YUH-YOU KNOW MY NAME?
"YOUR SISTER IS... WHAT?"

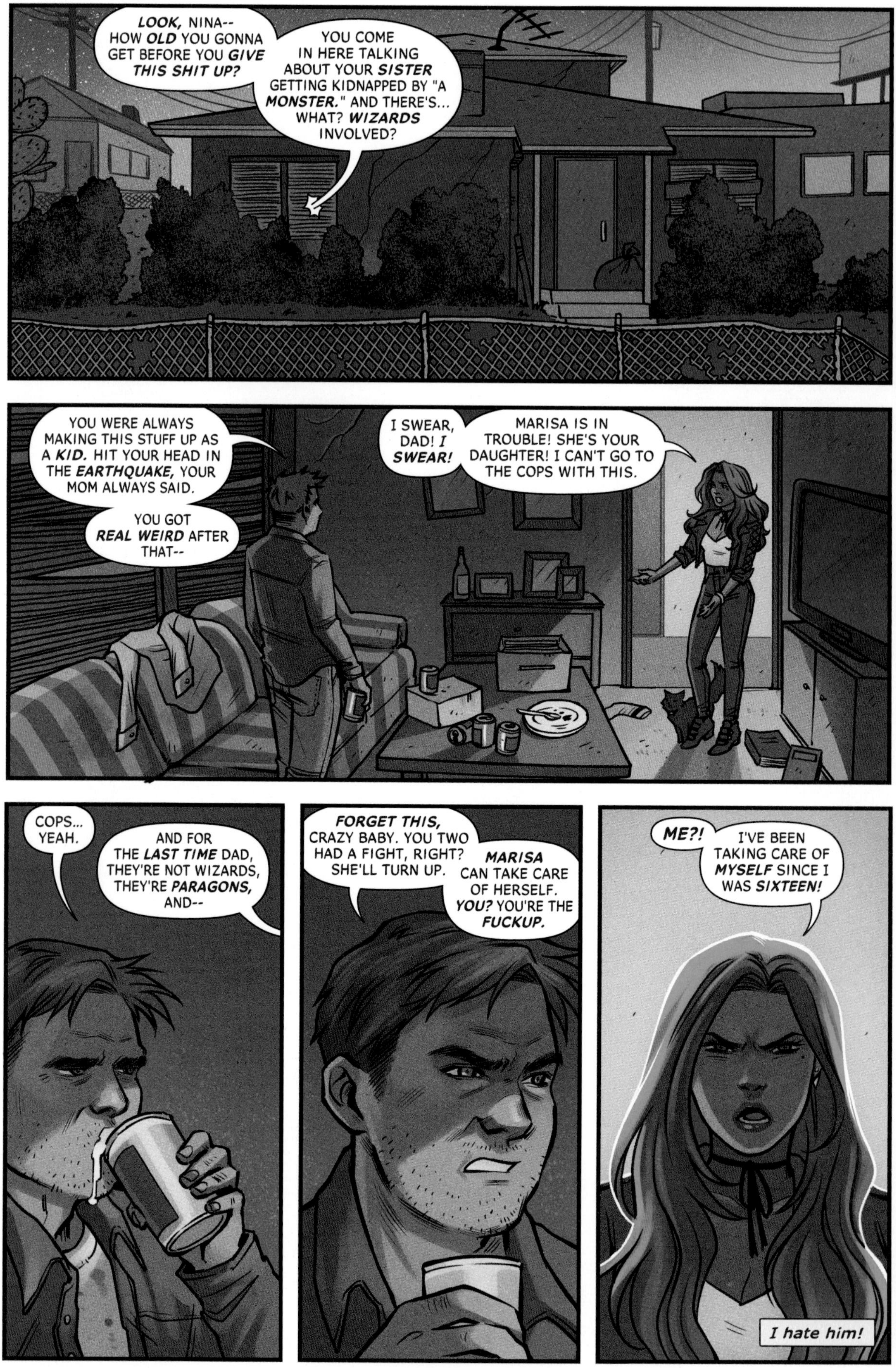
LOOK, NINA-- HOW OLD YOU GONNA GET BEFORE YOU GIVE THIS SHIT UP?
YOU COME IN HERE TALKING ABOUT YOUR SISTER GETTING KIDNAPPED BY "A MONSTER." AND THERE'S... WHAT? WIZARDS INVOLVED?
YOU WERE ALWAYS MAKING THIS STUFF UP AS A KID. HIT YOUR HEAD IN THE EARTHQUAKE, YOUR MOM ALWAYS SAID.
YOU GOT REAL WEIRD AFTER THAT--
I SWEAR, DAD! I SWEAR!
MARISA IS IN TROUBLE! SHE'S YOUR DAUGHTER! I CAN'T GO TO THE COPS WITH THIS.
COPS... YEAH.
AND FOR THE LAST TIME DAD, THEY'RE NOT WIZARDS, THEY'RE PARAGONS, AND--
FORGET THIS, CRAZY BABY. YOU TWO HAD A FIGHT, RIGHT? SHE'LL TURN UP.
MARISA CAN TAKE CARE OF HERSELF. YOU? YOU'RE THE FUCKUP.
ME?!
I'VE BEEN TAKING CARE OF MYSELF SINCE I WAS SIXTEEN!
I hate him!

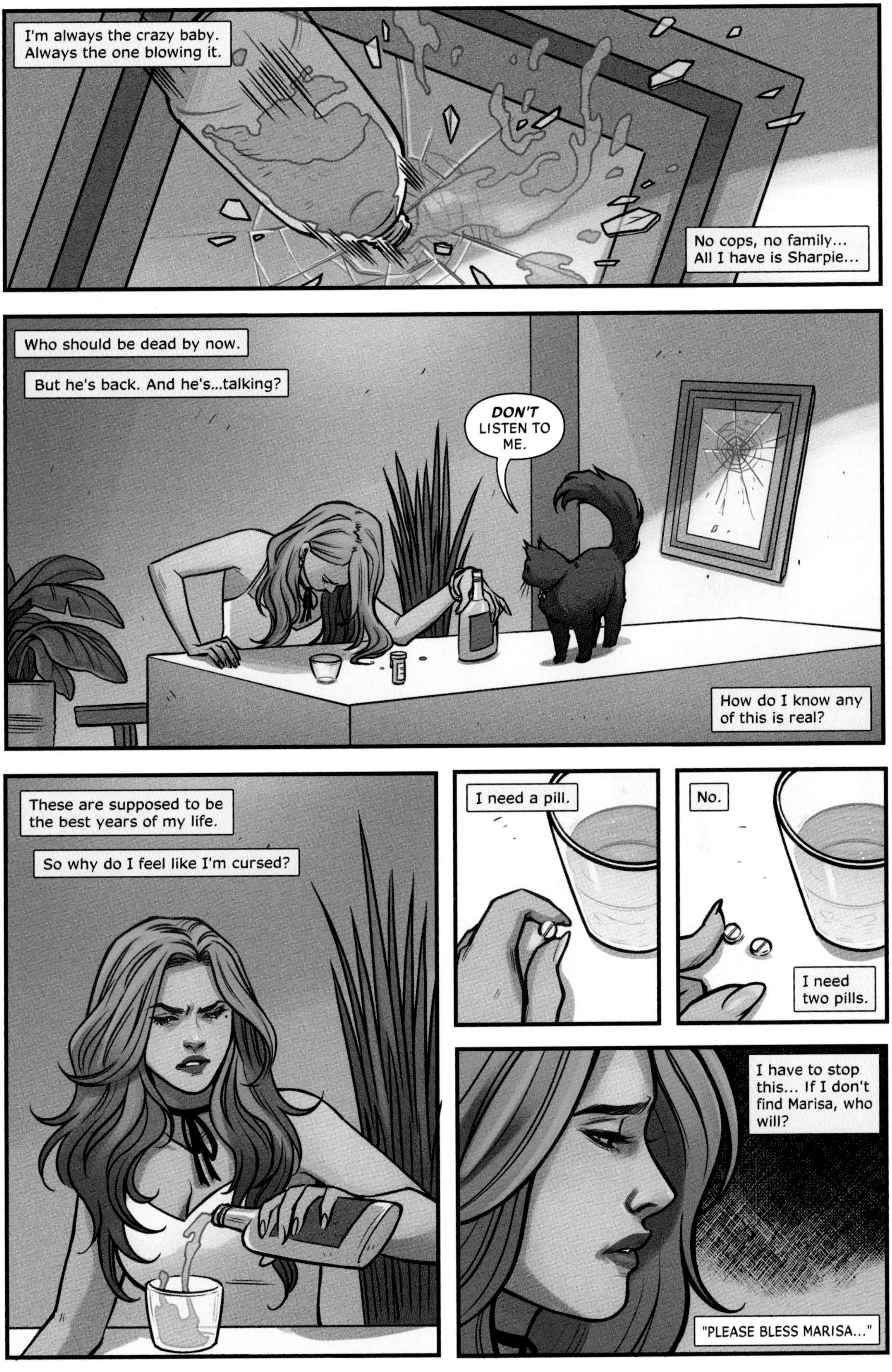
I'm always the crazy baby. Always the one blowing it.
No cops, no family... All I have is Sharpie...
Who should be dead by now.
But he's back. And he's...talking?
DON'T LISTEN TO ME.
How do I know any of this is real?
These are supposed to be the best years of my life.
So why do I feel like I'm cursed?
I need a pill.
No.
I need two pills.
I have to stop this... If I don't find Marisa, who will?
"PLEASE BLESS MARISA..."

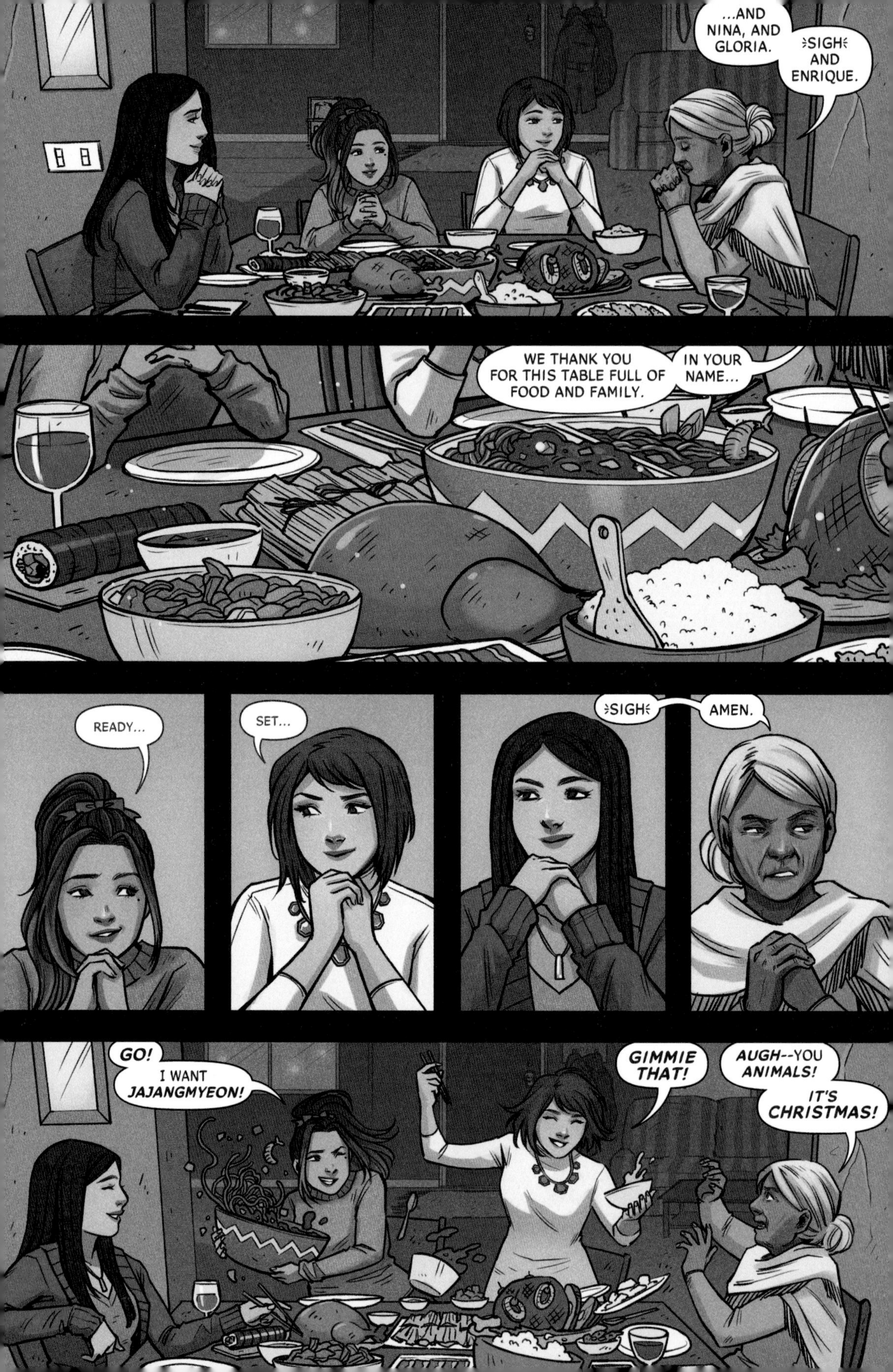
...AND NINA, AND GLORIA.
≷SIGH≶ AND ENRIQUE.
WE THANK YOU FOR THIS TABLE FULL OF FOOD AND FAMILY.
IN YOUR NAME...
READY...
SET...
≷SIGH≶
AMEN.
GO!
I WANT JAJANGMYEON!
GIMMIE THAT!
AUGH--YOU ANIMALS!
IT'S CHRISTMAS!

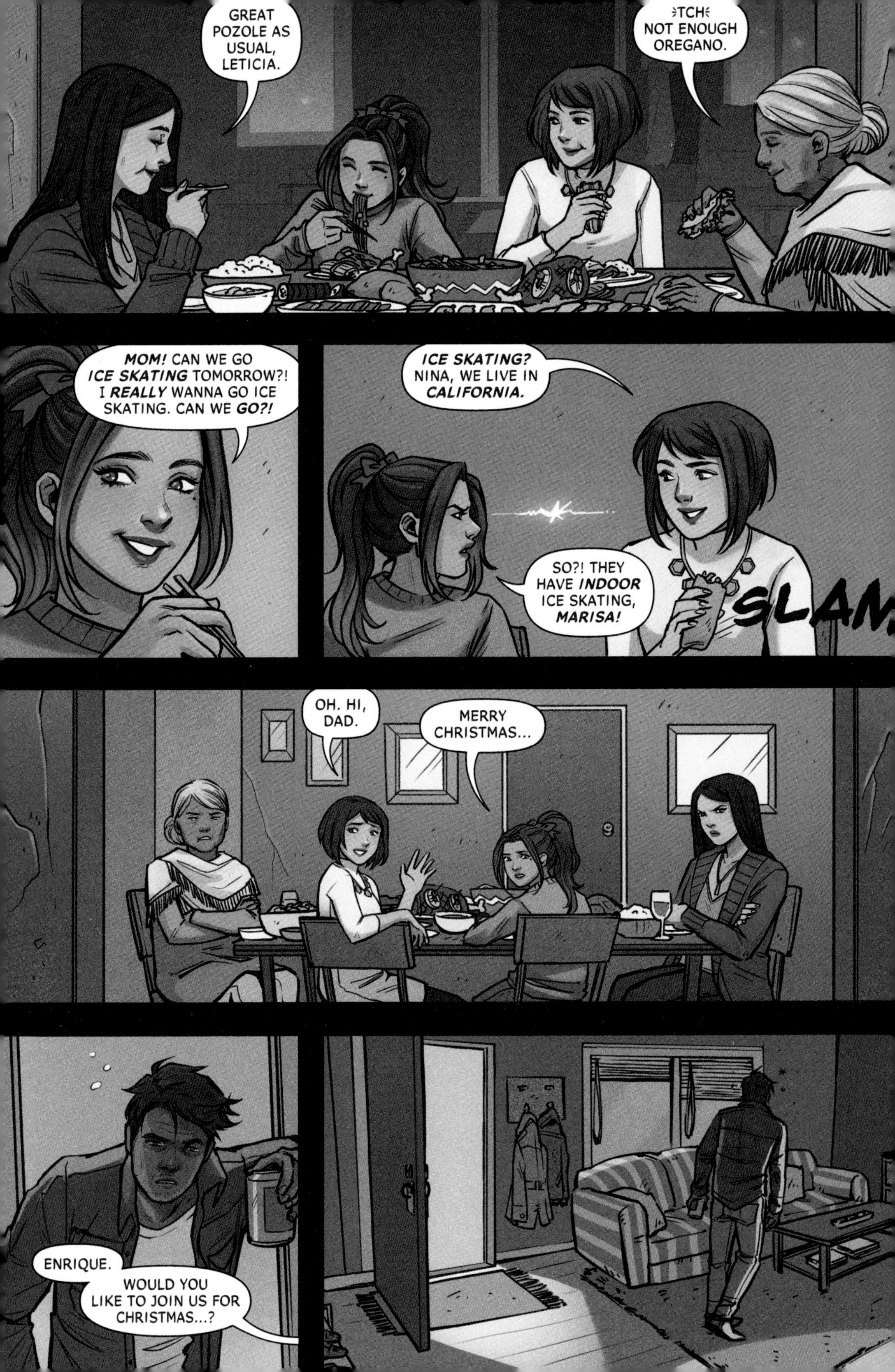
GREAT POZOLE AS USUAL, LETICIA.
TCH NOT ENOUGH OREGANO.
MOM! CAN WE GO ICE SKATING TOMORROW?! I REALLY WANNA GO ICE SKATING. CAN WE GO?!
ICE SKATING? NINA, WE LIVE IN CALIFORNIA.
SO?! THEY HAVE INDOOR ICE SKATING, MARISA!
SLAM
OH. HI, DAD.
MERRY CHRISTMAS...
ENRIQUE.
WOULD YOU LIKE TO JOIN US FOR CHRISTMAS...?

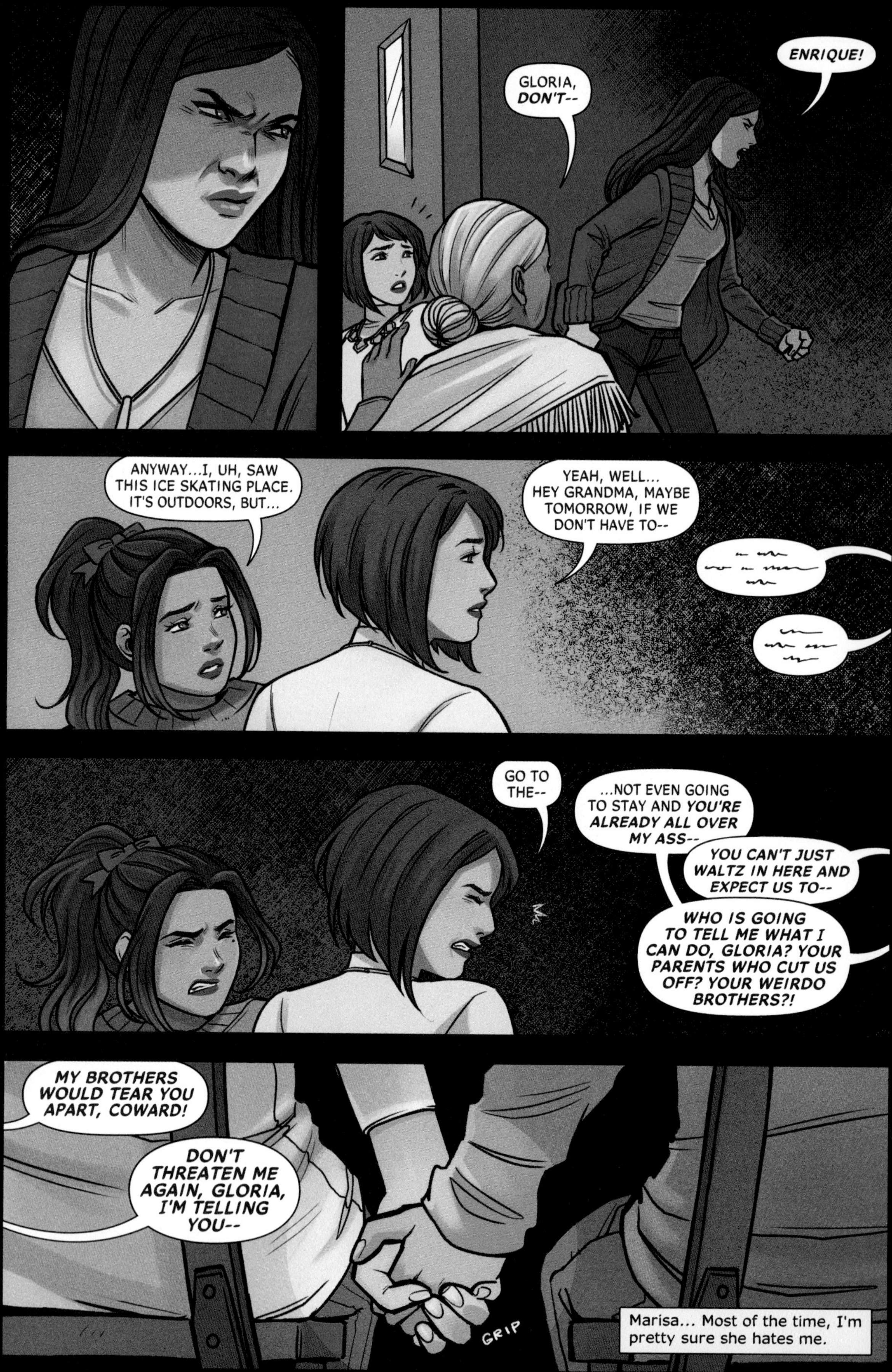
GLORIA, DON'T--
ENRIQUE!
ANYWAY...I, UH, SAW THIS ICE SKATING PLACE. IT'S OUTDOORS, BUT...
YEAH, WELL... HEY GRANDMA, MAYBE TOMORROW, IF WE DON'T HAVE TO--
GO TO THE--
...NOT EVEN GOING TO STAY AND YOU'RE ALREADY ALL OVER MY ASS--
YOU CAN'T JUST WALTZ IN HERE AND EXPECT US TO--
WHO IS GOING TO TELL ME WHAT I CAN DO, GLORIA? YOUR PARENTS WHO CUT US OFF? YOUR WEIRDO BROTHERS?!
MY BROTHERS WOULD TEAR YOU APART, COWARD!
DON'T THREATEN ME AGAIN, GLORIA, I'M TELLING YOU--
GRIP
Marisa... Most of the time, I'm pretty sure she hates me.

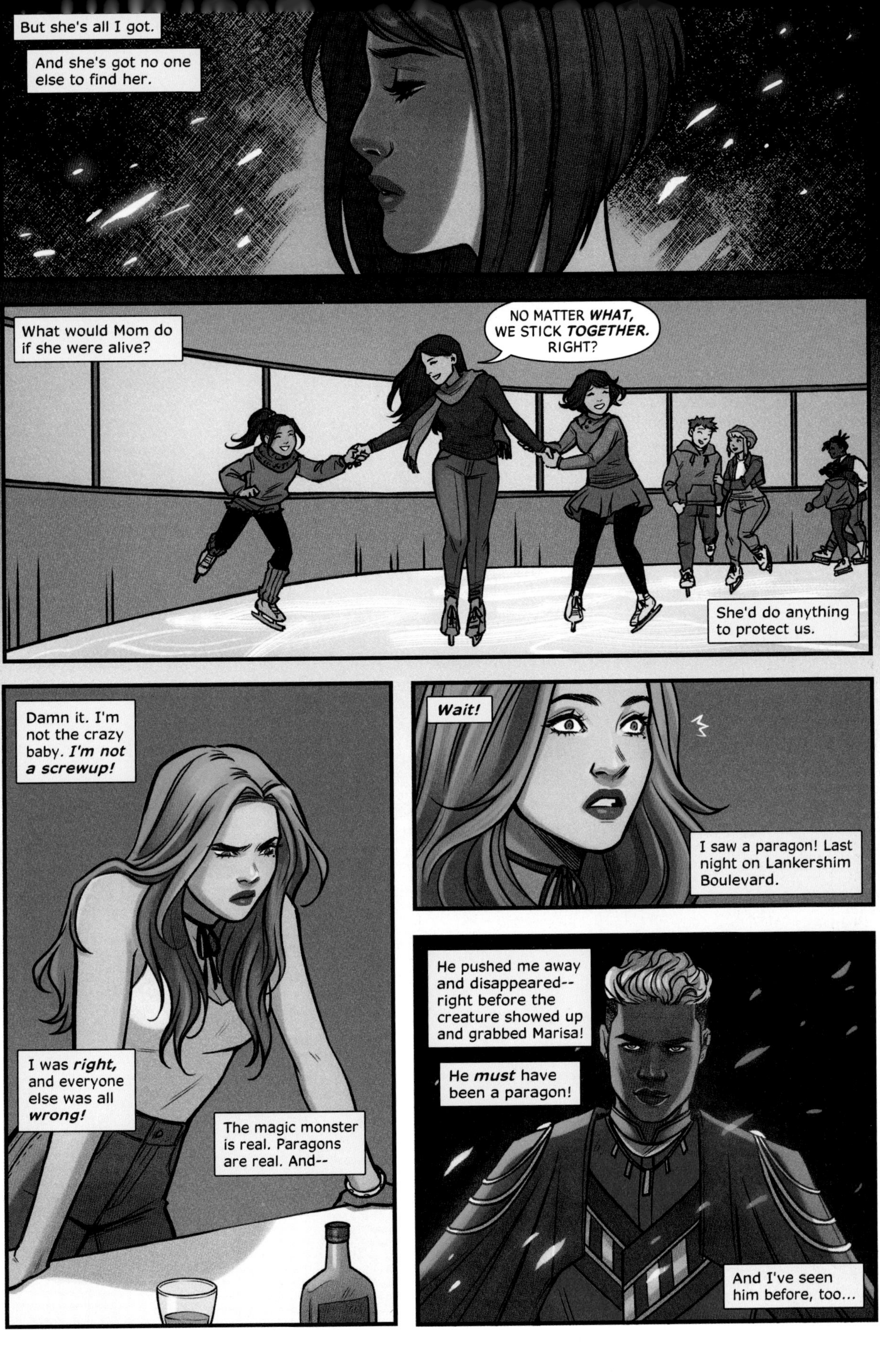
But she's all I got.
And she's got no one else to find her.
What would Mom do if she were alive?
NO MATTER *WHAT,* WE STICK *TOGETHER.* RIGHT?
She'd do anything to protect us.
Damn it. I'm not the crazy baby. ***I'm not a screwup!***
I was ***right,*** and everyone else was all ***wrong!***
The magic monster is real. Paragons are real. And--
Wait!
I saw a paragon! Last night on Lankershim Boulevard.
He pushed me away and disappeared-- right before the creature showed up and grabbed Marisa!
He ***must*** have been a paragon!
And I've seen him before, too...

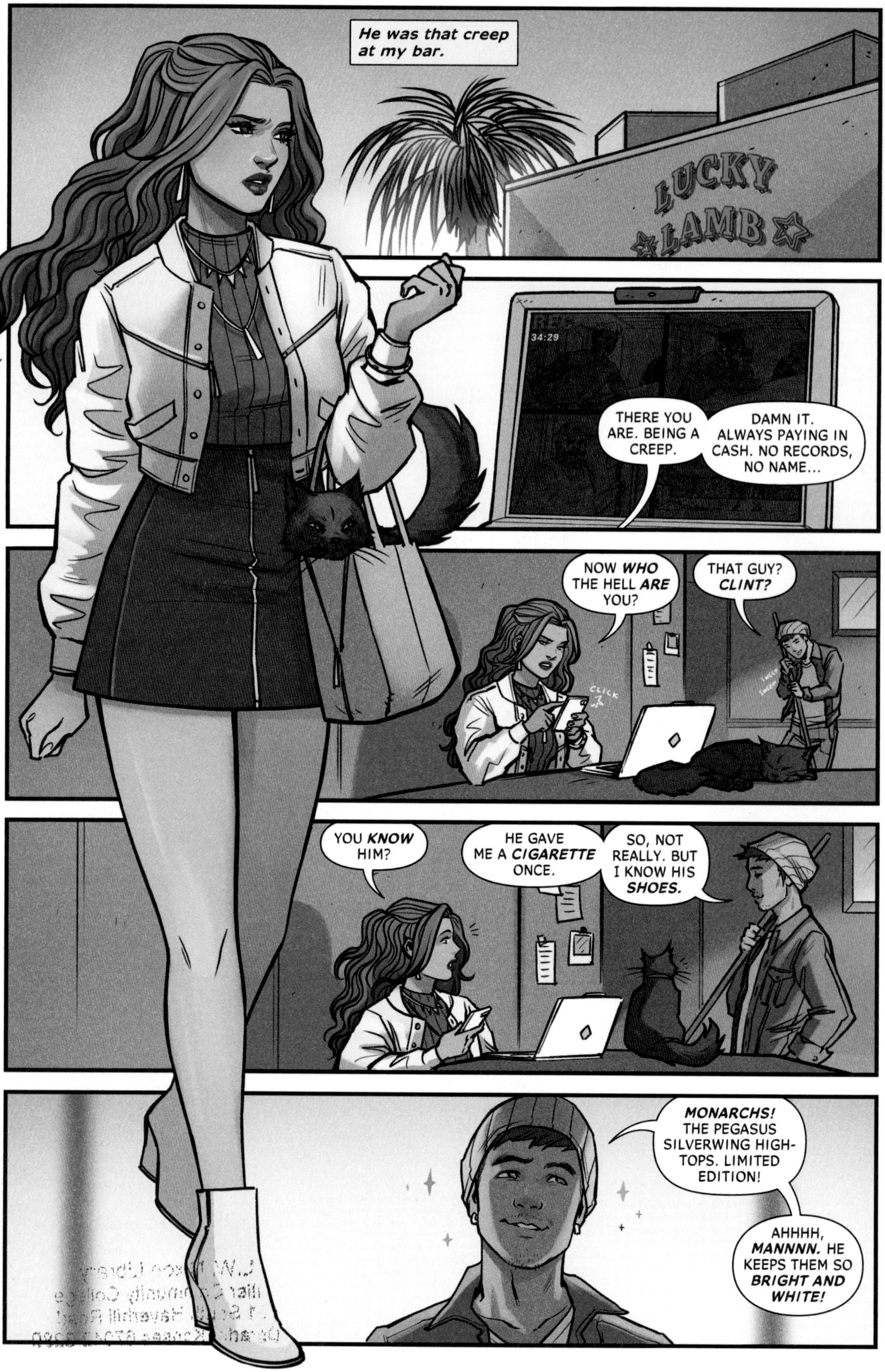
He was that creep at my bar.
LUCKY LAMB
34:29
THERE YOU ARE. BEING A CREEP.
DAMN IT. ALWAYS PAYING IN CASH. NO RECORDS, NO NAME...
NOW *WHO* THE HELL *ARE* YOU?
THAT GUY? *CLINT?*
CLICK
YOU *KNOW* HIM?
HE GAVE ME A *CIGARETTE* ONCE.
SO, NOT REALLY. BUT I KNOW HIS *SHOES.*
MONARCHS! THE PEGASUS SILVERWING HIGH-TOPS. LIMITED EDITION!
AHHHH, *MANNNN.* HE KEEPS THEM SO *BRIGHT AND WHITE!*

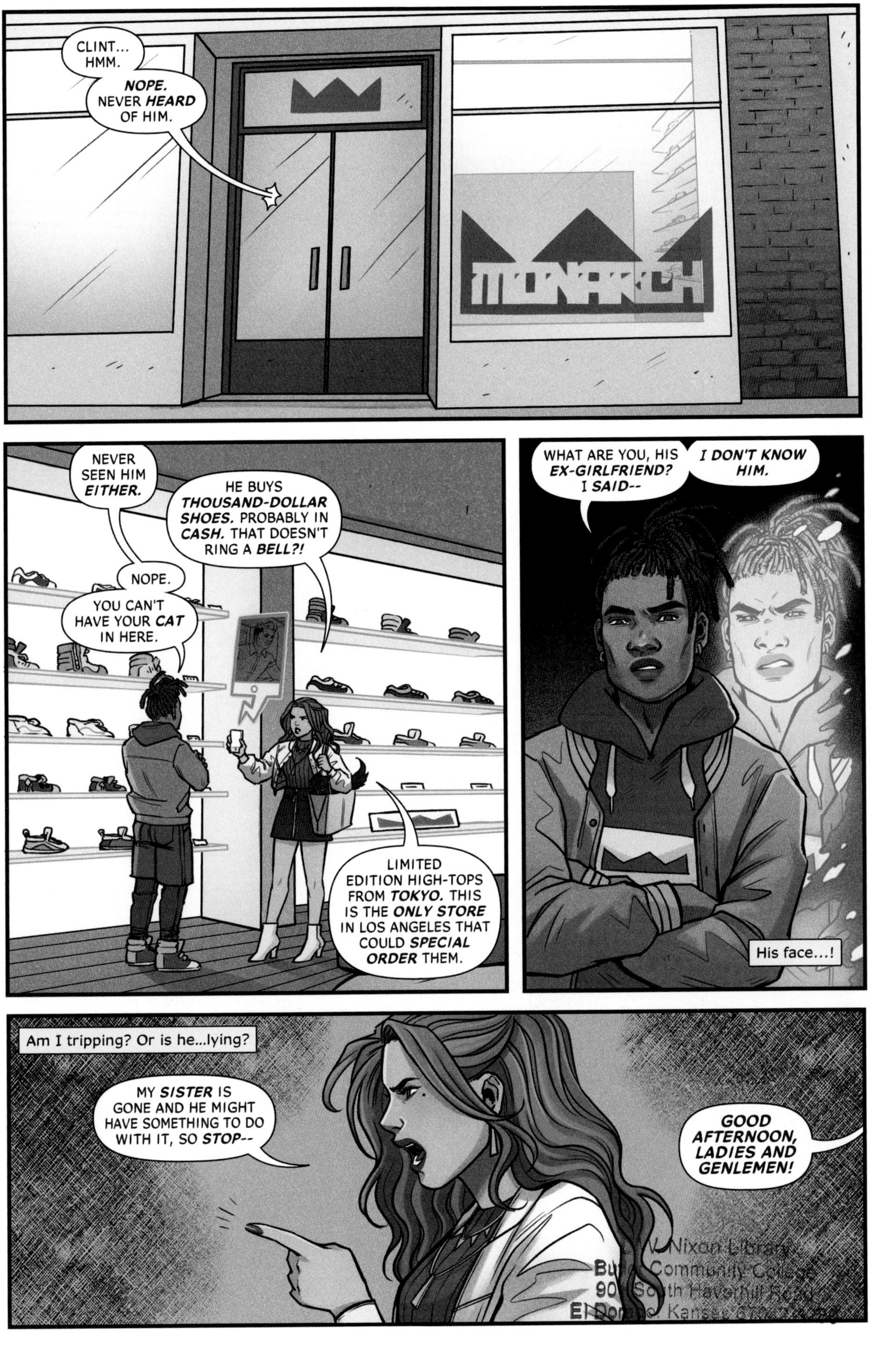
CLINT... HMM.
NOPE. NEVER HEARD OF HIM.
NEVER SEEN HIM EITHER.
HE BUYS THOUSAND-DOLLAR SHOES. PROBABLY IN CASH. THAT DOESN'T RING A BELL?!
NOPE.
YOU CAN'T HAVE YOUR CAT IN HERE.
LIMITED EDITION HIGH-TOPS FROM TOKYO. THIS IS THE ONLY STORE IN LOS ANGELES THAT COULD SPECIAL ORDER THEM.
WHAT ARE YOU, HIS EX-GIRLFRIEND? I SAID--
I DON'T KNOW HIM.
His face...!
Am I tripping? Or is he...lying?
MY SISTER IS GONE AND HE MIGHT HAVE SOMETHING TO DO WITH IT, SO STOP--
GOOD AFTERNOON, LADIES AND GENLEMEN!

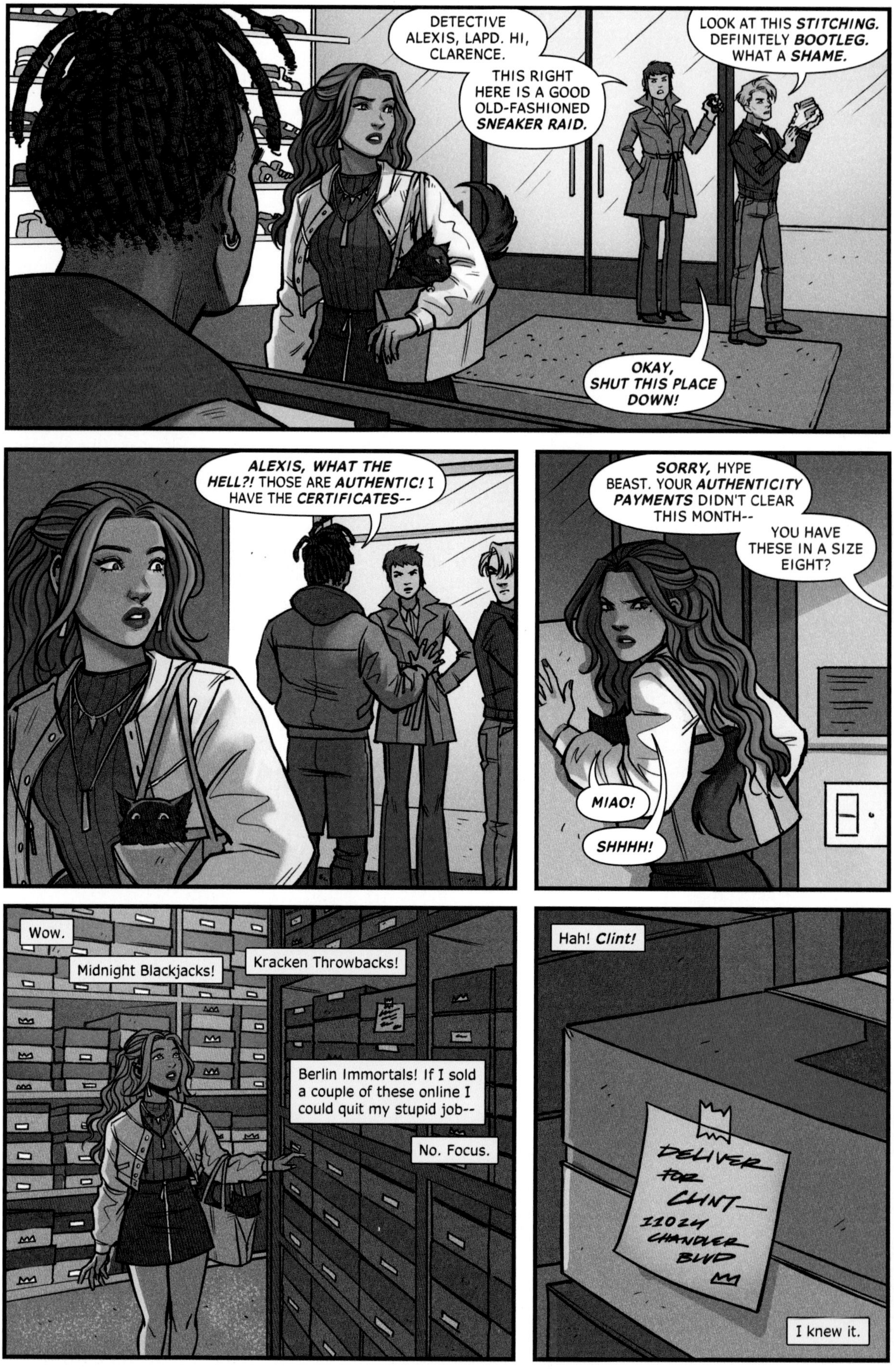

DETECTIVE ALEXIS, LAPD. HI, CLARENCE.
THIS RIGHT HERE IS A GOOD OLD-FASHIONED SNEAKER RAID.
LOOK AT THIS STITCHING. DEFINITELY BOOTLEG. WHAT A SHAME.
OKAY, SHUT THIS PLACE DOWN!
ALEXIS, WHAT THE HELL?! THOSE ARE AUTHENTIC! I HAVE THE CERTIFICATES--
SORRY, HYPE BEAST. YOUR AUTHENTICITY PAYMENTS DIDN'T CLEAR THIS MONTH--
YOU HAVE THESE IN A SIZE EIGHT?
MIAO!
SHHHH!
Wow.
Midnight Blackjacks!
Kracken Throwbacks!
Berlin Immortals! If I sold a couple of these online I could quit my stupid job--
No. Focus.
Hah! Clint!
DELIVER FOR CLINT 11024 CHANDLER BLVD
I knew it.

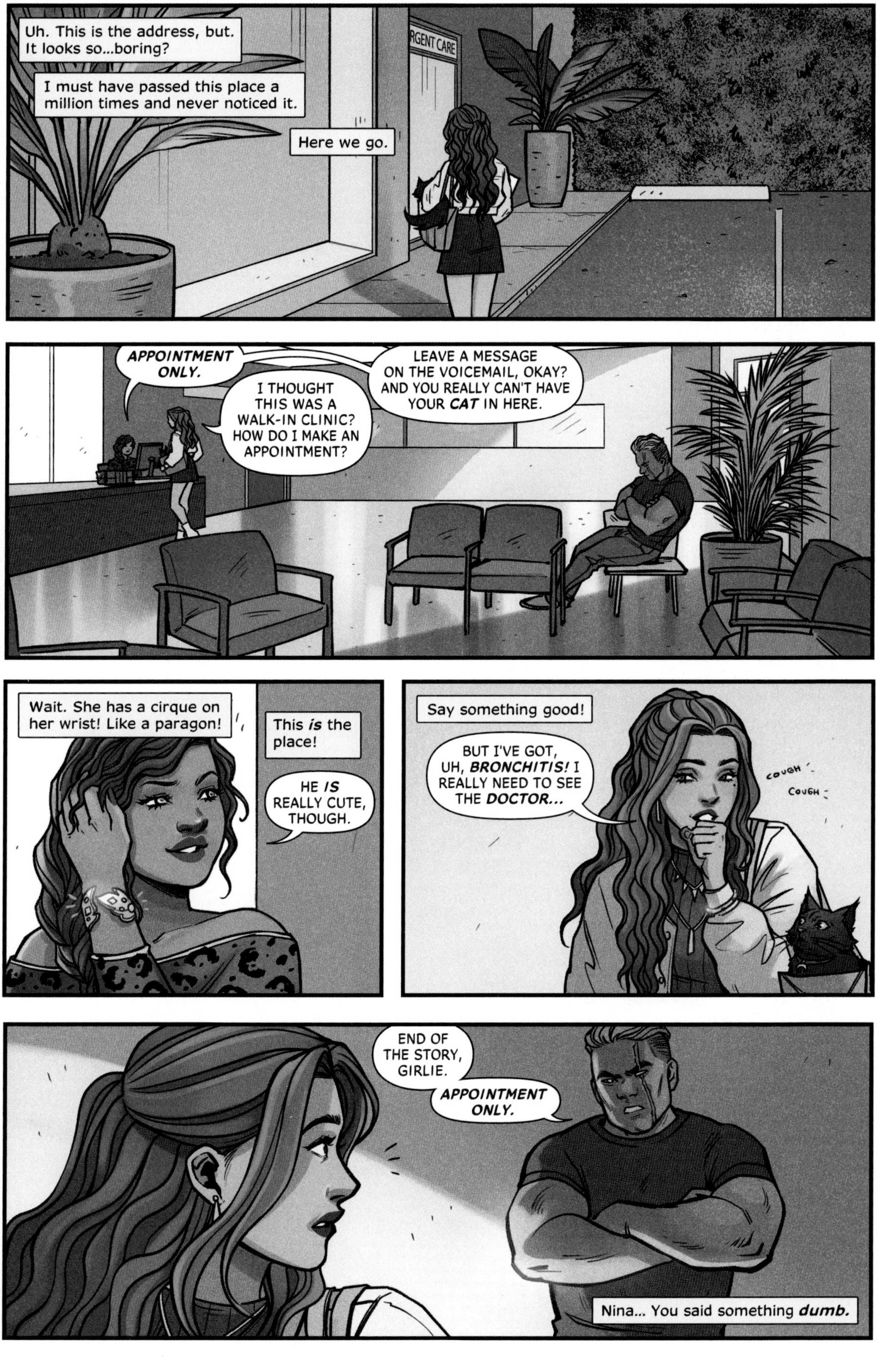
Uh. This is the address, but. It looks so...boring?
I must have passed this place a million times and never noticed it.
Here we go.
RGENT CARE
APPOINTMENT ONLY.
I THOUGHT THIS WAS A WALK-IN CLINIC? HOW DO I MAKE AN APPOINTMENT?
LEAVE A MESSAGE ON THE VOICEMAIL, OKAY? AND YOU REALLY CAN'T HAVE YOUR *CAT* IN HERE.
Wait. She has a cirque on her wrist! Like a paragon!
This *is* the place!
HE *IS* REALLY CUTE, THOUGH.
Say something good!
BUT I'VE GOT, UH, *BRONCHITIS!* I REALLY NEED TO SEE THE *DOCTOR...*
COUGH
COUGH
END OF THE STORY, GIRLIE.
APPOINTMENT ONLY.
Nina... You said something *dumb.*

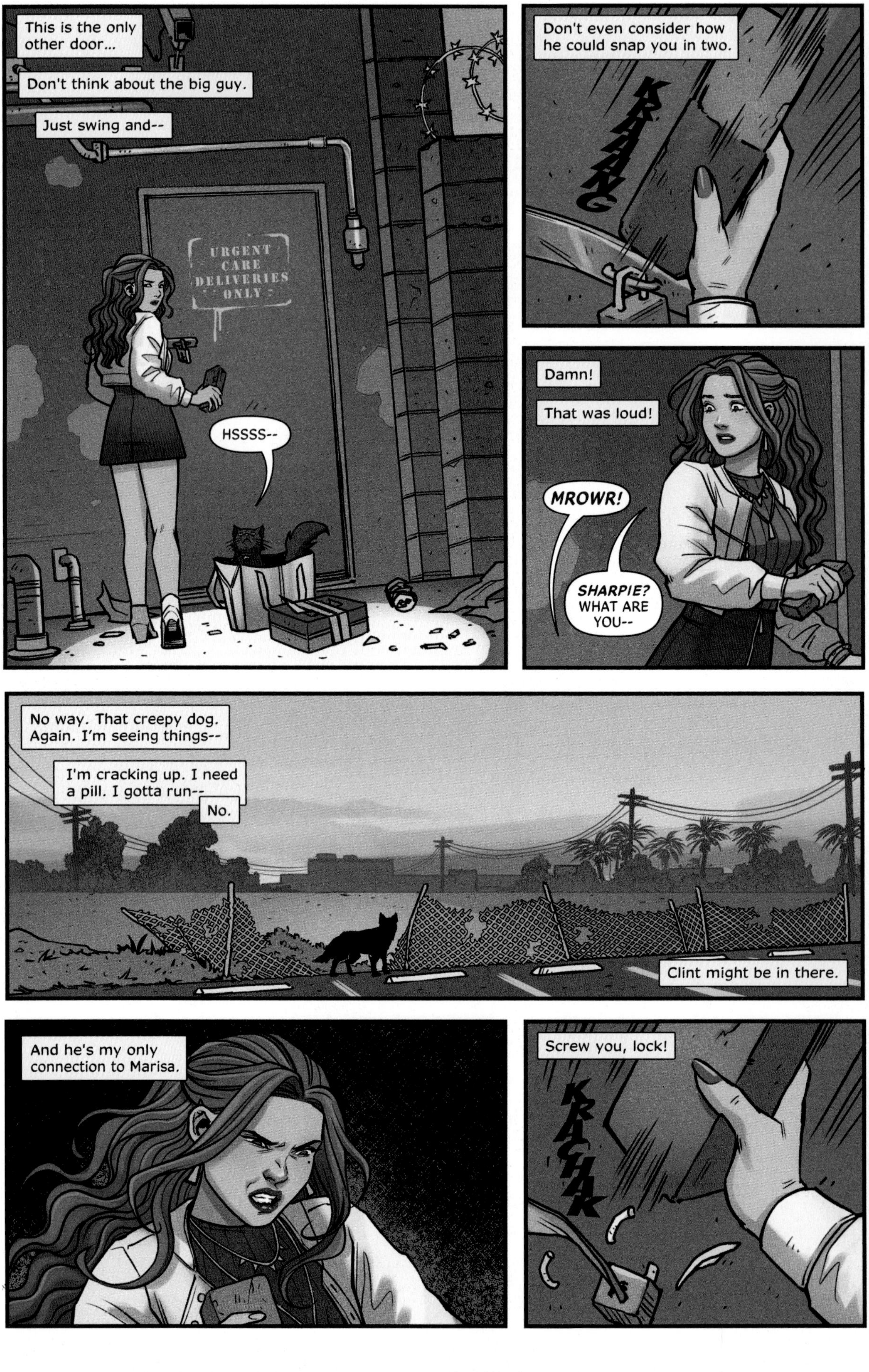
This is the only other door...
Don't think about the big guy.
Just swing and--
URGENT CARE DELIVERIES ONLY
HSSSS--
Don't even consider how he could snap you in two.
KRAAANG
Damn!
That was loud!
MROWR!
SHARPIE? WHAT ARE YOU--
No way. That creepy dog. Again. I'm seeing things--
I'm cracking up. I need a pill. I gotta run--
No.
Clint might be in there.
And he's my only connection to Marisa.
Screw you, lock!
KRACHAK

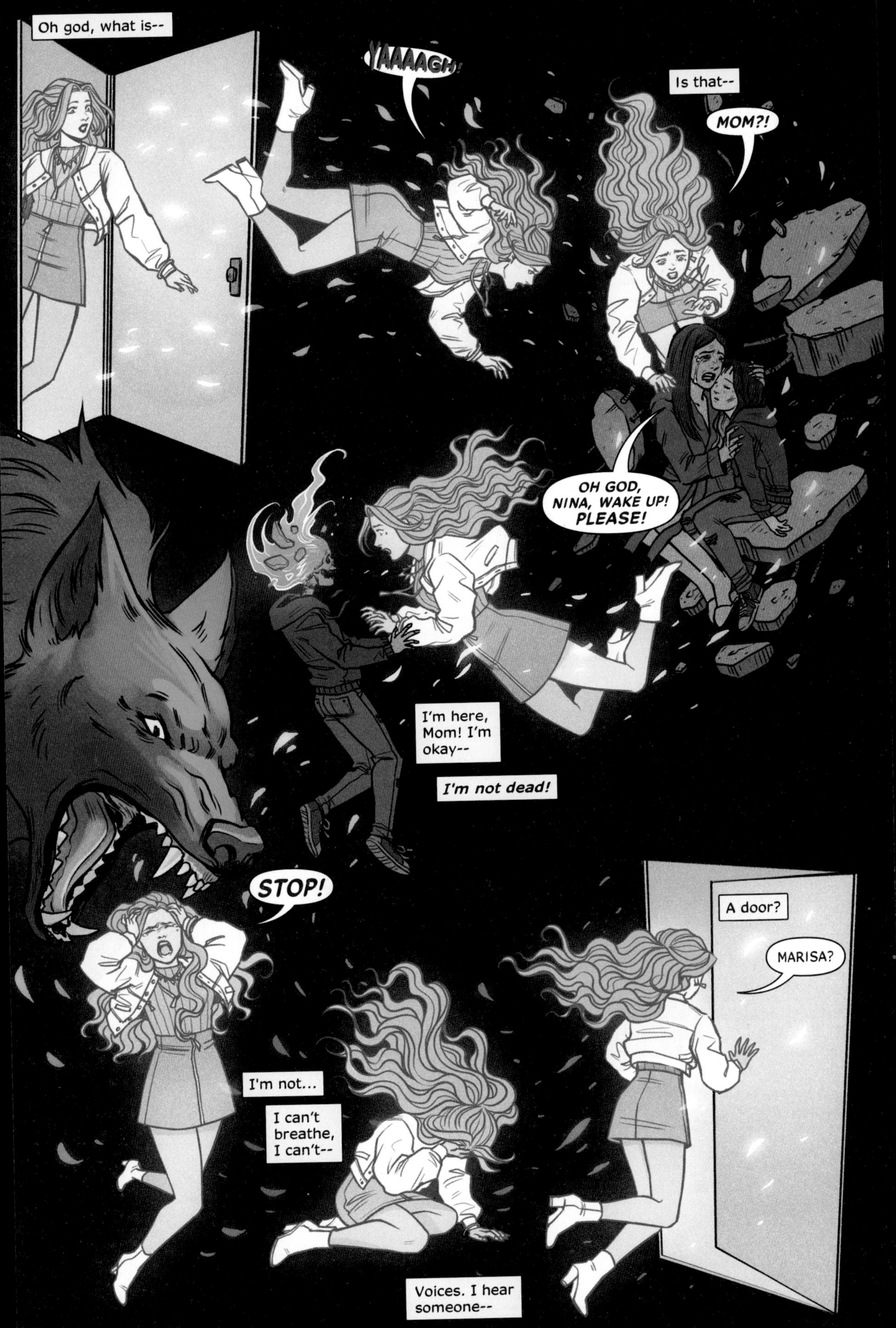
Oh god, what is--
YAAAAGH!
Is that--
MOM?!
OH GOD, NINA, WAKE UP! PLEASE!
I'm here, Mom! I'm okay--
I'm not dead!
STOP!
I'm not...
I can't breathe, I can't--
Voices. I hear someone--
A door?
MARISA?

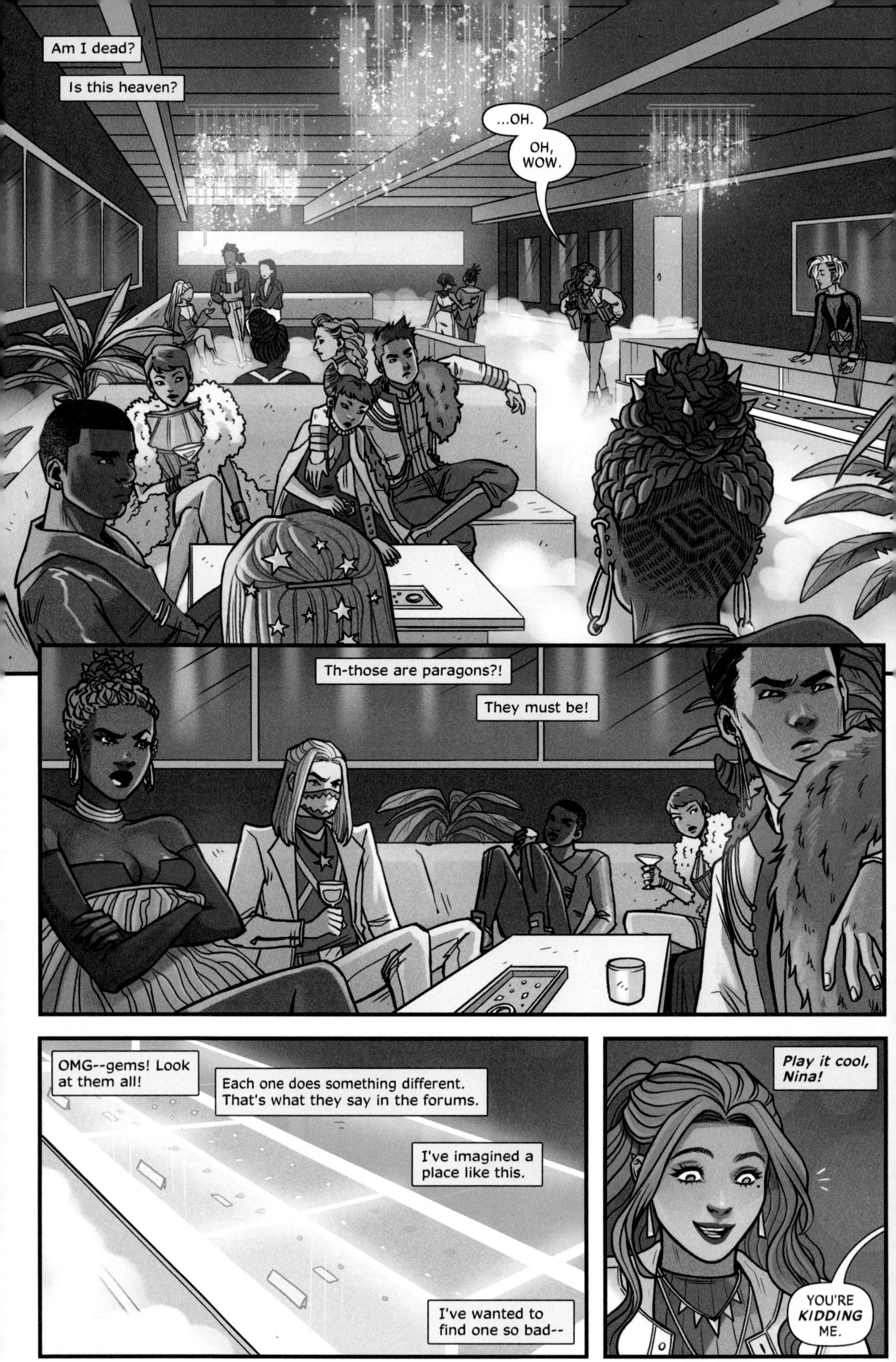
Am I dead?
Is this heaven?
...OH.
OH, WOW.
Th-those are paragons?!
They must be!
OMG--gems! Look at them all!
Each one does something different. That's what they say in the forums.
I've imagined a place like this.
I've wanted to find one so bad--
Play it cool, Nina!
YOU'RE *KIDDING* ME.

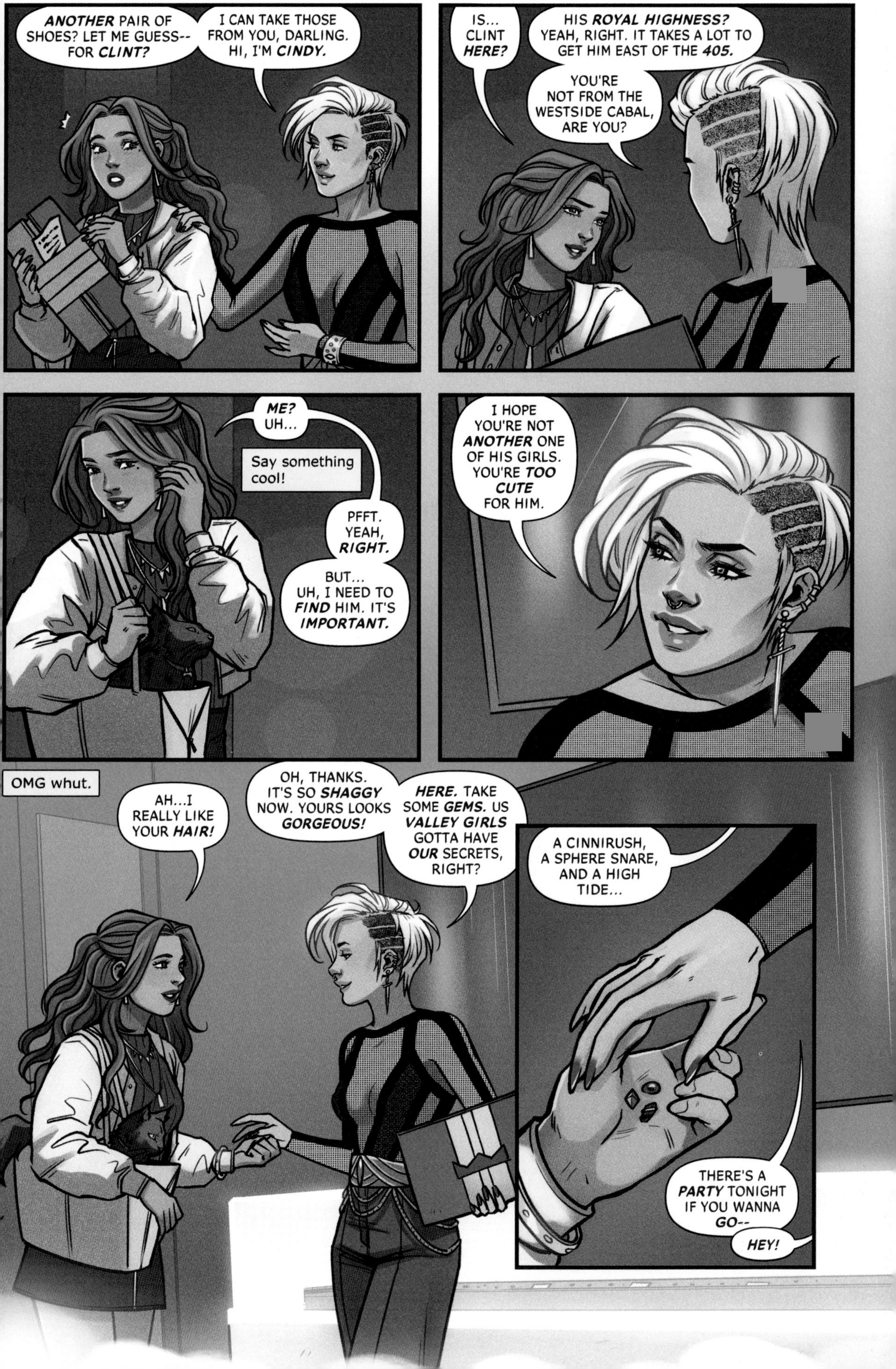

ANOTHER PAIR OF SHOES? LET ME GUESS-- FOR CLINT?
I CAN TAKE THOSE FROM YOU, DARLING. HI, I'M CINDY.
IS... CLINT HERE?
HIS ROYAL HIGHNESS? YEAH, RIGHT. IT TAKES A LOT TO GET HIM EAST OF THE 405.
YOU'RE NOT FROM THE WESTSIDE CABAL, ARE YOU?
ME? UH...
Say something cool!
PFFT. YEAH, RIGHT.
BUT... UH, I NEED TO FIND HIM. IT'S IMPORTANT.
I HOPE YOU'RE NOT ANOTHER ONE OF HIS GIRLS. YOU'RE TOO CUTE FOR HIM.
OMG whut.
AH...I REALLY LIKE YOUR HAIR!
OH, THANKS. IT'S SO SHAGGY NOW. YOURS LOOKS GORGEOUS!
HERE. TAKE SOME GEMS. US VALLEY GIRLS GOTTA HAVE OUR SECRETS, RIGHT?
A CINNIRUSH, A SPHERE SNARE, AND A HIGH TIDE...
THERE'S A PARTY TONIGHT IF YOU WANNA GO--
HEY!

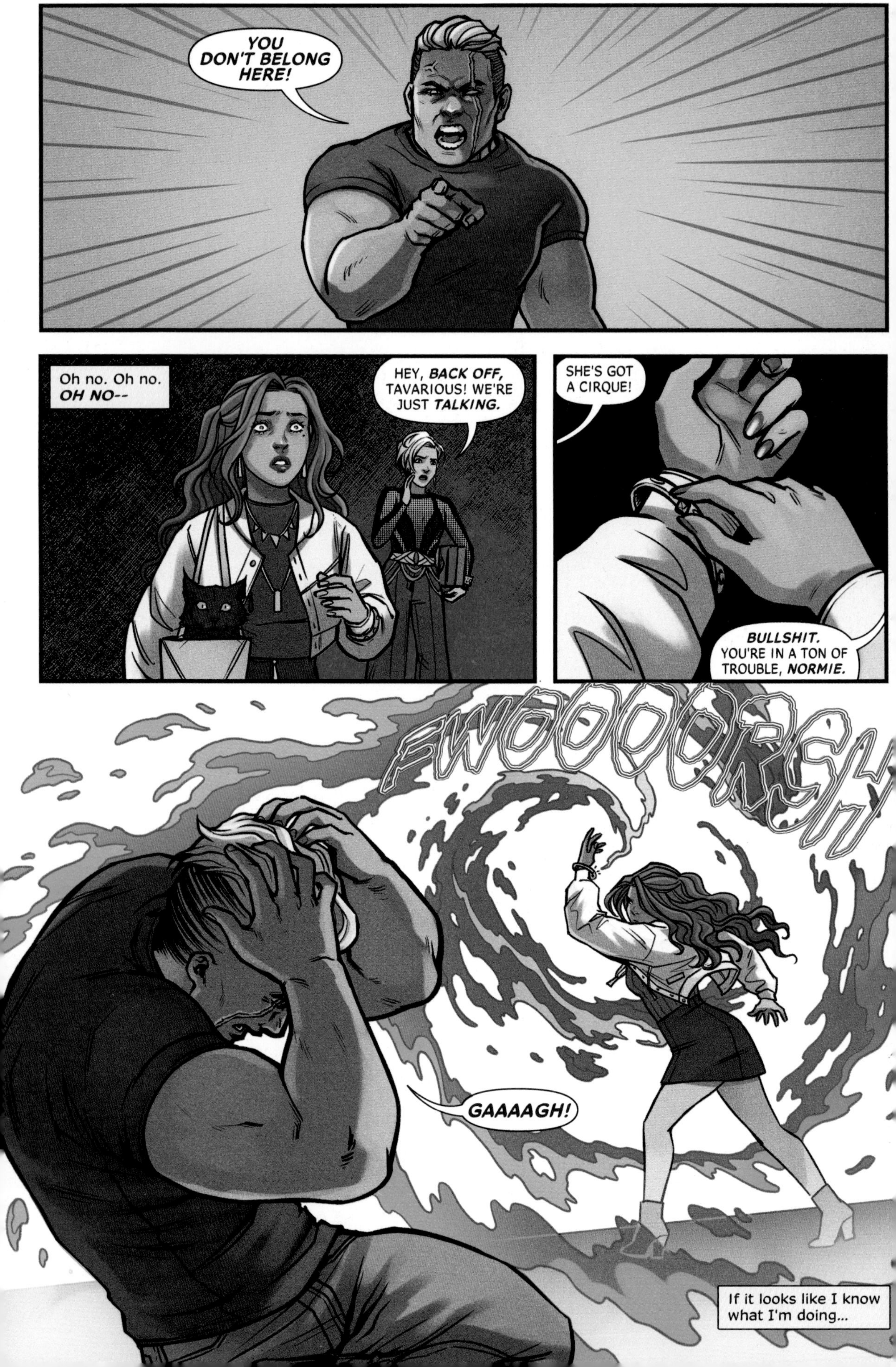

YOU DON'T BELONG HERE!
Oh no. Oh no. OH NO--
HEY, BACK OFF, TAVARIOUS! WE'RE JUST TALKING.
SHE'S GOT A CIRQUE!
BULLSHIT. YOU'RE IN A TON OF TROUBLE, NORMIE.
FWOOOOORSH
GAAAAGH!
If it looks like I know what I'm doing...

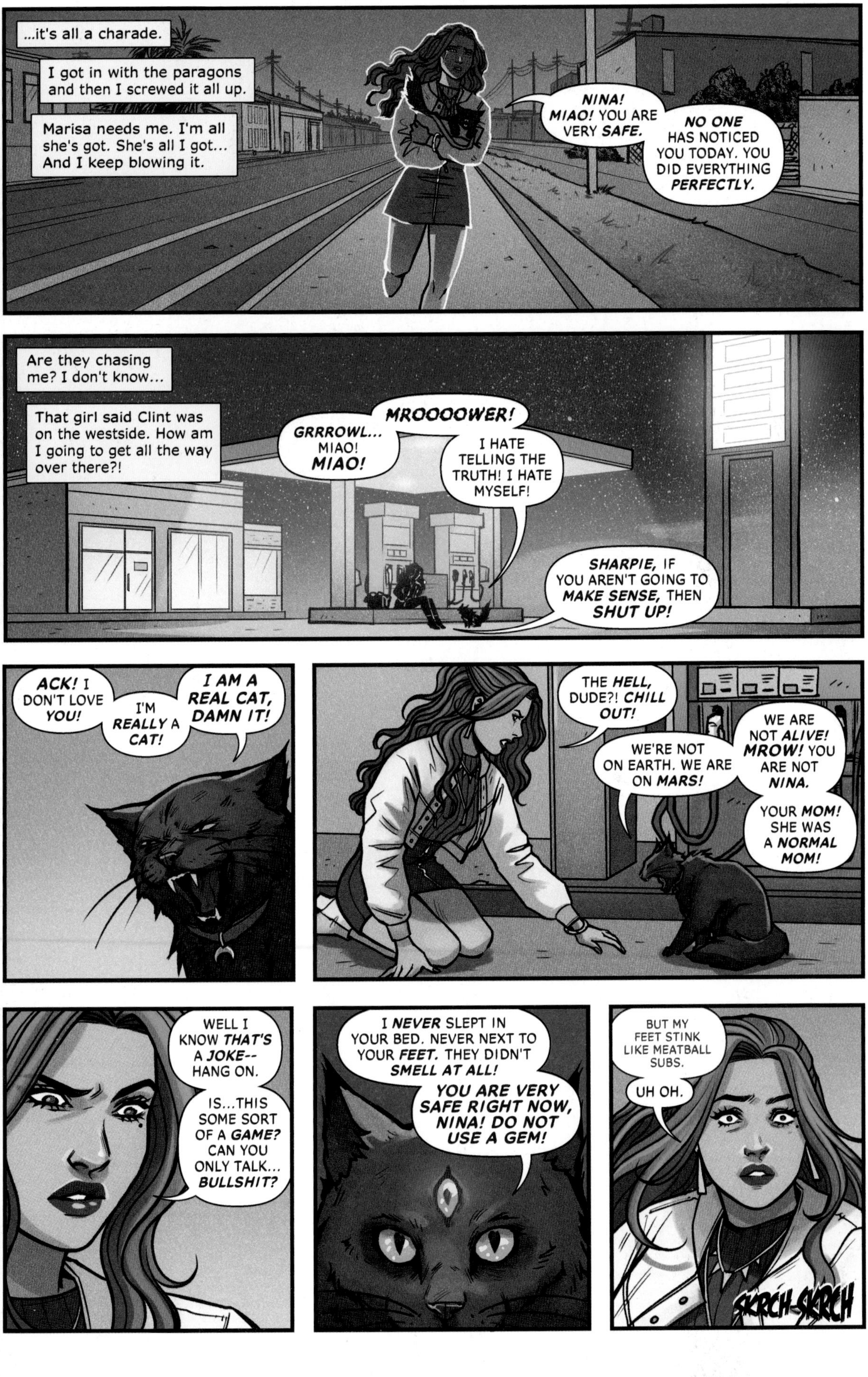
...it's all a charade.
I got in with the paragons and then I screwed it all up.
Marisa needs me. I'm all she's got. She's all I got... And I keep blowing it.
NINA! MIAO! YOU ARE VERY SAFE.
NO ONE HAS NOTICED YOU TODAY. YOU DID EVERYTHING PERFECTLY.
Are they chasing me? I don't know...
That girl said Clint was on the westside. How am I going to get all the way over there?!
GRRROWL... MIAO! MIAO!
MROOOOWER!
I HATE TELLING THE TRUTH! I HATE MYSELF!
SHARPIE, IF YOU AREN'T GOING TO MAKE SENSE, THEN SHUT UP!
ACK! I DON'T LOVE YOU!
I'M REALLY A CAT!
I AM A REAL CAT, DAMN IT!
THE HELL, DUDE?! CHILL OUT!
WE'RE NOT ON EARTH. WE ARE ON MARS!
WE ARE NOT ALIVE! MROW! YOU ARE NOT NINA.
YOUR MOM! SHE WAS A NORMAL MOM!
WELL I KNOW THAT'S A JOKE-- HANG ON.
IS...THIS SOME SORT OF A GAME? CAN YOU ONLY TALK... BULLSHIT?
I NEVER SLEPT IN YOUR BED. NEVER NEXT TO YOUR FEET. THEY DIDN'T SMELL AT ALL!
YOU ARE VERY SAFE RIGHT NOW, NINA! DO NOT USE A GEM!
BUT MY FEET STINK LIKE MEATBALL SUBS.
UH OH.
SKRCH-SKRCH

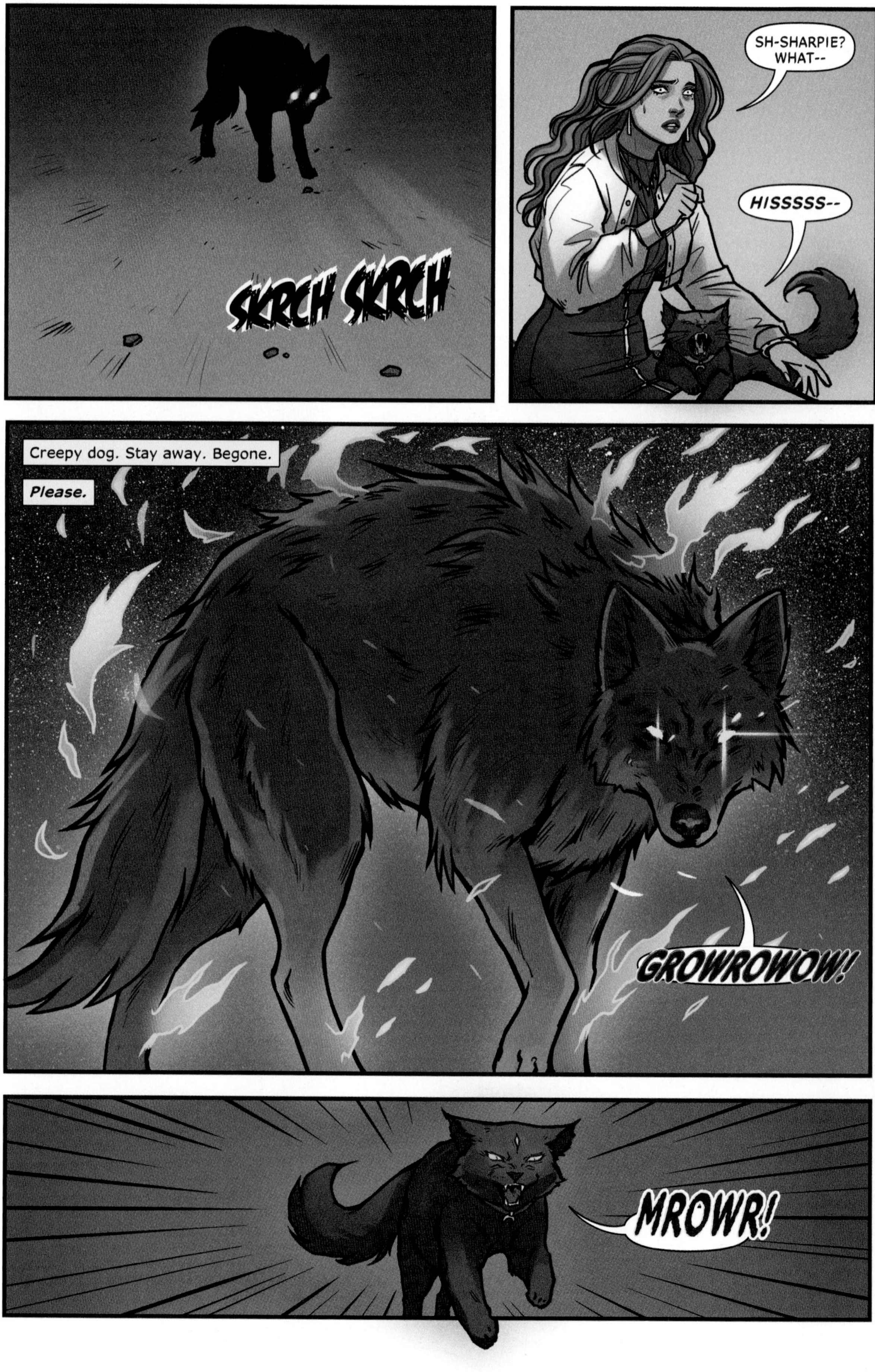

SKRCH SKRCH
SH-SHARPIE? WHAT--
HISSSSS--
Creepy dog. Stay away. Begone.
Please.
GROWROWOW!
MROWR!

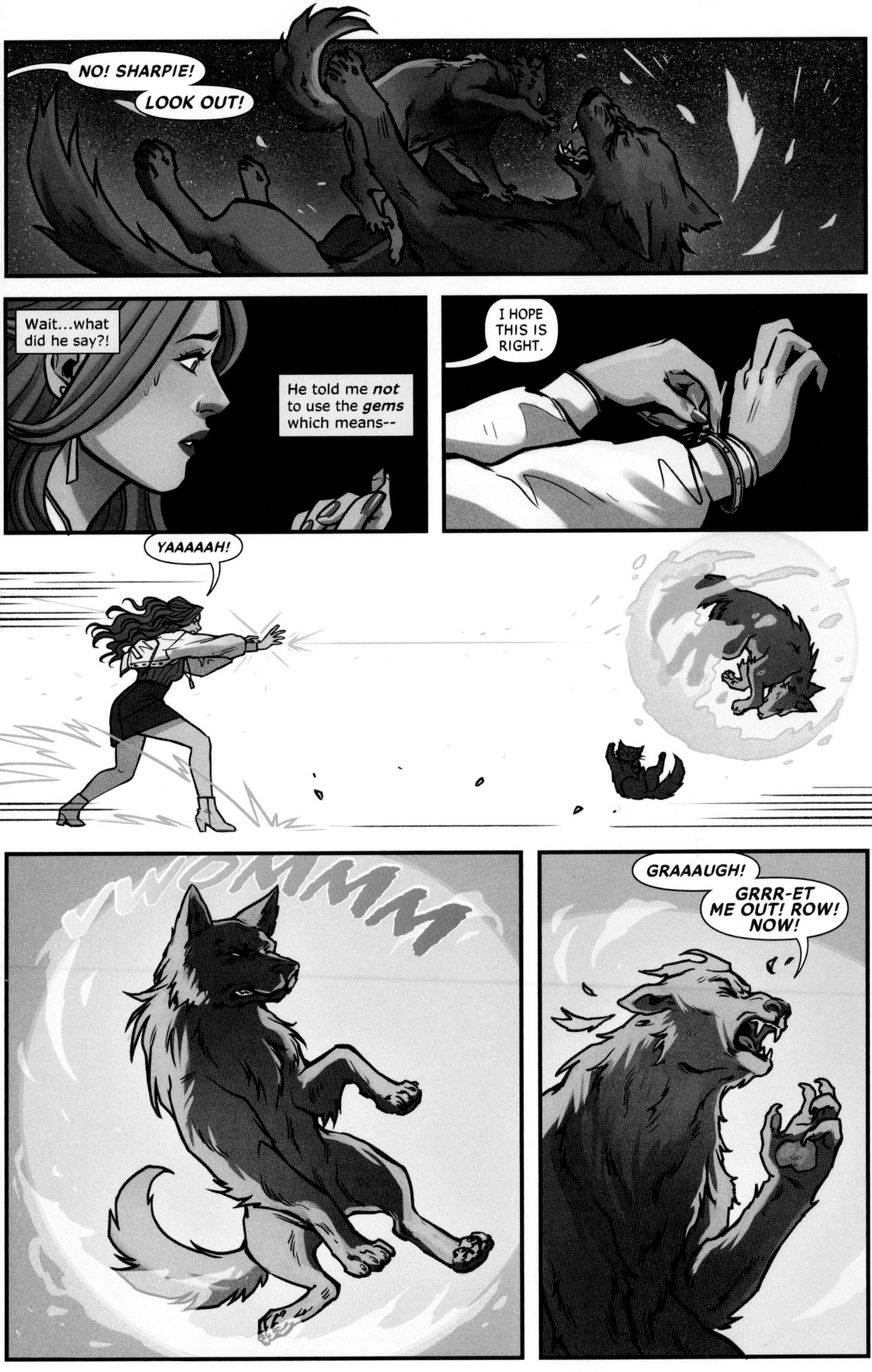
NO! SHARPIE!
LOOK OUT!
Wait...what did he say?!
He told me *not* to use the *gems* which means--
I HOPE THIS IS RIGHT.
YAAAAAH!
WOMMM
GRAAAUGH!
GRRR-ET ME OUT! ROW! NOW!

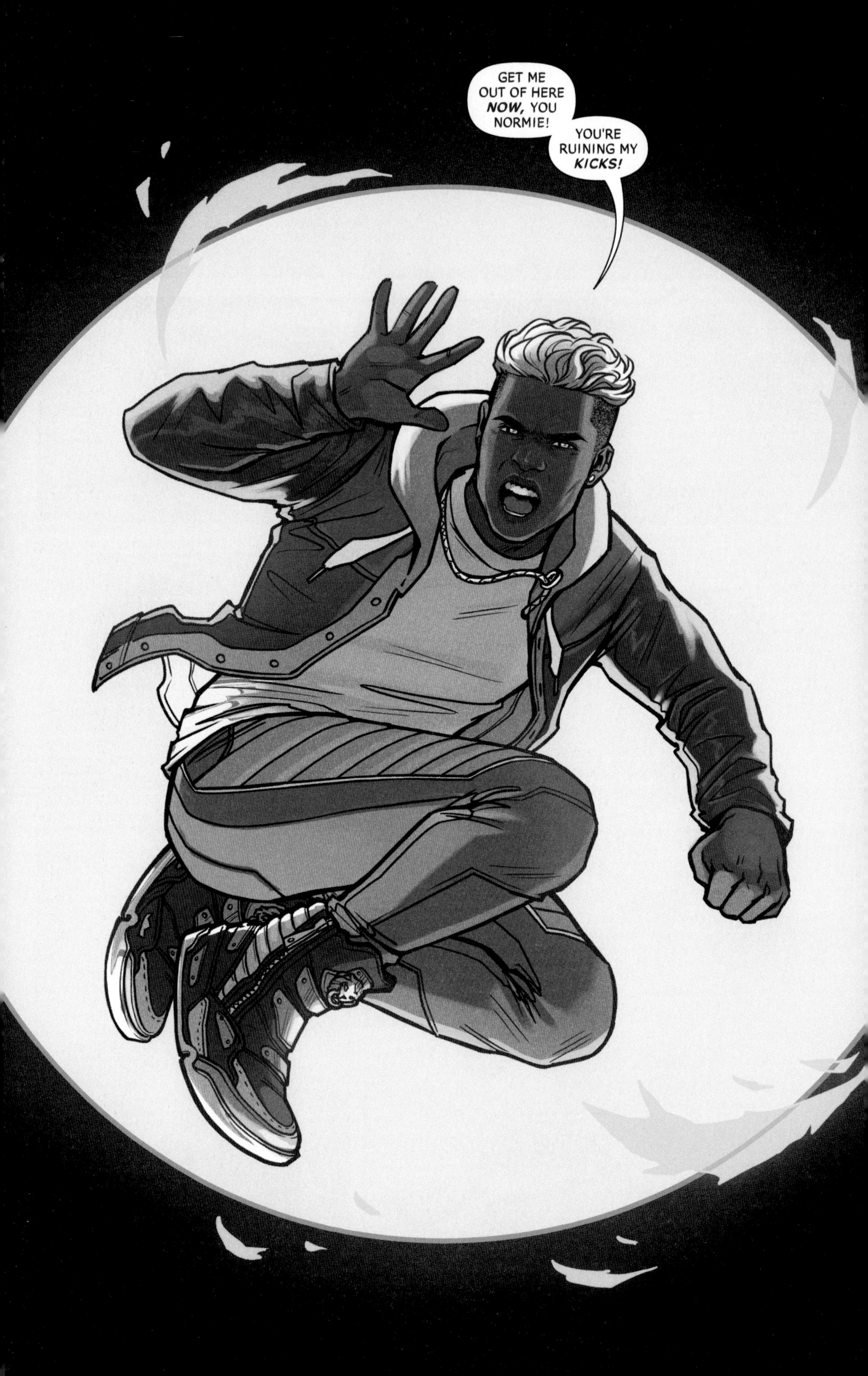
GET ME OUT OF HERE ***NOW,*** YOU NORMIE!
YOU'RE RUINING MY ***KICKS!***

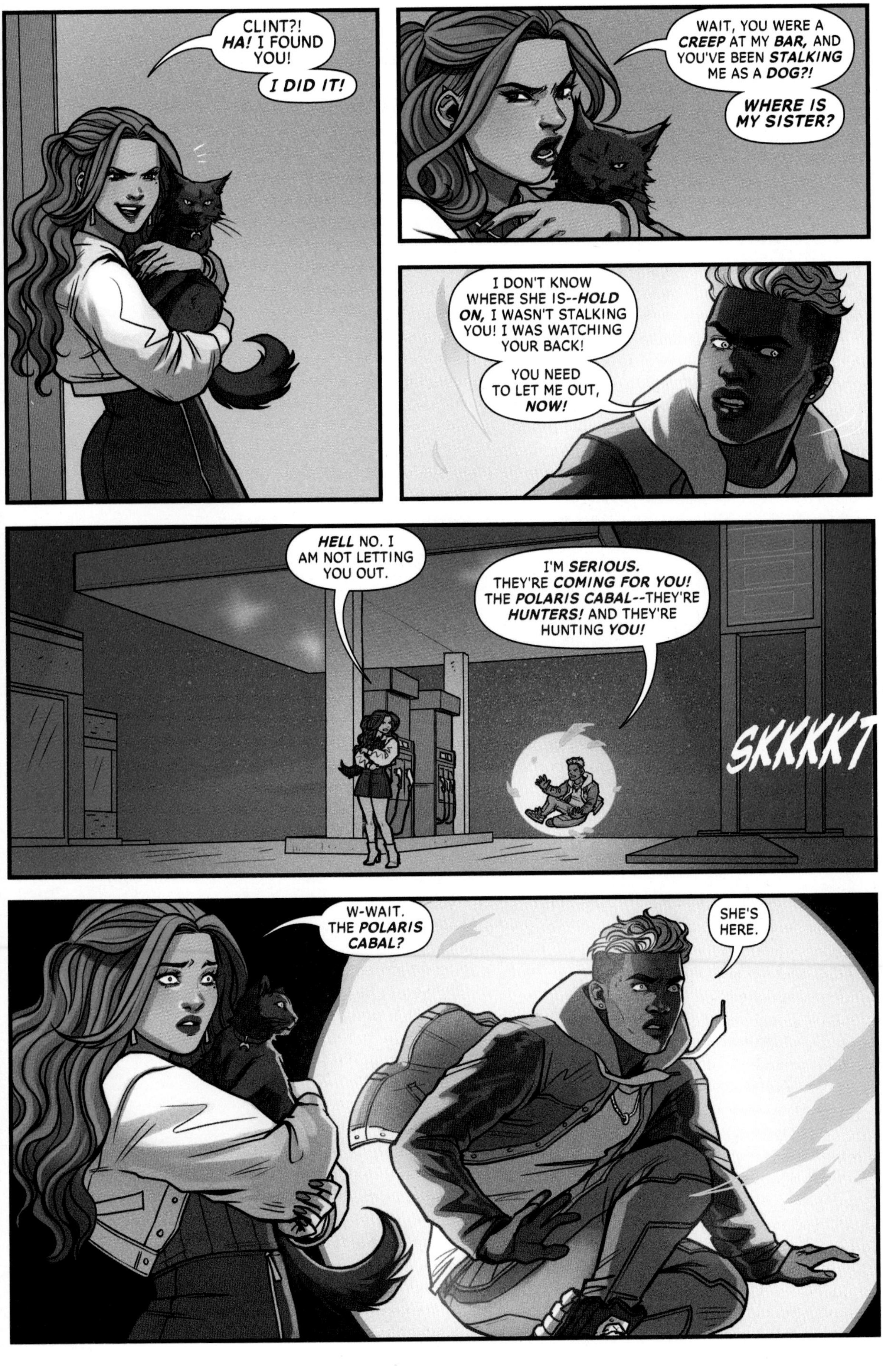
CLINT?! HA! I FOUND YOU!
I DID IT!
WAIT, YOU WERE A CREEP AT MY BAR, AND YOU'VE BEEN STALKING ME AS A DOG?!
WHERE IS MY SISTER?
I DON'T KNOW WHERE SHE IS--HOLD ON, I WASN'T STALKING YOU! I WAS WATCHING YOUR BACK!
YOU NEED TO LET ME OUT, NOW!
HELL NO. I AM NOT LETTING YOU OUT.
I'M SERIOUS. THEY'RE COMING FOR YOU! THE POLARIS CABAL--THEY'RE HUNTERS! AND THEY'RE HUNTING YOU!
SKKKKT
W-WAIT. THE POLARIS CABAL?
SHE'S HERE.

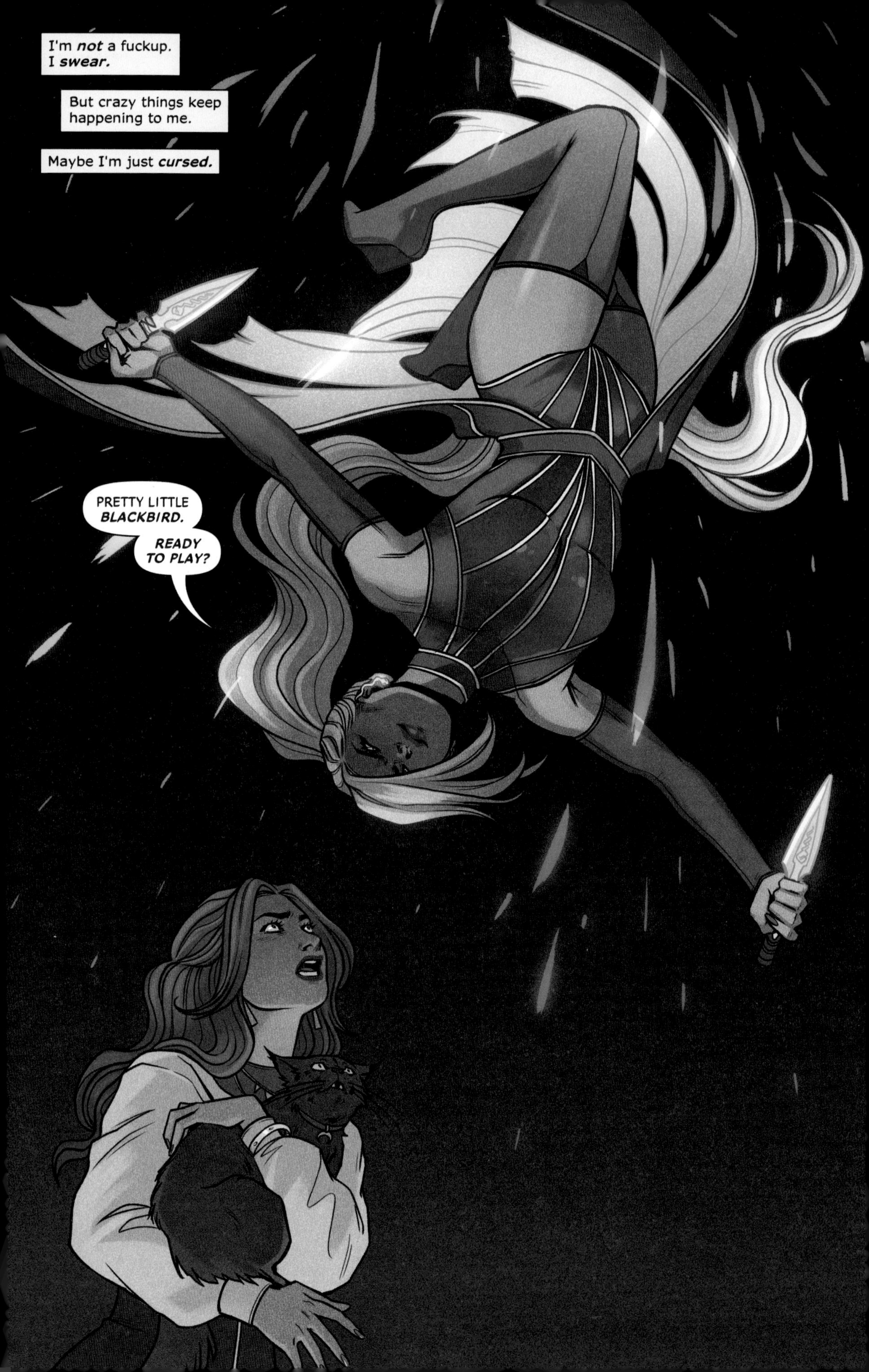
I'm *not* a fuckup. I *swear.*
But crazy things keep happening to me.
Maybe I'm just *cursed.*
PRETTY LITTLE *BLACKBIRD.*
READY TO PLAY?

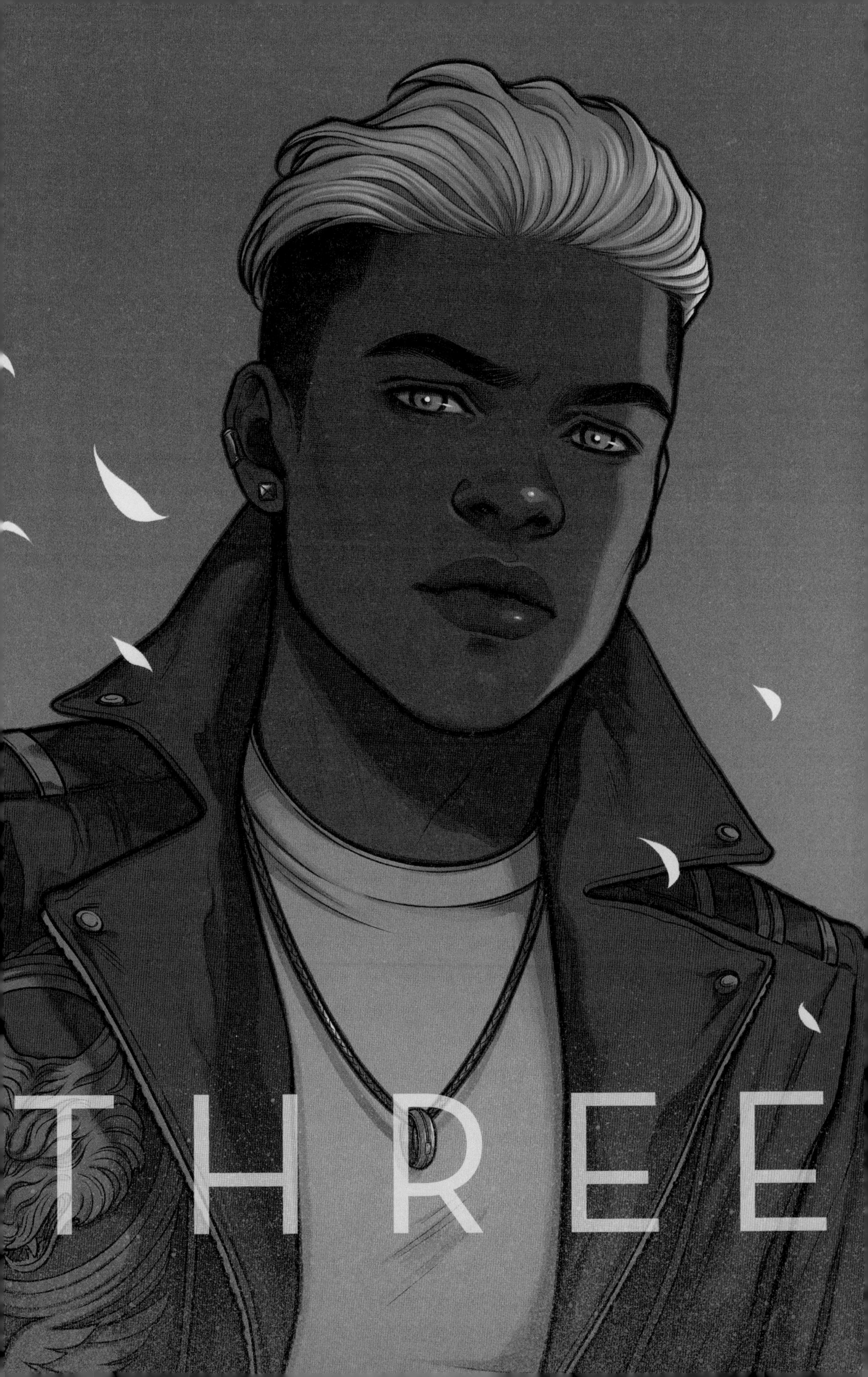
THREE

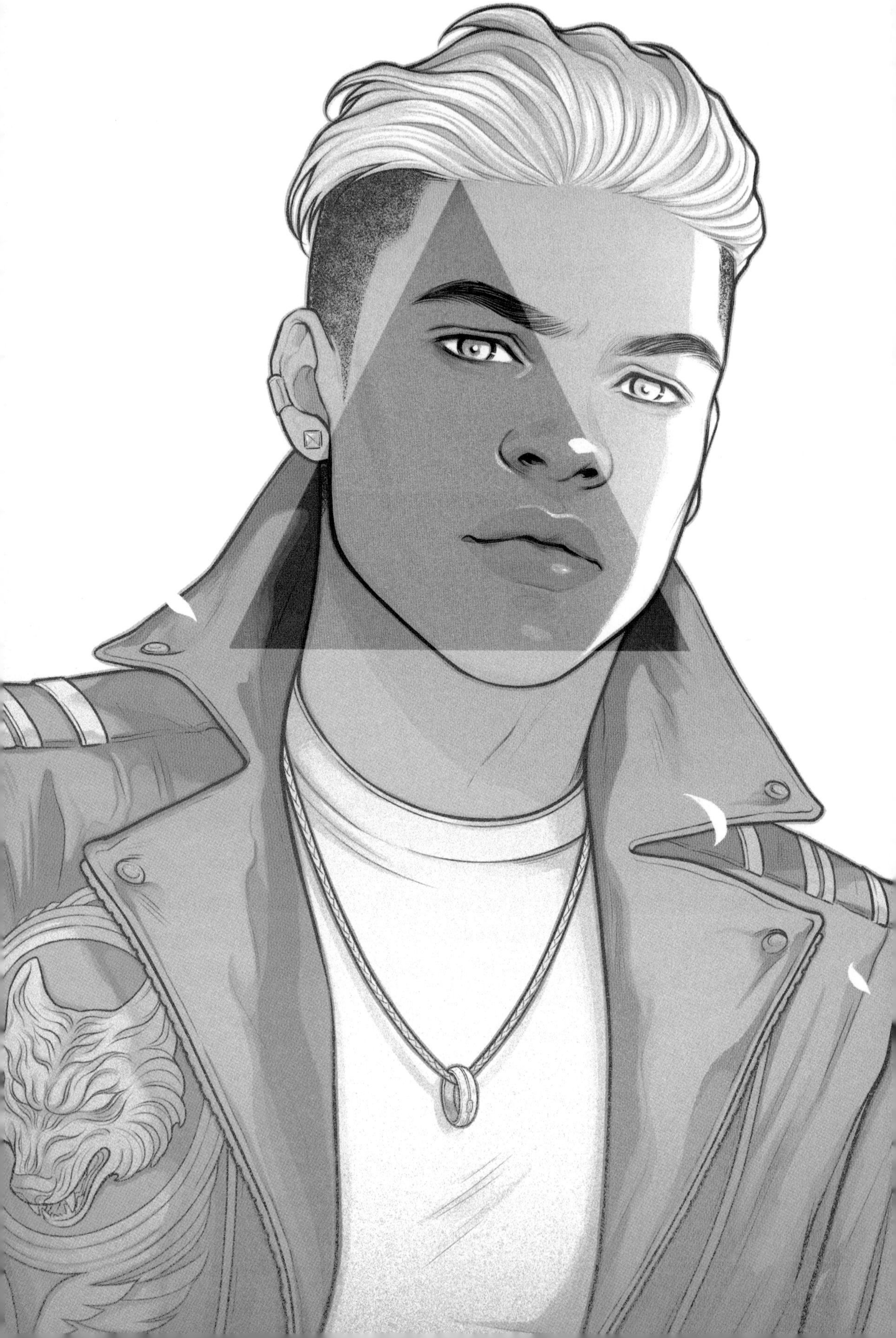

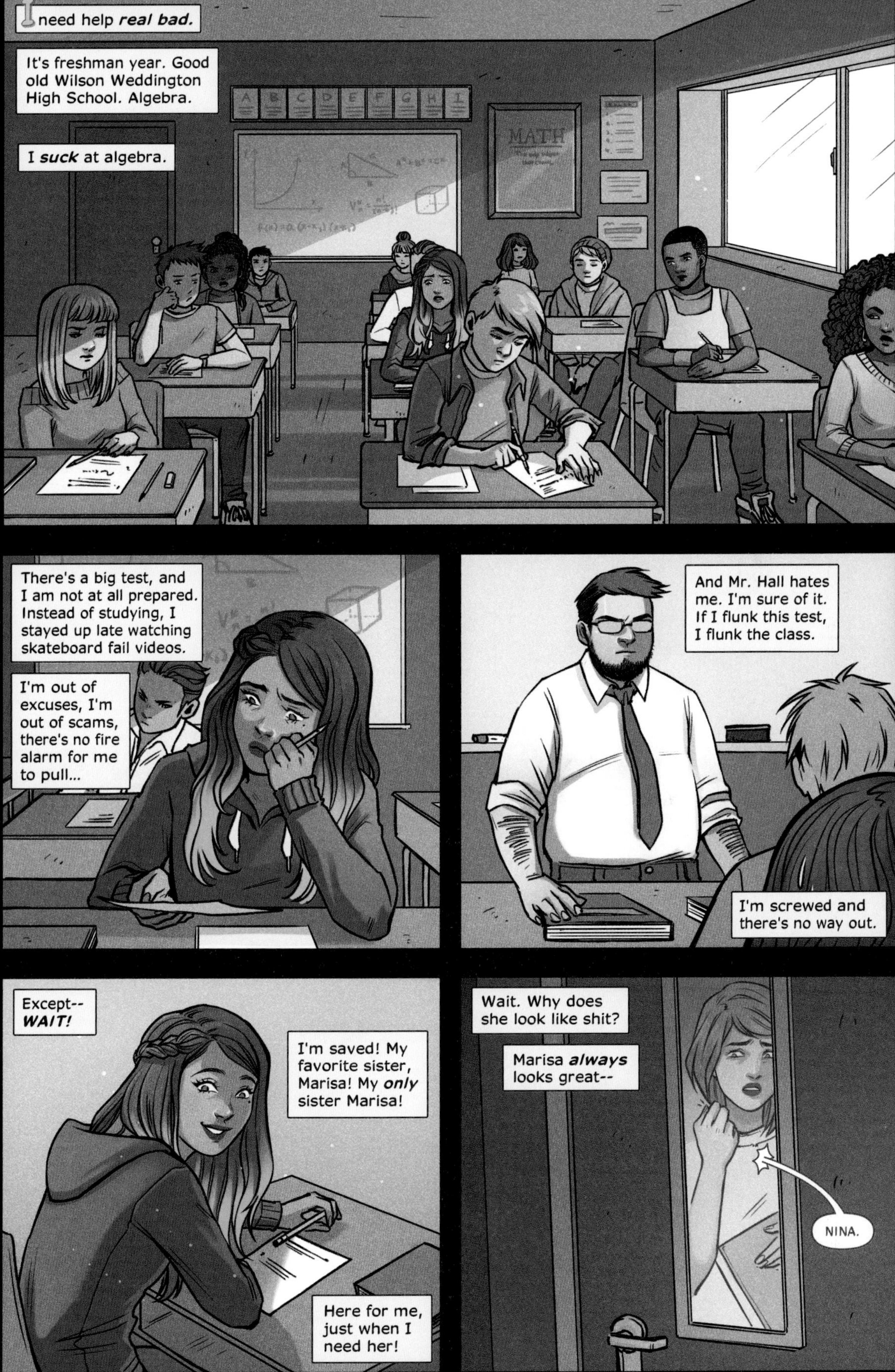
I need help *real bad.*
It's freshman year. Good old Wilson Weddington High School. Algebra.
I *suck* at algebra.
MATH
There's a big test, and I am not at all prepared. Instead of studying, I stayed up late watching skateboard fail videos.
I'm out of excuses, I'm out of scams, there's no fire alarm for me to pull...
And Mr. Hall hates me. I'm sure of it. If I flunk this test, I flunk the class.
I'm screwed and there's no way out.
Except-- ***WAIT!***
I'm saved! My favorite sister, Marisa! My *only* sister Marisa!
Here for me, just when I need her!
Wait. Why does she look like shit?
Marisa ***always*** looks great--
NINA.

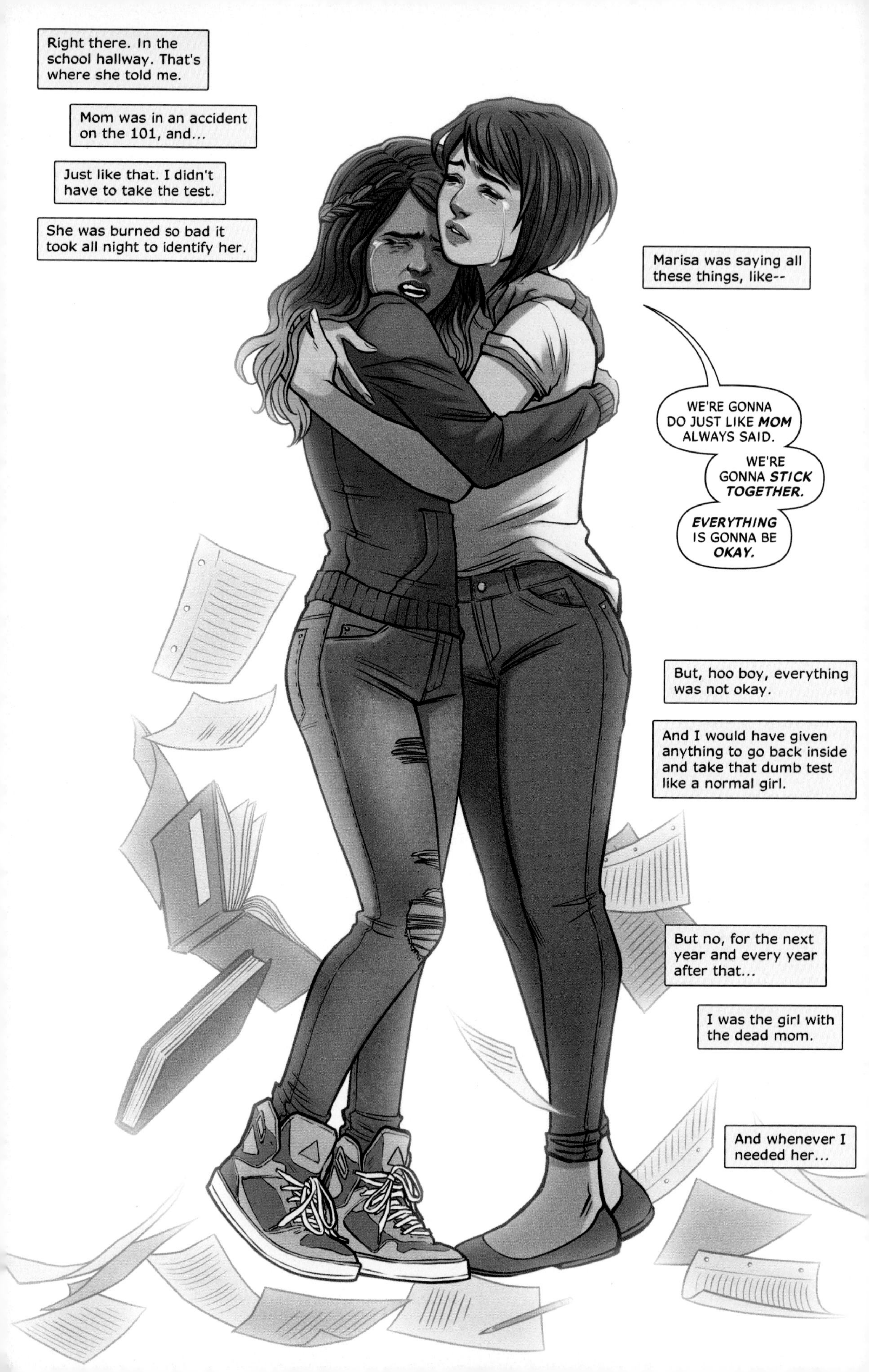
Right there. In the school hallway. That's where she told me.
Mom was in an accident on the 101, and...
Just like that. I didn't have to take the test.
She was burned so bad it took all night to identify her.
Marisa was saying all these things, like--
WE'RE GONNA DO JUST LIKE ***MOM*** ALWAYS SAID.
WE'RE GONNA ***STICK TOGETHER.***
EVERYTHING IS GONNA BE ***OKAY.***
But, hoo boy, everything was not okay.
And I would have given anything to go back inside and take that dumb test like a normal girl.
But no, for the next year and every year after that...
I was the girl with the dead mom.
And whenever I needed her...

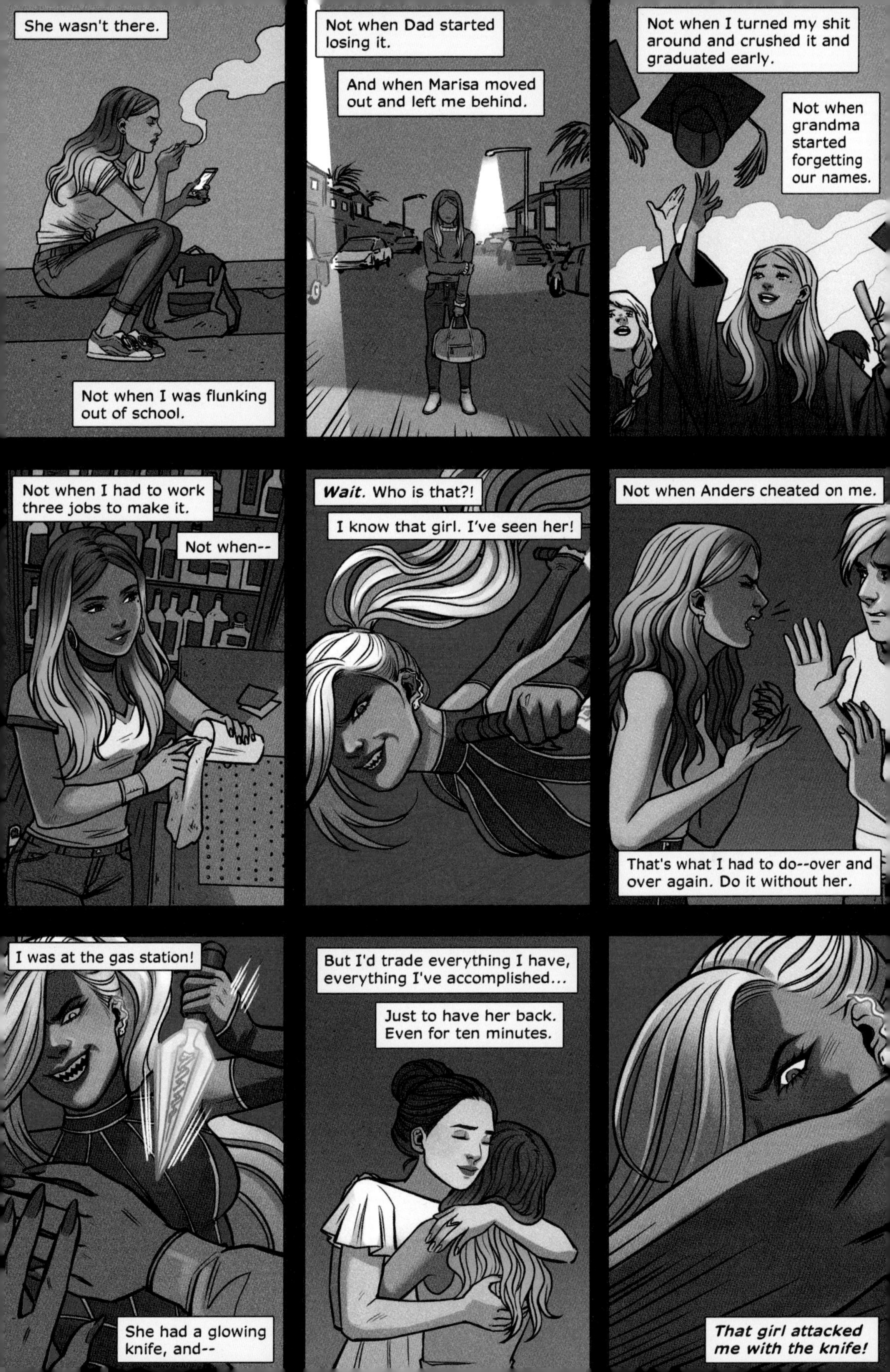
She wasn't there.
Not when I was flunking out of school.
Not when Dad started losing it.
And when Marisa moved out and left me behind.
Not when I turned my shit around and crushed it and graduated early.
Not when grandma started forgetting our names.
Not when I had to work three jobs to make it.
Not when--
Wait. Who is that?!
I know that girl. I've seen her!
Not when Anders cheated on me.
That's what I had to do--over and over again. Do it without her.
I was at the gas station!
She had a glowing knife, and--
But I'd trade everything I have, everything I've accomplished...
Just to have her back. Even for ten minutes.
That girl attacked me with the knife!

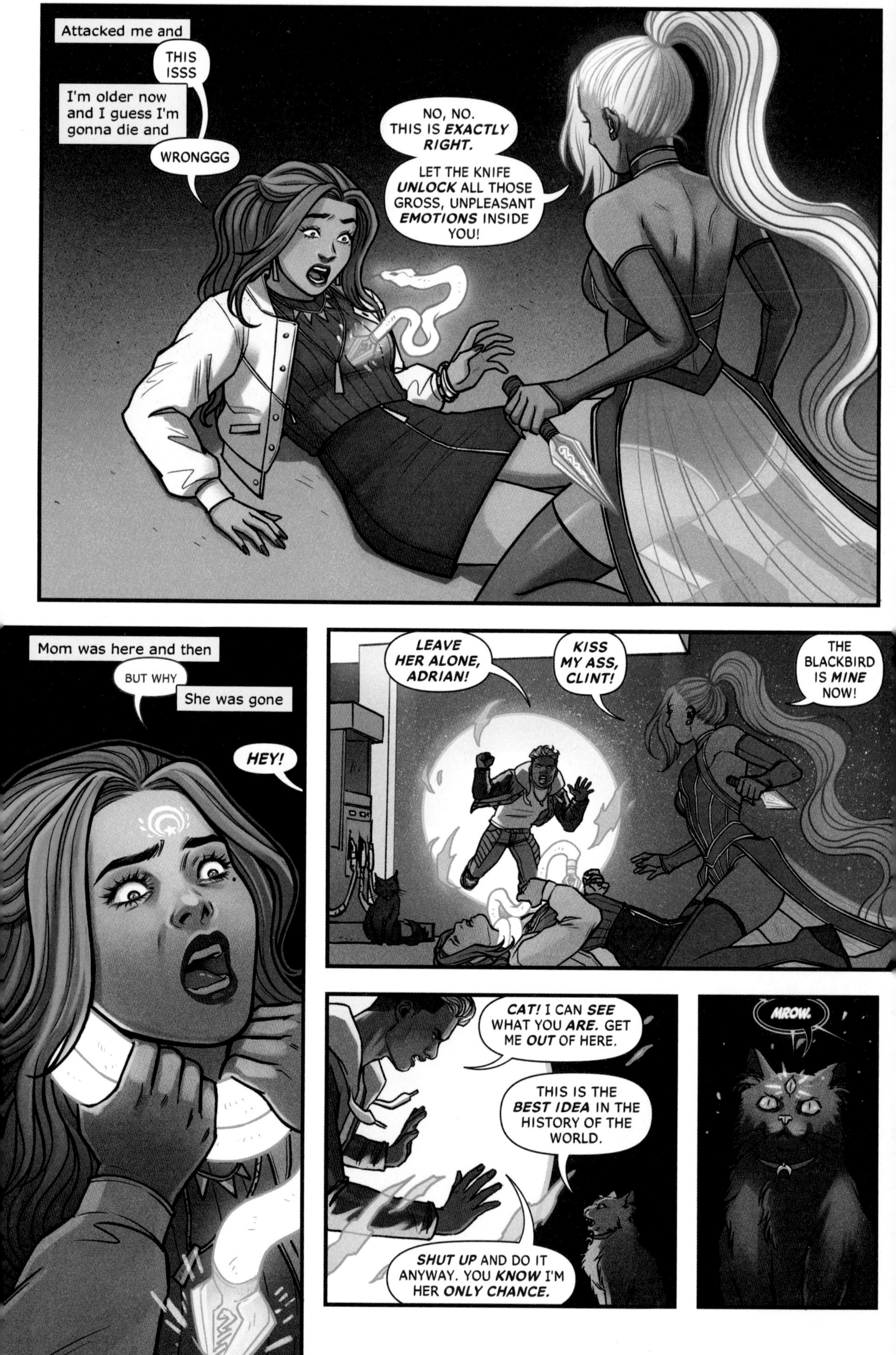
Attacked me and
THIS ISSS
I'm older now and I guess I'm gonna die and
WRONGGG
NO, NO. THIS IS EXACTLY RIGHT.
LET THE KNIFE UNLOCK ALL THOSE GROSS, UNPLEASANT EMOTIONS INSIDE YOU!
Mom was here and then
BUT WHY
She was gone
HEY!
LEAVE HER ALONE, ADRIAN!
KISS MY ASS, CLINT!
THE BLACKBIRD IS MINE NOW!
CAT! I CAN SEE WHAT YOU ARE. GET ME OUT OF HERE.
THIS IS THE BEST IDEA IN THE HISTORY OF THE WORLD.
SHUT UP AND DO IT ANYWAY. YOU KNOW I'M HER ONLY CHANCE.
MROW.

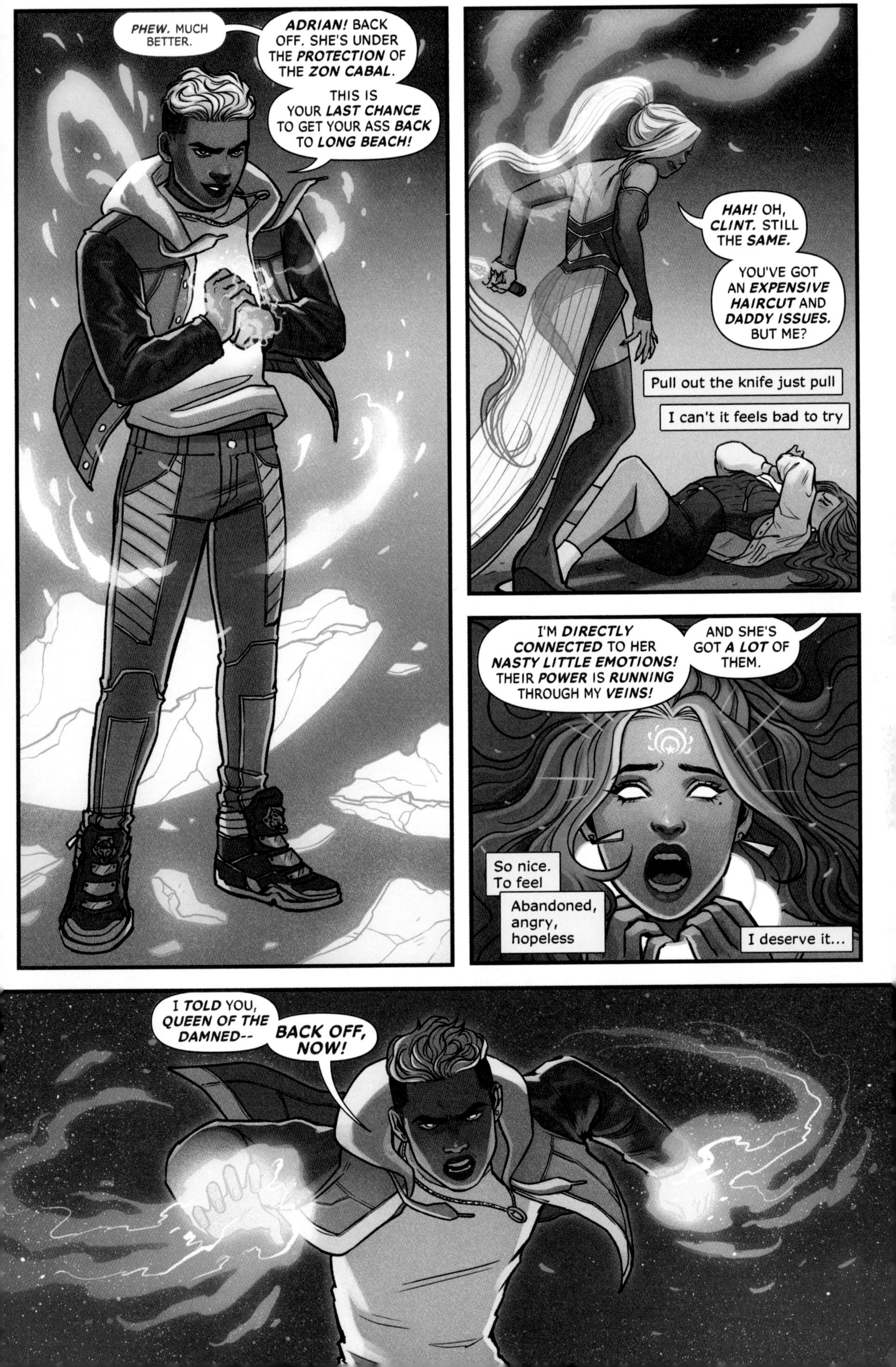
PHEW. MUCH BETTER.
ADRIAN! BACK OFF. SHE'S UNDER THE PROTECTION OF THE ZON CABAL.
THIS IS YOUR LAST CHANCE TO GET YOUR ASS BACK TO LONG BEACH!
HAH! OH, CLINT. STILL THE SAME.
YOU'VE GOT AN EXPENSIVE HAIRCUT AND DADDY ISSUES. BUT ME?
Pull out the knife just pull
I can't it feels bad to try
I'M DIRECTLY CONNECTED TO HER NASTY LITTLE EMOTIONS! THEIR POWER IS RUNNING THROUGH MY VEINS!
AND SHE'S GOT A LOT OF THEM.
So nice. To feel
Abandoned, angry, hopeless
I deserve it...
I TOLD YOU, QUEEN OF THE DAMNED--
BACK OFF, NOW!

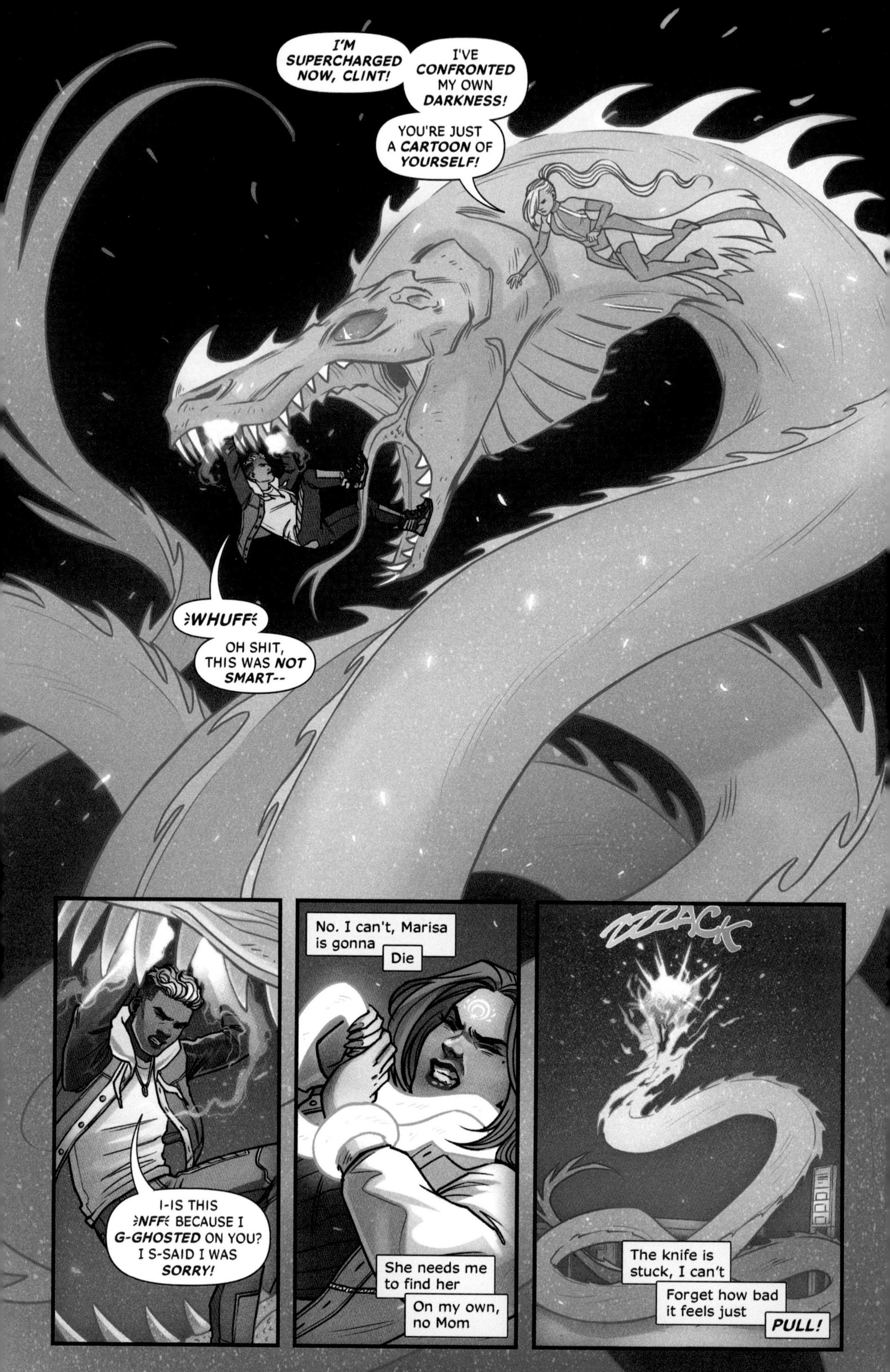
I'M SUPERCHARGED NOW, CLINT!
I'VE CONFRONTED MY OWN DARKNESS!
YOU'RE JUST A CARTOON OF YOURSELF!
WHUFF
OH SHIT, THIS WAS NOT SMART--
I-IS THIS NFF BECAUSE I G-GHOSTED ON YOU? I S-SAID I WAS SORRY!
No. I can't, Marisa is gonna
Die
She needs me to find her
On my own, no Mom
ZZZACK
The knife is stuck, I can't
Forget how bad it feels just
PULL!

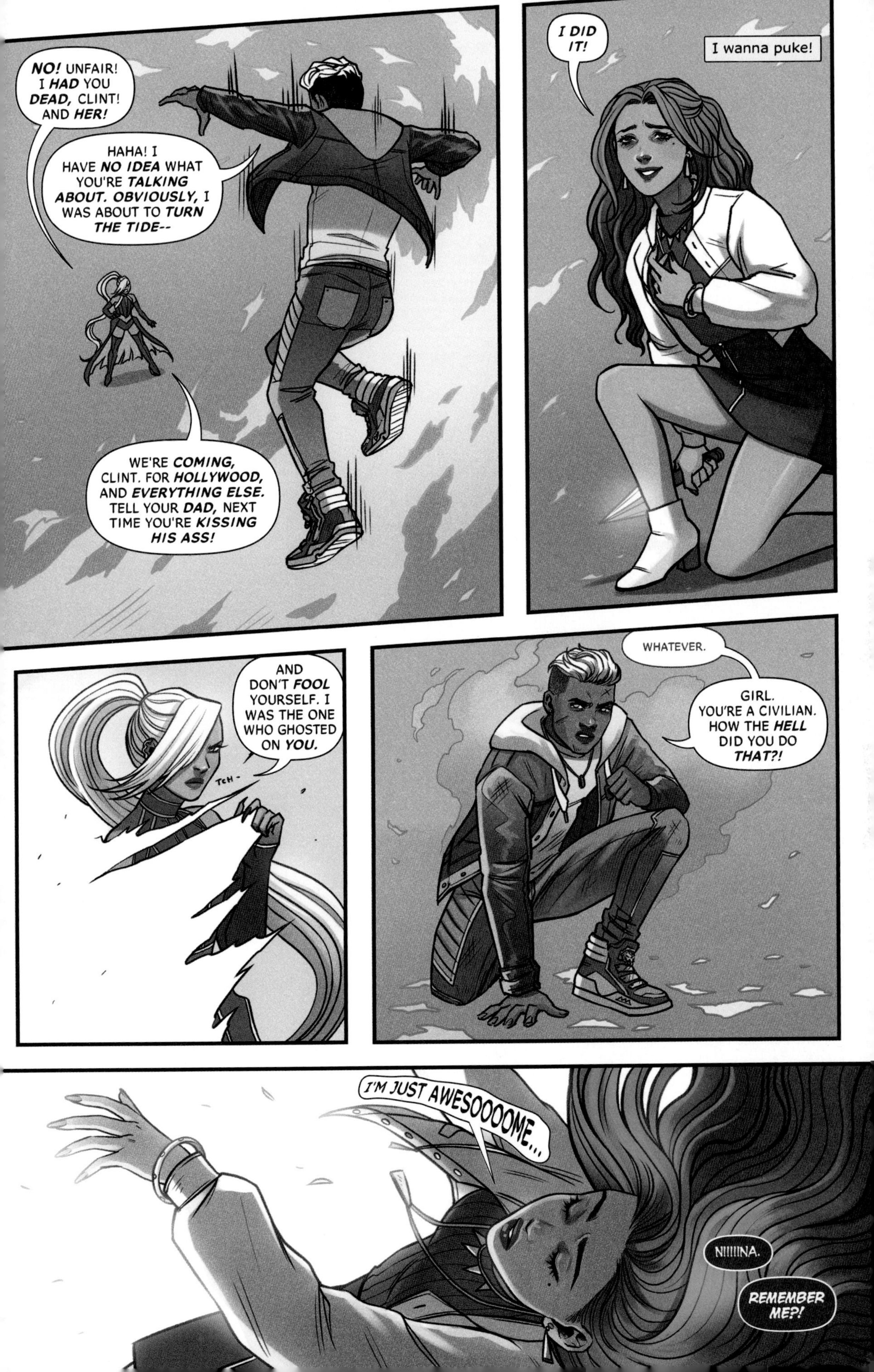
NO! UNFAIR! I HAD YOU DEAD, CLINT! AND HER!
HAHA! I HAVE NO IDEA WHAT YOU'RE TALKING ABOUT. OBVIOUSLY, I WAS ABOUT TO TURN THE TIDE--
WE'RE COMING, CLINT. FOR HOLLYWOOD, AND EVERYTHING ELSE. TELL YOUR DAD, NEXT TIME YOU'RE KISSING HIS ASS!
I DID IT!
I wanna puke!
AND DON'T FOOL YOURSELF. I WAS THE ONE WHO GHOSTED ON YOU.
TCH-
WHATEVER.
GIRL. YOU'RE A CIVILIAN. HOW THE HELL DID YOU DO THAT?!
I'M JUST AWESOOOOOME...
NIIIIINA.
REMEMBER ME?!

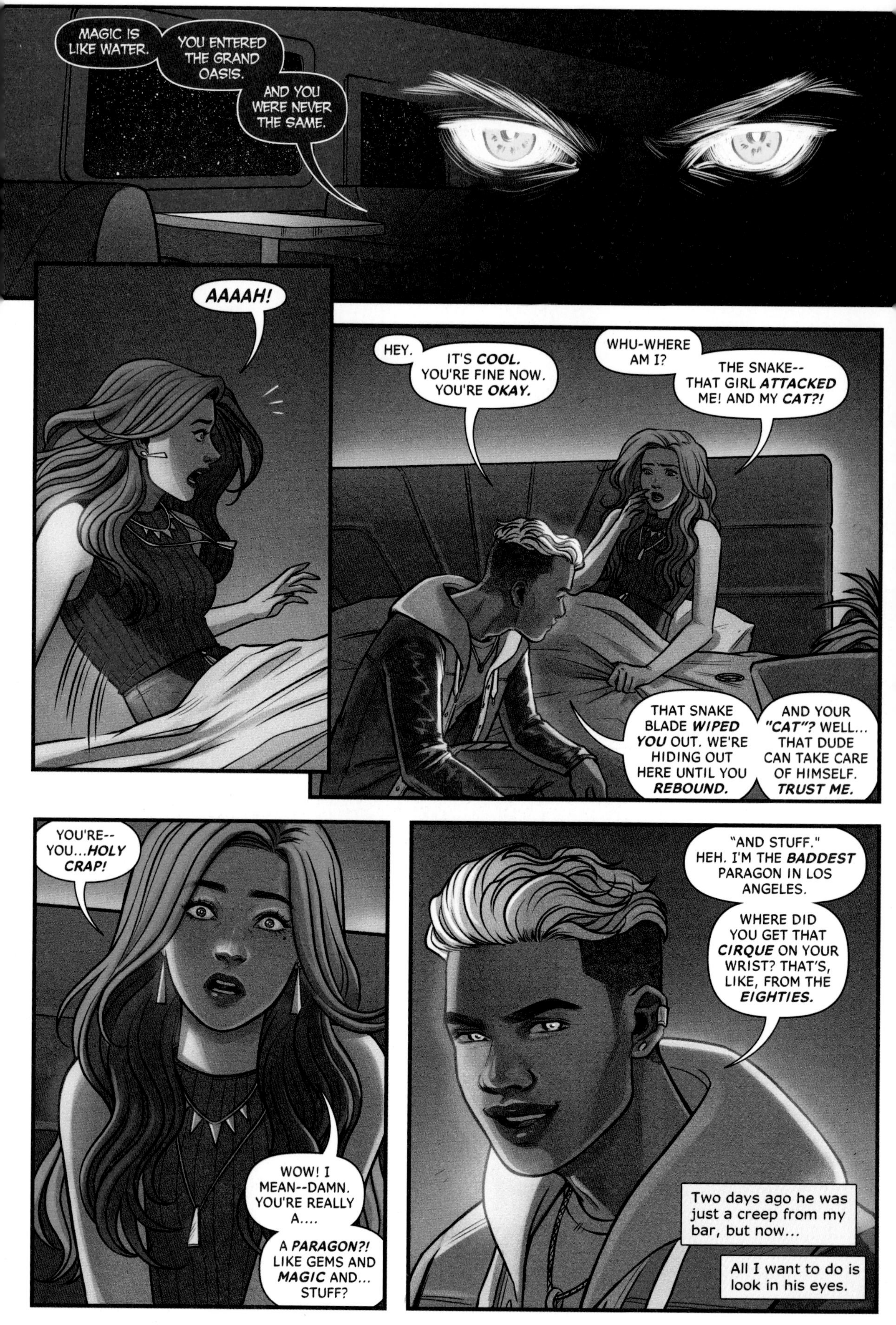
MAGIC IS LIKE WATER.
YOU ENTERED THE GRAND OASIS.
AND YOU WERE NEVER THE SAME.
AAAAH!
HEY.
IT'S COOL. YOU'RE FINE NOW. YOU'RE OKAY.
WHU-WHERE AM I?
THE SNAKE-- THAT GIRL ATTACKED ME! AND MY CAT?!
THAT SNAKE BLADE WIPED YOU OUT. WE'RE HIDING OUT HERE UNTIL YOU REBOUND.
AND YOUR "CAT"? WELL... THAT DUDE CAN TAKE CARE OF HIMSELF. TRUST ME.
YOU'RE-- YOU...HOLY CRAP!
WOW! I MEAN--DAMN. YOU'RE REALLY A....
A PARAGON?! LIKE GEMS AND MAGIC AND... STUFF?
"AND STUFF." HEH. I'M THE BADDEST PARAGON IN LOS ANGELES.
WHERE DID YOU GET THAT CIRQUE ON YOUR WRIST? THAT'S, LIKE, FROM THE EIGHTIES.
Two days ago he was just a creep from my bar, but now...
All I want to do is look in his eyes.

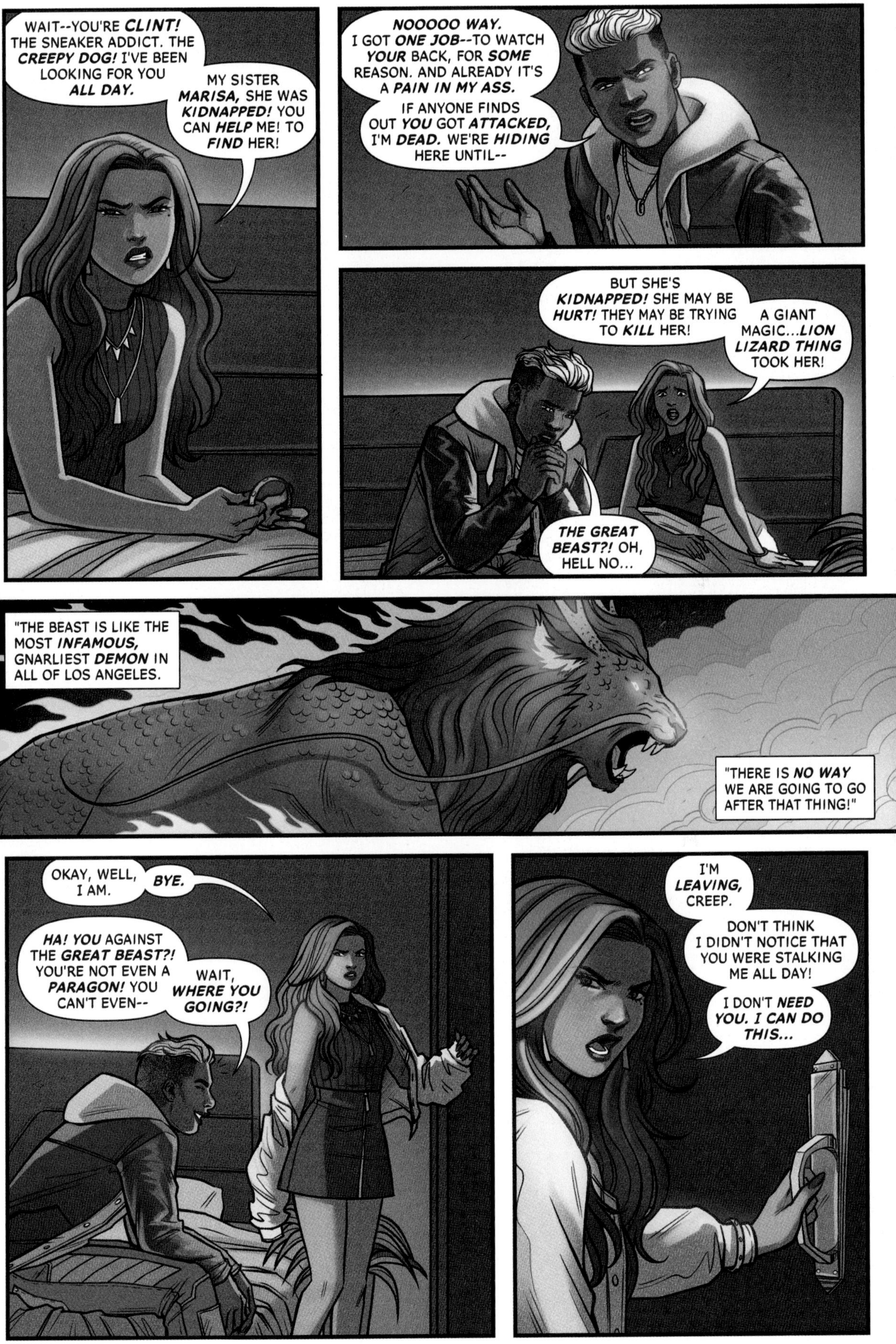

WAIT--YOU'RE CLINT! THE SNEAKER ADDICT. THE CREEPY DOG! I'VE BEEN LOOKING FOR YOU ALL DAY.
MY SISTER MARISA, SHE WAS KIDNAPPED! YOU CAN HELP ME! TO FIND HER!
NOOOOO WAY. I GOT ONE JOB--TO WATCH YOUR BACK, FOR SOME REASON. AND ALREADY IT'S A PAIN IN MY ASS.
IF ANYONE FINDS OUT YOU GOT ATTACKED, I'M DEAD. WE'RE HIDING HERE UNTIL--
BUT SHE'S KIDNAPPED! SHE MAY BE HURT! THEY MAY BE TRYING TO KILL HER!
A GIANT MAGIC...LION LIZARD THING TOOK HER!
THE GREAT BEAST?! OH, HELL NO...
"THE BEAST IS LIKE THE MOST INFAMOUS, GNARLIEST DEMON IN ALL OF LOS ANGELES.
"THERE IS NO WAY WE ARE GOING TO GO AFTER THAT THING!"
OKAY, WELL, I AM.
BYE.
HA! YOU AGAINST THE GREAT BEAST?! YOU'RE NOT EVEN A PARAGON! YOU CAN'T EVEN--
WAIT, WHERE YOU GOING?!
I'M LEAVING, CREEP.
DON'T THINK I DIDN'T NOTICE THAT YOU WERE STALKING ME ALL DAY!
I DON'T NEED YOU. I CAN DO THIS...

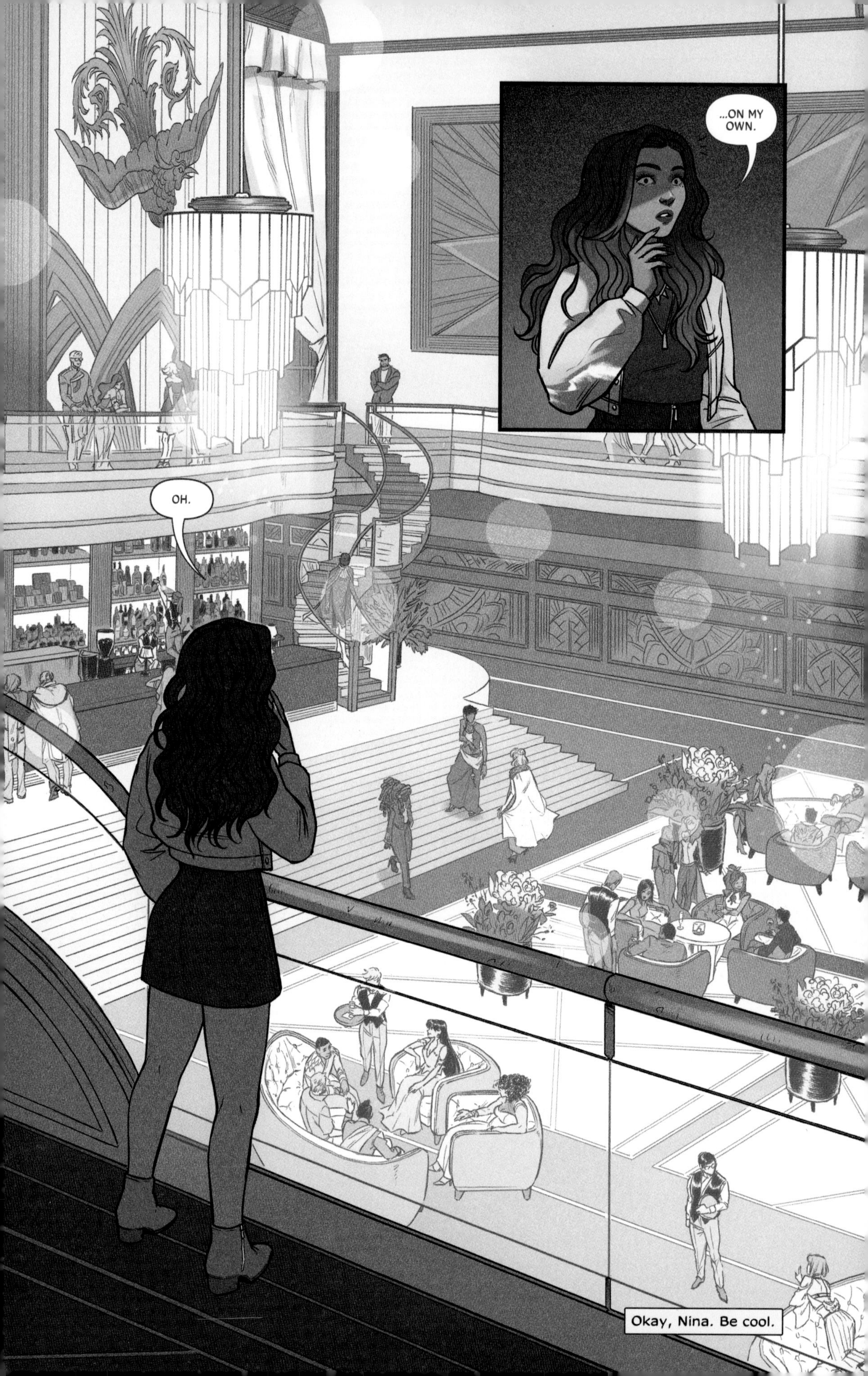
...ON MY OWN.
OH.
Okay, Nina. Be cool.

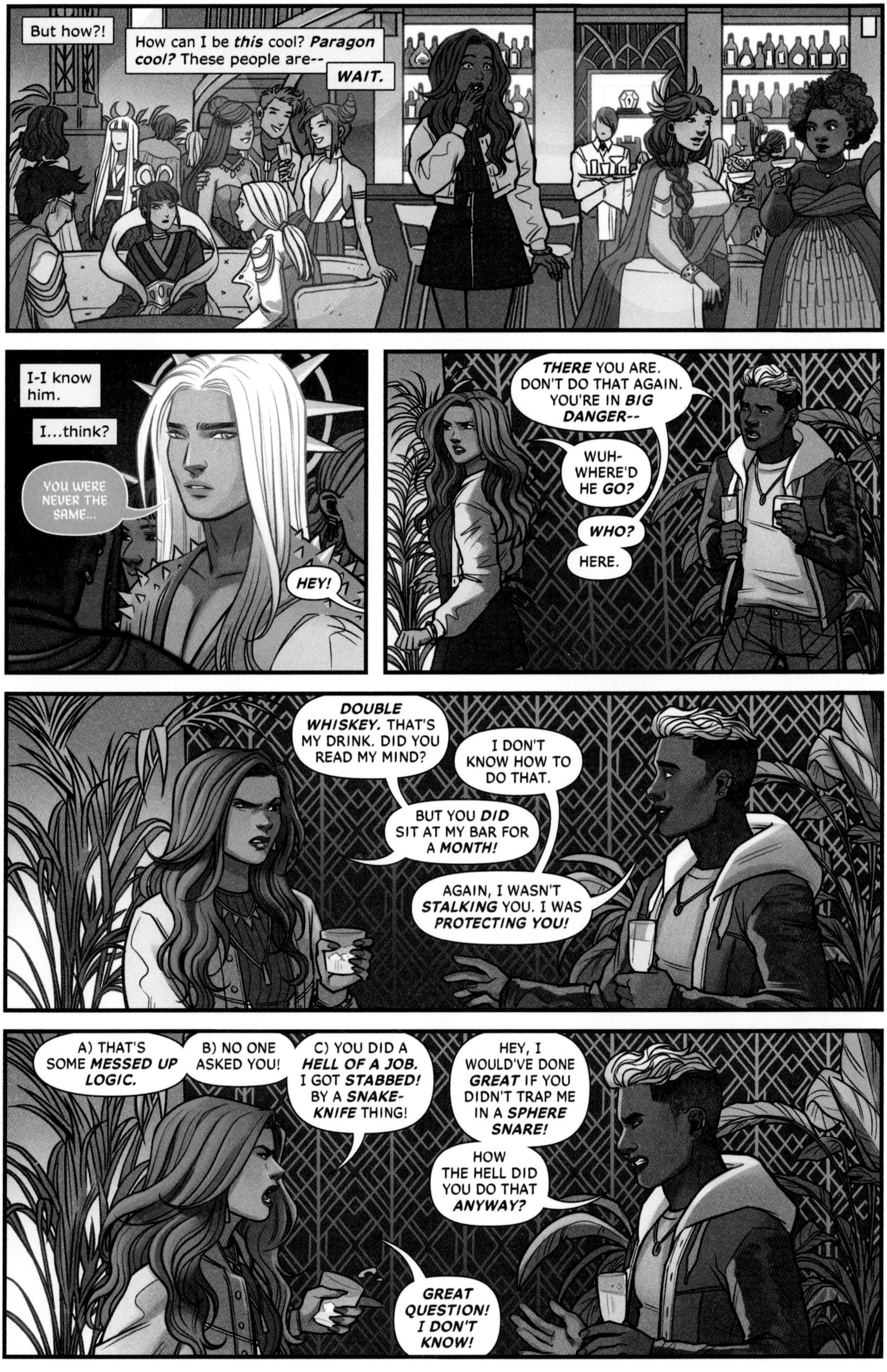
But how?!
How can I be this cool? Paragon cool? These people are--
WAIT.
I-I know him.
I...think?
YOU WERE NEVER THE SAME...
HEY!
THERE YOU ARE. DON'T DO THAT AGAIN. YOU'RE IN BIG DANGER--
WUH-WHERE'D HE GO?
WHO?
HERE.
DOUBLE WHISKEY. THAT'S MY DRINK. DID YOU READ MY MIND?
I DON'T KNOW HOW TO DO THAT.
BUT YOU DID SIT AT MY BAR FOR A MONTH!
AGAIN, I WASN'T STALKING YOU. I WAS PROTECTING YOU!
A) THAT'S SOME MESSED UP LOGIC.
B) NO ONE ASKED YOU!
C) YOU DID A HELL OF A JOB. I GOT STABBED! BY A SNAKE-KNIFE THING!
HEY, I WOULD'VE DONE GREAT IF YOU DIDN'T TRAP ME IN A SPHERE SNARE!
HOW THE HELL DID YOU DO THAT ANYWAY?
GREAT QUESTION! I DON'T KNOW!

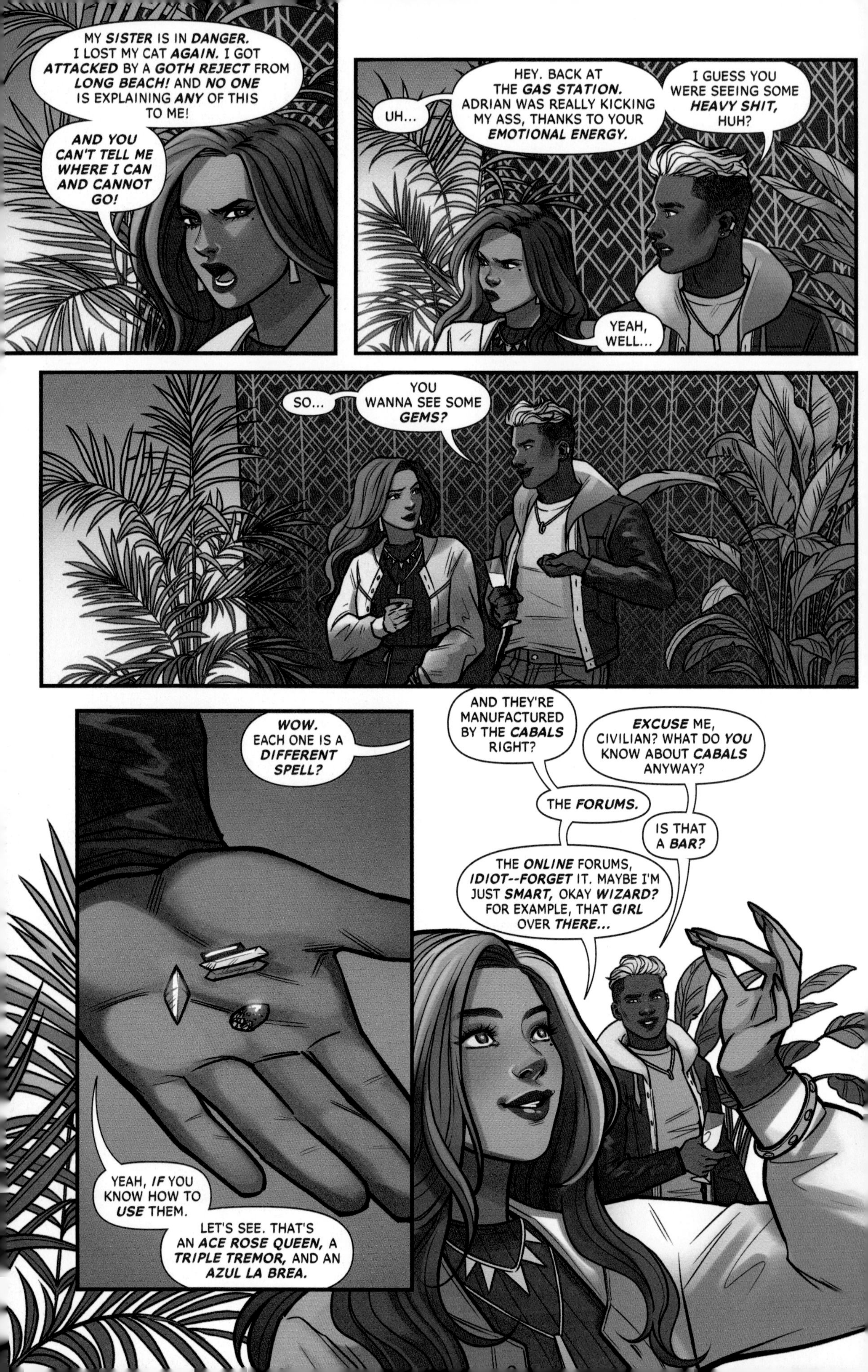
MY SISTER IS IN DANGER. I LOST MY CAT AGAIN. I GOT ATTACKED BY A GOTH REJECT FROM LONG BEACH! AND NO ONE IS EXPLAINING ANY OF THIS TO ME!
AND YOU CAN'T TELL ME WHERE I CAN AND CANNOT GO!
UH...
HEY. BACK AT THE GAS STATION. ADRIAN WAS REALLY KICKING MY ASS, THANKS TO YOUR EMOTIONAL ENERGY.
I GUESS YOU WERE SEEING SOME HEAVY SHIT, HUH?
YEAH, WELL...
SO...
YOU WANNA SEE SOME GEMS?
WOW. EACH ONE IS A DIFFERENT SPELL?
YEAH, IF YOU KNOW HOW TO USE THEM.
LET'S SEE. THAT'S AN ACE ROSE QUEEN, A TRIPLE TREMOR, AND AN AZUL LA BREA.
AND THEY'RE MANUFACTURED BY THE CABALS RIGHT?
EXCUSE ME, CIVILIAN? WHAT DO YOU KNOW ABOUT CABALS ANYWAY?
THE FORUMS.
IS THAT A BAR?
THE ONLINE FORUMS, IDIOT--FORGET IT. MAYBE I'M JUST SMART, OKAY WIZARD? FOR EXAMPLE, THAT GIRL OVER THERE...

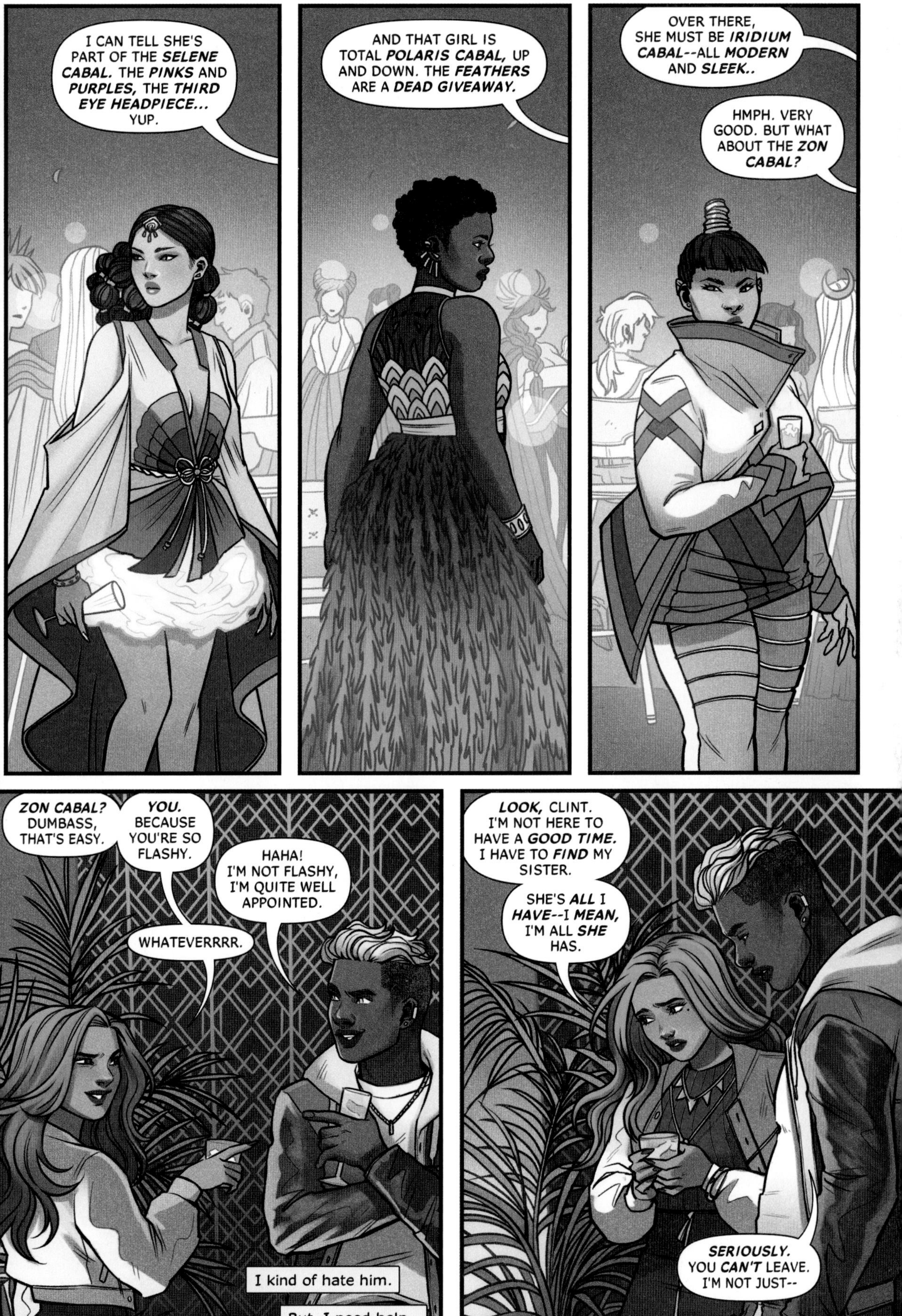
I CAN TELL SHE'S PART OF THE SELENE CABAL. THE PINKS AND PURPLES, THE THIRD EYE HEADPIECE... YUP.
AND THAT GIRL IS TOTAL POLARIS CABAL, UP AND DOWN. THE FEATHERS ARE A DEAD GIVEAWAY.
OVER THERE, SHE MUST BE IRIDIUM CABAL--ALL MODERN AND SLEEK..
HMPH. VERY GOOD. BUT WHAT ABOUT THE ZON CABAL?
ZON CABAL? DUMBASS, THAT'S EASY.
YOU. BECAUSE YOU'RE SO FLASHY.
HAHA! I'M NOT FLASHY, I'M QUITE WELL APPOINTED.
WHATEVERRRR.
I kind of hate him.
But. I need help from someone...
LOOK, CLINT. I'M NOT HERE TO HAVE A GOOD TIME. I HAVE TO FIND MY SISTER.
SHE'S ALL I HAVE--I MEAN, I'M ALL SHE HAS.
SERIOUSLY. YOU CAN'T LEAVE. I'M NOT JUST--

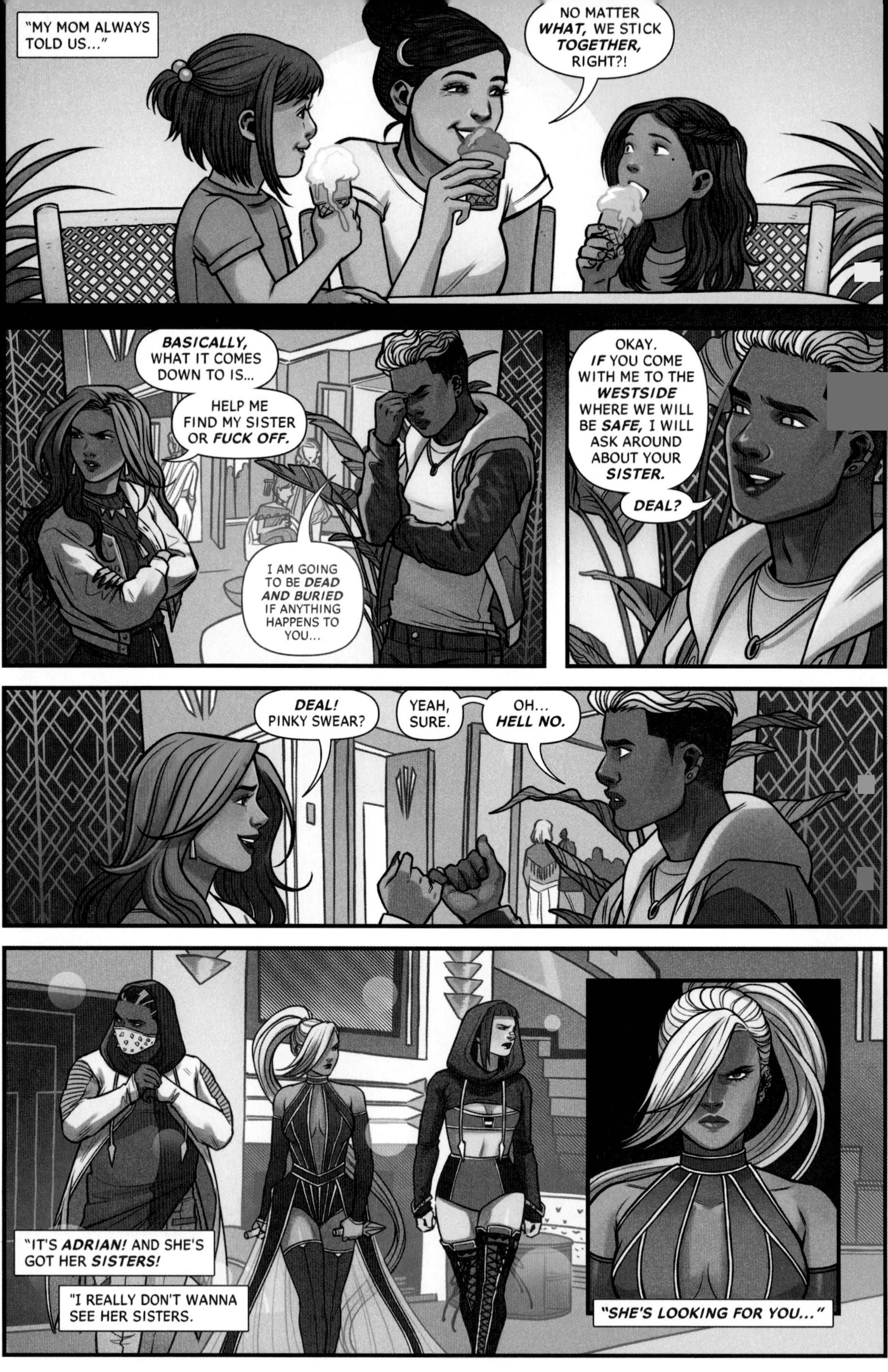
"MY MOM ALWAYS TOLD US..."
NO MATTER WHAT, WE STICK TOGETHER, RIGHT?!
BASICALLY, WHAT IT COMES DOWN TO IS...
HELP ME FIND MY SISTER OR FUCK OFF.
I AM GOING TO BE DEAD AND BURIED IF ANYTHING HAPPENS TO YOU...
OKAY. IF YOU COME WITH ME TO THE WESTSIDE WHERE WE WILL BE SAFE, I WILL ASK AROUND ABOUT YOUR SISTER.
DEAL?
DEAL! PINKY SWEAR?
YEAH, SURE.
OH... HELL NO.
"IT'S ADRIAN! AND SHE'S GOT HER SISTERS!
"I REALLY DON'T WANNA SEE HER SISTERS.
"SHE'S LOOKING FOR YOU..."

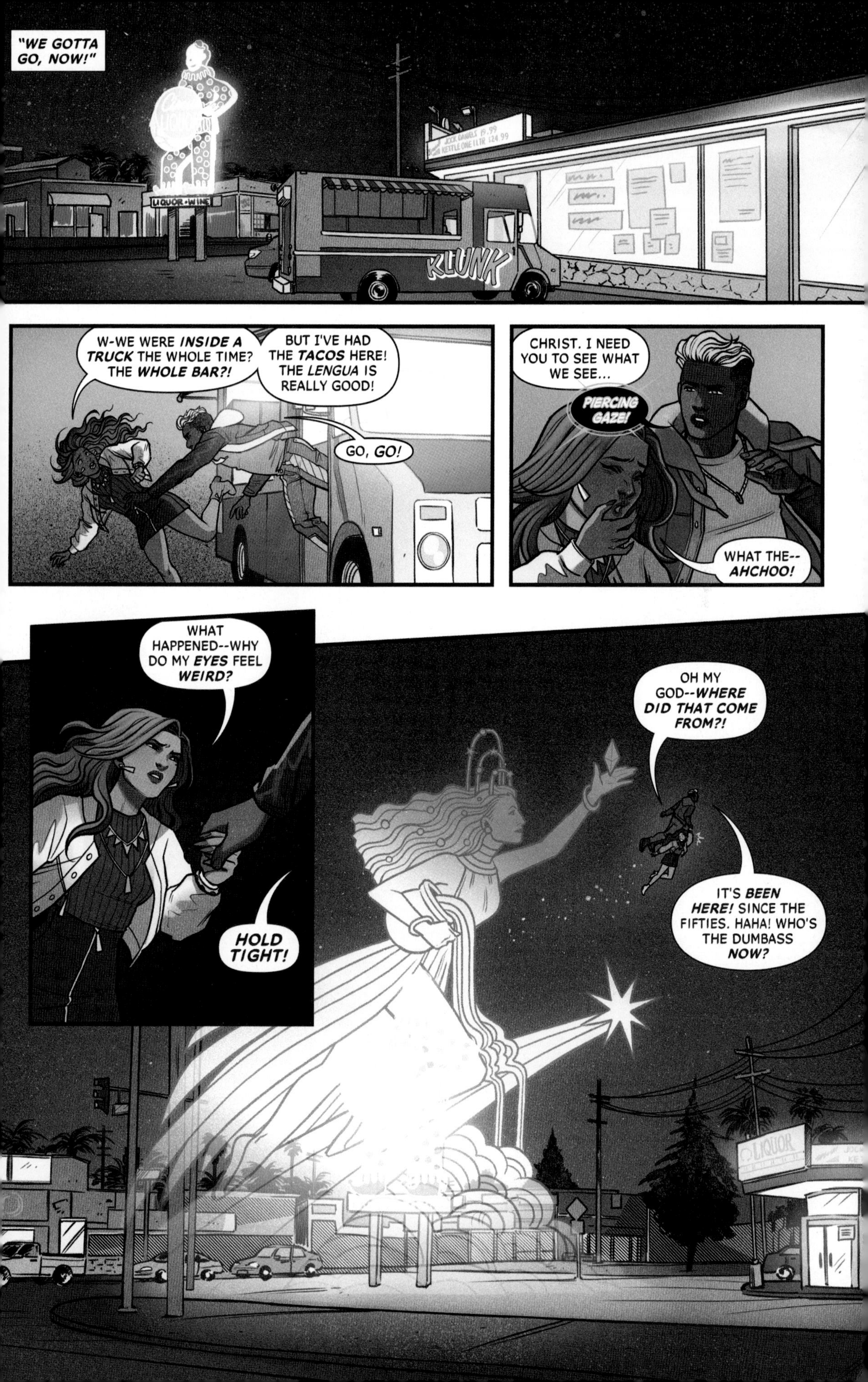
"WE GOTTA GO, NOW!"
LIQUOR • WINE
KLUNK
W-WE WERE INSIDE A TRUCK THE WHOLE TIME? THE WHOLE BAR?!
BUT I'VE HAD THE TACOS HERE! THE LENGUA IS REALLY GOOD!
GO, GO!
CHRIST. I NEED YOU TO SEE WHAT WE SEE...
PIERCING GAZE!
WHAT THE-- AHCHOO!
WHAT HAPPENED--WHY DO MY EYES FEEL WEIRD?
HOLD TIGHT!
OH MY GOD--WHERE DID THAT COME FROM?!
IT'S BEEN HERE! SINCE THE FIFTIES. HAHA! WHO'S THE DUMBASS NOW?
LIQUOR

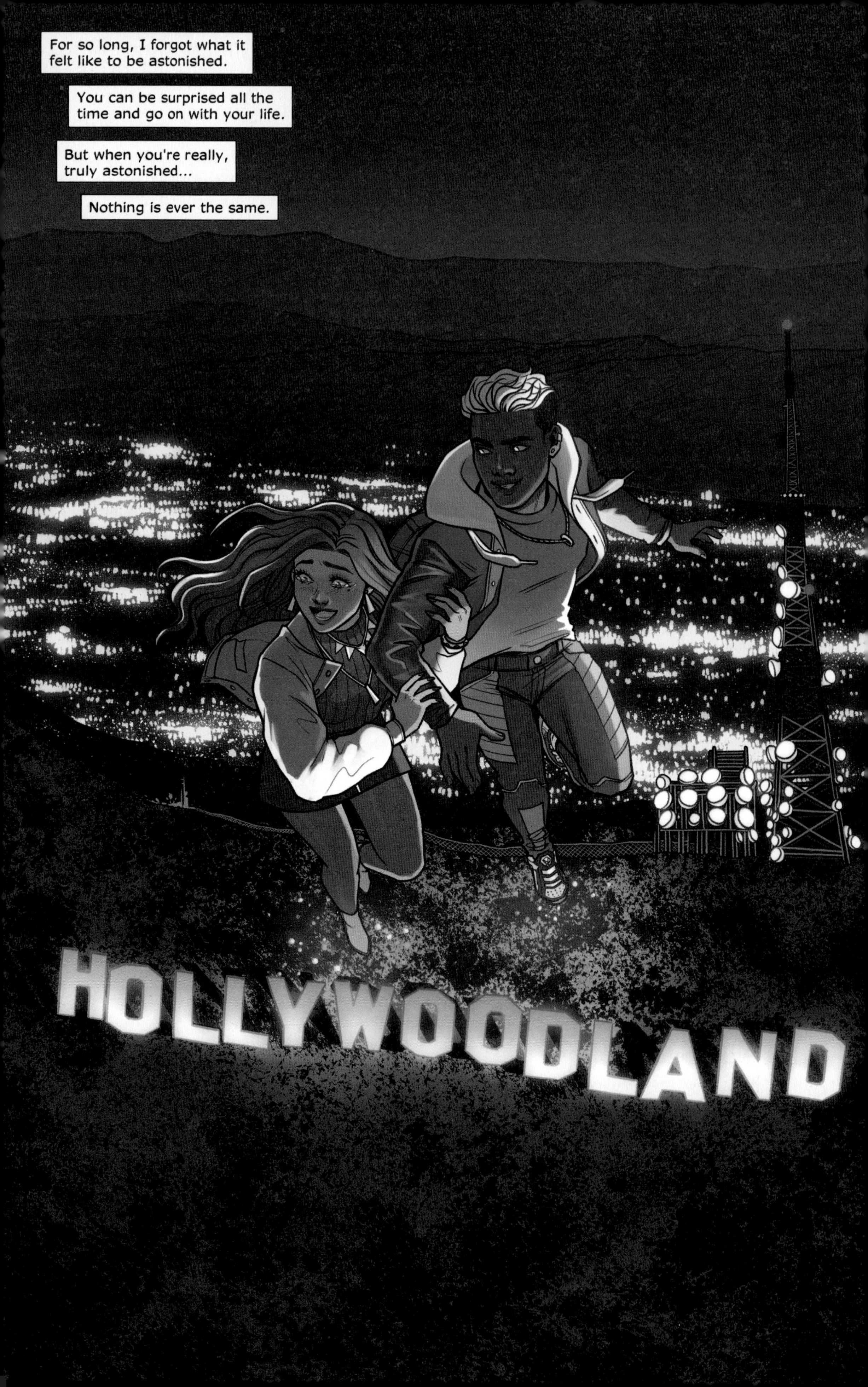
For so long, I forgot what it felt like to be astonished.
You can be surprised all the time and go on with your life.
But when you're really, truly astonished...
Nothing is ever the same.
HOLLYWOODLAND

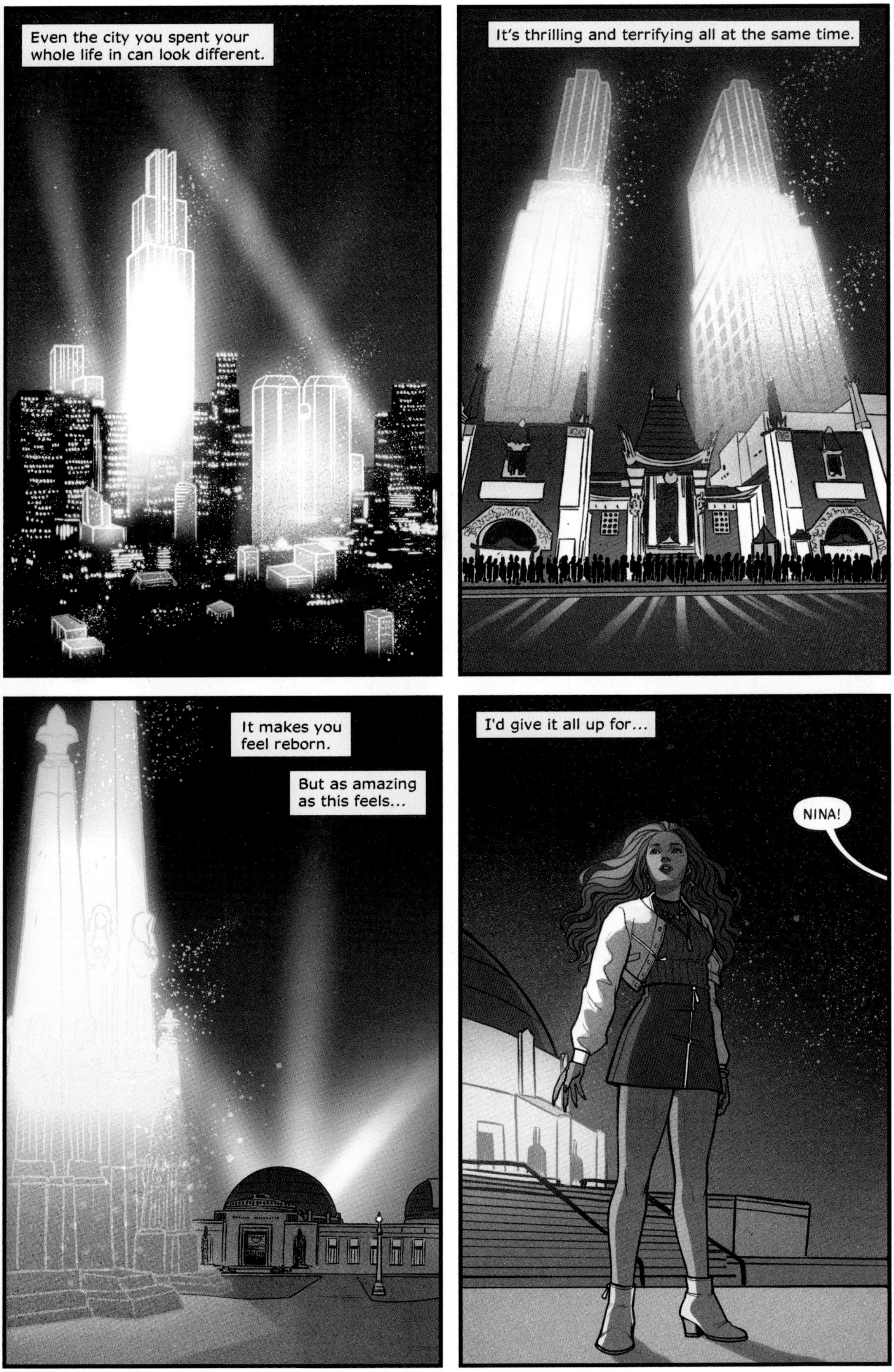
Even the city you spent your whole life in can look different.
It's thrilling and terrifying all at the same time.
It makes you feel reborn.
But as amazing as this feels...
I'd give it all up for...
NINA!

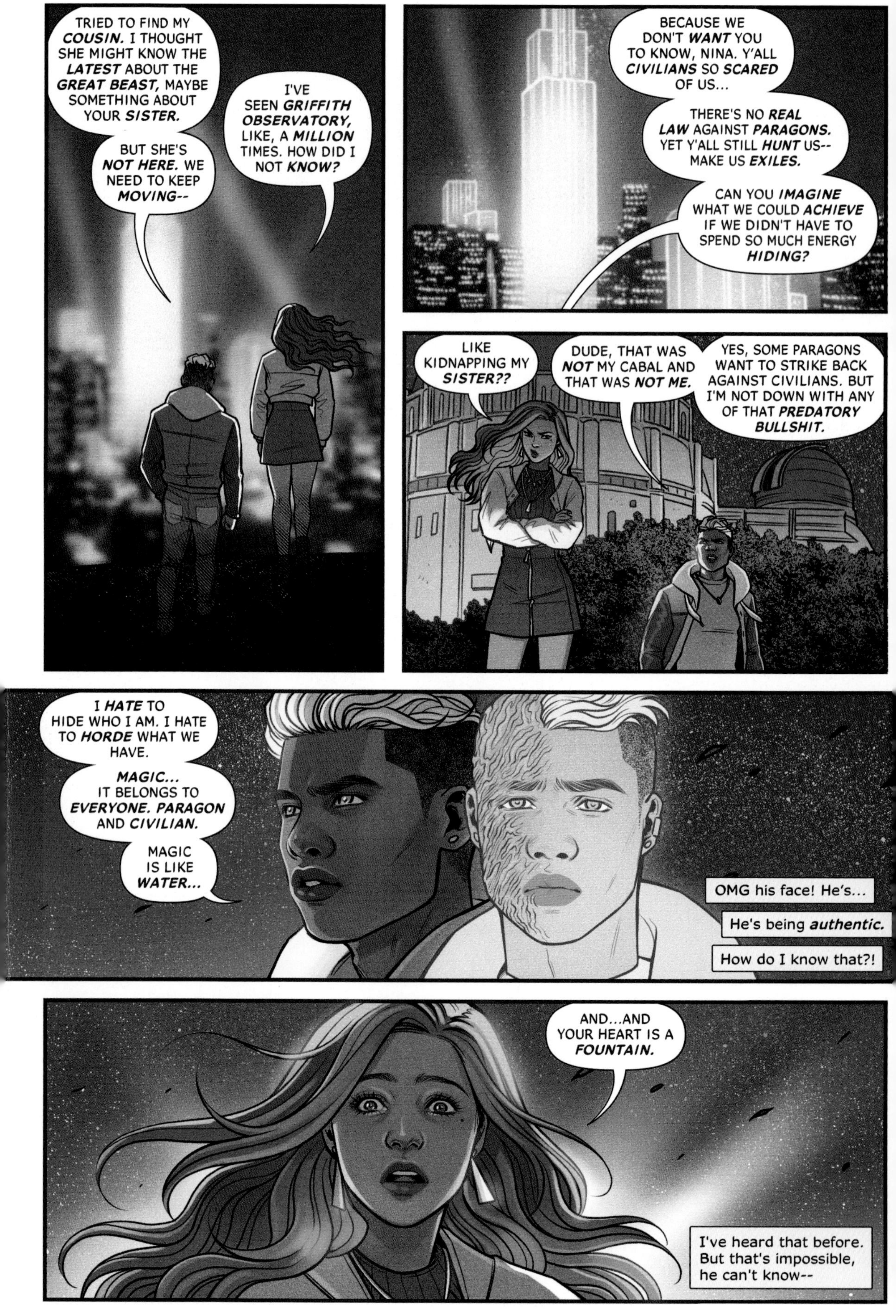

TRIED TO FIND MY COUSIN. I THOUGHT SHE MIGHT KNOW THE LATEST ABOUT THE GREAT BEAST, MAYBE SOMETHING ABOUT YOUR SISTER.
BUT SHE'S NOT HERE. WE NEED TO KEEP MOVING--
I'VE SEEN GRIFFITH OBSERVATORY, LIKE, A MILLION TIMES. HOW DID I NOT KNOW?
BECAUSE WE DON'T WANT YOU TO KNOW, NINA. Y'ALL CIVILIANS SO SCARED OF US...
THERE'S NO REAL LAW AGAINST PARAGONS. YET Y'ALL STILL HUNT US-- MAKE US EXILES.
CAN YOU IMAGINE WHAT WE COULD ACHIEVE IF WE DIDN'T HAVE TO SPEND SO MUCH ENERGY HIDING?
LIKE KIDNAPPING MY SISTER??
DUDE, THAT WAS NOT MY CABAL AND THAT WAS NOT ME.
YES, SOME PARAGONS WANT TO STRIKE BACK AGAINST CIVILIANS. BUT I'M NOT DOWN WITH ANY OF THAT PREDATORY BULLSHIT.
I HATE TO HIDE WHO I AM. I HATE TO HORDE WHAT WE HAVE.
MAGIC... IT BELONGS TO EVERYONE. PARAGON AND CIVILIAN.
MAGIC IS LIKE WATER...
OMG his face! He's...
He's being authentic.
How do I know that?!
AND...AND YOUR HEART IS A FOUNTAIN.
I've heard that before. But that's impossible, he can't know--

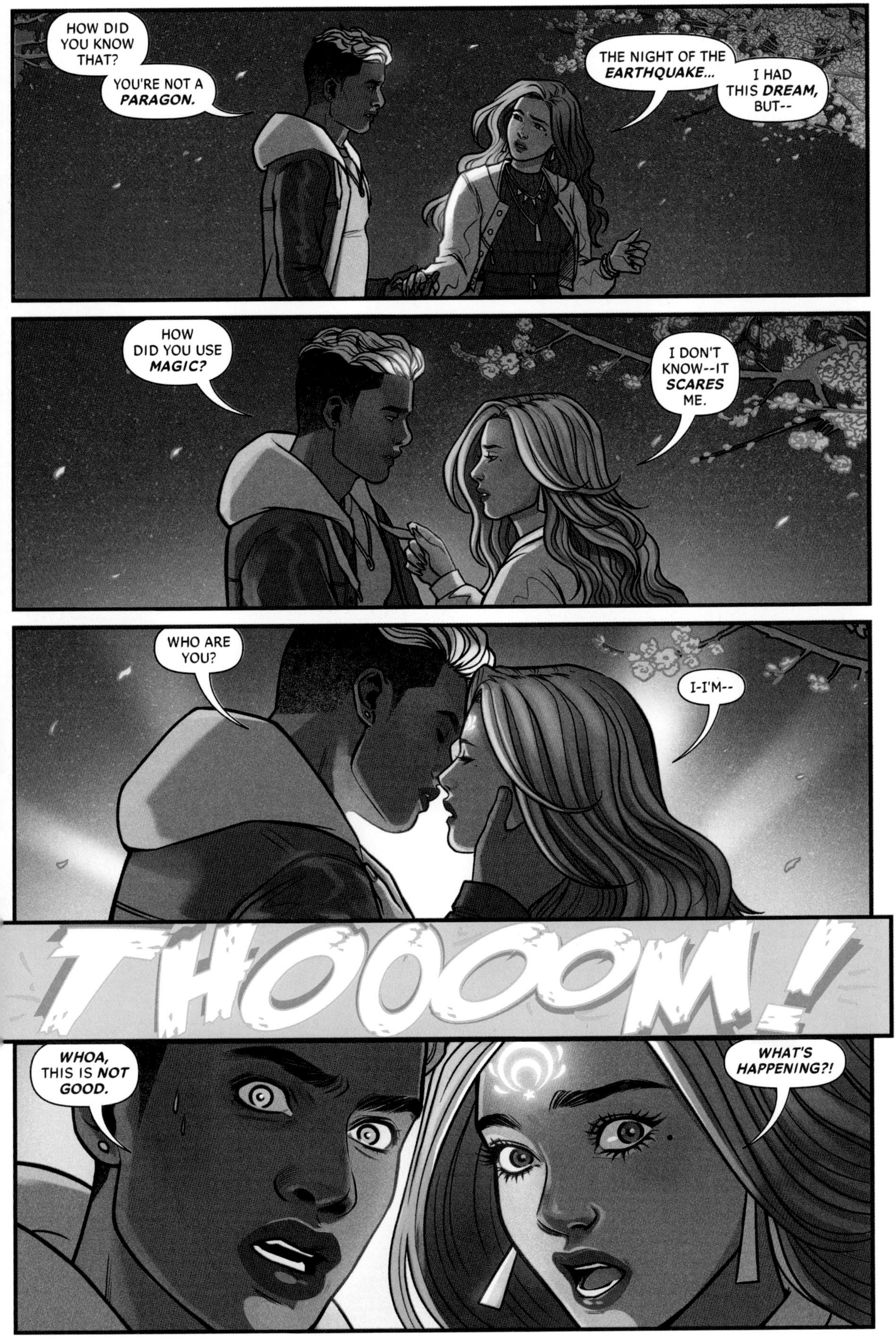
HOW DID YOU KNOW THAT?
YOU'RE NOT A PARAGON.
THE NIGHT OF THE EARTHQUAKE...
I HAD THIS DREAM, BUT--
HOW DID YOU USE MAGIC?
I DON'T KNOW--IT SCARES ME.
WHO ARE YOU?
I-I'M--
THOOOOM!
WHOA, THIS IS NOT GOOD.
WHAT'S HAPPENING?!

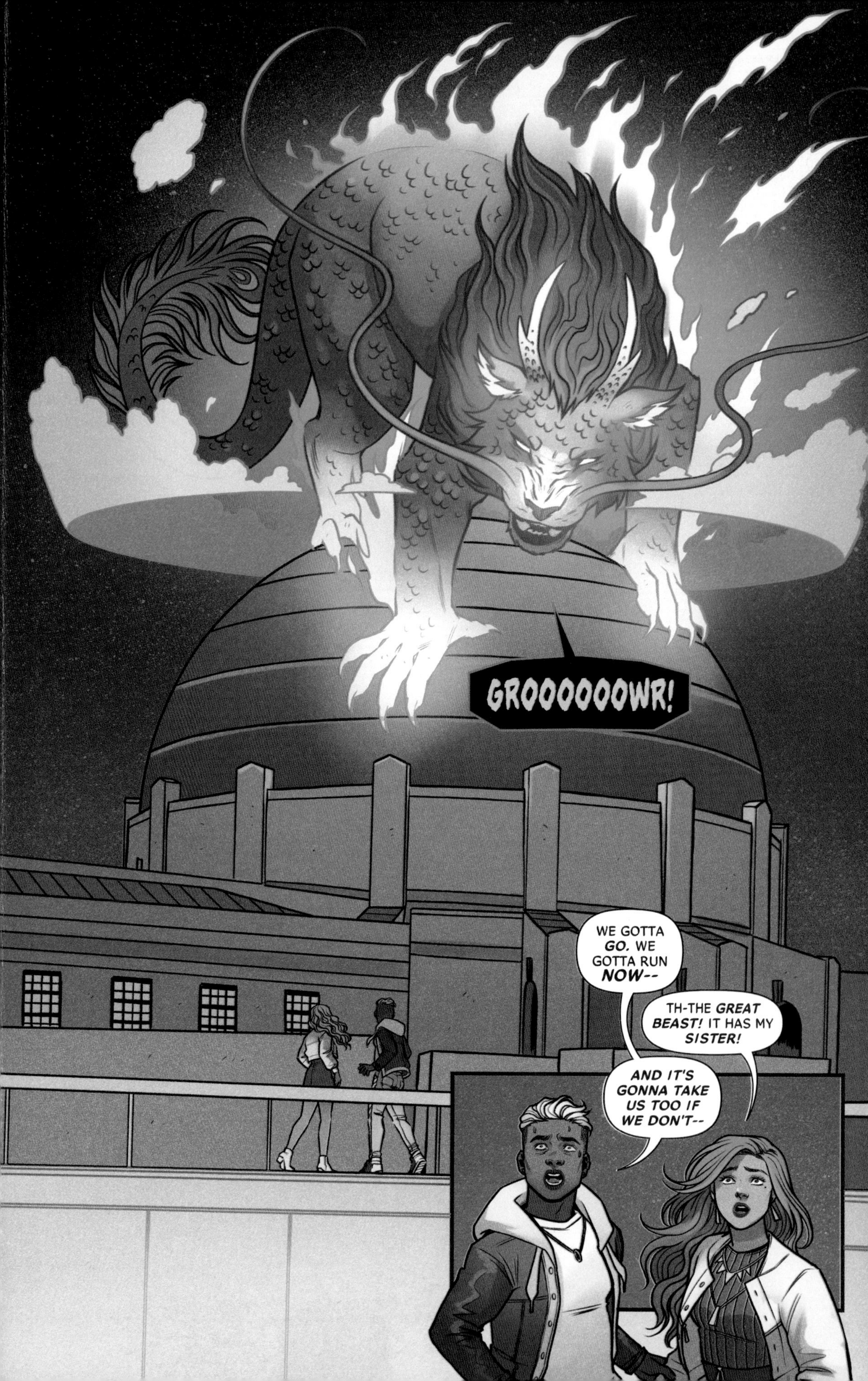
GROOOOOOWR!
WE GOTTA GO. WE GOTTA RUN NOW--
TH-THE GREAT BEAST! IT HAS MY SISTER!
AND IT'S GONNA TAKE US TOO IF WE DON'T--

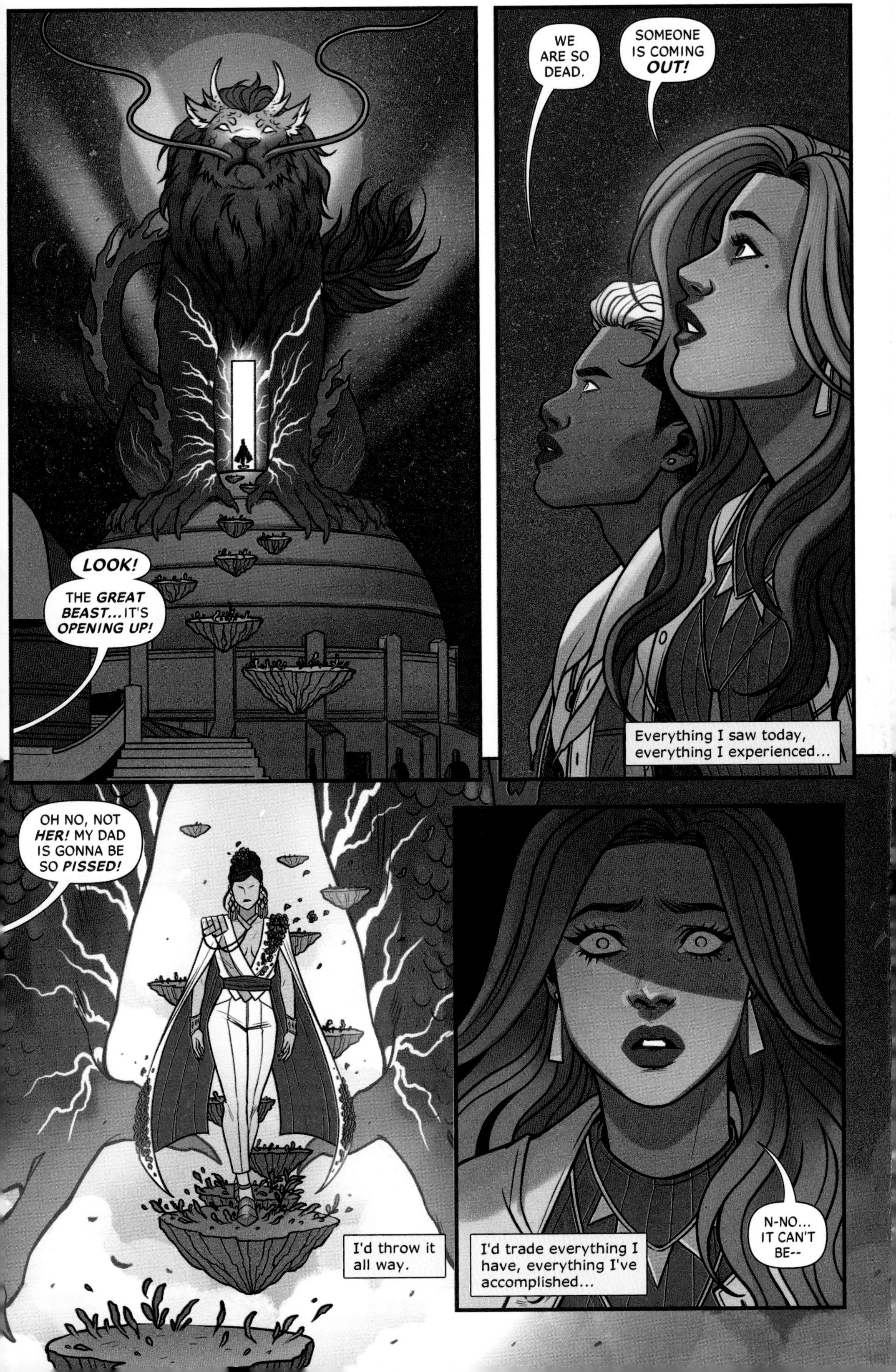
LOOK!
THE GREAT BEAST...IT'S OPENING UP!
WE ARE SO DEAD.
SOMEONE IS COMING OUT!
Everything I saw today, everything I experienced...
OH NO, NOT HER! MY DAD IS GONNA BE SO PISSED!
I'd throw it all way.
I'd trade everything I have, everything I've accomplished...
N-NO... IT CAN'T BE--

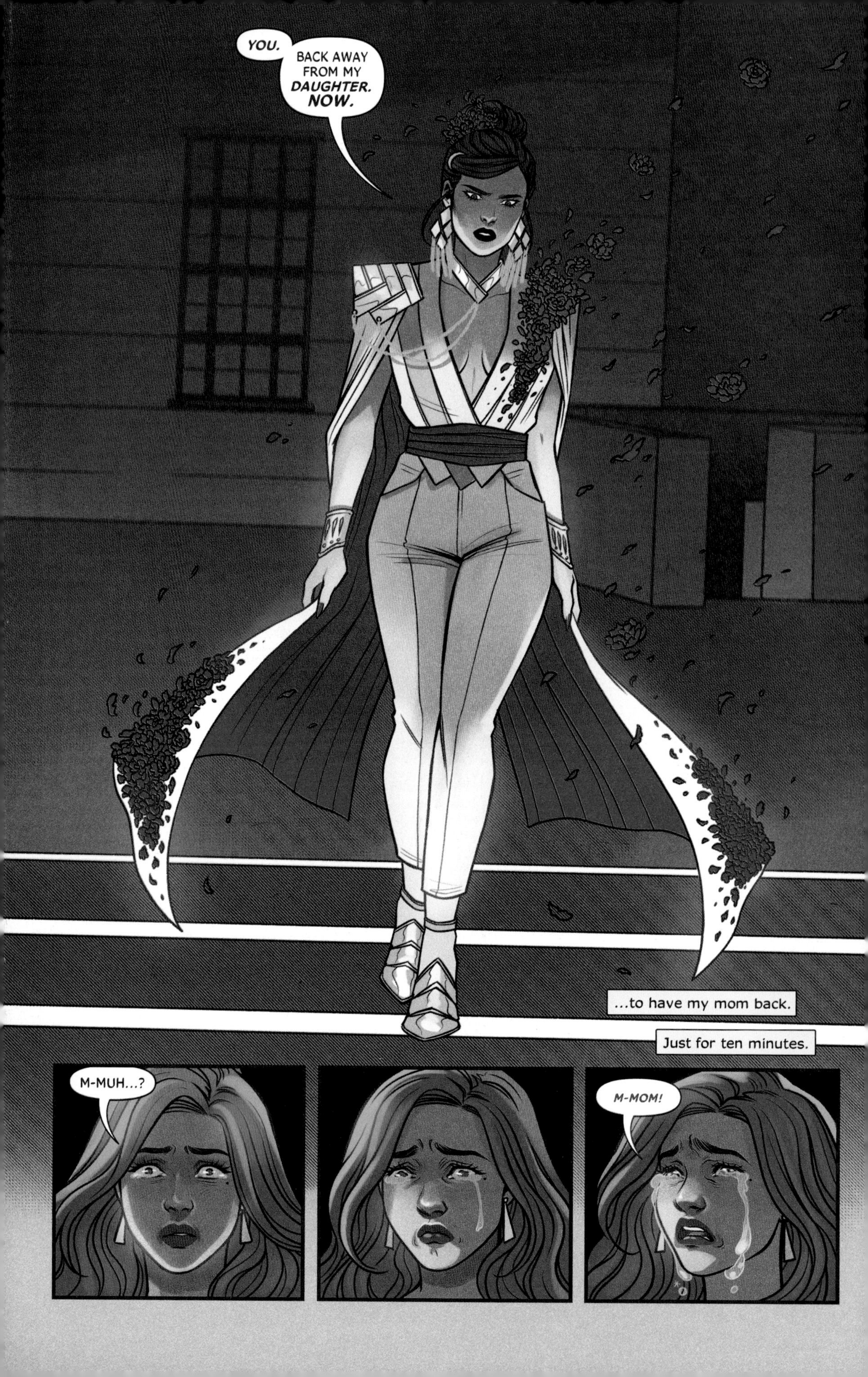
YOU.
BACK AWAY FROM MY DAUGHTER. NOW.
...to have my mom back.
Just for ten minutes.
M-MUH...?
M-MOM!

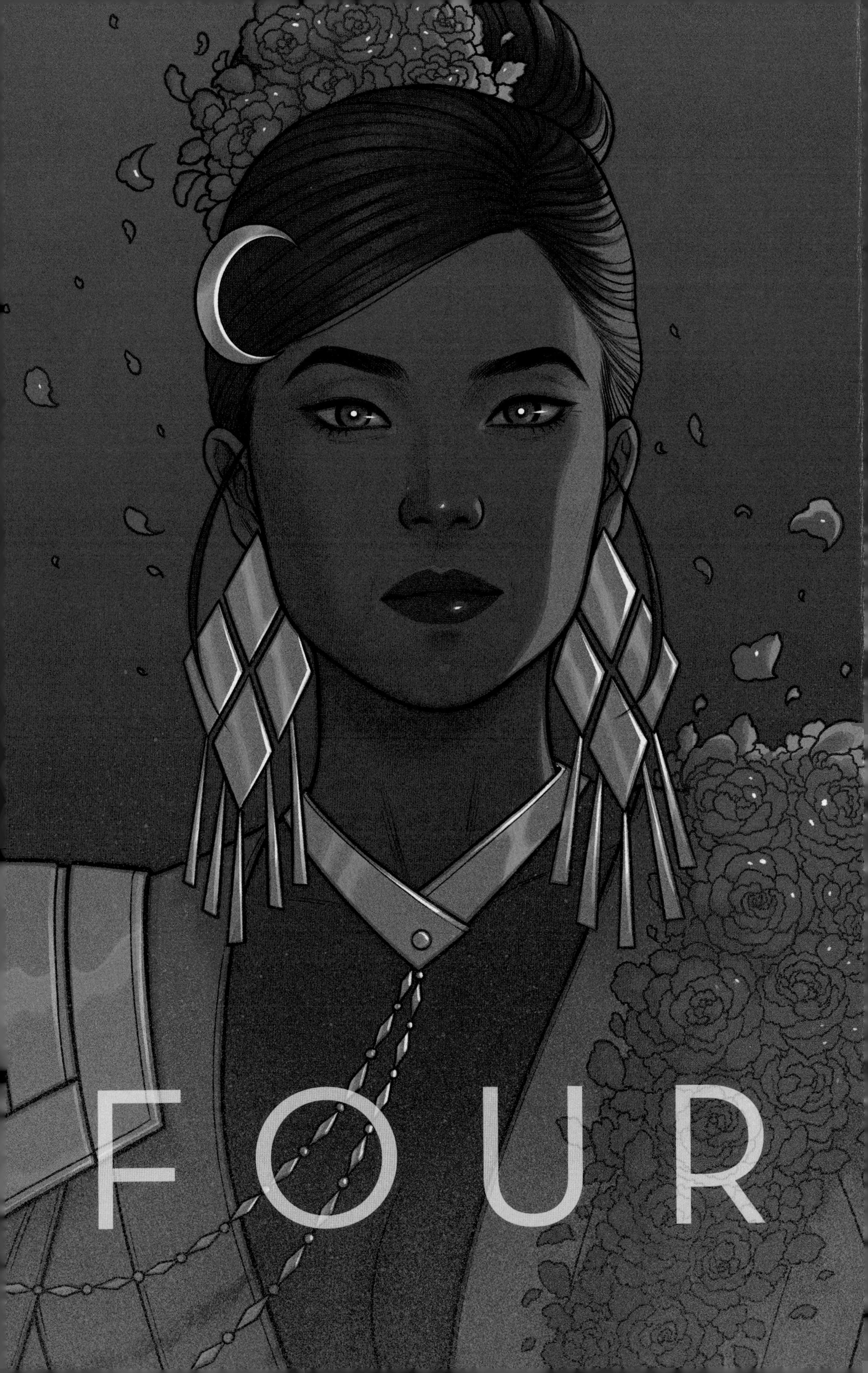
FOUR

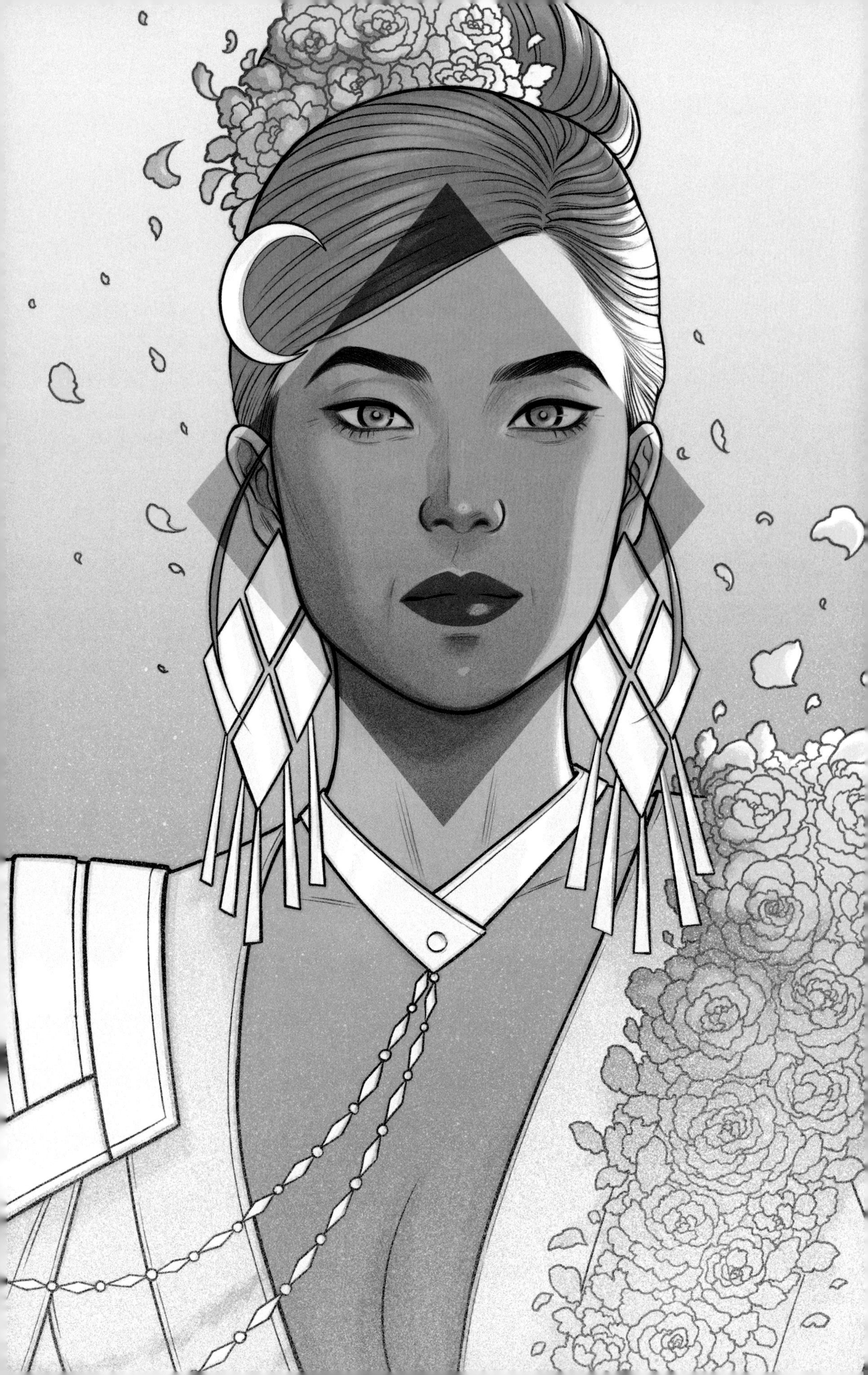

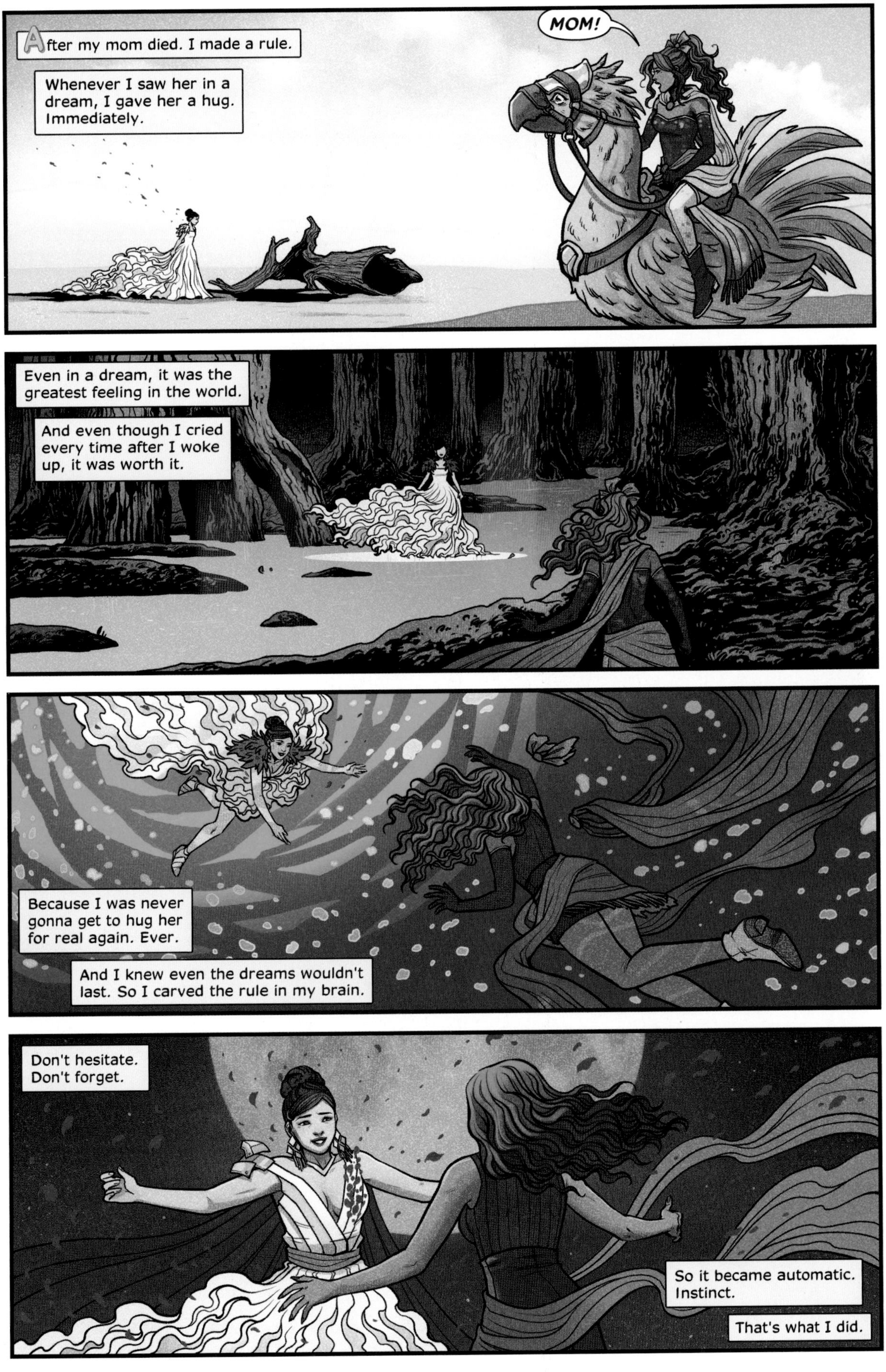
After my mom died. I made a rule.
Whenever I saw her in a dream, I gave her a hug. Immediately.
MOM!
Even in a dream, it was the greatest feeling in the world.
And even though I cried every time after I woke up, it was worth it.
Because I was never gonna get to hug her for real again. Ever.
And I knew even the dreams wouldn't last. So I carved the rule in my brain.
Don't hesitate. Don't forget.
So it became automatic. Instinct.
That's what I did.

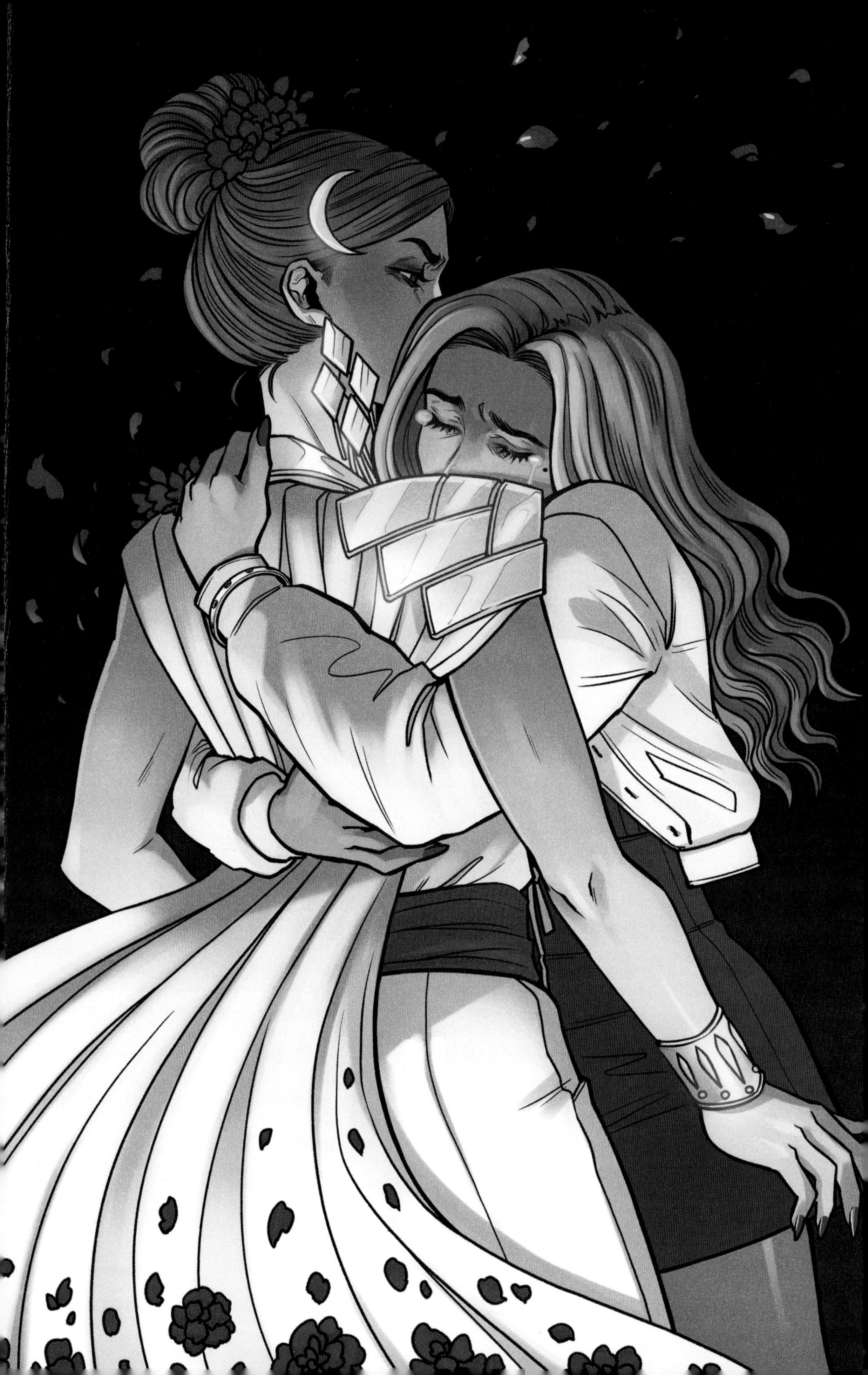

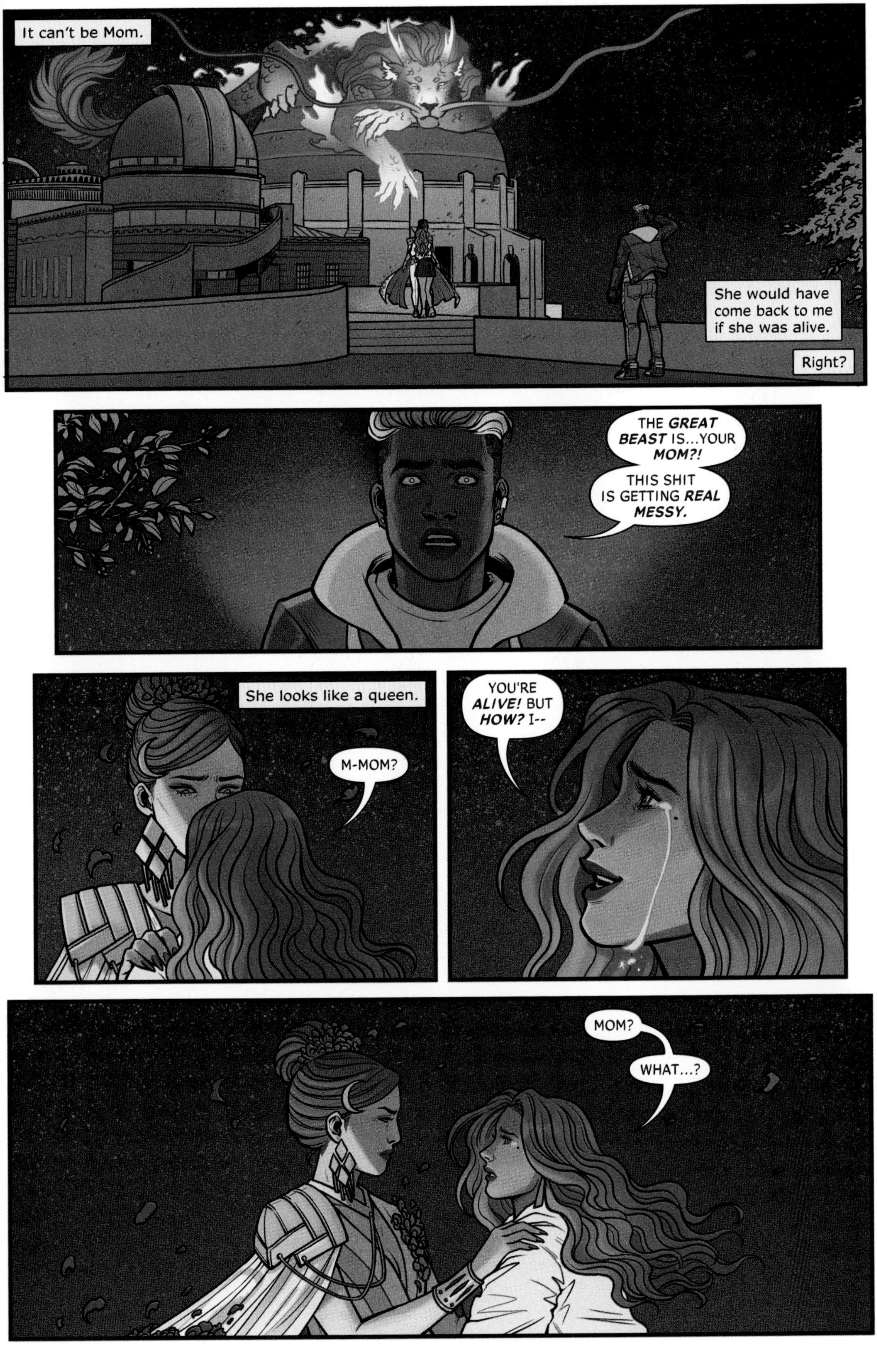
It can't be Mom.
She would have come back to me if she was alive.
Right?
THE GREAT BEAST IS...YOUR MOM?!
THIS SHIT IS GETTING REAL MESSY.
She looks like a queen.
M-MOM?
YOU'RE ALIVE! BUT HOW? I--
MOM?
WHAT...?

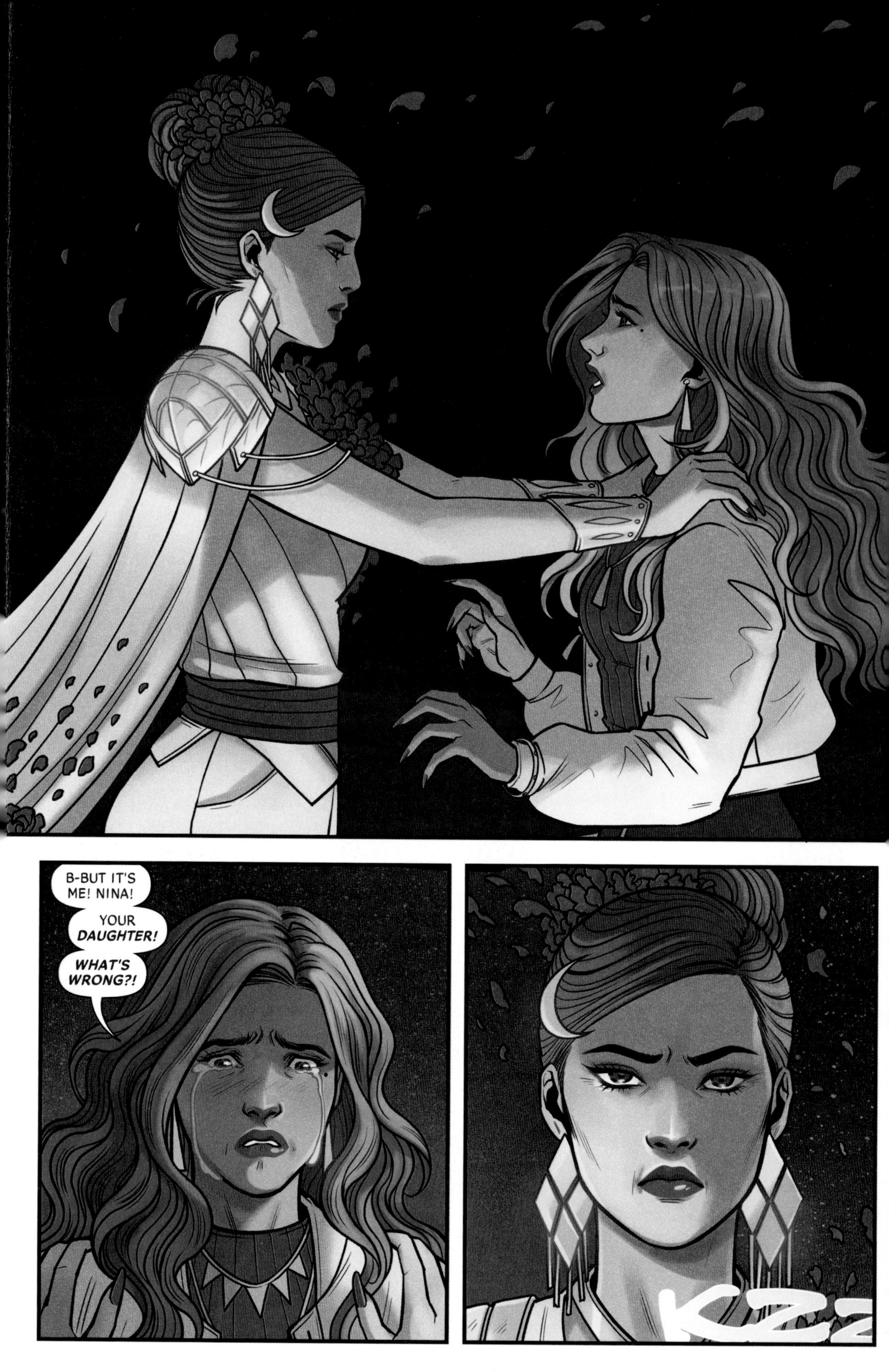
B-BUT IT'S ME! NINA!
YOUR *DAUGHTER!*
WHAT'S WRONG?!
KZZ

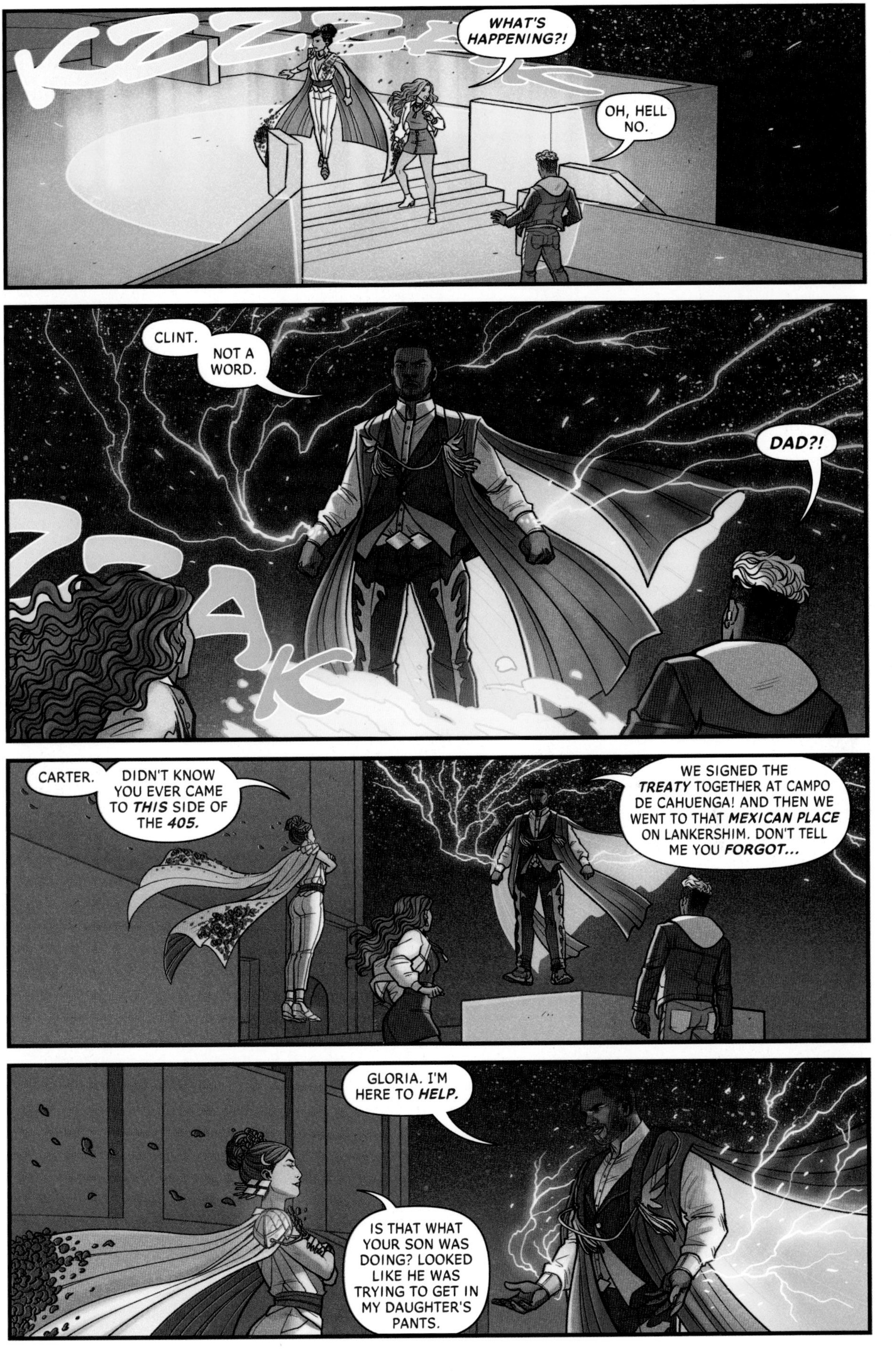
KZZZKK
WHAT'S HAPPENING?!
OH, HELL NO.
CLINT.
NOT A WORD.
DAD?!
ZZAK
CARTER.
DIDN'T KNOW YOU EVER CAME TO THIS SIDE OF THE 405.
WE SIGNED THE TREATY TOGETHER AT CAMPO DE CAHUENGA! AND THEN WE WENT TO THAT MEXICAN PLACE ON LANKERSHIM. DON'T TELL ME YOU FORGOT...
GLORIA. I'M HERE TO HELP.
IS THAT WHAT YOUR SON WAS DOING? LOOKED LIKE HE WAS TRYING TO GET IN MY DAUGHTER'S PANTS.

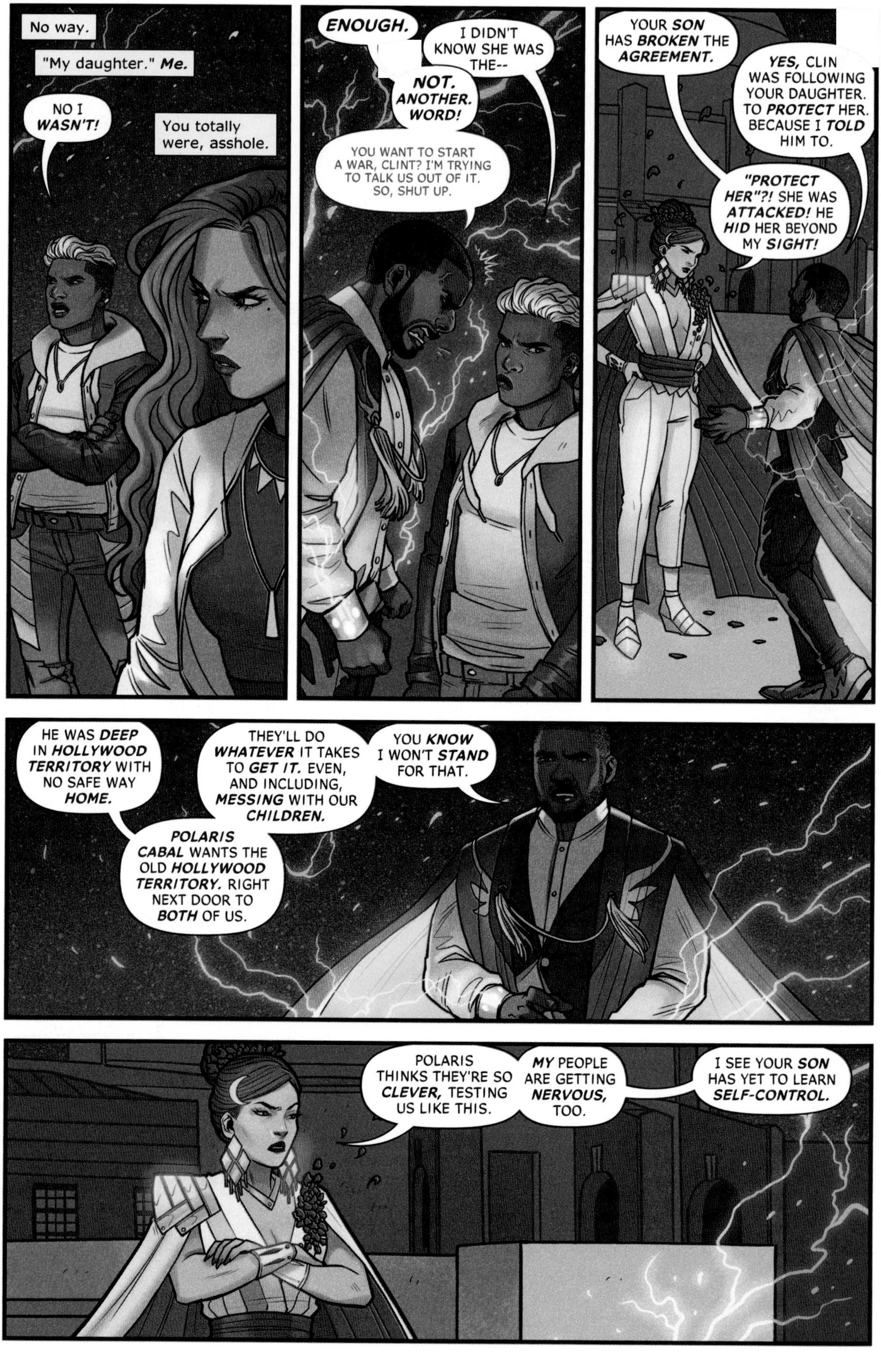

No way.
"My daughter." Me.
NO I WASN'T!
You totally were, asshole.
ENOUGH.
I DIDN'T KNOW SHE WAS THE--
NOT. ANOTHER. WORD!
YOU WANT TO START A WAR, CLINT? I'M TRYING TO TALK US OUT OF IT. SO, SHUT UP.
YOUR SON HAS BROKEN THE AGREEMENT.
YES, CLIN WAS FOLLOWING YOUR DAUGHTER. TO PROTECT HER. BECAUSE I TOLD HIM TO.
"PROTECT HER"?! SHE WAS ATTACKED! HE HID HER BEYOND MY SIGHT!
HE WAS DEEP IN HOLLYWOOD TERRITORY WITH NO SAFE WAY HOME.
POLARIS CABAL WANTS THE OLD HOLLYWOOD TERRITORY. RIGHT NEXT DOOR TO BOTH OF US.
THEY'LL DO WHATEVER IT TAKES TO GET IT. EVEN, AND INCLUDING, MESSING WITH OUR CHILDREN.
YOU KNOW I WON'T STAND FOR THAT.
POLARIS THINKS THEY'RE SO CLEVER, TESTING US LIKE THIS.
MY PEOPLE ARE GETTING NERVOUS, TOO.
I SEE YOUR SON HAS YET TO LEARN SELF-CONTROL.

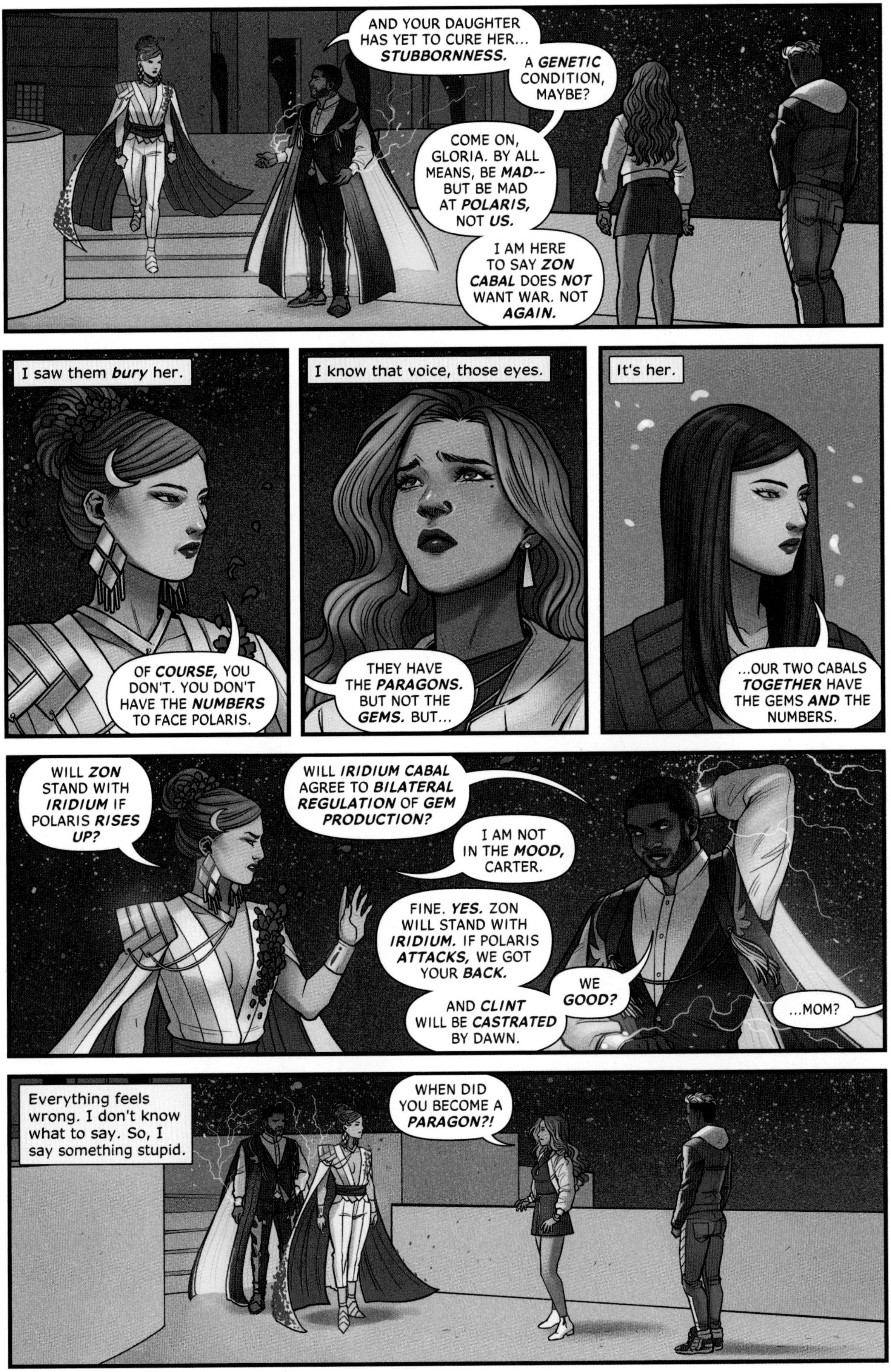
AND YOUR DAUGHTER HAS YET TO CURE HER... STUBBORNNESS.
A GENETIC CONDITION, MAYBE?
COME ON, GLORIA. BY ALL MEANS, BE MAD-- BUT BE MAD AT POLARIS, NOT US.
I AM HERE TO SAY ZON CABAL DOES NOT WANT WAR. NOT AGAIN.
I saw them bury her.
OF COURSE, YOU DON'T. YOU DON'T HAVE THE NUMBERS TO FACE POLARIS.
I know that voice, those eyes.
THEY HAVE THE PARAGONS. BUT NOT THE GEMS. BUT...
It's her.
...OUR TWO CABALS TOGETHER HAVE THE GEMS AND THE NUMBERS.
WILL ZON STAND WITH IRIDIUM IF POLARIS RISES UP?
WILL IRIDIUM CABAL AGREE TO BILATERAL REGULATION OF GEM PRODUCTION?
I AM NOT IN THE MOOD, CARTER.
FINE. YES. ZON WILL STAND WITH IRIDIUM. IF POLARIS ATTACKS, WE GOT YOUR BACK.
WE GOOD?
AND CLINT WILL BE CASTRATED BY DAWN.
...MOM?
Everything feels wrong. I don't know what to say. So, I say something stupid.
WHEN DID YOU BECOME A PARAGON?!

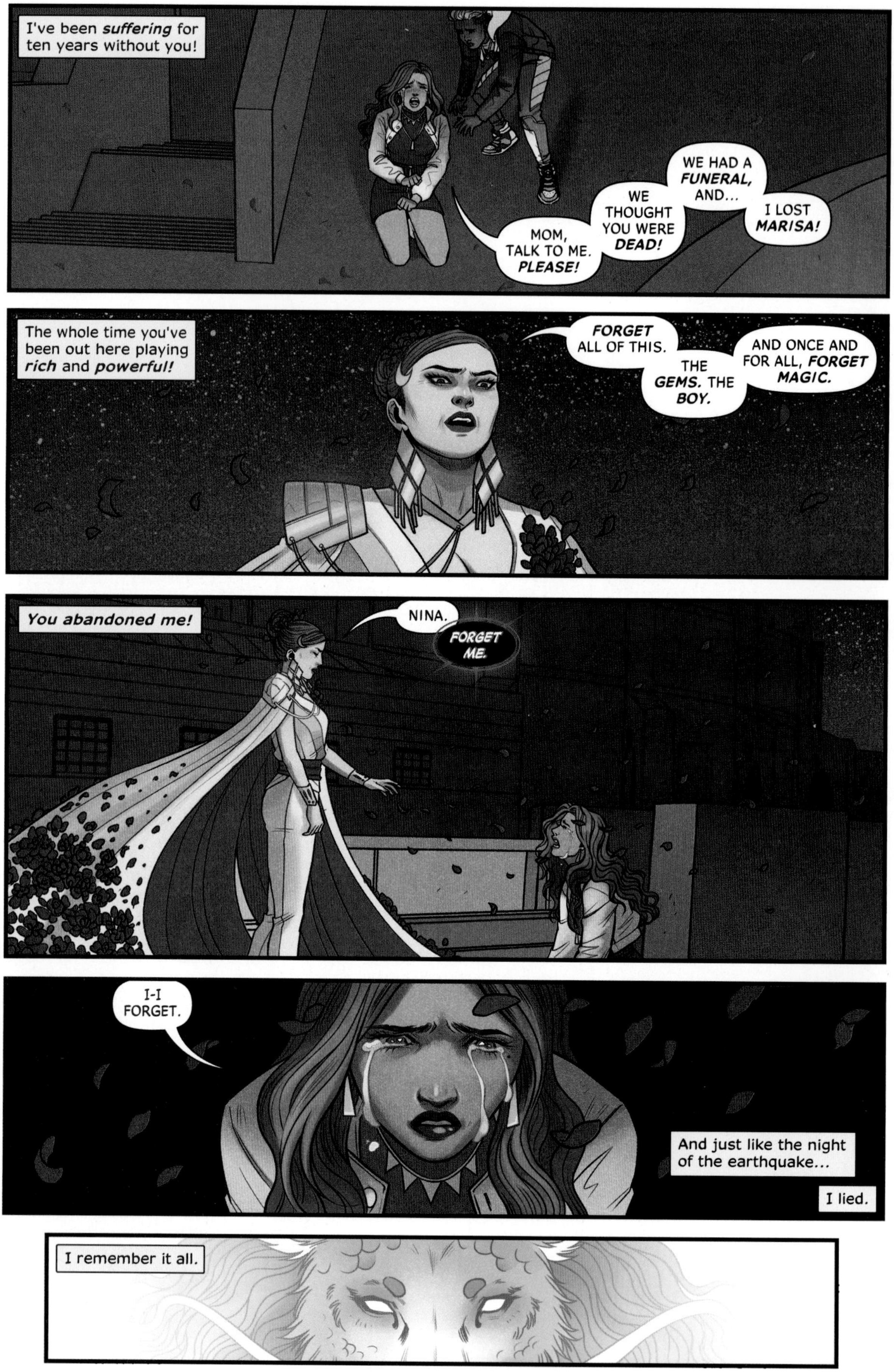

I've been *suffering* for ten years without you!
MOM, TALK TO ME. *PLEASE!*
WE THOUGHT YOU WERE *DEAD!*
WE HAD A *FUNERAL,* AND...
I LOST *MARISA!*
The whole time you've been out here playing *rich* and *powerful!*
FORGET ALL OF THIS.
THE *GEMS.* THE *BOY.*
AND ONCE AND FOR ALL, *FORGET MAGIC.*
You abandoned me!
NINA.
FORGET ME.
I-I FORGET.
And just like the night of the earthquake...
I lied.
I remember it all.

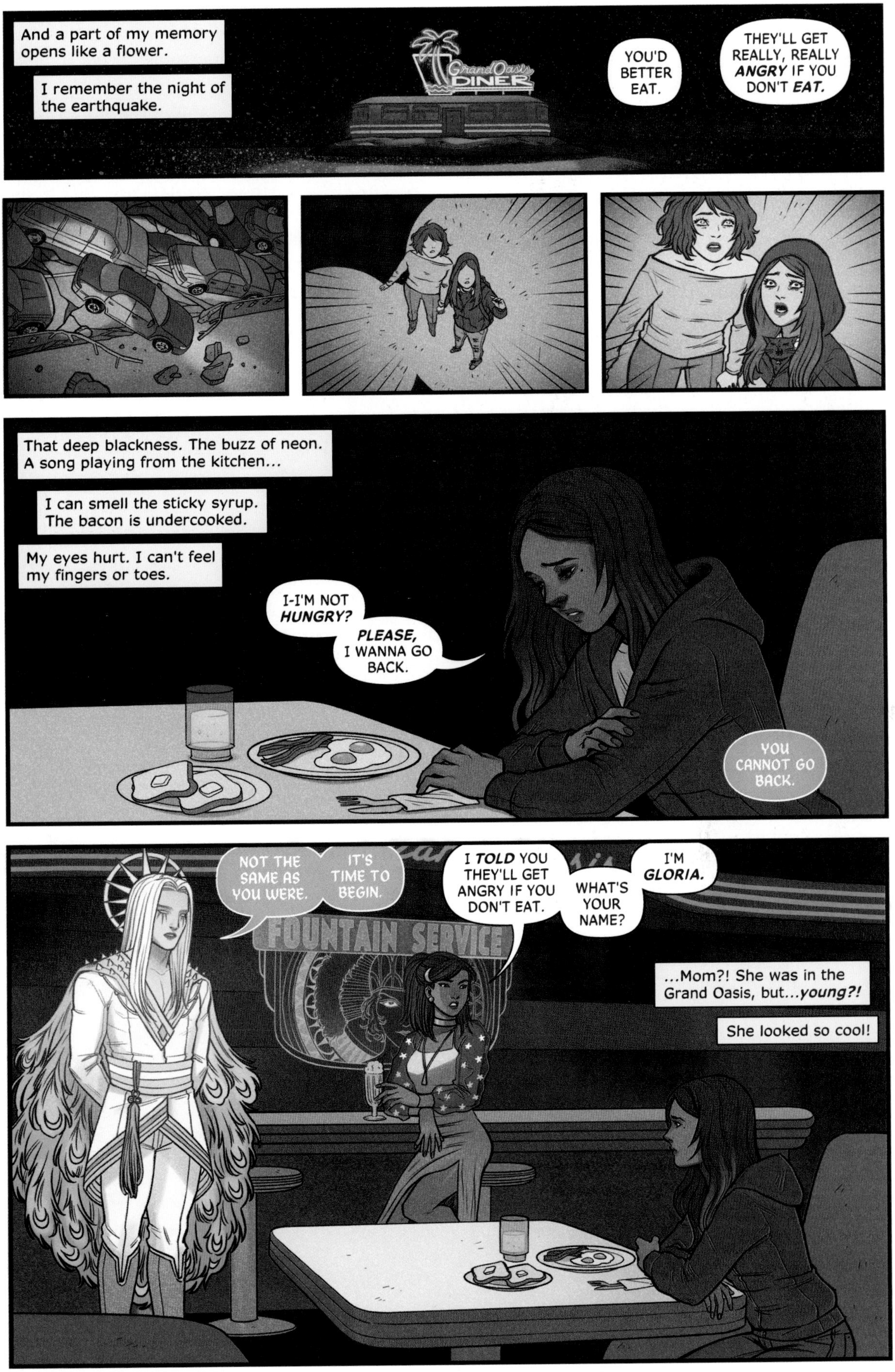
And a part of my memory opens like a flower.
I remember the night of the earthquake.
Grand Oasis DINER
YOU'D BETTER EAT.
THEY'LL GET REALLY, REALLY ANGRY IF YOU DON'T EAT.
That deep blackness. The buzz of neon. A song playing from the kitchen...
I can smell the sticky syrup. The bacon is undercooked.
My eyes hurt. I can't feel my fingers or toes.
I-I'M NOT HUNGRY?
PLEASE, I WANNA GO BACK.
YOU CANNOT GO BACK.
NOT THE SAME AS YOU WERE.
IT'S TIME TO BEGIN.
I TOLD YOU THEY'LL GET ANGRY IF YOU DON'T EAT.
WHAT'S YOUR NAME?
I'M GLORIA.
FOUNTAIN SERVICE
...Mom?! She was in the Grand Oasis, but...young?!
She looked so cool!

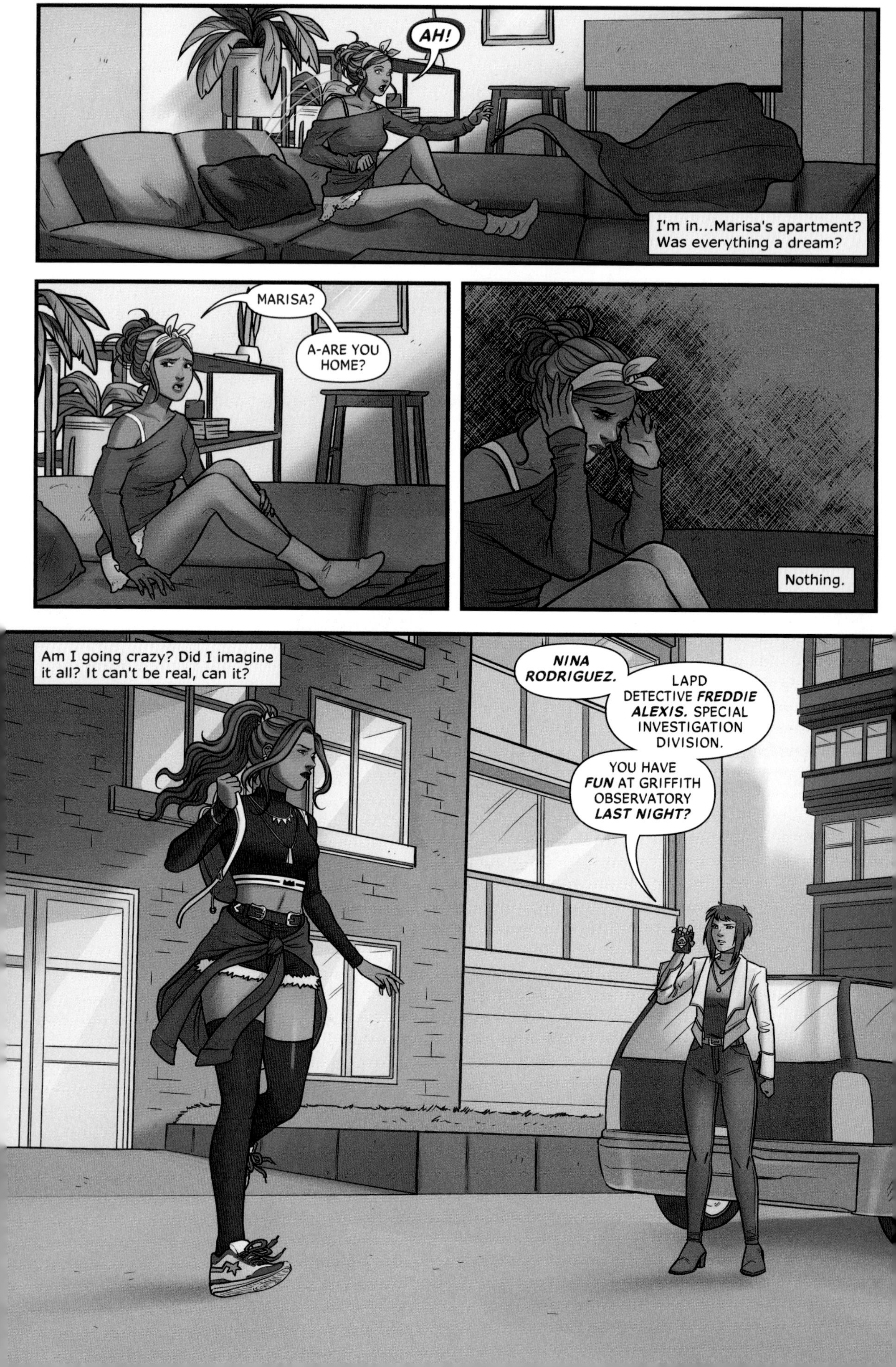
AH!
I'm in...Marisa's apartment? Was everything a dream?
MARISA?
A-ARE YOU HOME?
Nothing.
Am I going crazy? Did I imagine it all? It can't be real, can it?
NINA RODRIGUEZ.
LAPD DETECTIVE FREDDIE ALEXIS. SPECIAL INVESTIGATION DIVISION.
YOU HAVE FUN AT GRIFFITH OBSERVATORY LAST NIGHT?

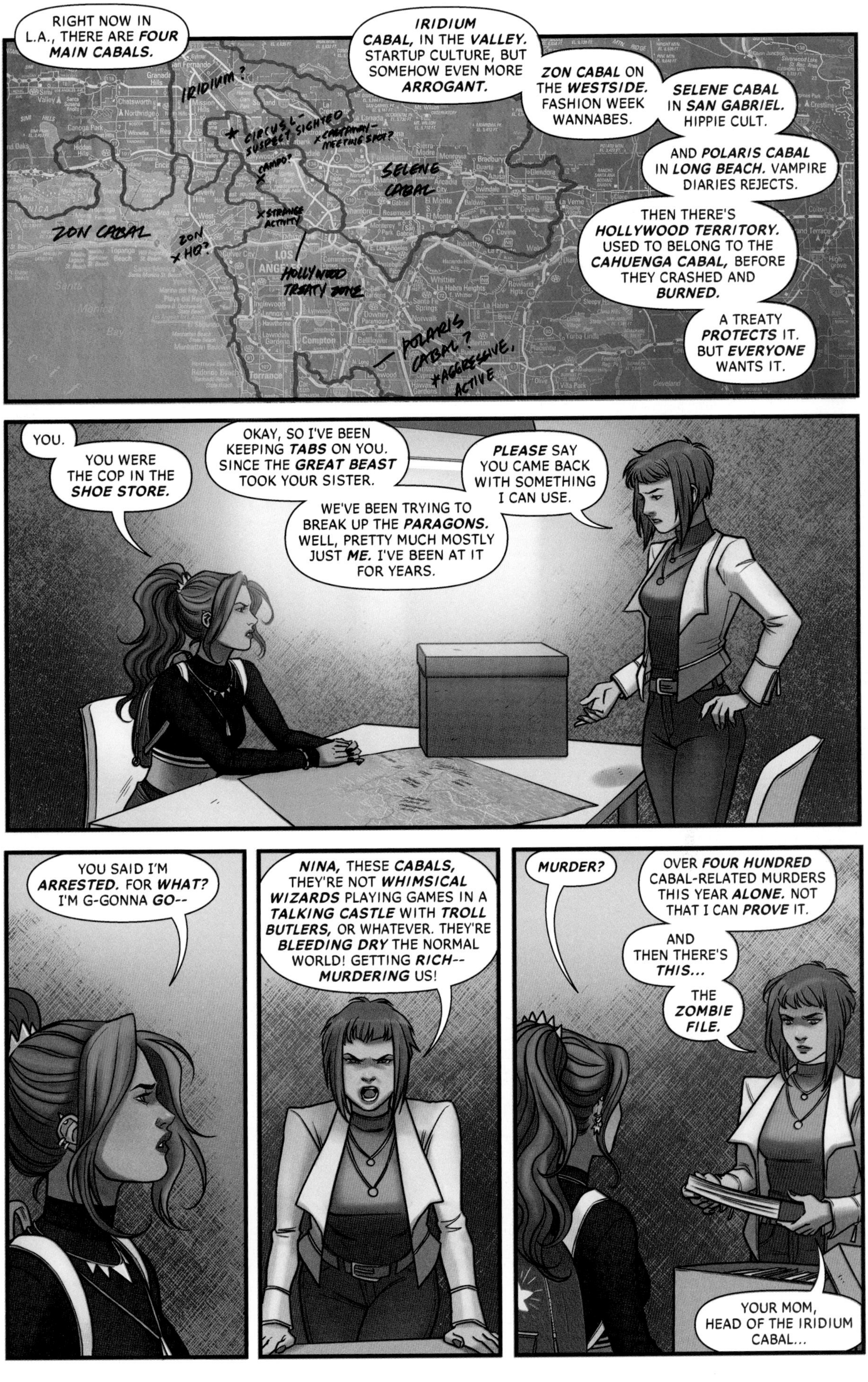

RIGHT NOW IN L.A., THERE ARE FOUR MAIN CABALS.
IRIDIUM CABAL, IN THE VALLEY. STARTUP CULTURE, BUT SOMEHOW EVEN MORE ARROGANT.
ZON CABAL ON THE WESTSIDE. FASHION WEEK WANNABES.
SELENE CABAL IN SAN GABRIEL. HIPPIE CULT.
AND POLARIS CABAL IN LONG BEACH. VAMPIRE DIARIES REJECTS.
THEN THERE'S HOLLYWOOD TERRITORY. USED TO BELONG TO THE CAHUENGA CABAL, BEFORE THEY CRASHED AND BURNED.
A TREATY PROTECTS IT. BUT EVERYONE WANTS IT.
IRIDIUM?
SELENE CABAL
ZON CABAL
ZON HQ?
STRANGE ACTIVITY
HOLLYWOOD TREATY ZONE
POLARIS CABAL? AGGRESSIVE, ACTIVE
YOU.
YOU WERE THE COP IN THE SHOE STORE.
OKAY, SO I'VE BEEN KEEPING TABS ON YOU. SINCE THE GREAT BEAST TOOK YOUR SISTER.
WE'VE BEEN TRYING TO BREAK UP THE PARAGONS. WELL, PRETTY MUCH MOSTLY JUST ME. I'VE BEEN AT IT FOR YEARS.
PLEASE SAY YOU CAME BACK WITH SOMETHING I CAN USE.
YOU SAID I'M ARRESTED. FOR WHAT? I'M G-GONNA GO--
NINA, THESE CABALS, THEY'RE NOT WHIMSICAL WIZARDS PLAYING GAMES IN A TALKING CASTLE WITH TROLL BUTLERS, OR WHATEVER. THEY'RE BLEEDING DRY THE NORMAL WORLD! GETTING RICH--MURDERING US!
MURDER?
OVER FOUR HUNDRED CABAL-RELATED MURDERS THIS YEAR ALONE. NOT THAT I CAN PROVE IT.
AND THEN THERE'S THIS...
THE ZOMBIE FILE.
YOUR MOM, HEAD OF THE IRIDIUM CABAL...

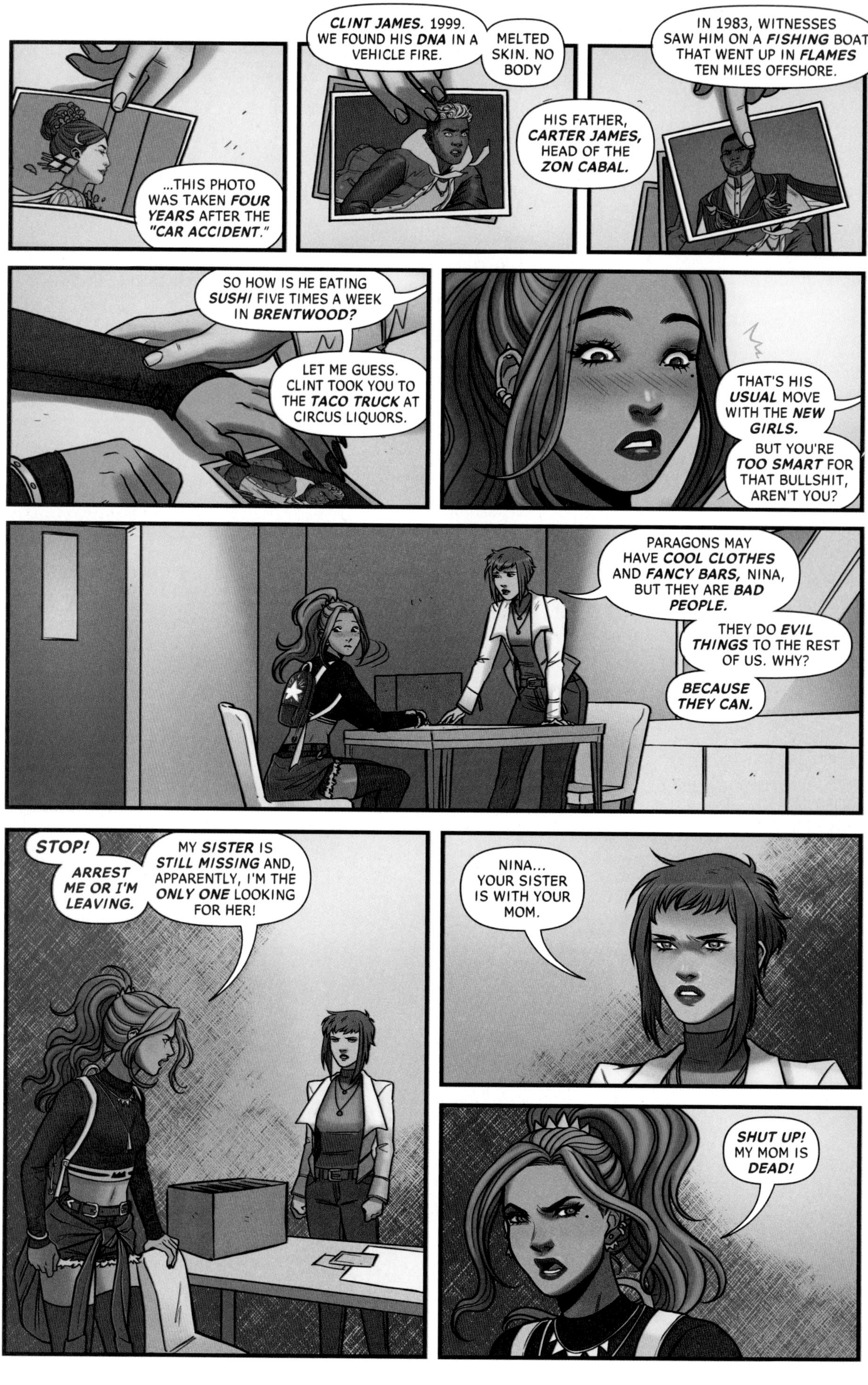
...THIS PHOTO WAS TAKEN FOUR YEARS AFTER THE "CAR ACCIDENT."
CLINT JAMES. 1999. WE FOUND HIS DNA IN A VEHICLE FIRE.
MELTED SKIN. NO BODY
HIS FATHER, CARTER JAMES, HEAD OF THE ZON CABAL.
IN 1983, WITNESSES SAW HIM ON A FISHING BOAT THAT WENT UP IN FLAMES TEN MILES OFFSHORE.
SO HOW IS HE EATING SUSHI FIVE TIMES A WEEK IN BRENTWOOD?
LET ME GUESS. CLINT TOOK YOU TO THE TACO TRUCK AT CIRCUS LIQUORS.
THAT'S HIS USUAL MOVE WITH THE NEW GIRLS.
BUT YOU'RE TOO SMART FOR THAT BULLSHIT, AREN'T YOU?
PARAGONS MAY HAVE COOL CLOTHES AND FANCY BARS, NINA, BUT THEY ARE BAD PEOPLE.
THEY DO EVIL THINGS TO THE REST OF US. WHY?
BECAUSE THEY CAN.
STOP!
ARREST ME OR I'M LEAVING.
MY SISTER IS STILL MISSING AND, APPARENTLY, I'M THE ONLY ONE LOOKING FOR HER!
NINA... YOUR SISTER IS WITH YOUR MOM.
SHUT UP! MY MOM IS DEAD!

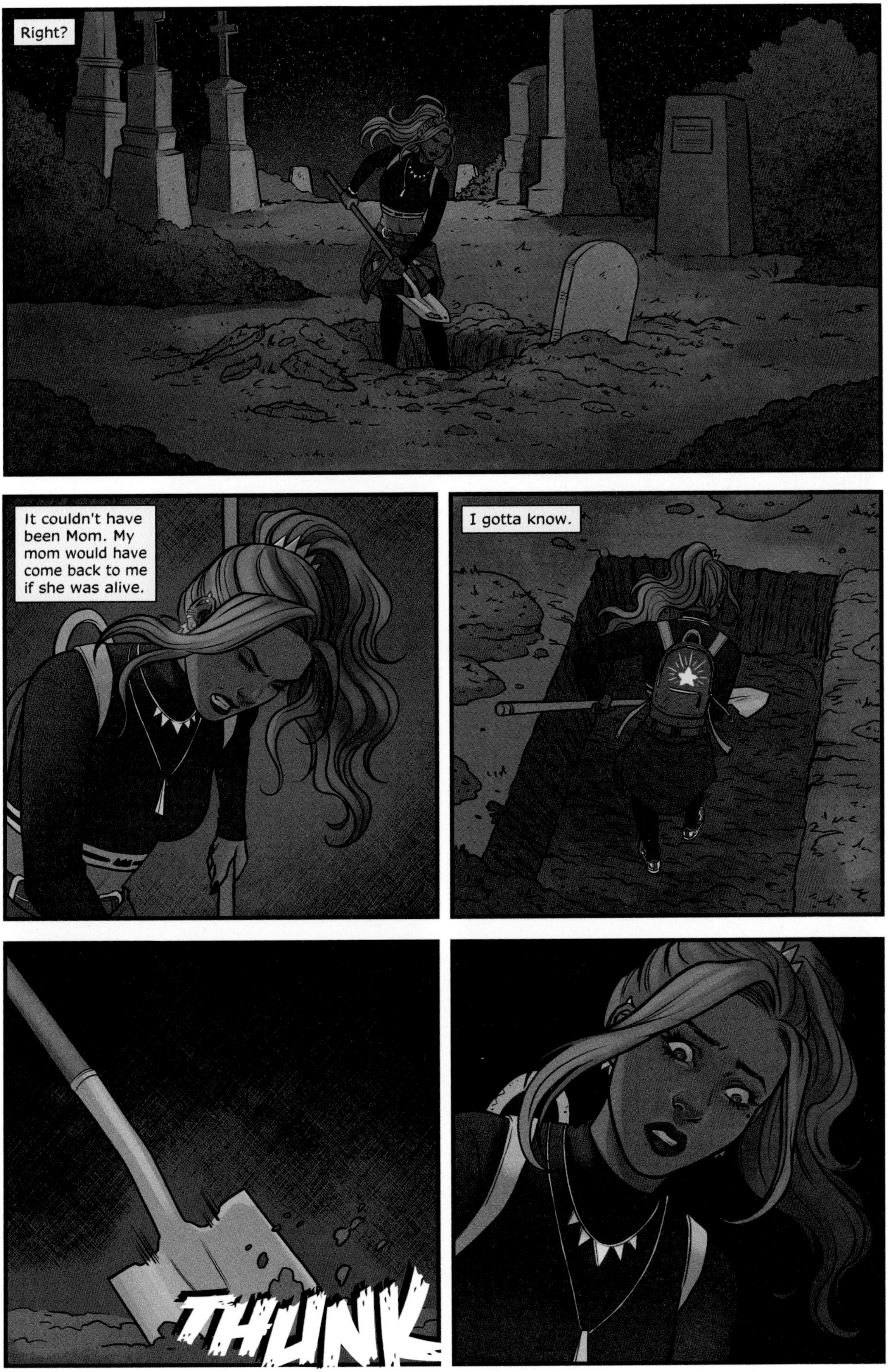
Right?
It couldn't have been Mom. My mom would have come back to me if she was alive.
I gotta know.
THUNK

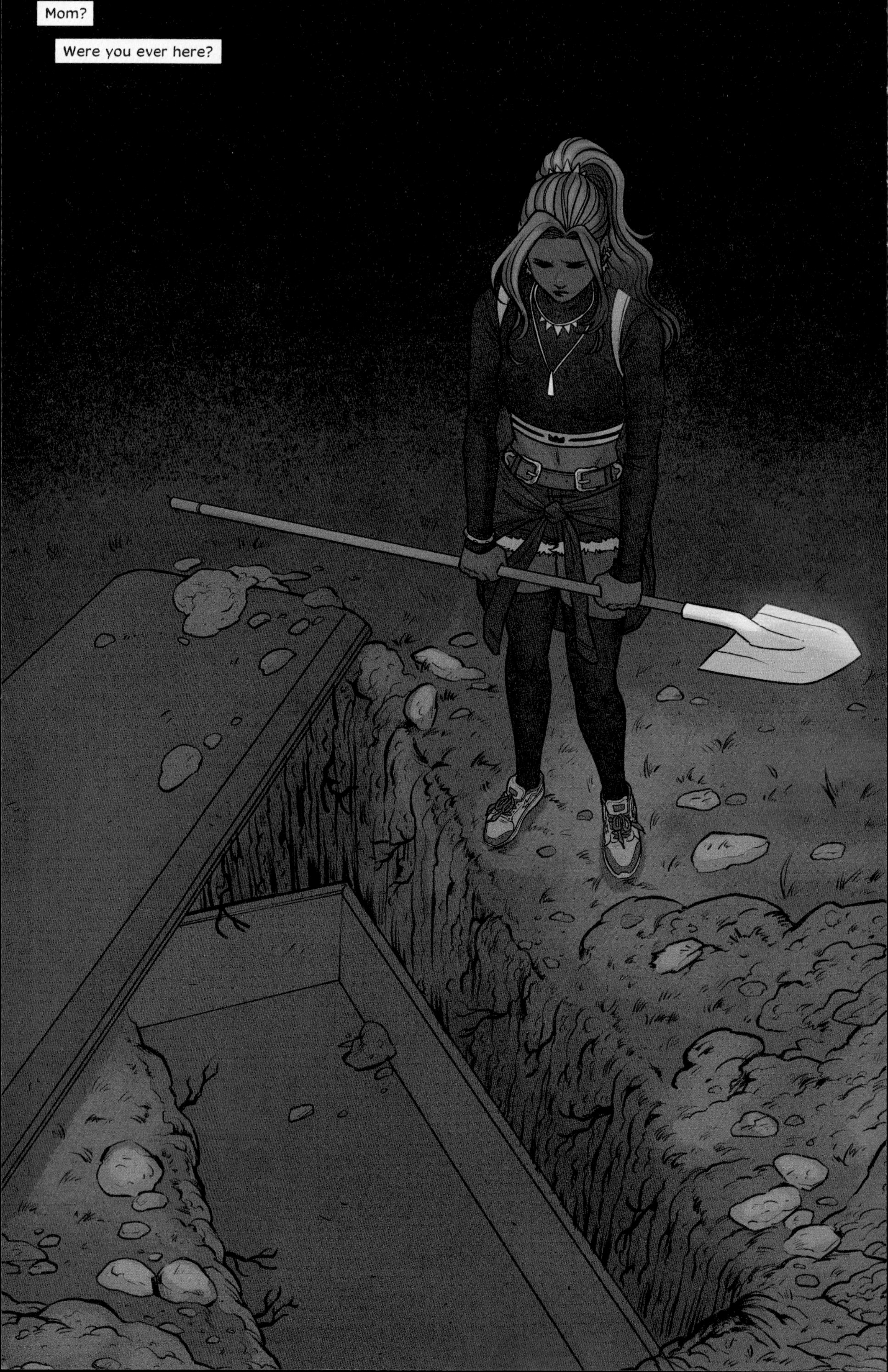
Mom?
Were you ever here?

She came back for Marisa and not me.

I wanted this so bad. More than anything.

I wanted her to be alive.

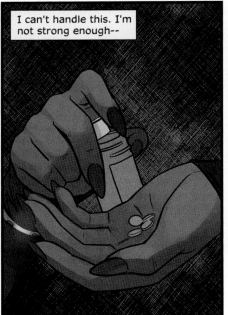

I can't handle this. I'm not strong enough--

MIAO.

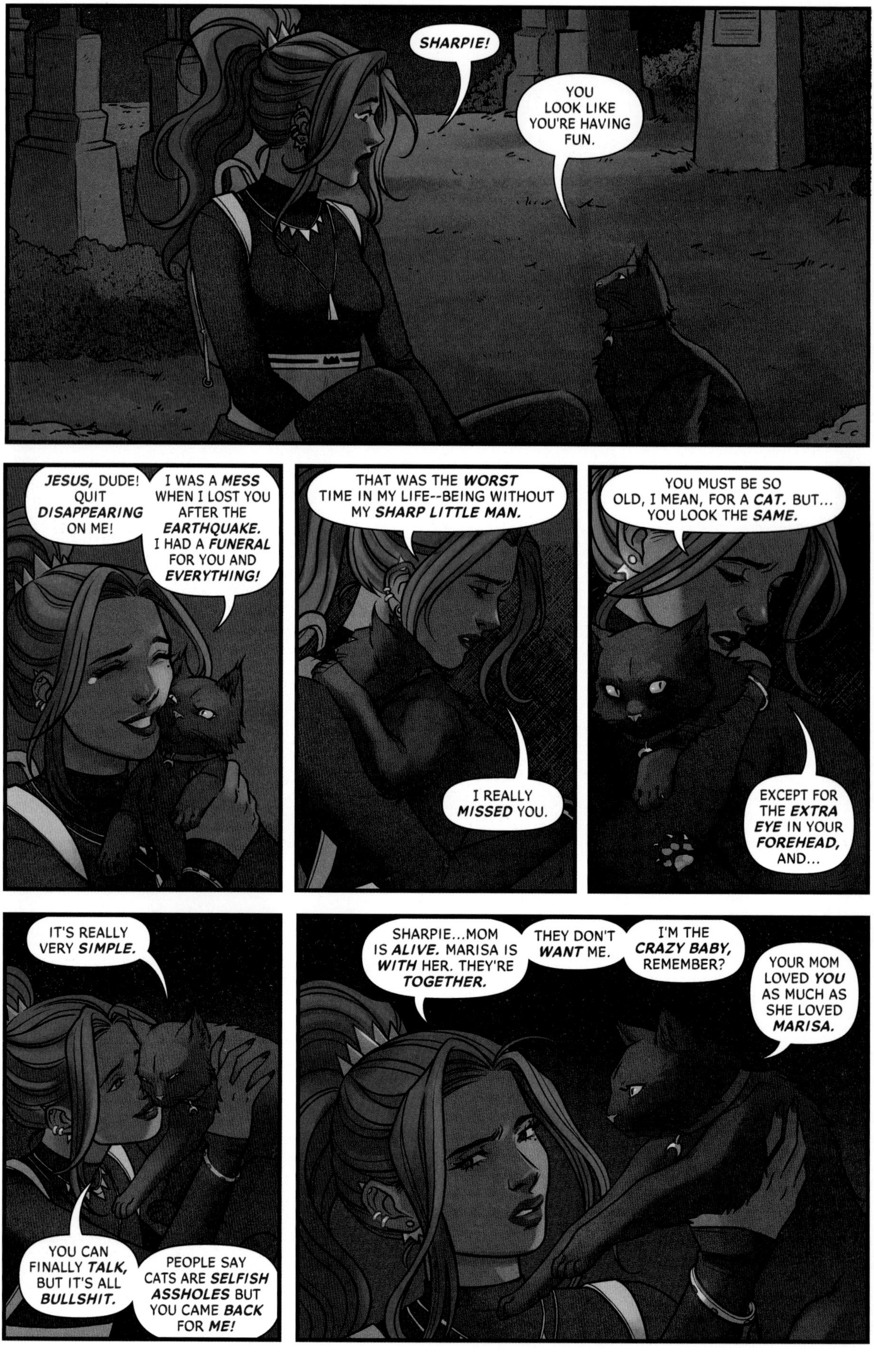
SHARPIE!
YOU LOOK LIKE YOU'RE HAVING FUN.
JESUS, DUDE! QUIT DISAPPEARING ON ME!
I WAS A MESS WHEN I LOST YOU AFTER THE EARTHQUAKE. I HAD A FUNERAL FOR YOU AND EVERYTHING!
THAT WAS THE WORST TIME IN MY LIFE--BEING WITHOUT MY SHARP LITTLE MAN.
I REALLY MISSED YOU.
YOU MUST BE SO OLD, I MEAN, FOR A CAT. BUT... YOU LOOK THE SAME.
EXCEPT FOR THE EXTRA EYE IN YOUR FOREHEAD, AND...
IT'S REALLY VERY SIMPLE.
YOU CAN FINALLY TALK, BUT IT'S ALL BULLSHIT.
PEOPLE SAY CATS ARE SELFISH ASSHOLES BUT YOU CAME BACK FOR ME!
SHARPIE...MOM IS ALIVE. MARISA IS WITH HER. THEY'RE TOGETHER.
THEY DON'T WANT ME.
I'M THE CRAZY BABY, REMEMBER?
YOUR MOM LOVED YOU AS MUCH AS SHE LOVED MARISA.

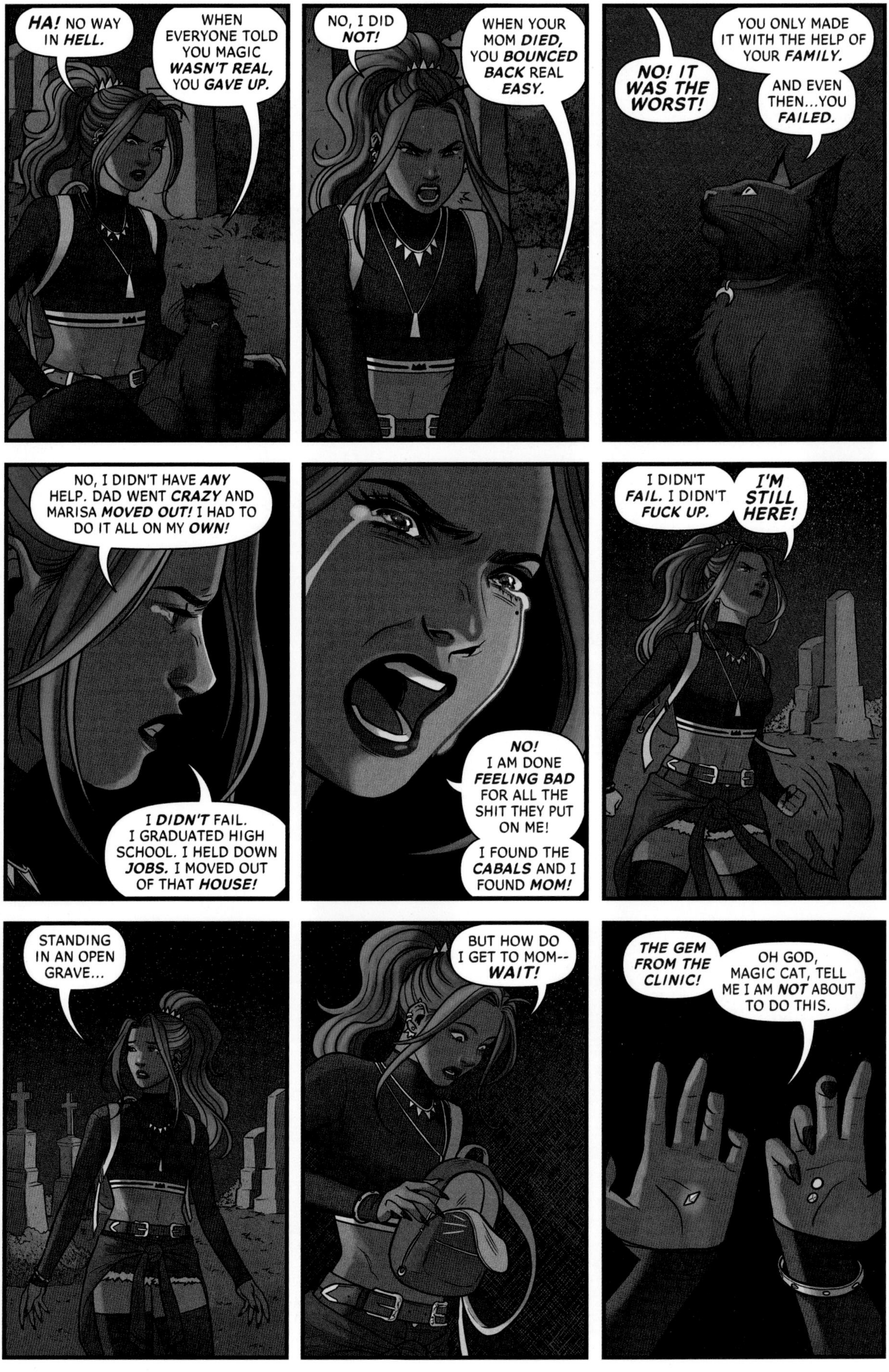
HA! NO WAY IN HELL.
WHEN EVERYONE TOLD YOU MAGIC WASN'T REAL, YOU GAVE UP.
NO, I DID NOT!
WHEN YOUR MOM DIED, YOU BOUNCED BACK REAL EASY.
NO! IT WAS THE WORST!
YOU ONLY MADE IT WITH THE HELP OF YOUR FAMILY.
AND EVEN THEN...YOU FAILED.
NO, I DIDN'T HAVE ANY HELP. DAD WENT CRAZY AND MARISA MOVED OUT! I HAD TO DO IT ALL ON MY OWN!
I DIDN'T FAIL. I GRADUATED HIGH SCHOOL. I HELD DOWN JOBS. I MOVED OUT OF THAT HOUSE!
NO! I AM DONE FEELING BAD FOR ALL THE SHIT THEY PUT ON ME!
I FOUND THE CABALS AND I FOUND MOM!
I DIDN'T FAIL. I DIDN'T FUCK UP.
I'M STILL HERE!
STANDING IN AN OPEN GRAVE...
BUT HOW DO I GET TO MOM-- WAIT!
THE GEM FROM THE CLINIC!
OH GOD, MAGIC CAT, TELL ME I AM NOT ABOUT TO DO THIS.

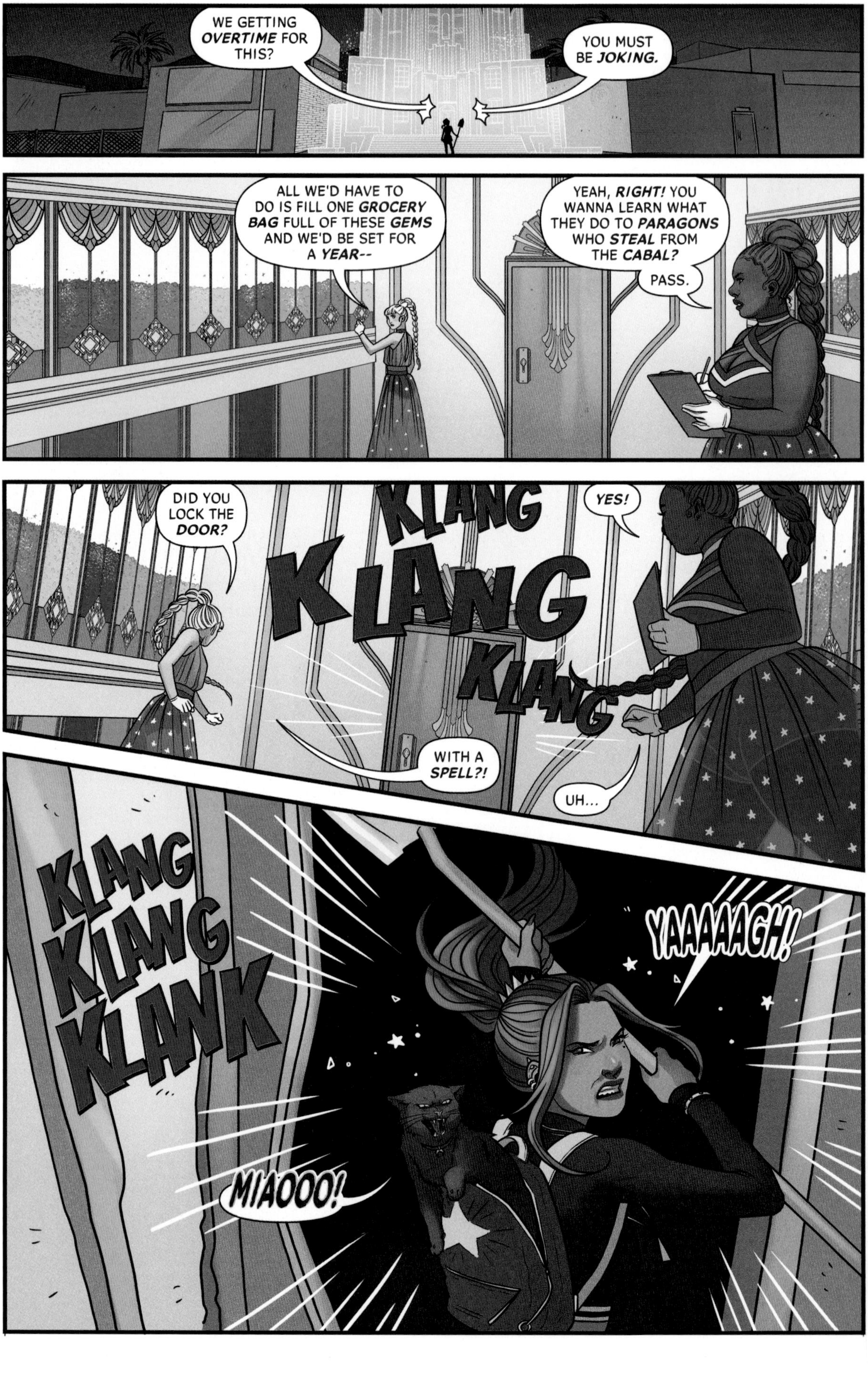

WE GETTING OVERTIME FOR THIS?
YOU MUST BE JOKING.
ALL WE'D HAVE TO DO IS FILL ONE GROCERY BAG FULL OF THESE GEMS AND WE'D BE SET FOR A YEAR--
YEAH, RIGHT! YOU WANNA LEARN WHAT THEY DO TO PARAGONS WHO STEAL FROM THE CABAL?
PASS.
DID YOU LOCK THE DOOR?
KLANG
KLANG
KLANG
YES!
KLANG
WITH A SPELL?!
UH...
KLANG
KLANG
KLANK
YAAAAAGH!
MIAOOO!

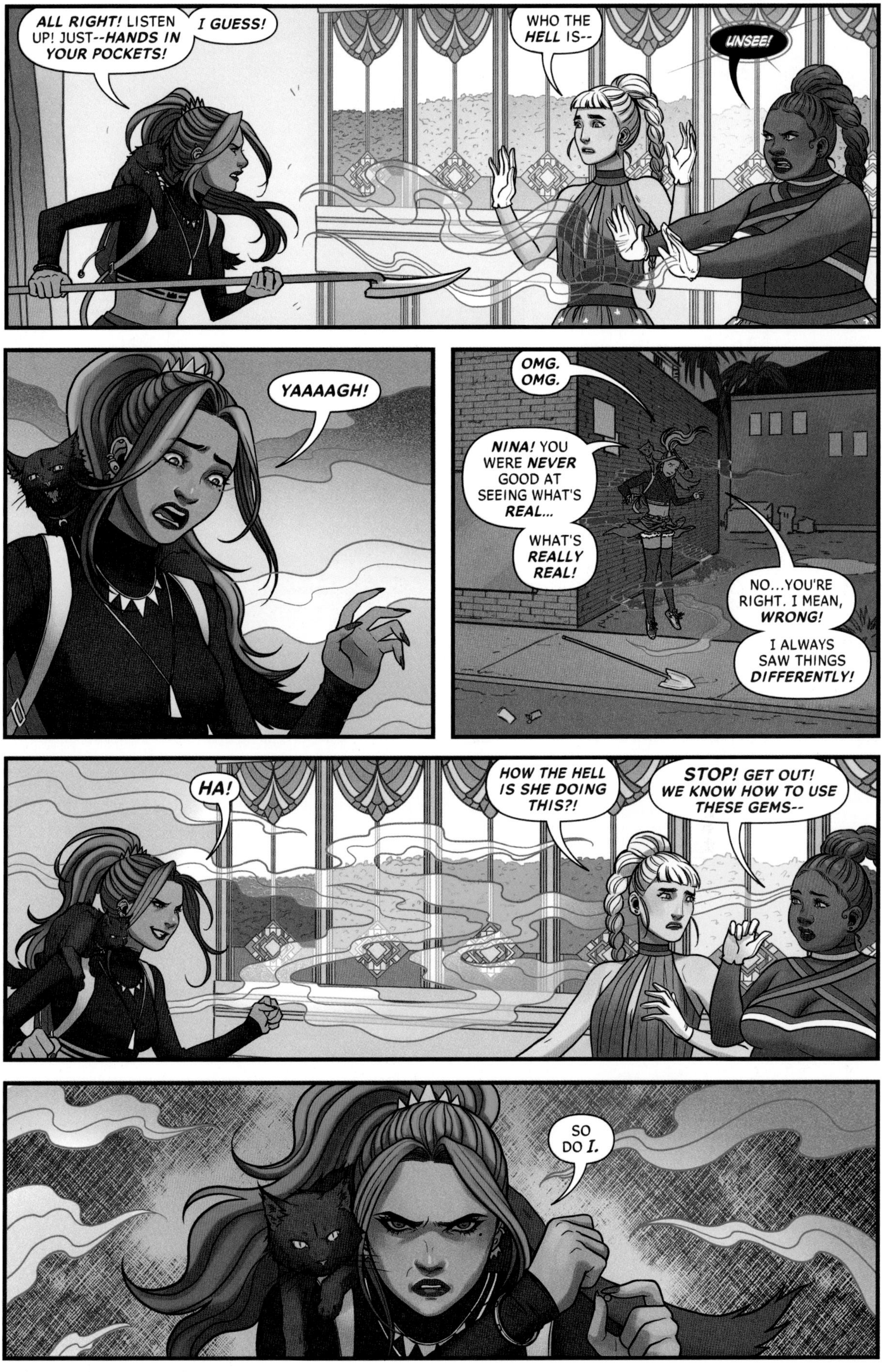
ALL RIGHT! LISTEN UP! JUST--HANDS IN YOUR POCKETS!
I GUESS!
WHO THE HELL IS--
UNSEE!
YAAAAGH!
OMG. OMG.
NINA! YOU WERE NEVER GOOD AT SEEING WHAT'S REAL...
WHAT'S REALLY REAL!
NO...YOU'RE RIGHT. I MEAN, WRONG!
I ALWAYS SAW THINGS DIFFERENTLY!
HA!
HOW THE HELL IS SHE DOING THIS?!
STOP! GET OUT! WE KNOW HOW TO USE THESE GEMS--
SO DO I.

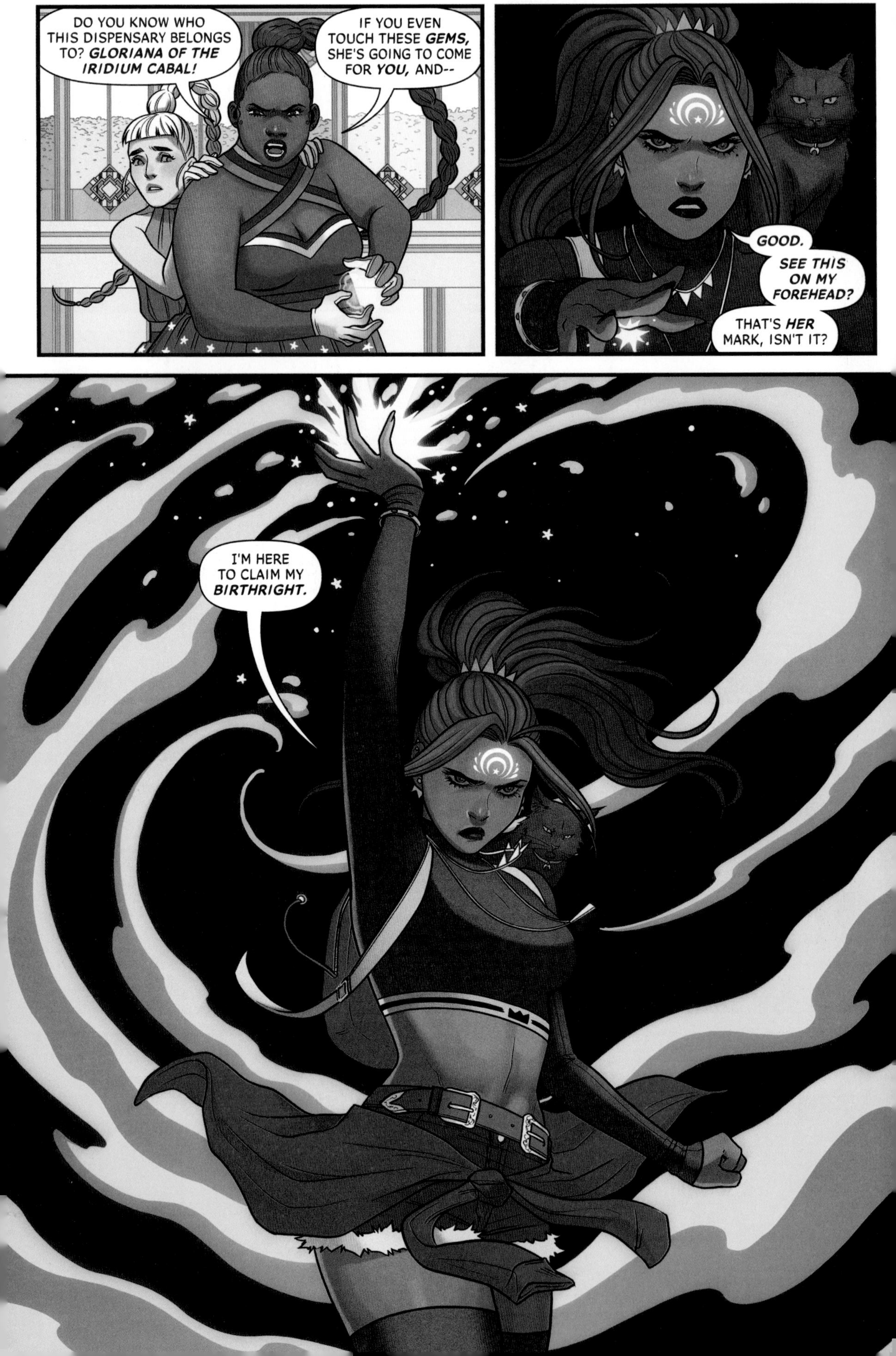
DO YOU KNOW WHO THIS DISPENSARY BELONGS TO? ***GLORIANA OF THE IRIDIUM CABAL!***
IF YOU EVEN TOUCH THESE ***GEMS,*** SHE'S GOING TO COME FOR ***YOU,*** AND--
GOOD.
SEE THIS ON MY FOREHEAD?
THAT'S ***HER*** MARK, ISN'T IT?
I'M HERE TO CLAIM MY ***BIRTHRIGHT.***

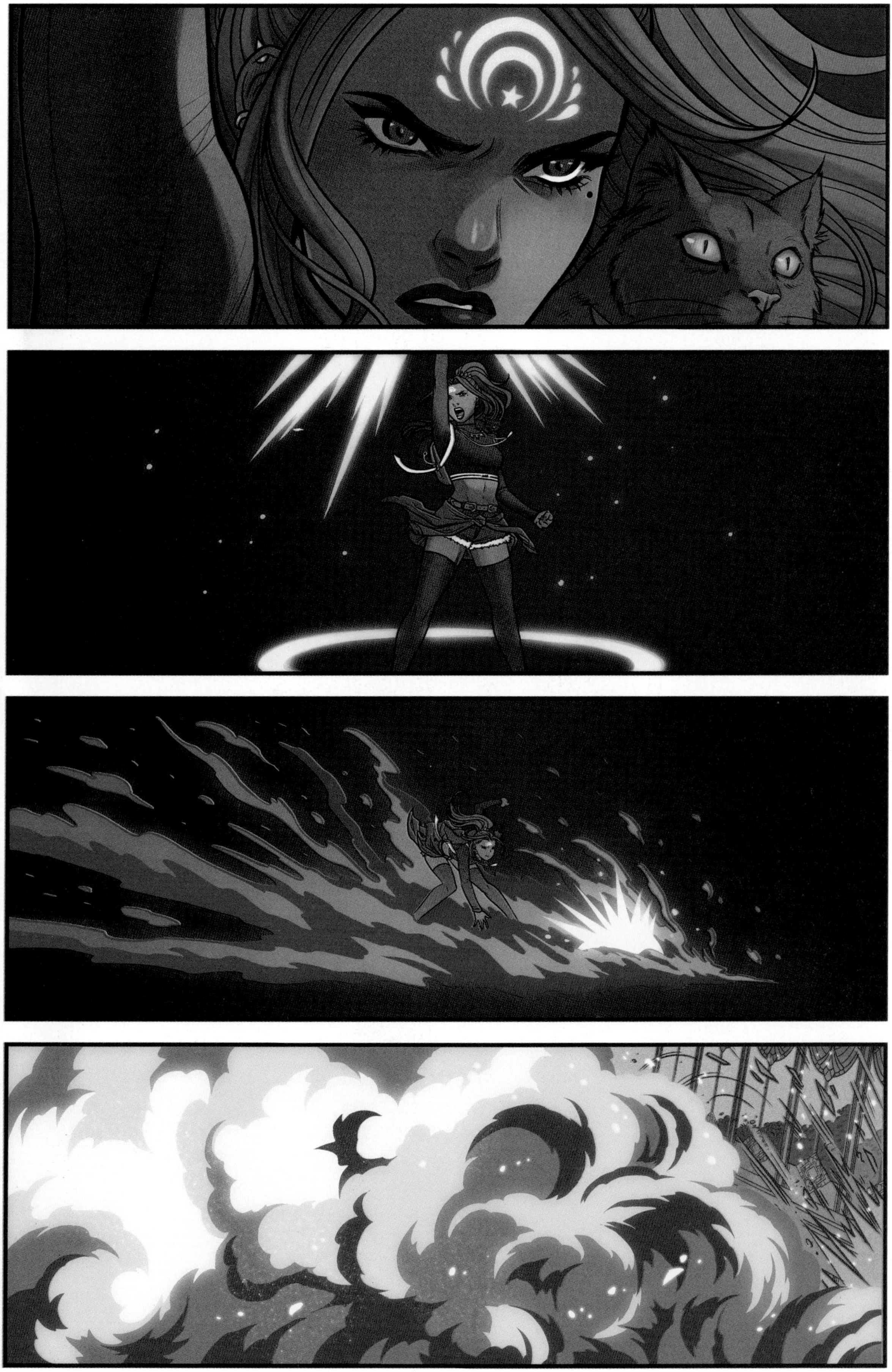

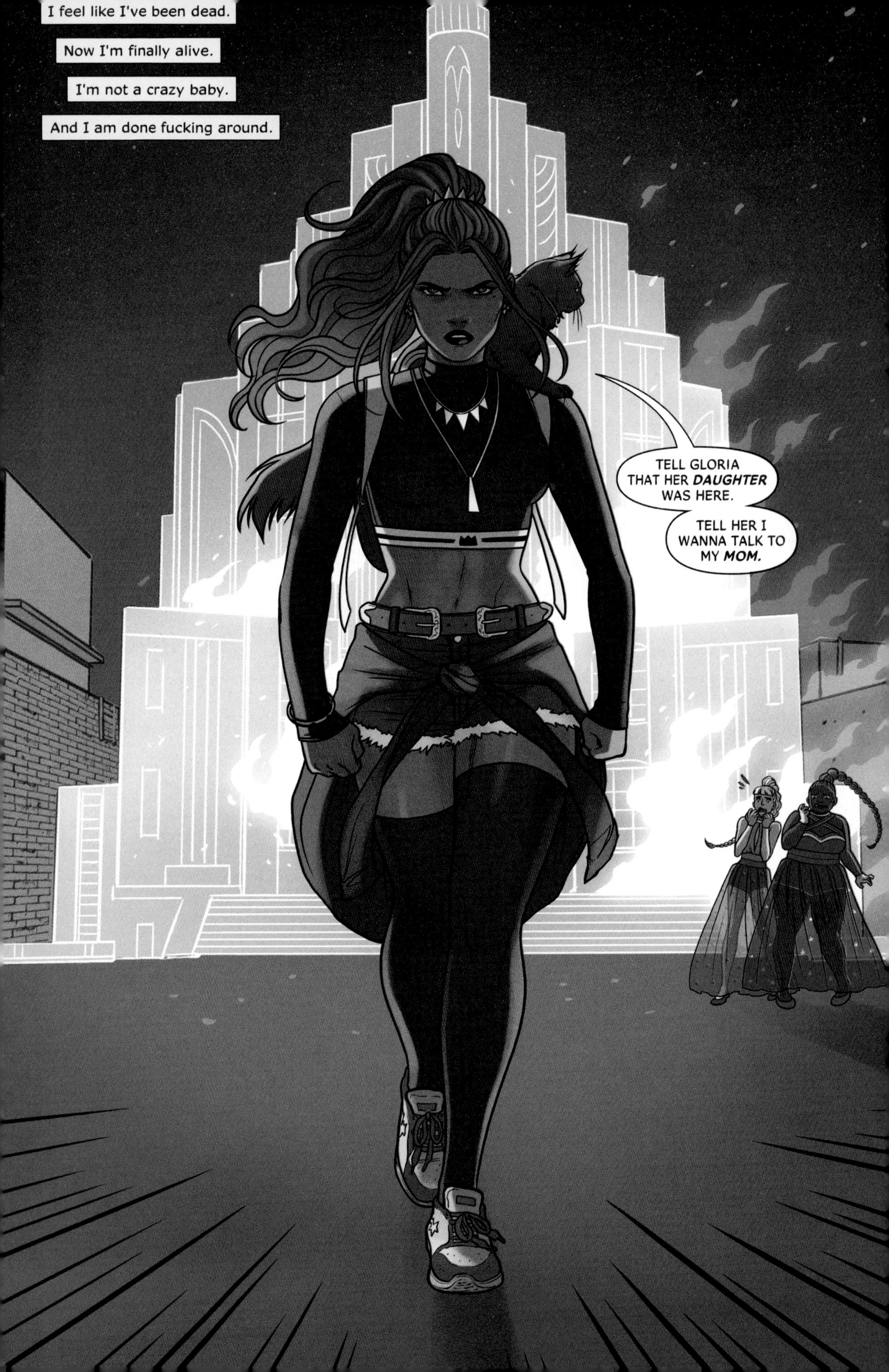
I feel like I've been dead.
Now I'm finally alive.
I'm not a crazy baby.
And I am done fucking around.
TELL GLORIA THAT HER ***DAUGHTER*** WAS HERE.
TELL HER I WANNA TALK TO MY ***MOM.***

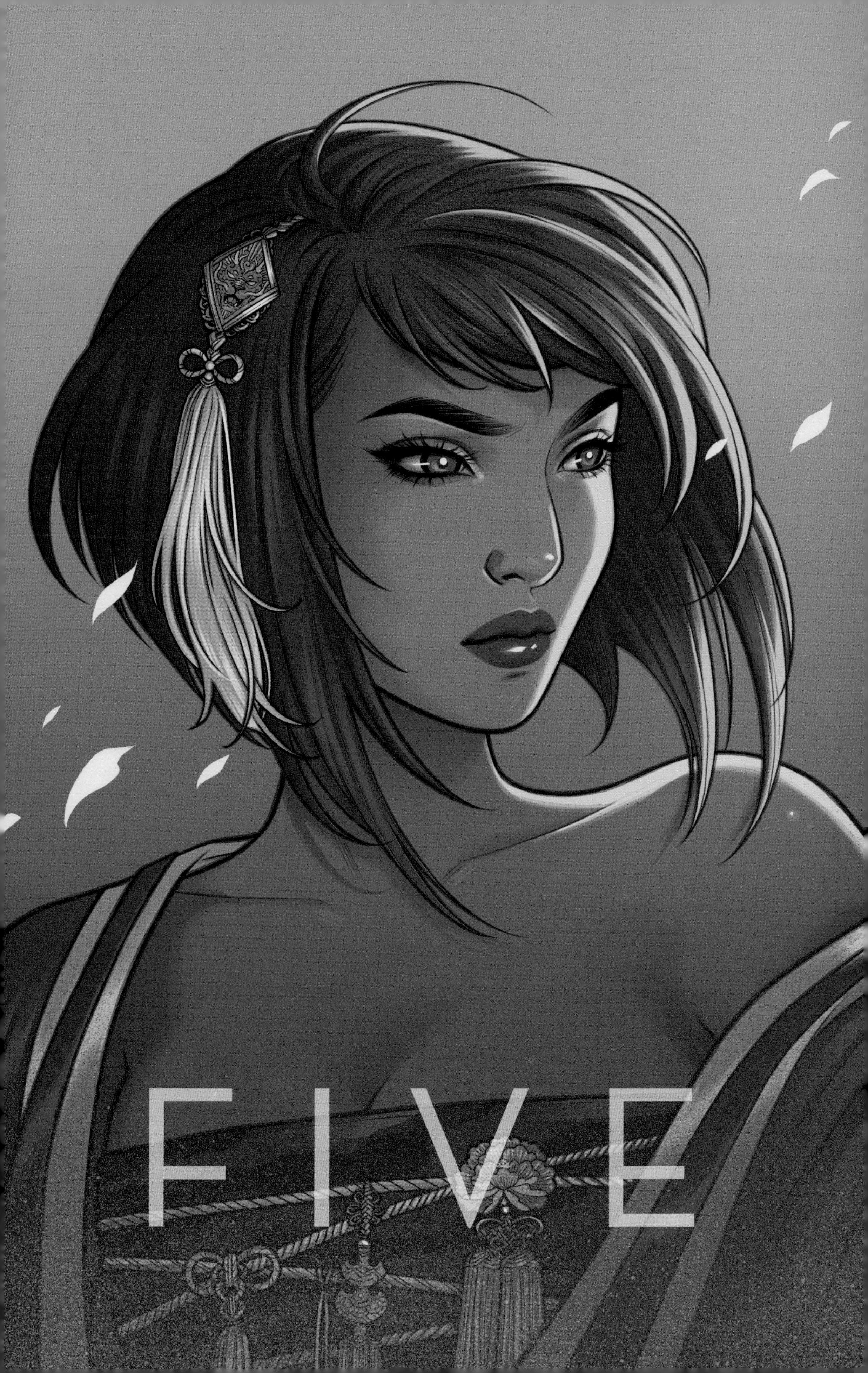
FIVE

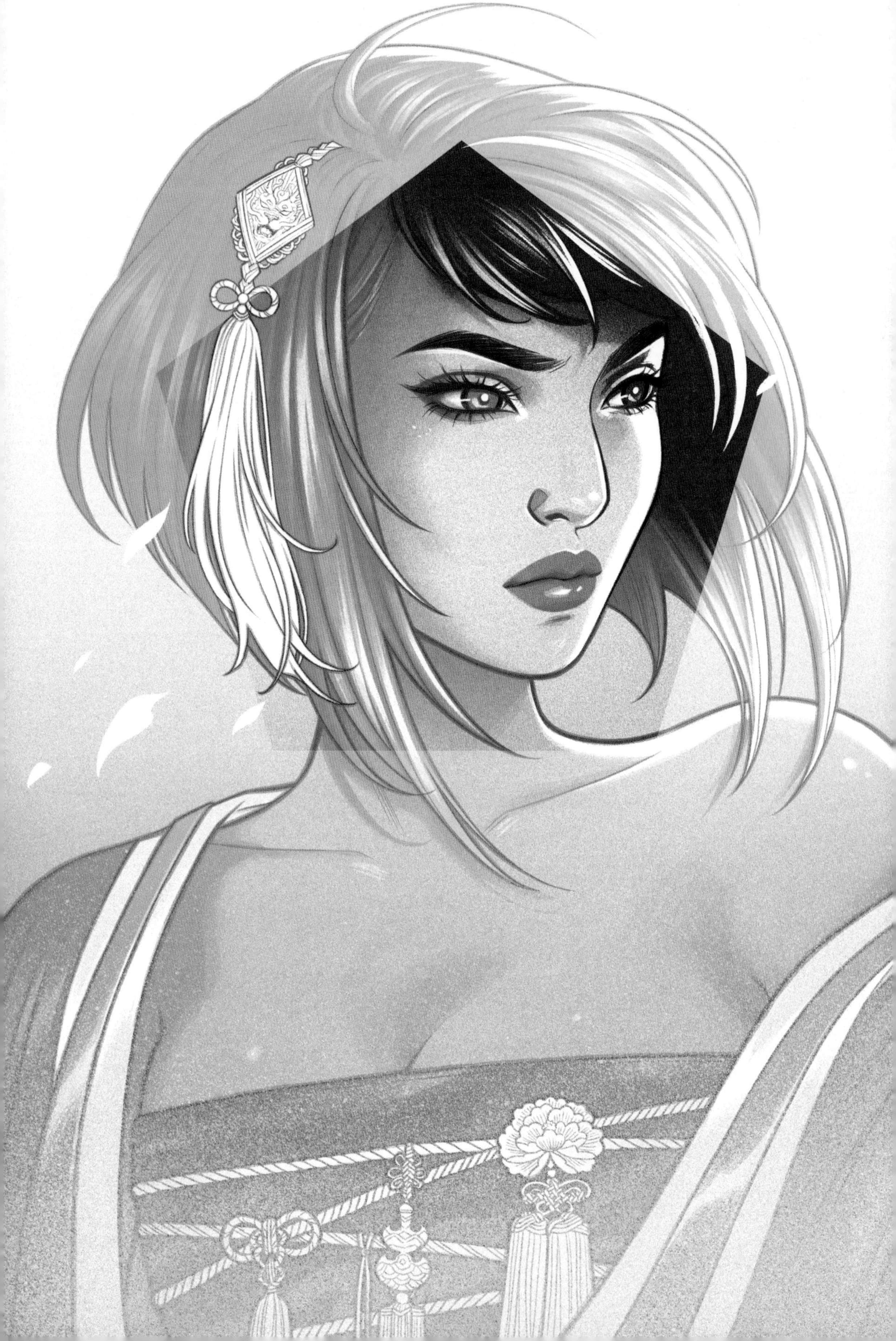

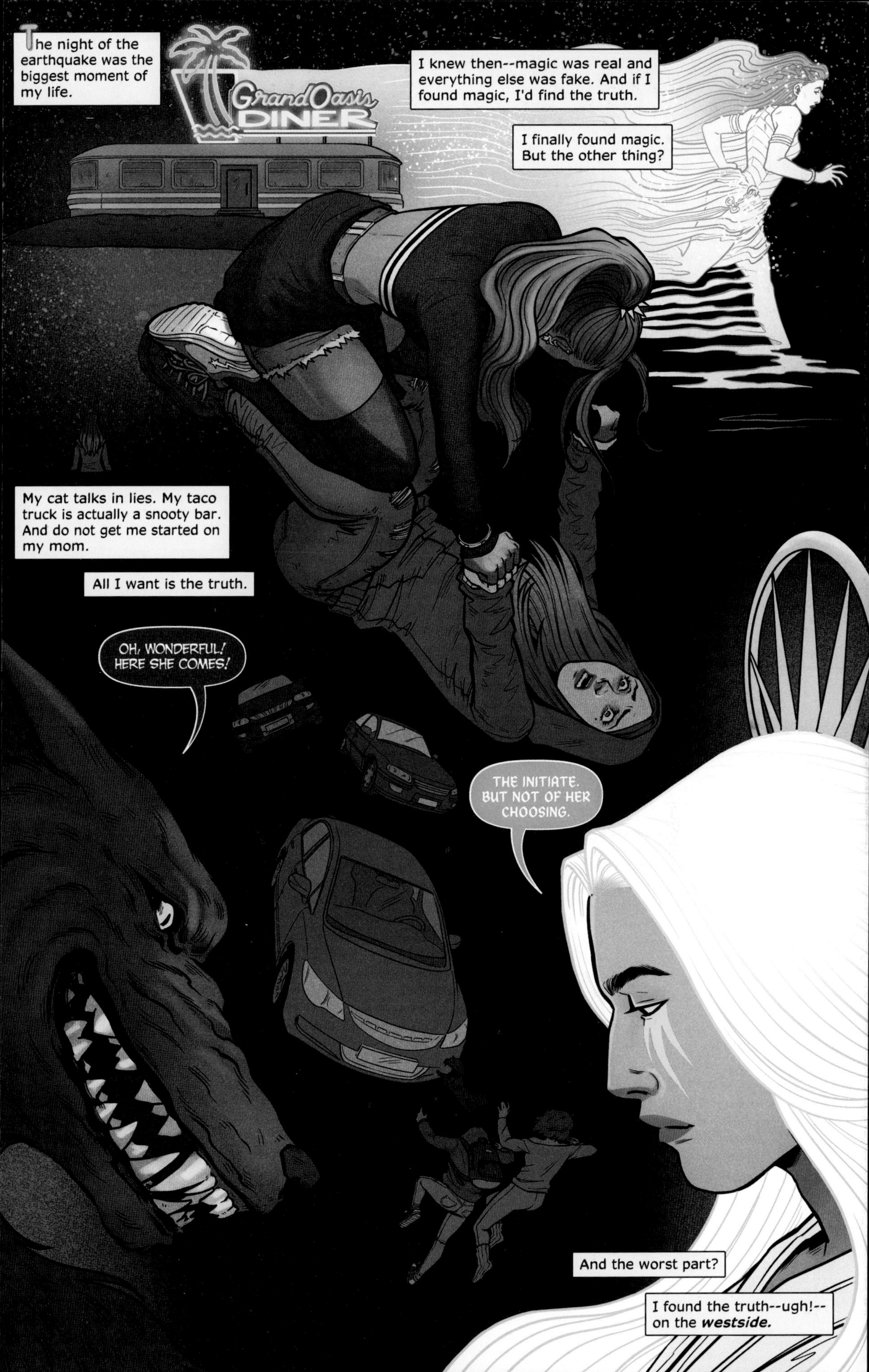

GrandOasis DINER
The night of the earthquake was the biggest moment of my life.
I knew then--magic was real and everything else was fake. And if I found magic, I'd find the truth.
I finally found magic. But the other thing?
My cat talks in lies. My taco truck is actually a snooty bar. And do not get me started on my mom.
All I want is the truth.
OH, WONDERFUL! HERE SHE COMES!
THE INITIATE. BUT NOT OF HER CHOOSING.
And the worst part?
I found the truth--ugh!-- on the *westside.*

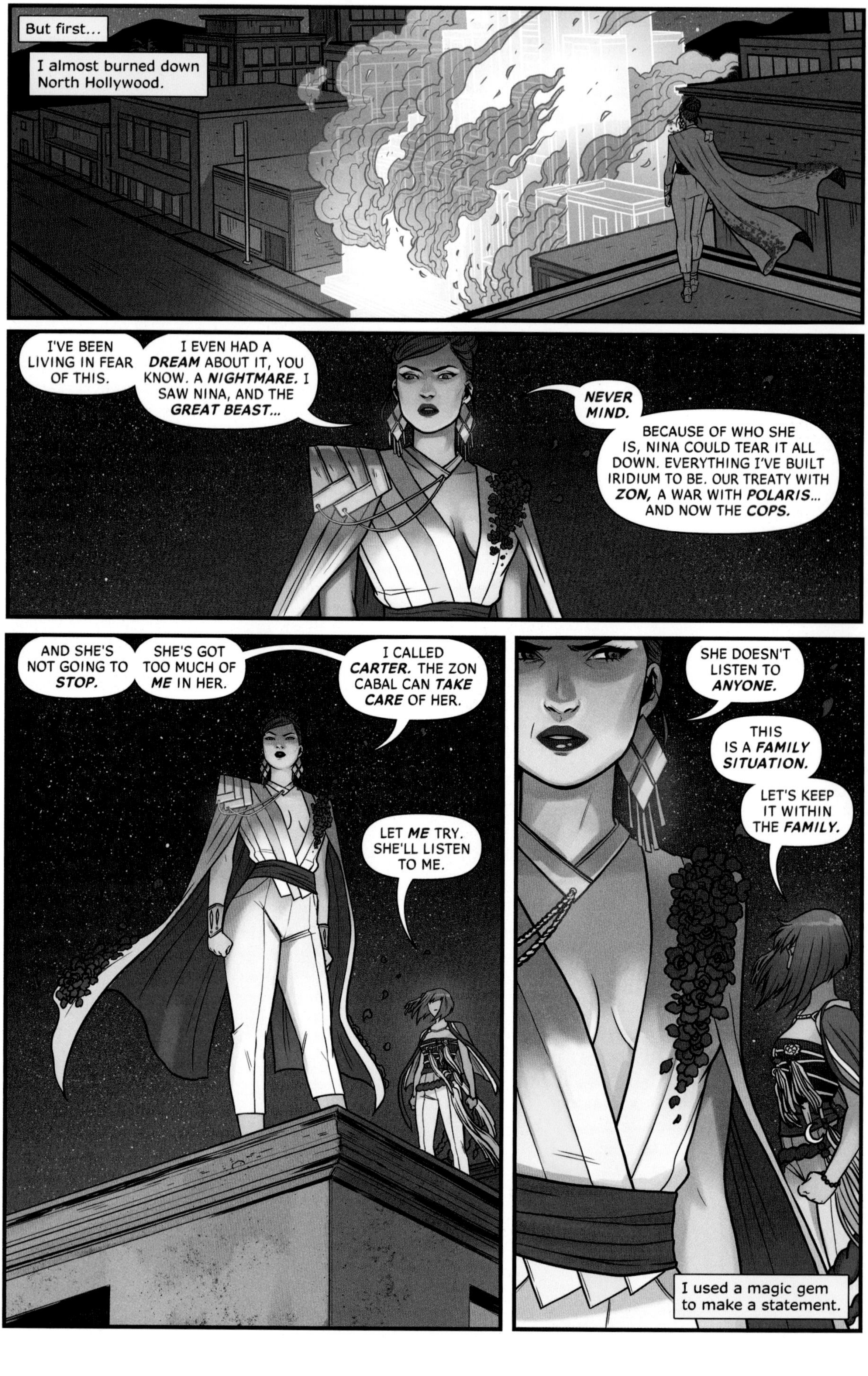
But first...
I almost burned down North Hollywood.
I'VE BEEN LIVING IN FEAR OF THIS.
I EVEN HAD A DREAM ABOUT IT, YOU KNOW. A NIGHTMARE. I SAW NINA, AND THE GREAT BEAST...
NEVER MIND.
BECAUSE OF WHO SHE IS, NINA COULD TEAR IT ALL DOWN. EVERYTHING I'VE BUILT IRIDIUM TO BE. OUR TREATY WITH ZON, A WAR WITH POLARIS... AND NOW THE COPS.
AND SHE'S NOT GOING TO STOP.
SHE'S GOT TOO MUCH OF ME IN HER.
I CALLED CARTER. THE ZON CABAL CAN TAKE CARE OF HER.
LET ME TRY. SHE'LL LISTEN TO ME.
SHE DOESN'T LISTEN TO ANYONE.
THIS IS A FAMILY SITUATION.
LET'S KEEP IT WITHIN THE FAMILY.
I used a magic gem to make a statement.

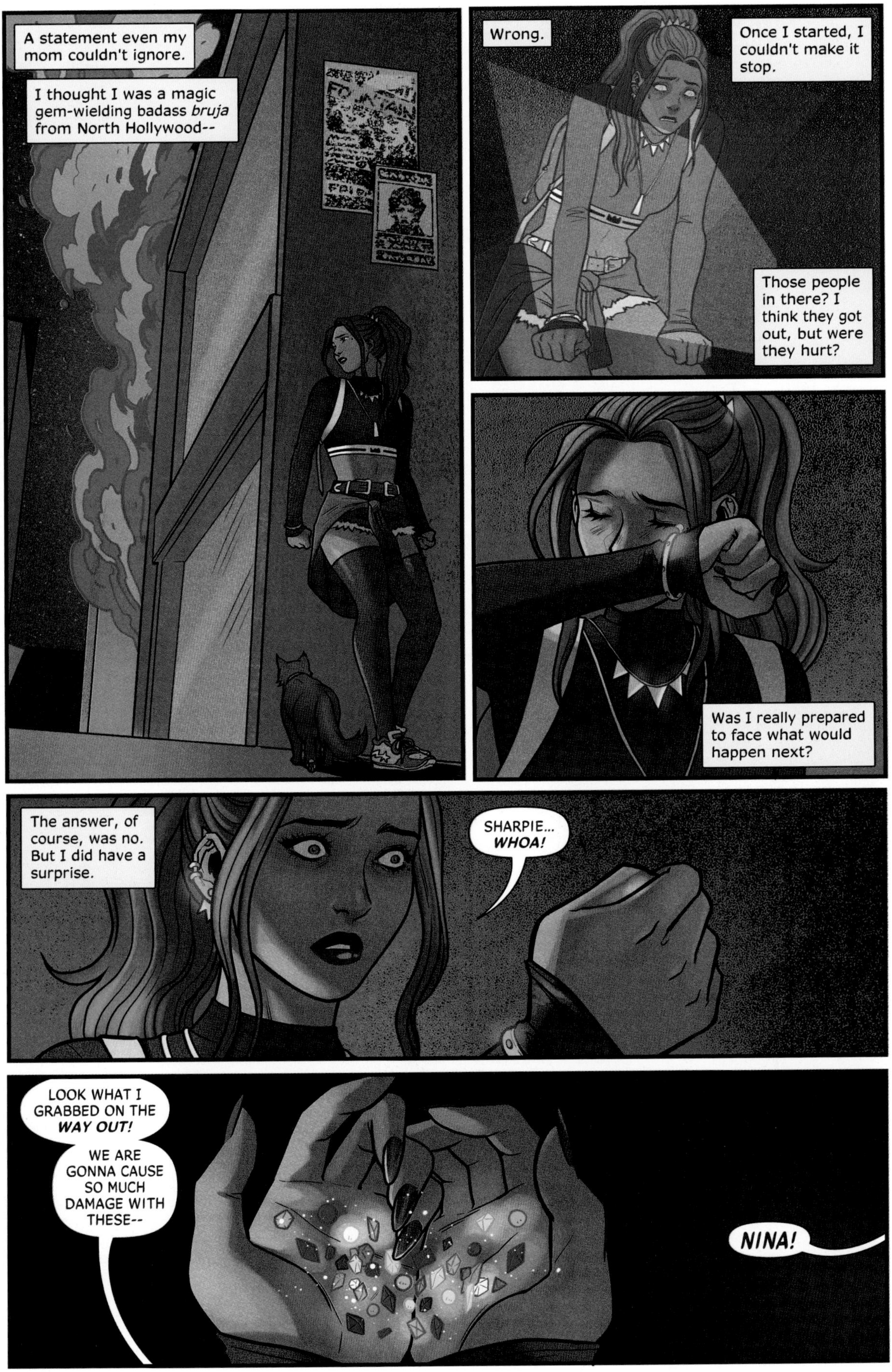
A statement even my mom couldn't ignore.
I thought I was a magic gem-wielding badass *bruja* from North Hollywood--
Wrong.
Once I started, I couldn't make it stop.
Those people in there? I think they got out, but were they hurt?
Was I really prepared to face what would happen next?
The answer, of course, was no. But I did have a surprise.
SHARPIE... **WHOA!**
LOOK WHAT I GRABBED ON THE **WAY OUT!**
WE ARE GONNA CAUSE SO MUCH DAMAGE WITH THESE--
NINA!

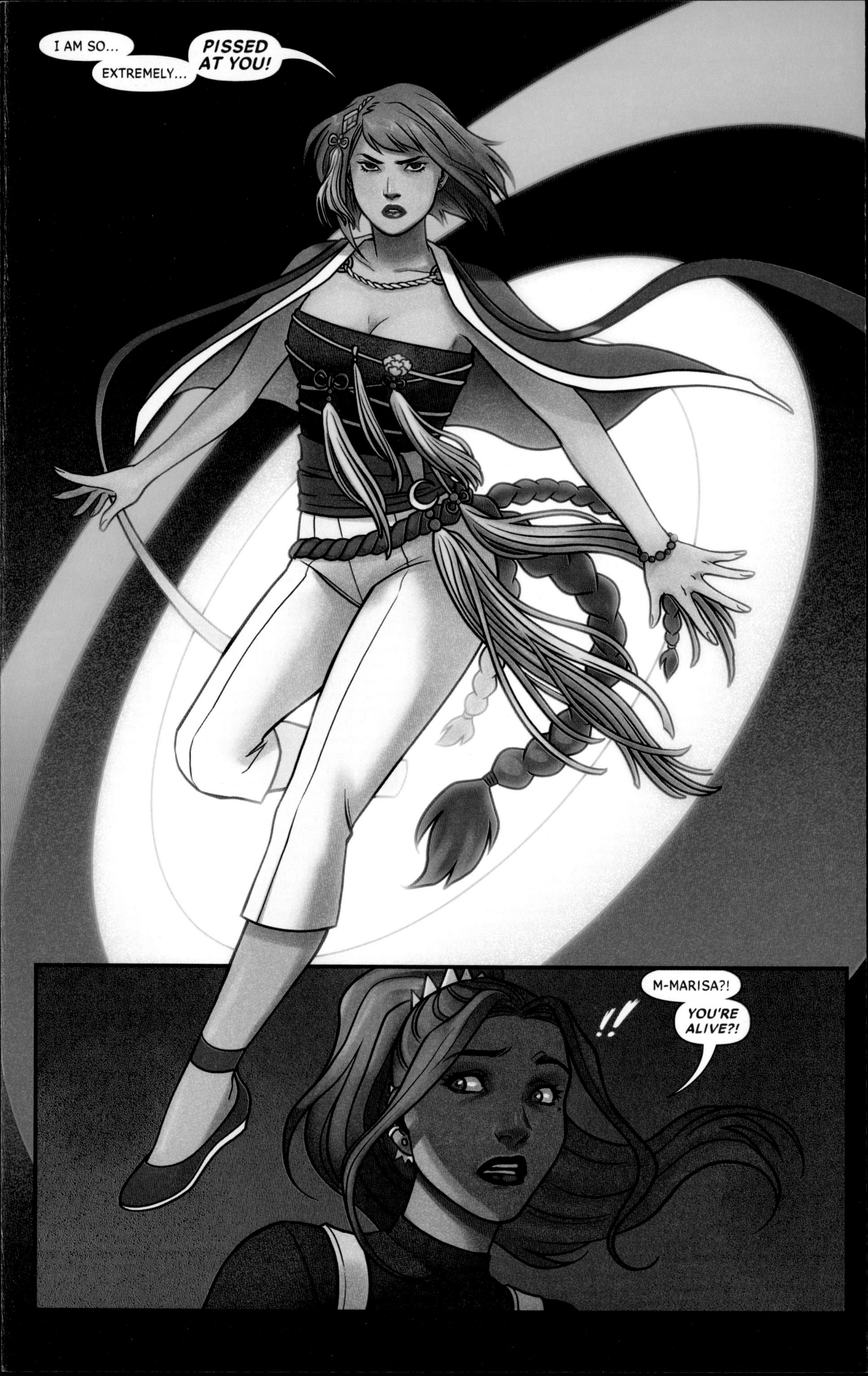
I AM SO...
EXTREMELY...
PISSED AT YOU!
!!
M-MARISA?!
YOU'RE ALIVE?!

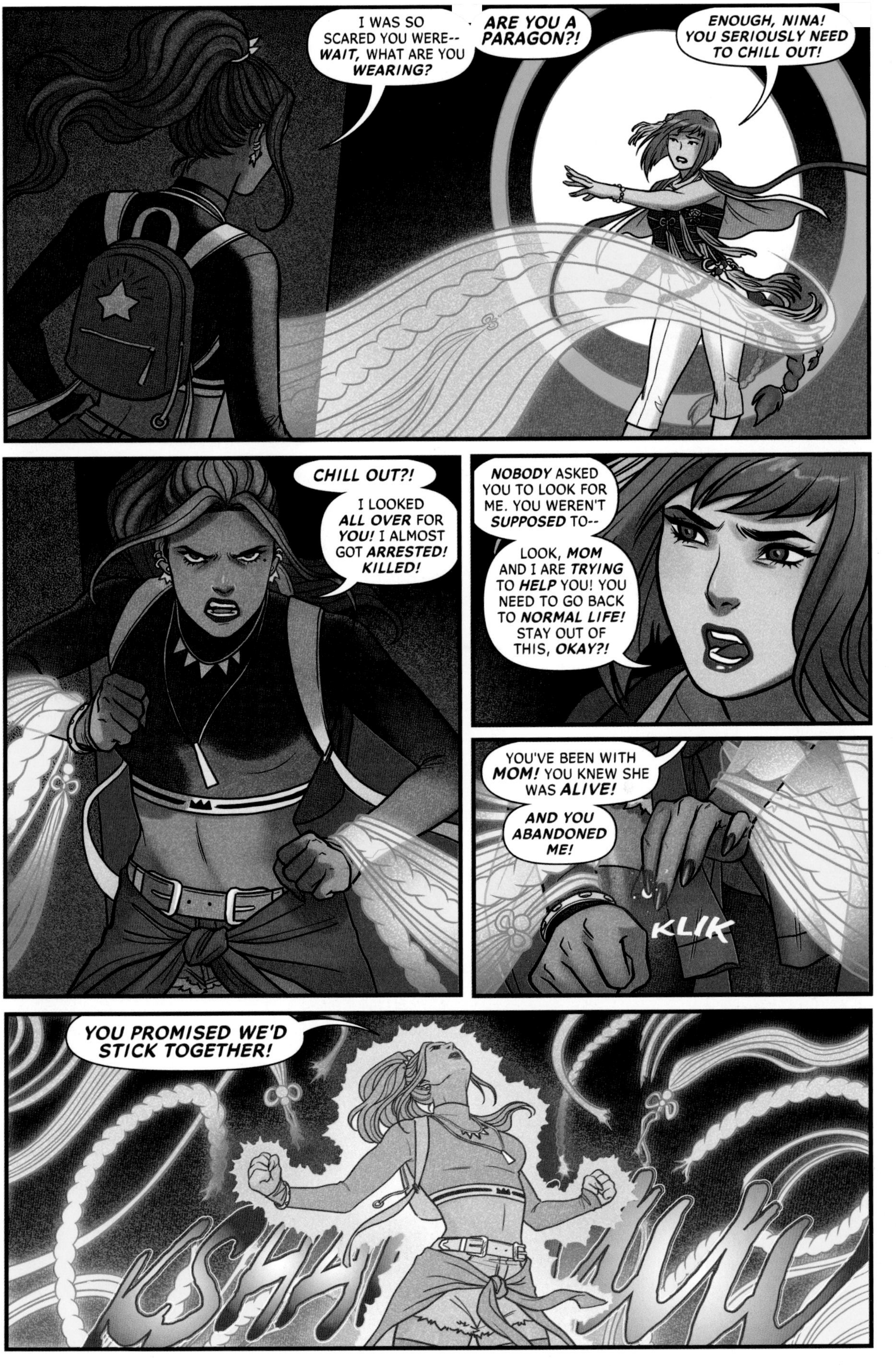
I WAS SO SCARED YOU WERE-- WAIT, WHAT ARE YOU WEARING?
ARE YOU A PARAGON?!
ENOUGH, NINA! YOU SERIOUSLY NEED TO CHILL OUT!
CHILL OUT?!
I LOOKED ALL OVER FOR YOU! I ALMOST GOT ARRESTED! KILLED!
NOBODY ASKED YOU TO LOOK FOR ME. YOU WEREN'T SUPPOSED TO--
LOOK, MOM AND I ARE TRYING TO HELP YOU! YOU NEED TO GO BACK TO NORMAL LIFE! STAY OUT OF THIS, OKAY?!
YOU'VE BEEN WITH MOM! YOU KNEW SHE WAS ALIVE!
AND YOU ABANDONED ME!
KLIK
YOU PROMISED WE'D STICK TOGETHER!
KSHHHHH

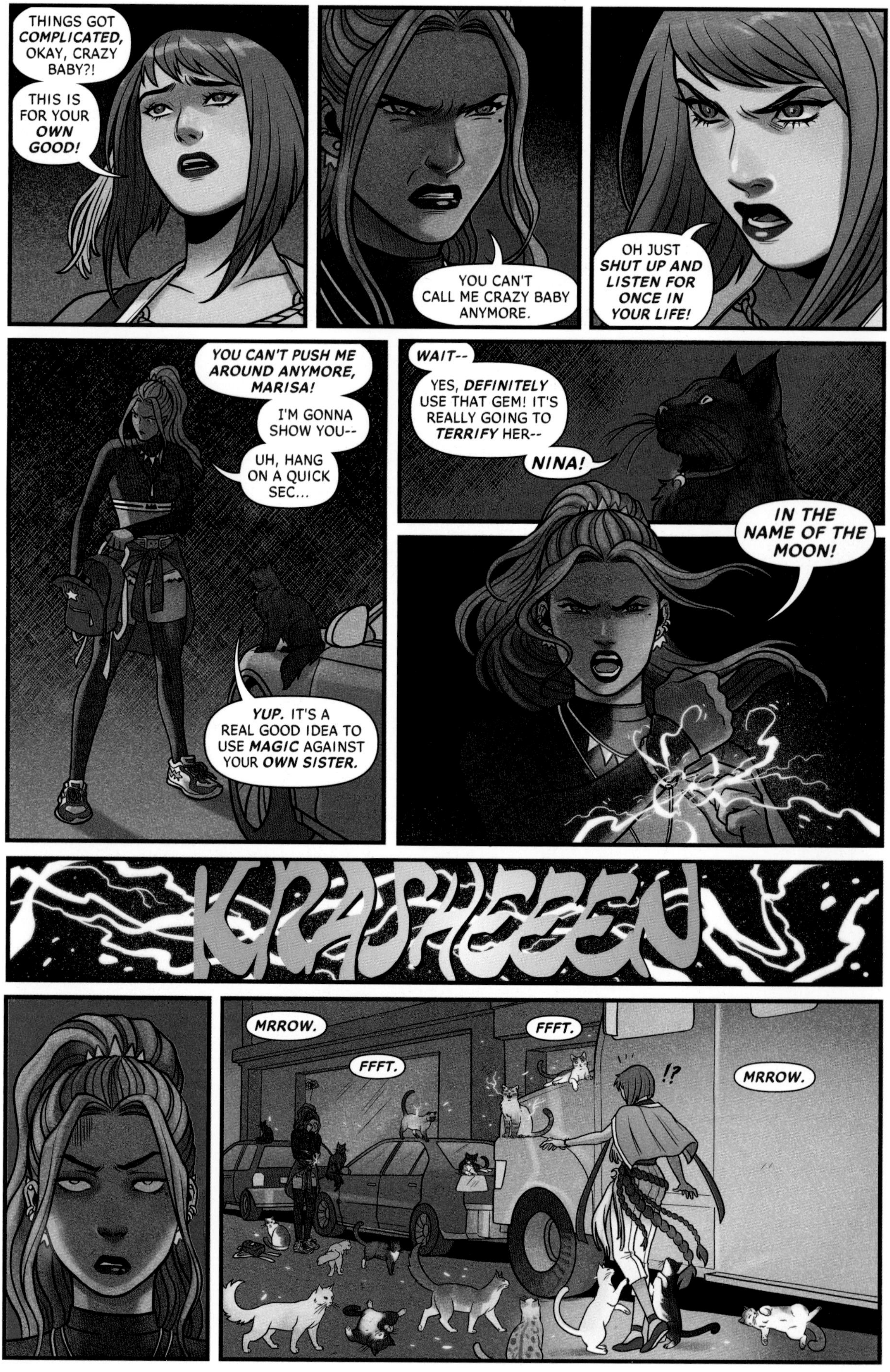
THINGS GOT COMPLICATED, OKAY, CRAZY BABY?!
THIS IS FOR YOUR OWN GOOD!
YOU CAN'T CALL ME CRAZY BABY ANYMORE.
OH JUST SHUT UP AND LISTEN FOR ONCE IN YOUR LIFE!
YOU CAN'T PUSH ME AROUND ANYMORE, MARISA!
I'M GONNA SHOW YOU--
UH, HANG ON A QUICK SEC...
YUP. IT'S A REAL GOOD IDEA TO USE MAGIC AGAINST YOUR OWN SISTER.
WAIT--
YES, DEFINITELY USE THAT GEM! IT'S REALLY GOING TO TERRIFY HER--
NINA!
IN THE NAME OF THE MOON!
KRASHEEEEN
MRROW.
FFFT.
FFFT.
!?
MRROW.

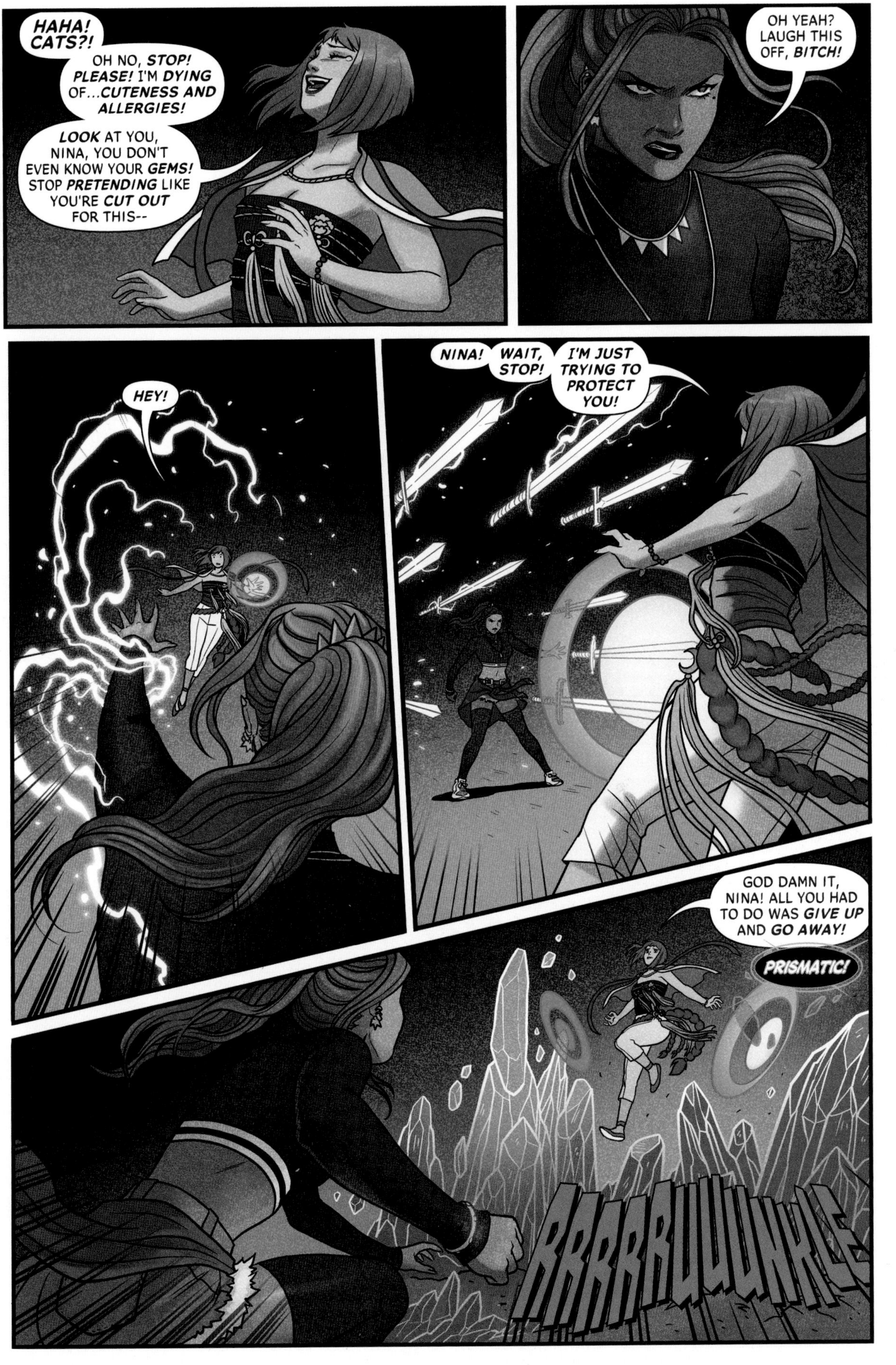
HAHA! CATS?!
OH NO, STOP! PLEASE! I'M DYING OF...CUTENESS AND ALLERGIES!
LOOK AT YOU, NINA, YOU DON'T EVEN KNOW YOUR GEMS! STOP PRETENDING LIKE YOU'RE CUT OUT FOR THIS--
OH YEAH? LAUGH THIS OFF, BITCH!
HEY!
NINA!
WAIT, STOP!
I'M JUST TRYING TO PROTECT YOU!
GOD DAMN IT, NINA! ALL YOU HAD TO DO WAS GIVE UP AND GO AWAY!
PRISMATIC!
RRRRRUUUNKLE

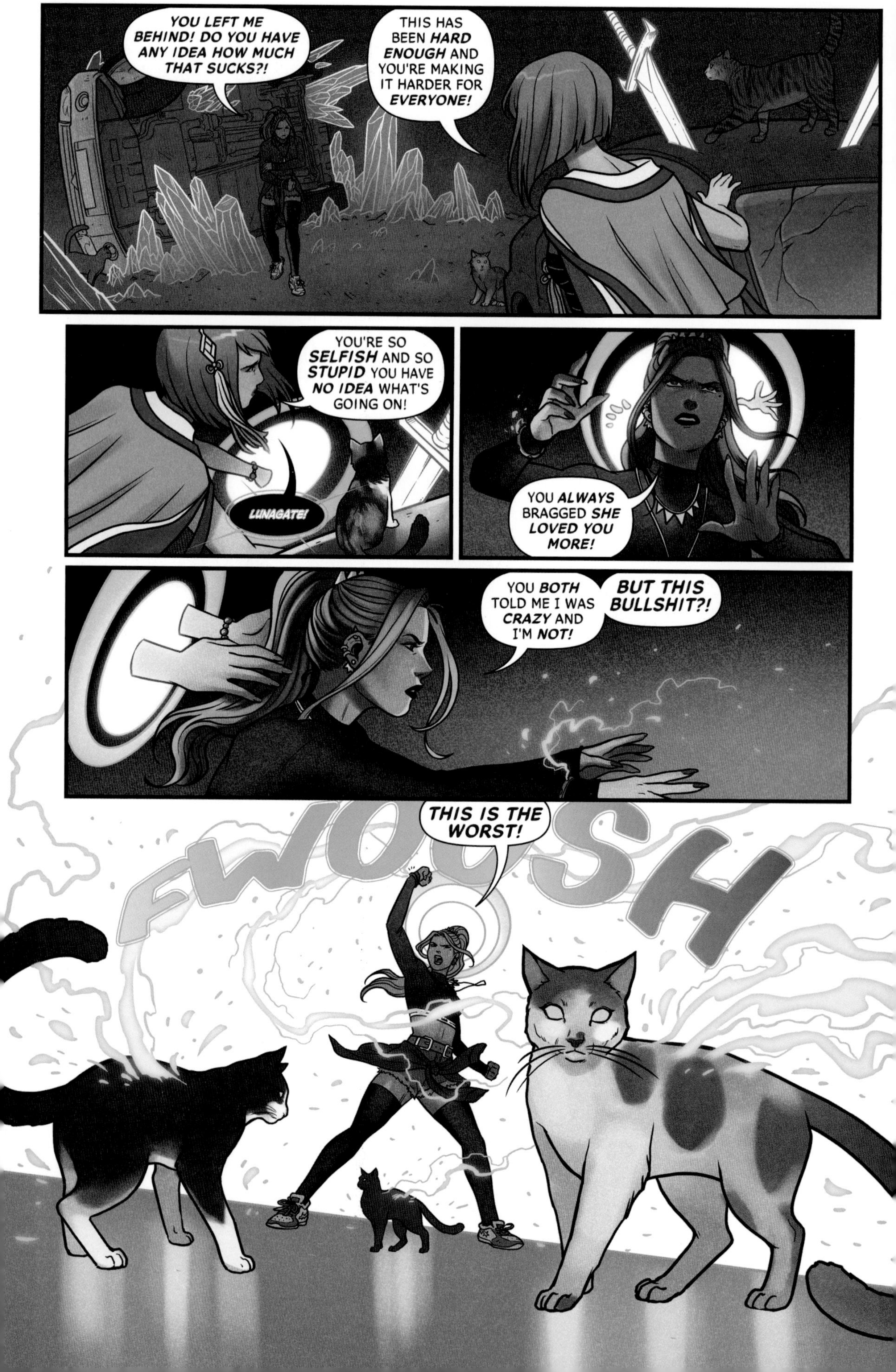
YOU LEFT ME BEHIND! DO YOU HAVE ANY IDEA HOW MUCH THAT SUCKS?!
THIS HAS BEEN HARD ENOUGH AND YOU'RE MAKING IT HARDER FOR EVERYONE!
YOU'RE SO SELFISH AND SO STUPID YOU HAVE NO IDEA WHAT'S GOING ON!
LUNAGATE!
YOU ALWAYS BRAGGED SHE LOVED YOU MORE!
YOU BOTH TOLD ME I WAS CRAZY AND I'M NOT!
BUT THIS BULLSHIT?!
THIS IS THE WORST!
FWOOSH

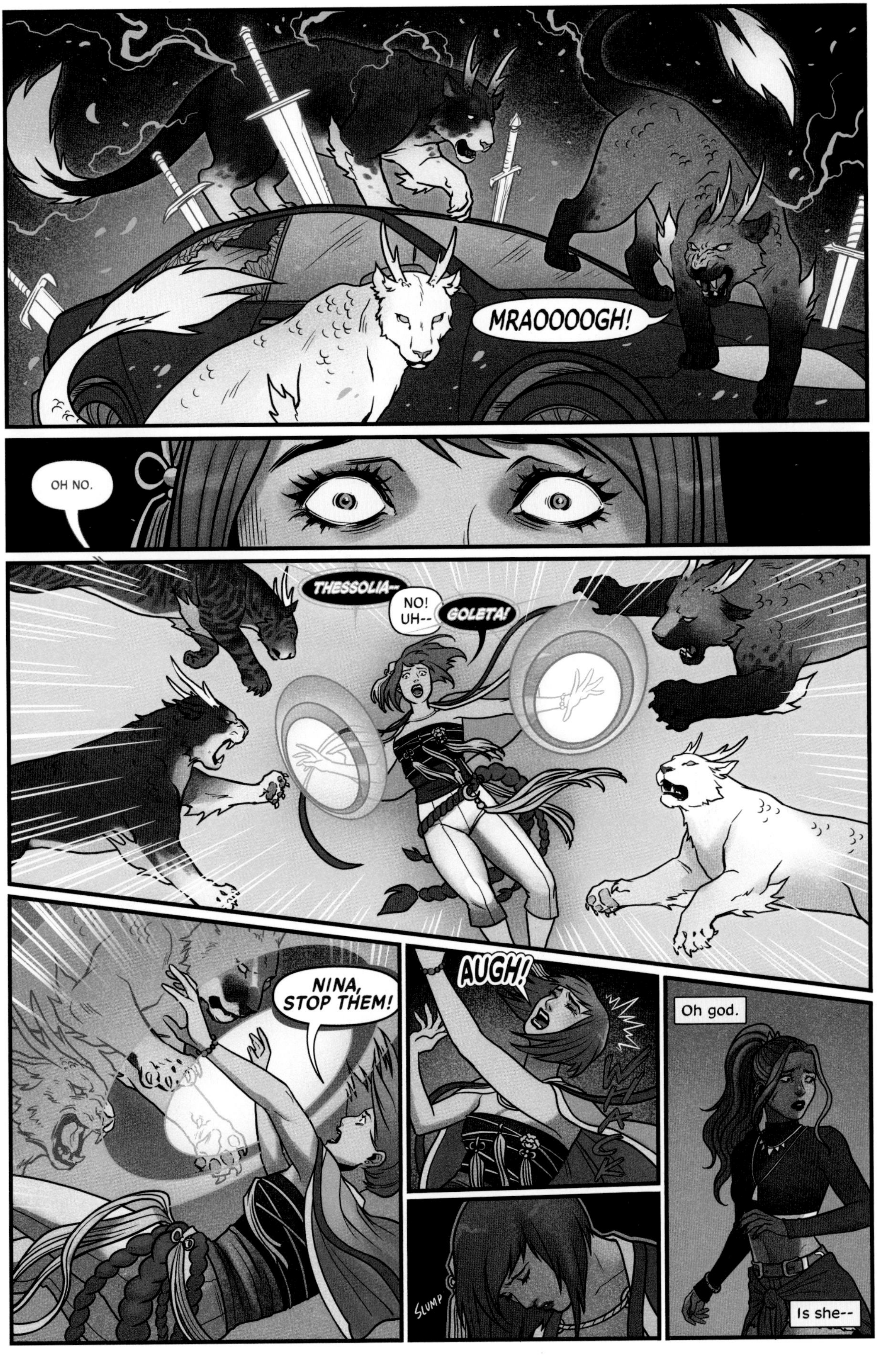
MRAOOOOGH!
OH NO.
THESSOLIA--
NO! UH--
GOLETA!
NINA, STOP THEM!
AUGH!
Oh god.
SLUMP
Is she--

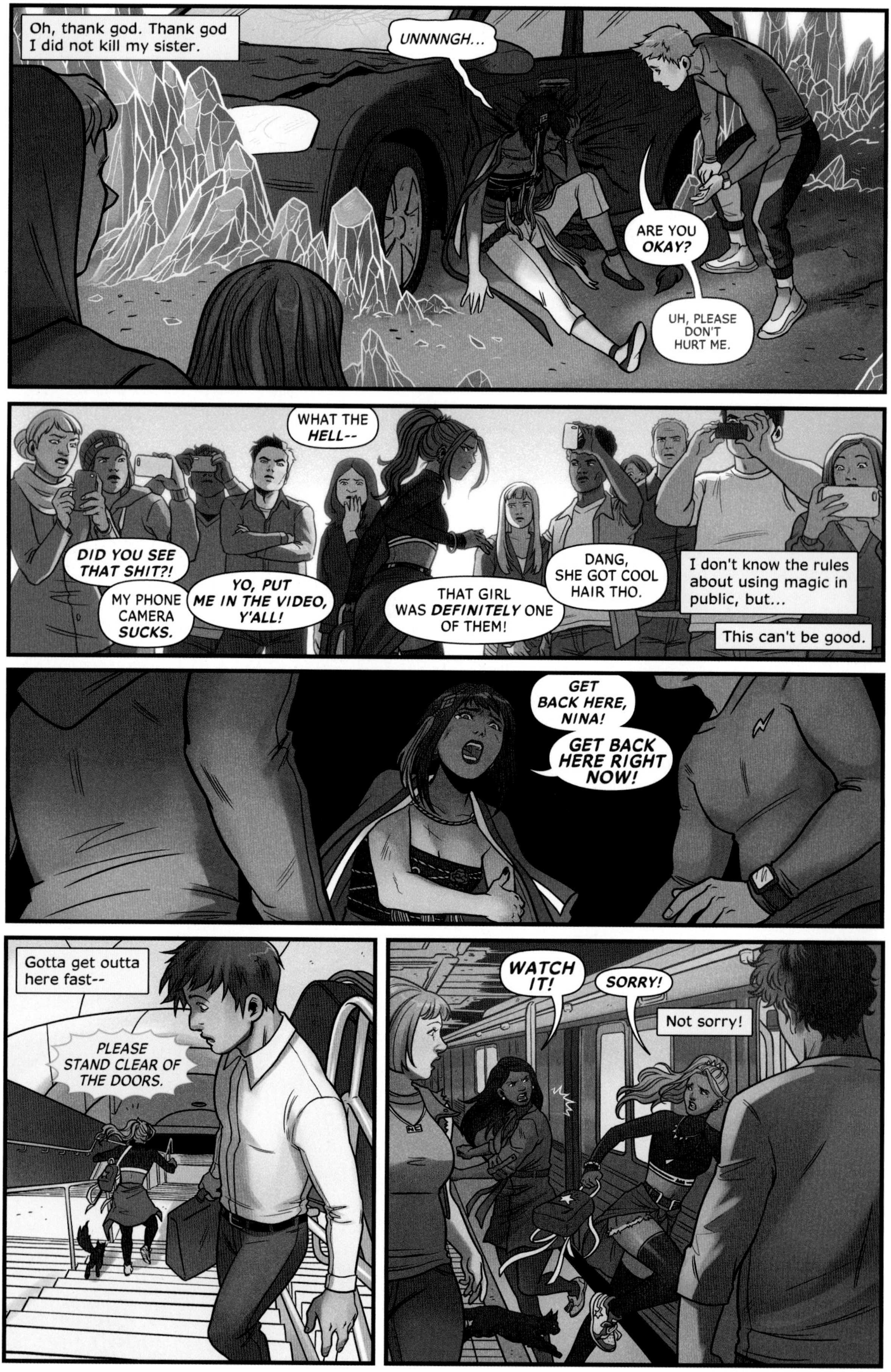
Oh, thank god. Thank god I did not kill my sister.
UNNNNGH...
ARE YOU OKAY?
UH, PLEASE DON'T HURT ME.
WHAT THE HELL--
DID YOU SEE THAT SHIT?!
MY PHONE CAMERA SUCKS.
YO, PUT ME IN THE VIDEO, Y'ALL!
THAT GIRL WAS DEFINITELY ONE OF THEM!
DANG, SHE GOT COOL HAIR THO.
I don't know the rules about using magic in public, but...
This can't be good.
GET BACK HERE, NINA!
GET BACK HERE RIGHT NOW!
Gotta get outta here fast--
PLEASE STAND CLEAR OF THE DOORS.
WATCH IT!
SORRY!
Not sorry!

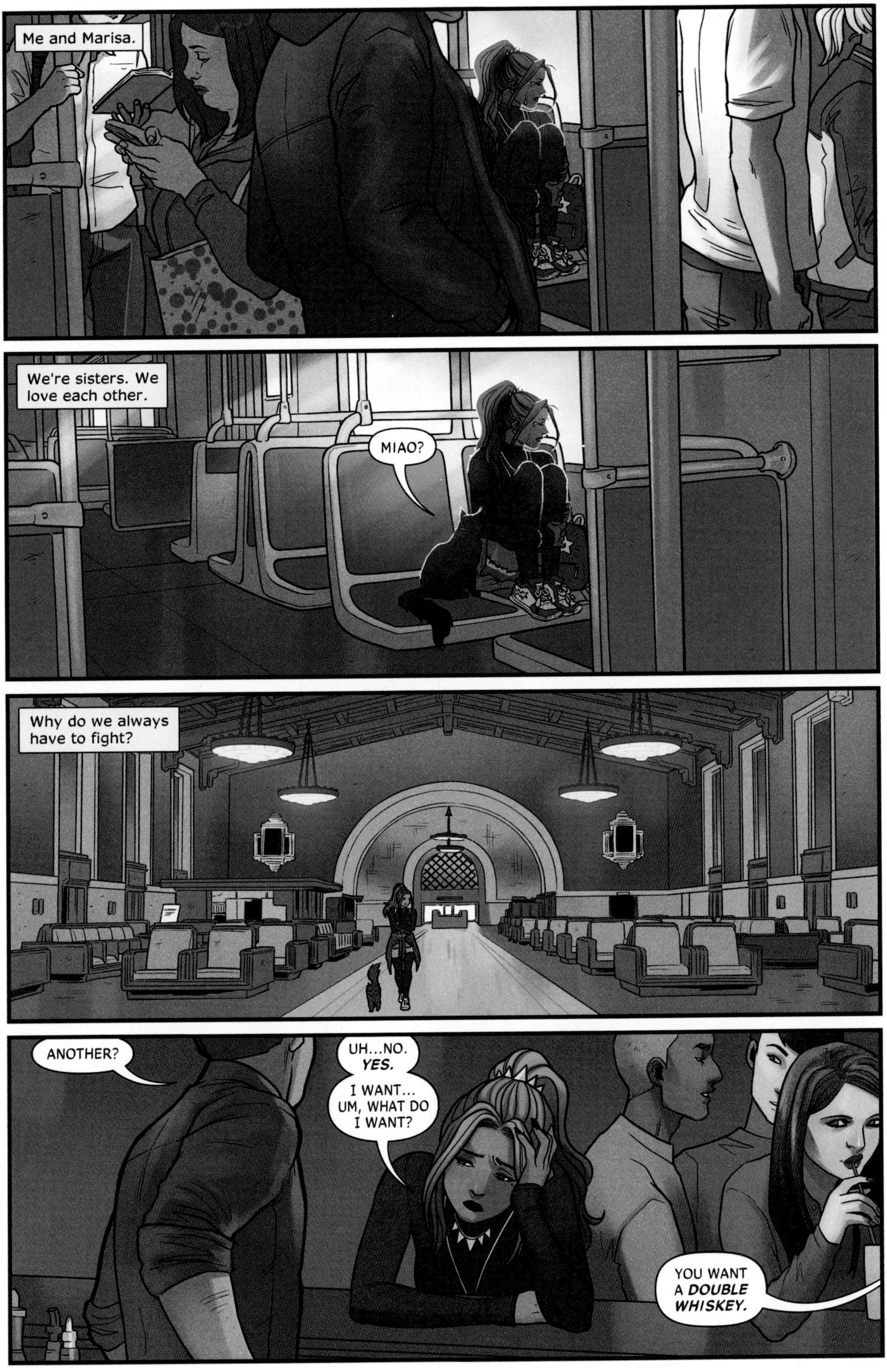

Me and Marisa.
We're sisters. We love each other.
MIAO?
Why do we always have to fight?
ANOTHER?
UH...NO. *YES.*
I WANT... UM, WHAT DO I WANT?
YOU WANT A *DOUBLE WHISKEY.*

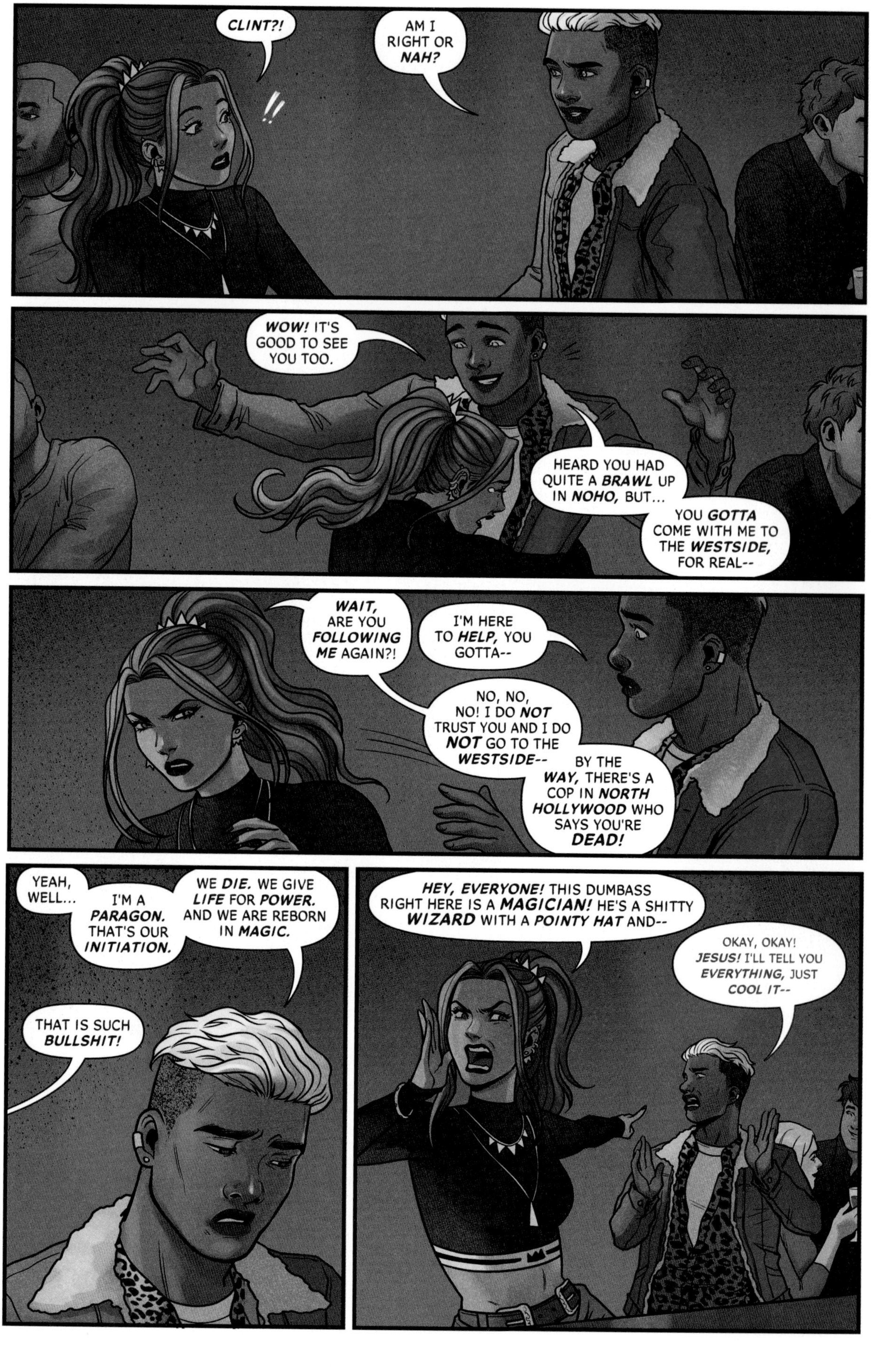
CLINT?!
AM I RIGHT OR NAH?
!!
WOW! IT'S GOOD TO SEE YOU TOO.
HEARD YOU HAD QUITE A BRAWL UP IN NOHO, BUT...
YOU GOTTA COME WITH ME TO THE WESTSIDE, FOR REAL--
WAIT, ARE YOU FOLLOWING ME AGAIN?!
I'M HERE TO HELP, YOU GOTTA--
NO, NO, NO! I DO NOT TRUST YOU AND I DO NOT GO TO THE WESTSIDE--
BY THE WAY, THERE'S A COP IN NORTH HOLLYWOOD WHO SAYS YOU'RE DEAD!
YEAH, WELL...
I'M A PARAGON. THAT'S OUR INITIATION.
WE DIE. WE GIVE LIFE FOR POWER. AND WE ARE REBORN IN MAGIC.
THAT IS SUCH BULLSHIT!
HEY, EVERYONE! THIS DUMBASS RIGHT HERE IS A MAGICIAN! HE'S A SHITTY WIZARD WITH A POINTY HAT AND--
OKAY, OKAY! JESUS! I'LL TELL YOU EVERYTHING, JUST COOL IT--

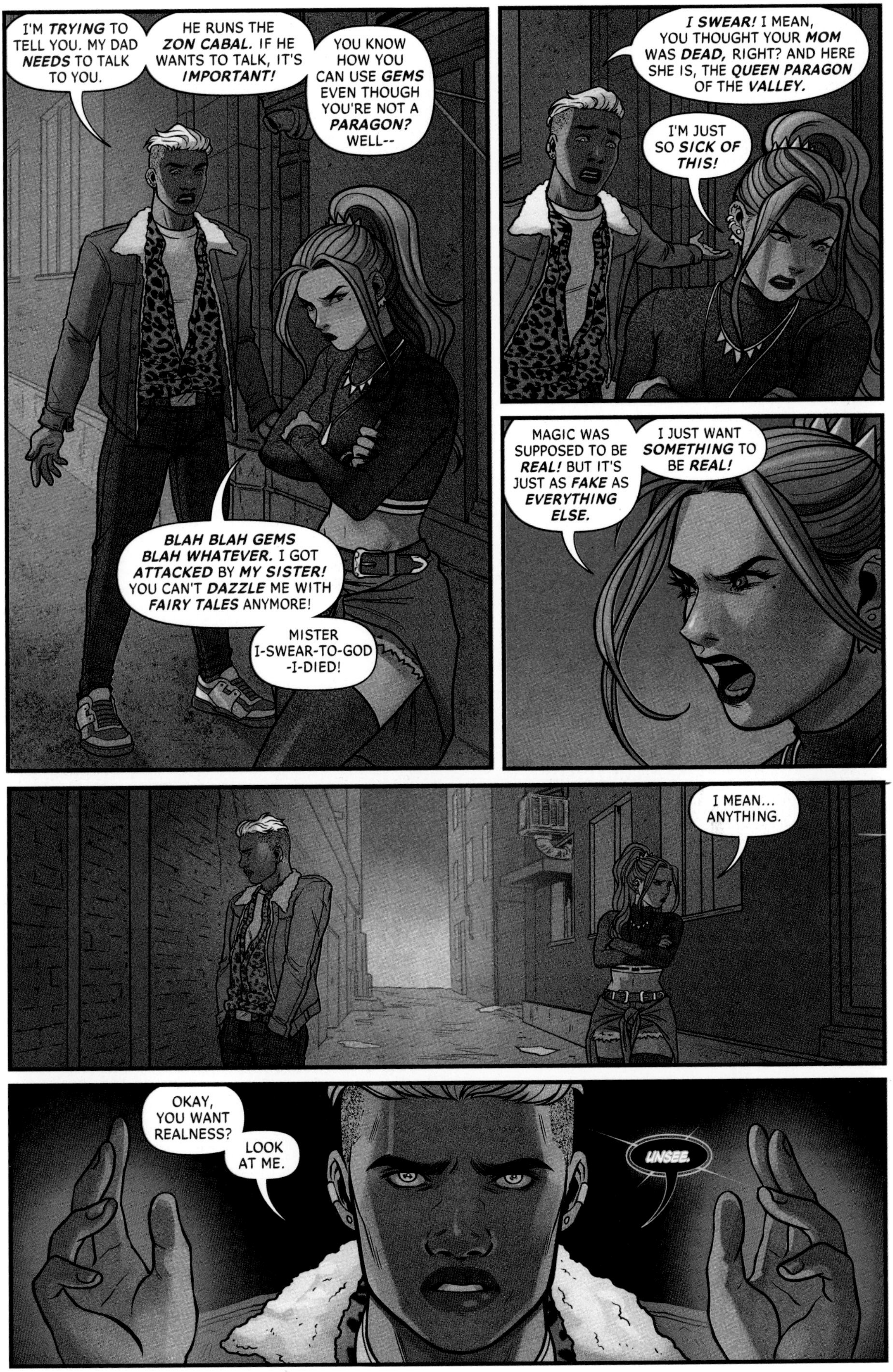
I'M TRYING TO TELL YOU. MY DAD NEEDS TO TALK TO YOU.
HE RUNS THE ZON CABAL. IF HE WANTS TO TALK, IT'S IMPORTANT!
YOU KNOW HOW YOU CAN USE GEMS EVEN THOUGH YOU'RE NOT A PARAGON? WELL--
BLAH BLAH GEMS BLAH WHATEVER. I GOT ATTACKED BY MY SISTER! YOU CAN'T DAZZLE ME WITH FAIRY TALES ANYMORE!
MISTER I-SWEAR-TO-GOD -I-DIED!
I SWEAR! I MEAN, YOU THOUGHT YOUR MOM WAS DEAD, RIGHT? AND HERE SHE IS, THE QUEEN PARAGON OF THE VALLEY.
I'M JUST SO SICK OF THIS!
MAGIC WAS SUPPOSED TO BE REAL! BUT IT'S JUST AS FAKE AS EVERYTHING ELSE.
I JUST WANT SOMETHING TO BE REAL!
I MEAN... ANYTHING.
OKAY, YOU WANT REALNESS?
LOOK AT ME.
UNSEE.

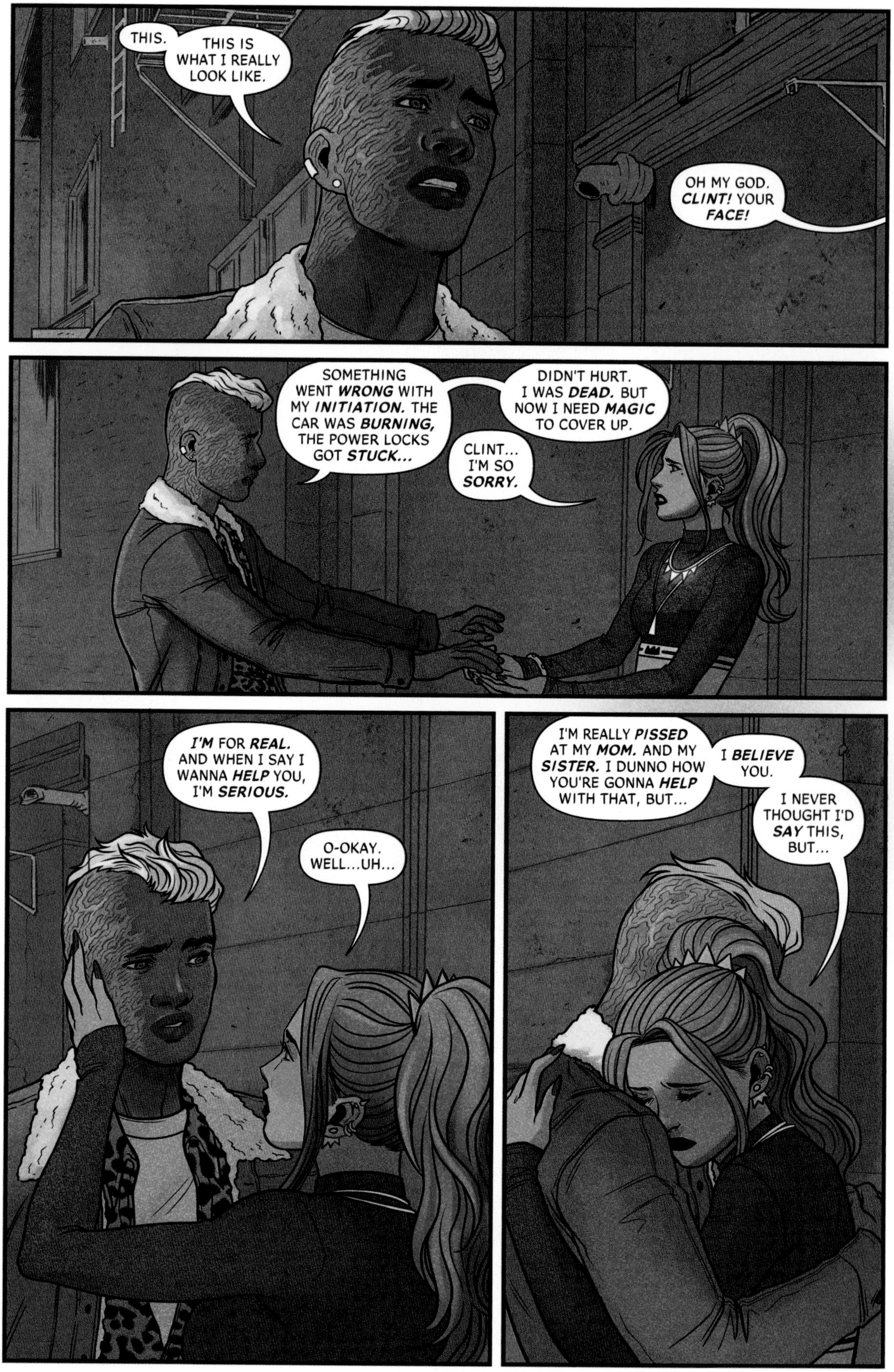

THIS.
THIS IS WHAT I REALLY LOOK LIKE.
OH MY GOD. *CLINT!* YOUR *FACE!*
SOMETHING WENT *WRONG* WITH MY *INITIATION.* THE CAR WAS *BURNING,* THE POWER LOCKS GOT *STUCK...*
DIDN'T HURT. I WAS *DEAD.* BUT NOW I NEED *MAGIC* TO COVER UP.
CLINT... I'M SO *SORRY.*
I'M FOR *REAL.* AND WHEN I SAY I WANNA *HELP* YOU, I'M *SERIOUS.*
O-OKAY. WELL...UH...
I'M REALLY *PISSED* AT MY *MOM.* AND MY *SISTER.* I DUNNO HOW YOU'RE GONNA *HELP* WITH THAT, BUT...
I *BELIEVE* YOU.
I NEVER THOUGHT I'D *SAY* THIS, BUT...

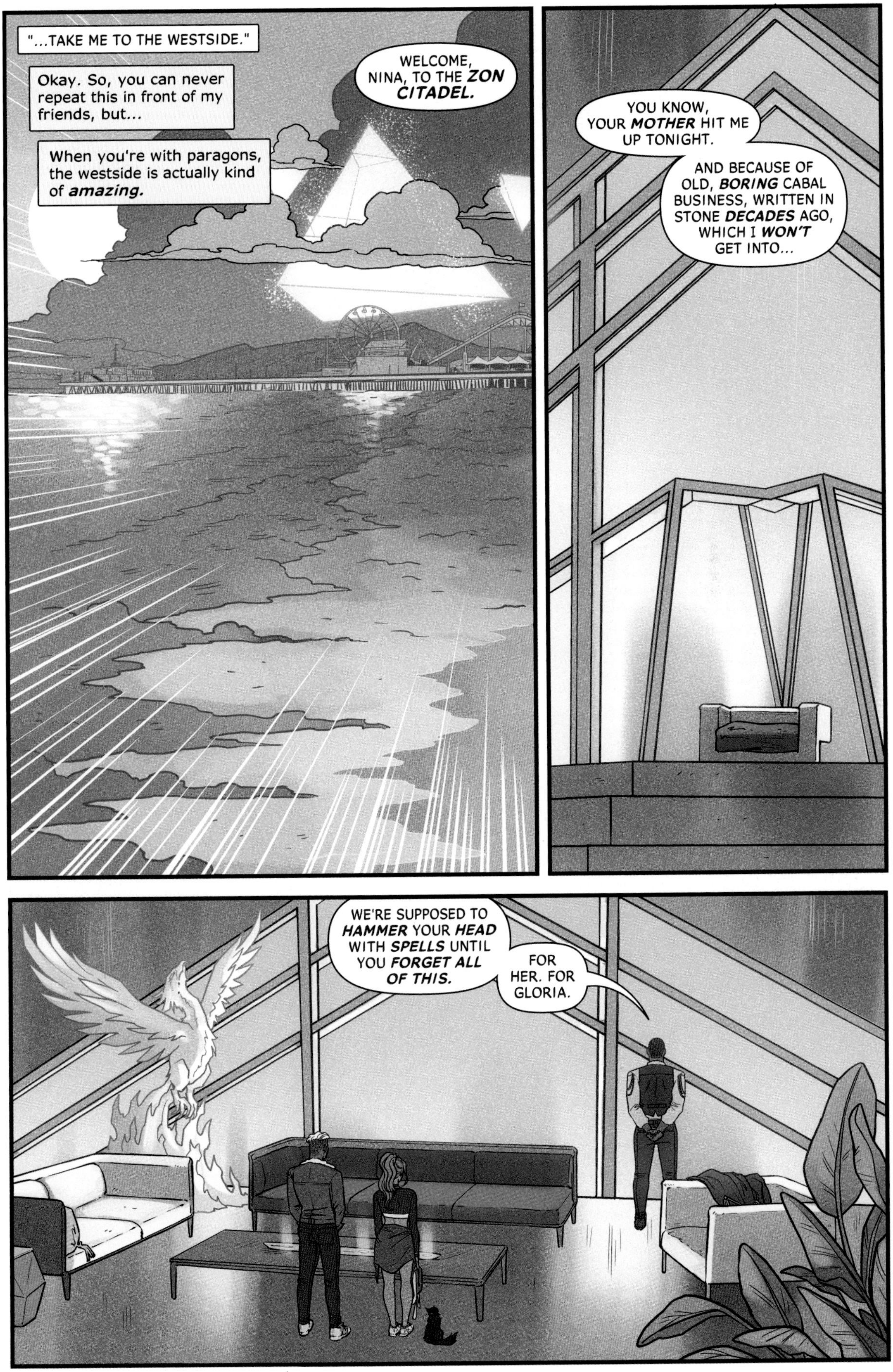

"...TAKE ME TO THE WESTSIDE."
Okay. So, you can never repeat this in front of my friends, but...
When you're with paragons, the westside is actually kind of *amazing.*
WELCOME, NINA, TO THE *ZON CITADEL.*
YOU KNOW, YOUR *MOTHER* HIT ME UP TONIGHT.
AND BECAUSE OF OLD, *BORING* CABAL BUSINESS, WRITTEN IN STONE *DECADES* AGO, WHICH I *WON'T* GET INTO...
WE'RE SUPPOSED TO *HAMMER* YOUR *HEAD* WITH *SPELLS* UNTIL YOU *FORGET ALL OF THIS.*
FOR HER. FOR GLORIA.

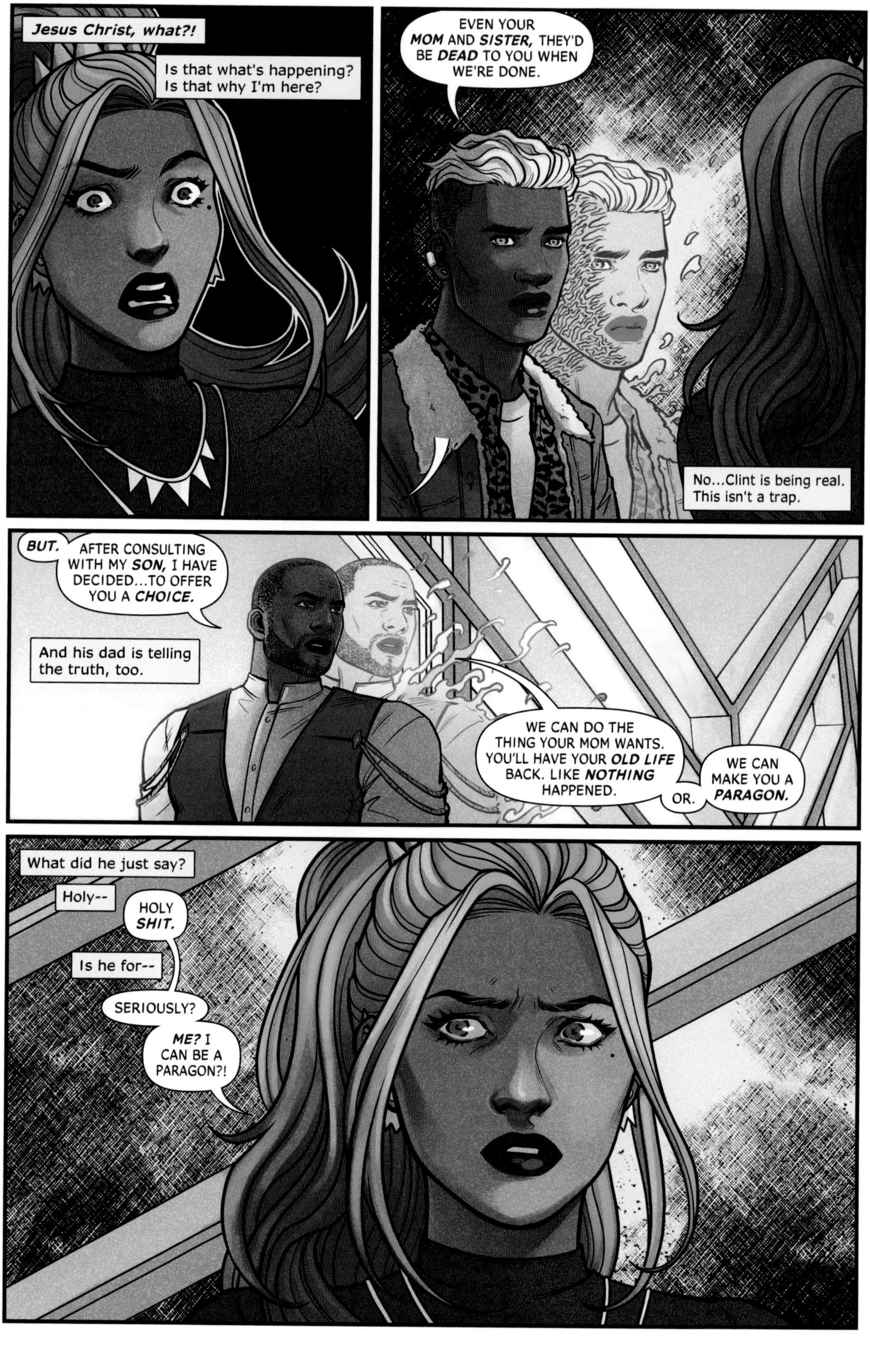

Jesus Christ, what?!
Is that what's happening? Is that why I'm here?
EVEN YOUR MOM AND SISTER, THEY'D BE DEAD TO YOU WHEN WE'RE DONE.
No...Clint is being real. This isn't a trap.
BUT.
AFTER CONSULTING WITH MY SON, I HAVE DECIDED...TO OFFER YOU A CHOICE.
And his dad is telling the truth, too.
WE CAN DO THE THING YOUR MOM WANTS. YOU'LL HAVE YOUR OLD LIFE BACK. LIKE NOTHING HAPPENED.
OR.
WE CAN MAKE YOU A PARAGON.
What did he just say?
Holy--
HOLY SHIT.
Is he for--
SERIOUSLY?
ME? I CAN BE A PARAGON?!

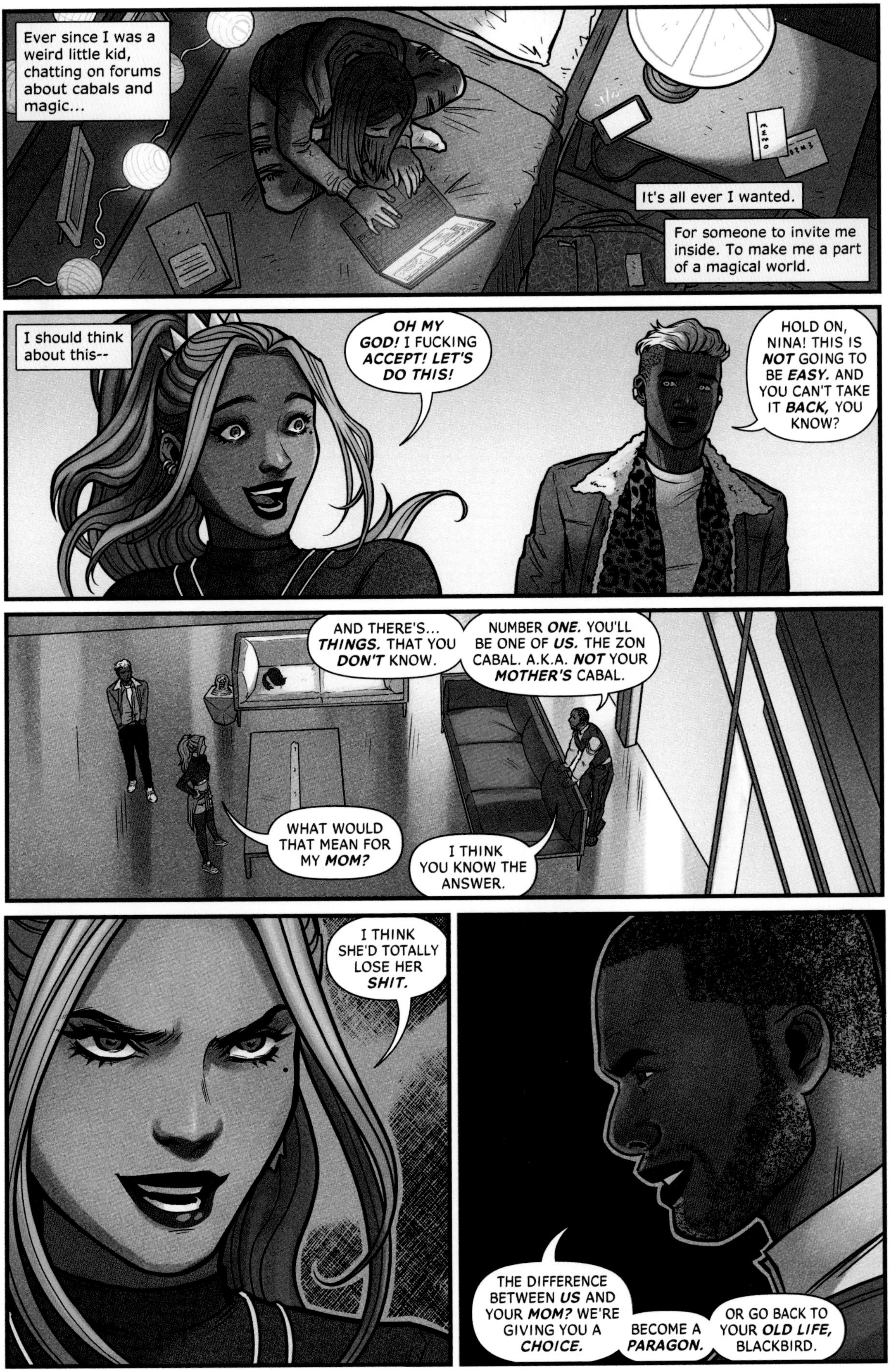
Ever since I was a weird little kid, chatting on forums about cabals and magic...
It's all ever I wanted.
For someone to invite me inside. To make me a part of a magical world.
I should think about this--
OH MY GOD! I FUCKING ACCEPT! LET'S DO THIS!
HOLD ON, NINA! THIS IS NOT GOING TO BE EASY. AND YOU CAN'T TAKE IT BACK, YOU KNOW?
AND THERE'S... THINGS. THAT YOU DON'T KNOW.
NUMBER ONE. YOU'LL BE ONE OF US. THE ZON CABAL. A.K.A. NOT YOUR MOTHER'S CABAL.
WHAT WOULD THAT MEAN FOR MY MOM?
I THINK YOU KNOW THE ANSWER.
I THINK SHE'D TOTALLY LOSE HER SHIT.
THE DIFFERENCE BETWEEN US AND YOUR MOM? WE'RE GIVING YOU A CHOICE.
BECOME A PARAGON.
OR GO BACK TO YOUR OLD LIFE, BLACKBIRD.

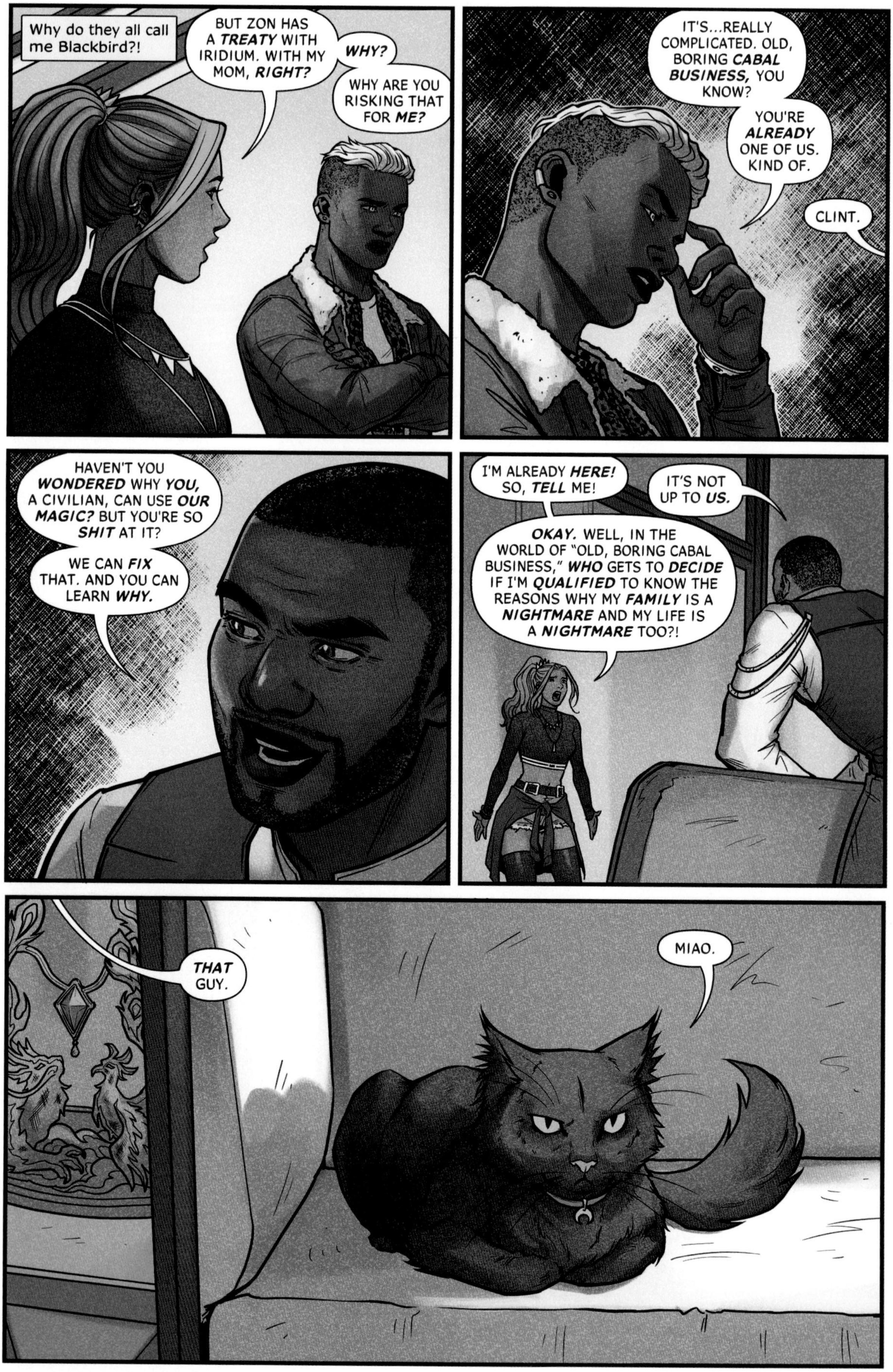
Why do they all call me Blackbird?!
BUT ZON HAS A TREATY WITH IRIDIUM. WITH MY MOM, RIGHT?
WHY?
WHY ARE YOU RISKING THAT FOR ME?
IT'S...REALLY COMPLICATED. OLD, BORING CABAL BUSINESS, YOU KNOW?
YOU'RE ALREADY ONE OF US. KIND OF.
CLINT.
HAVEN'T YOU WONDERED WHY YOU, A CIVILIAN, CAN USE OUR MAGIC? BUT YOU'RE SO SHIT AT IT?
WE CAN FIX THAT. AND YOU CAN LEARN WHY.
I'M ALREADY HERE! SO, TELL ME!
IT'S NOT UP TO US.
OKAY. WELL, IN THE WORLD OF "OLD, BORING CABAL BUSINESS," WHO GETS TO DECIDE IF I'M QUALIFIED TO KNOW THE REASONS WHY MY FAMILY IS A NIGHTMARE AND MY LIFE IS A NIGHTMARE TOO?!
THAT GUY.
MIAO.

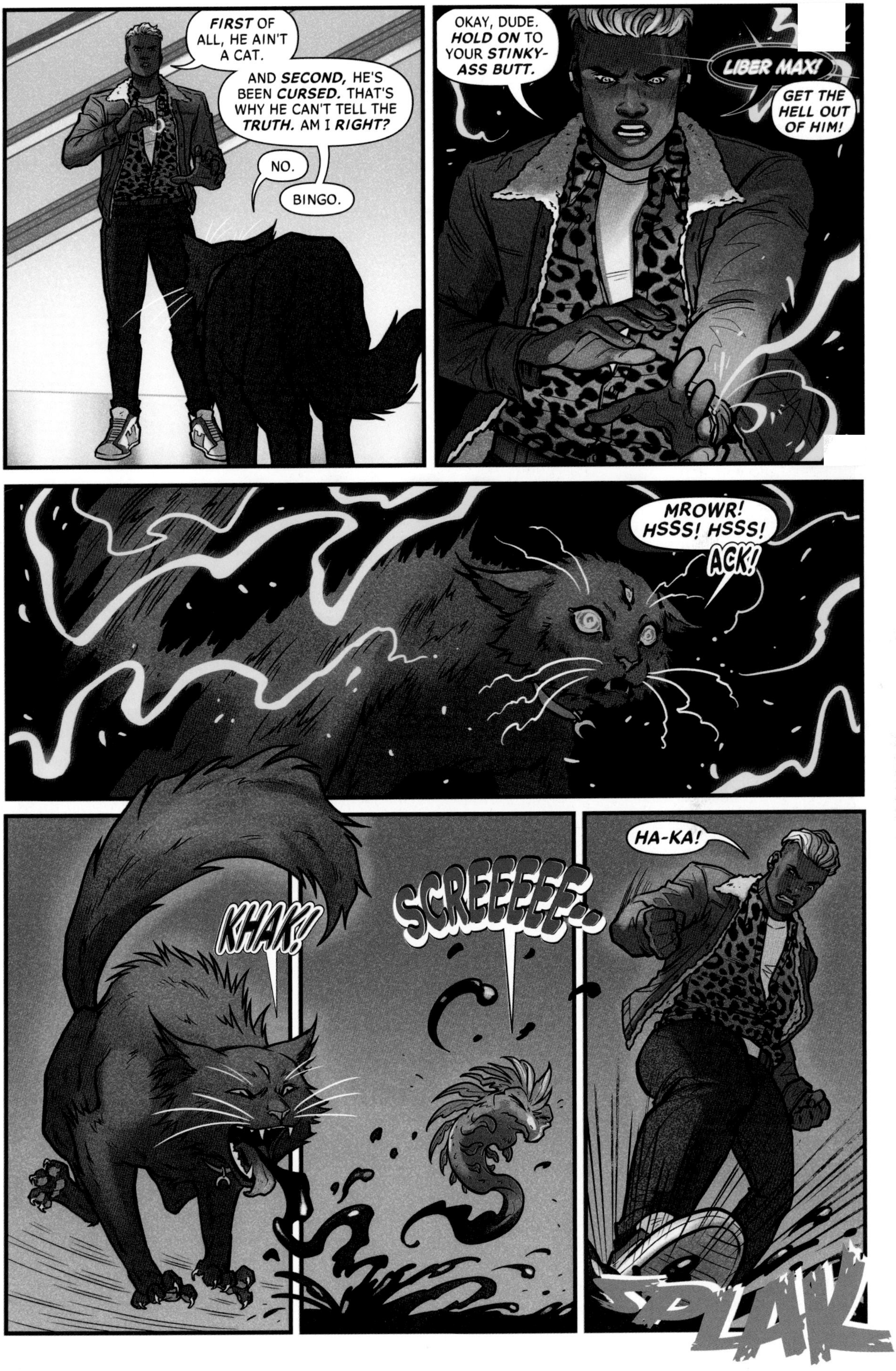

FIRST OF ALL, HE AIN'T A CAT.
AND SECOND, HE'S BEEN CURSED. THAT'S WHY HE CAN'T TELL THE TRUTH. AM I RIGHT?
NO.
BINGO.
OKAY, DUDE. HOLD ON TO YOUR STINKY-ASS BUTT.
LIBER MAX!
GET THE HELL OUT OF HIM!
MROWR! HSSS! HSSS!
ACK!
KHAK!
SCREEEEEE..
HA-KA!
SPLAK

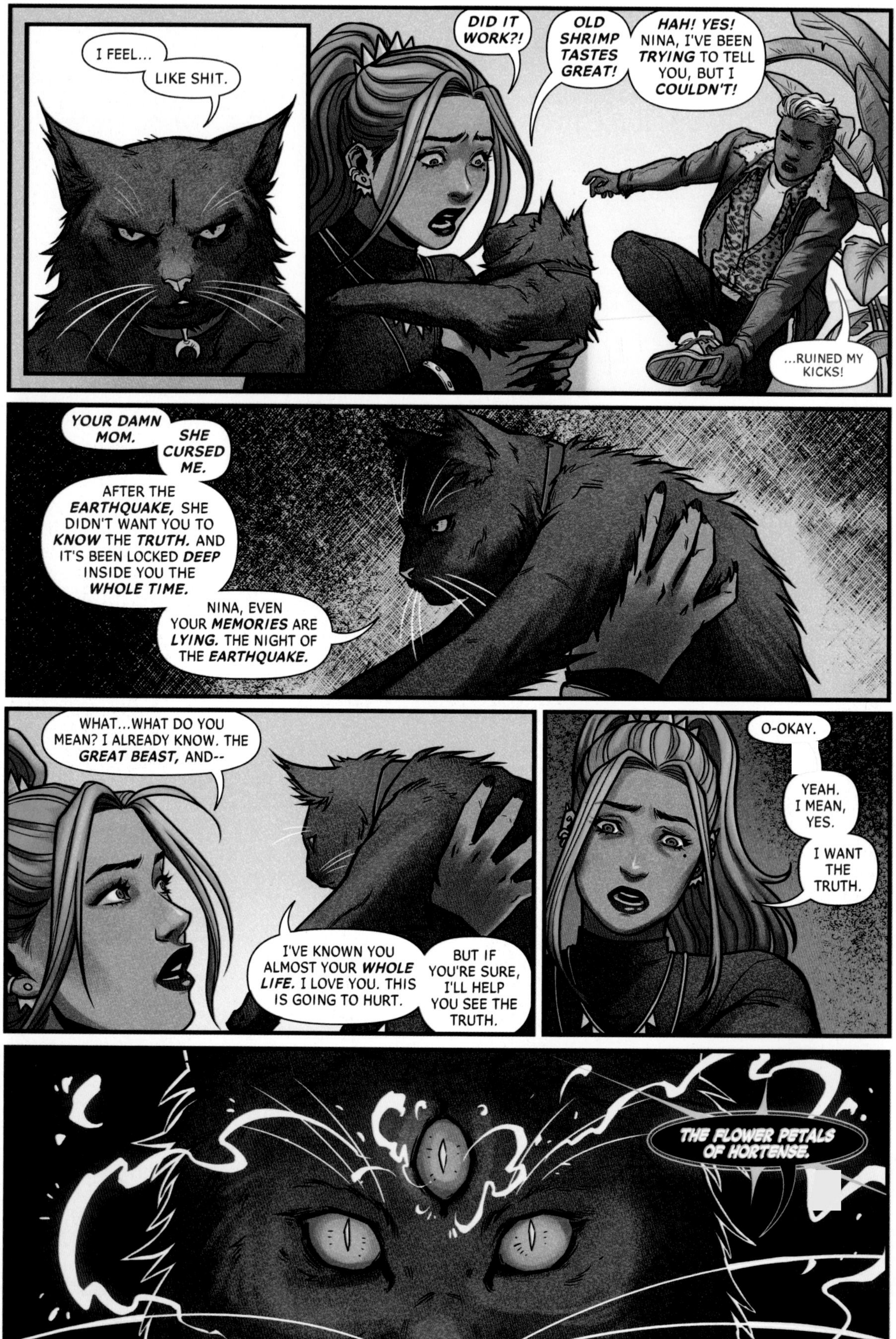
I FEEL...
LIKE SHIT.
DID IT WORK?!
OLD SHRIMP TASTES GREAT!
HAH! YES! NINA, I'VE BEEN TRYING TO TELL YOU, BUT I COULDN'T!
...RUINED MY KICKS!
YOUR DAMN MOM.
SHE CURSED ME.
AFTER THE EARTHQUAKE, SHE DIDN'T WANT YOU TO KNOW THE TRUTH. AND IT'S BEEN LOCKED DEEP INSIDE YOU THE WHOLE TIME.
NINA, EVEN YOUR MEMORIES ARE LYING. THE NIGHT OF THE EARTHQUAKE.
WHAT...WHAT DO YOU MEAN? I ALREADY KNOW. THE GREAT BEAST, AND--
I'VE KNOWN YOU ALMOST YOUR WHOLE LIFE. I LOVE YOU. THIS IS GOING TO HURT.
BUT IF YOU'RE SURE, I'LL HELP YOU SEE THE TRUTH.
O-OKAY.
YEAH. I MEAN, YES.
I WANT THE TRUTH.
THE FLOWER PETALS OF HORTENSE.

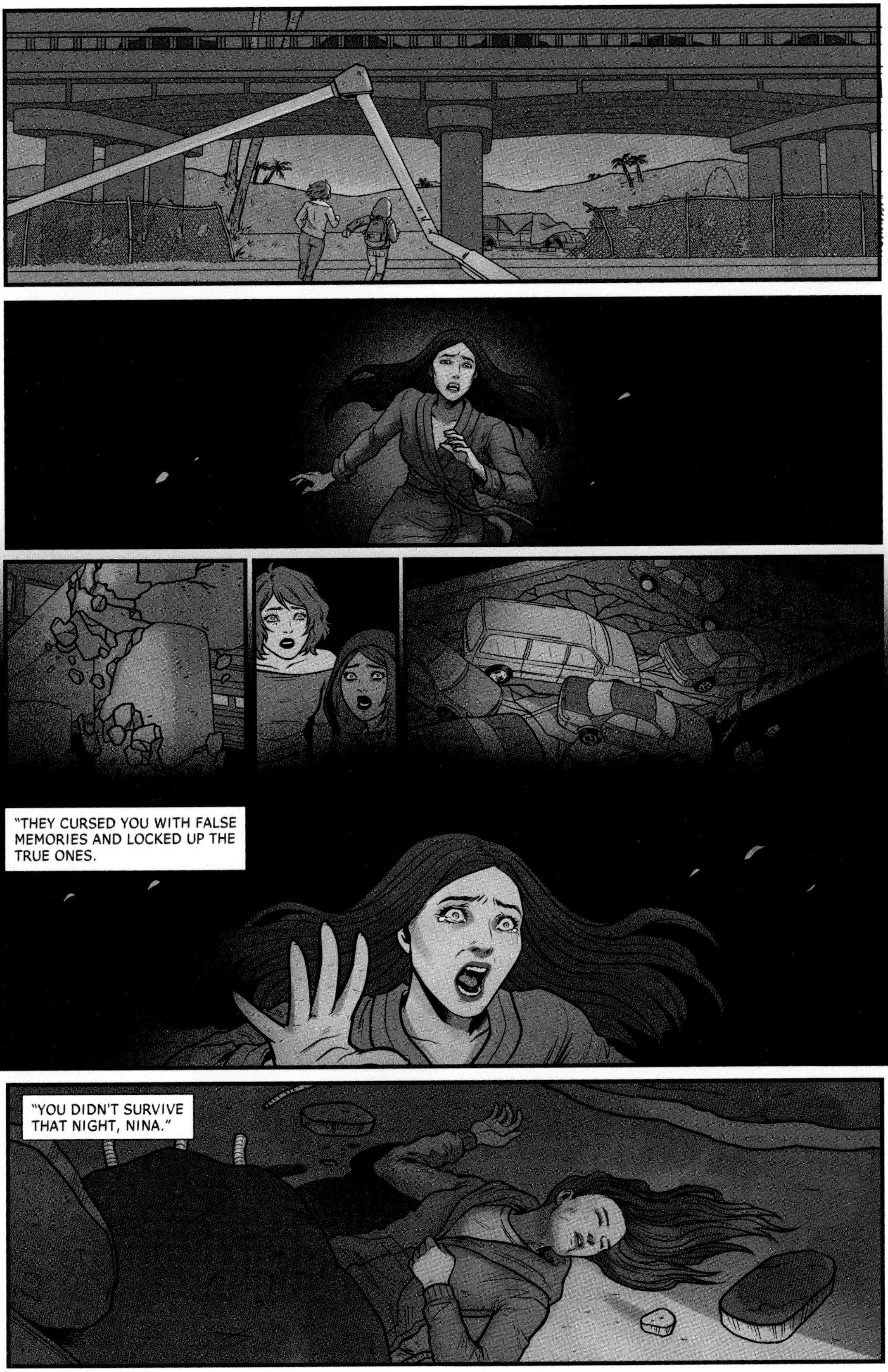
"THEY CURSED YOU WITH FALSE MEMORIES AND LOCKED UP THE TRUE ONES.
"YOU DIDN'T SURVIVE THAT NIGHT, NINA."

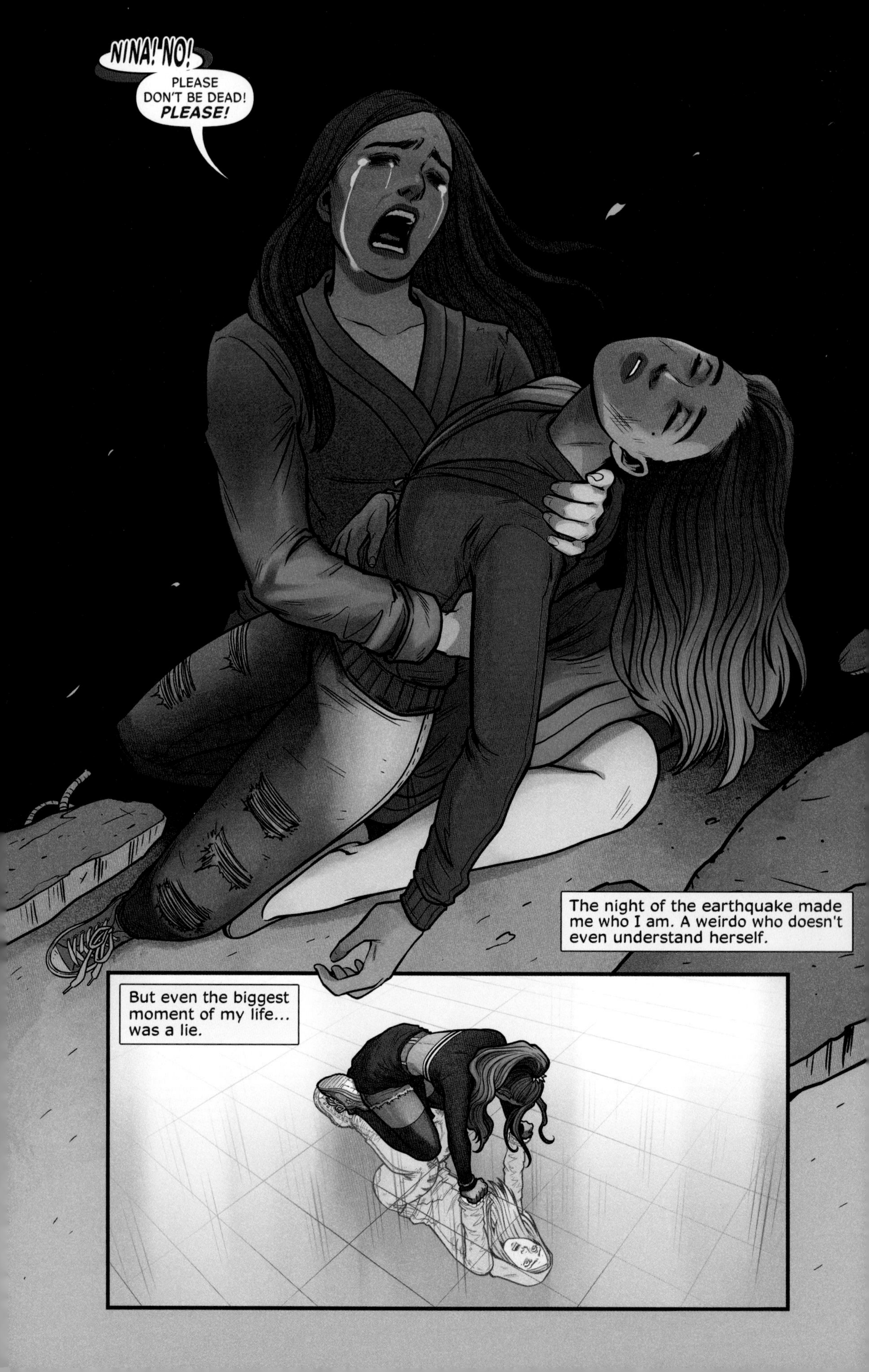
NINA! NO!
PLEASE DON'T BE DEAD! PLEASE!
The night of the earthquake made me who I am. A weirdo who doesn't even understand herself.
But even the biggest moment of my life... was a lie.

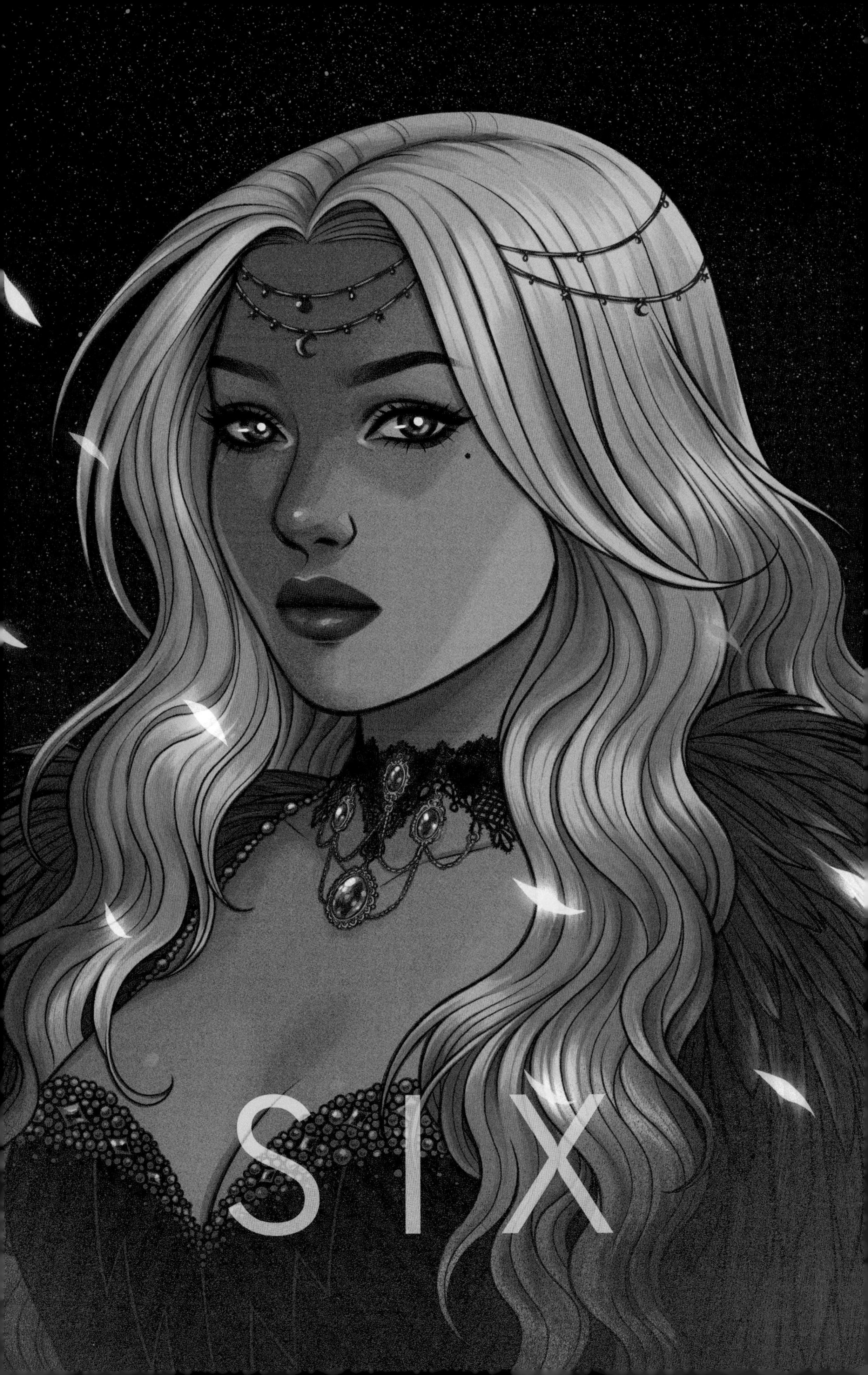
SIX

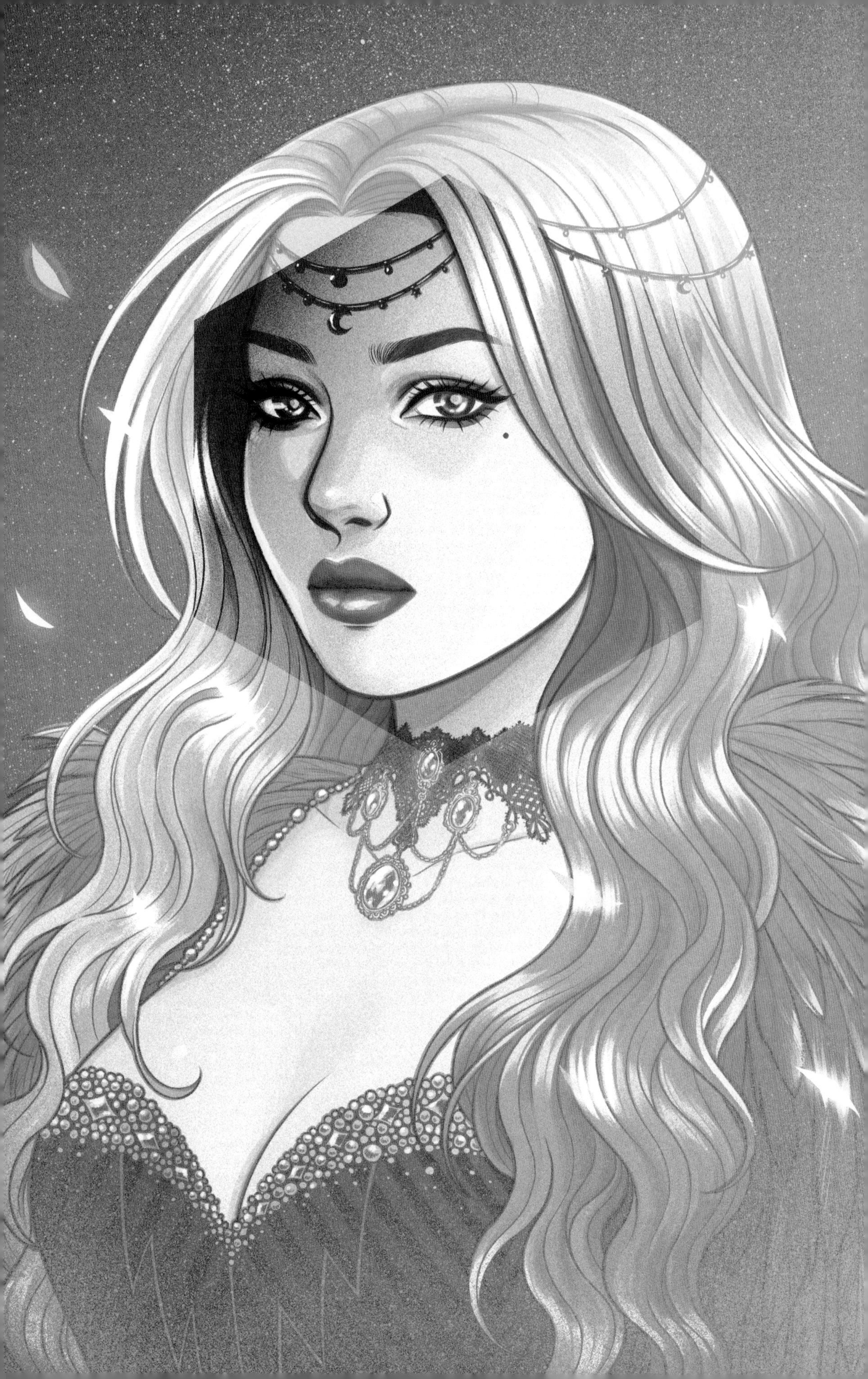

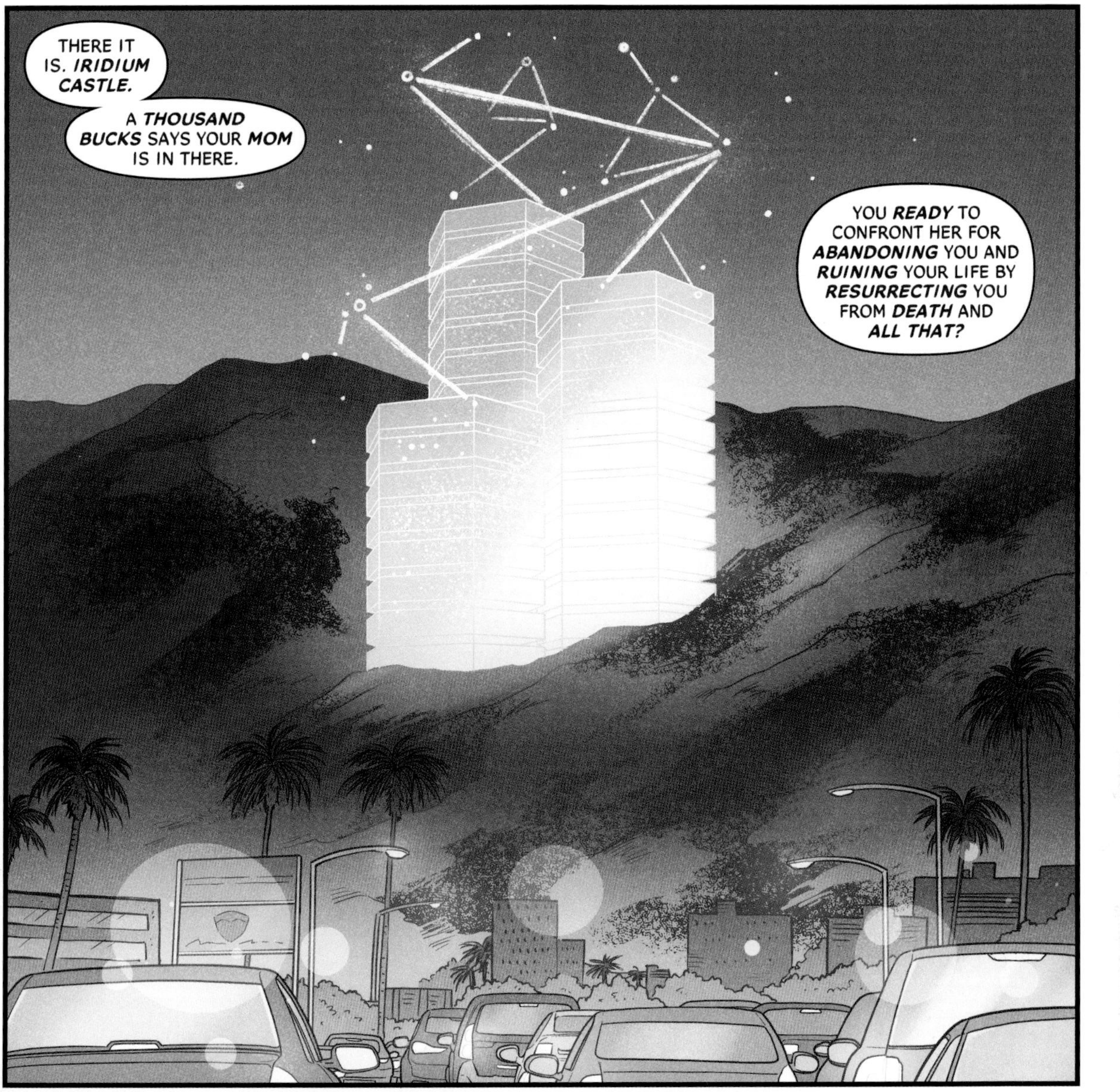
THERE IT IS. IRIDIUM CASTLE.
A THOUSAND BUCKS SAYS YOUR MOM IS IN THERE.
YOU READY TO CONFRONT HER FOR ABANDONING YOU AND RUINING YOUR LIFE BY RESURRECTING YOU FROM DEATH AND ALL THAT?

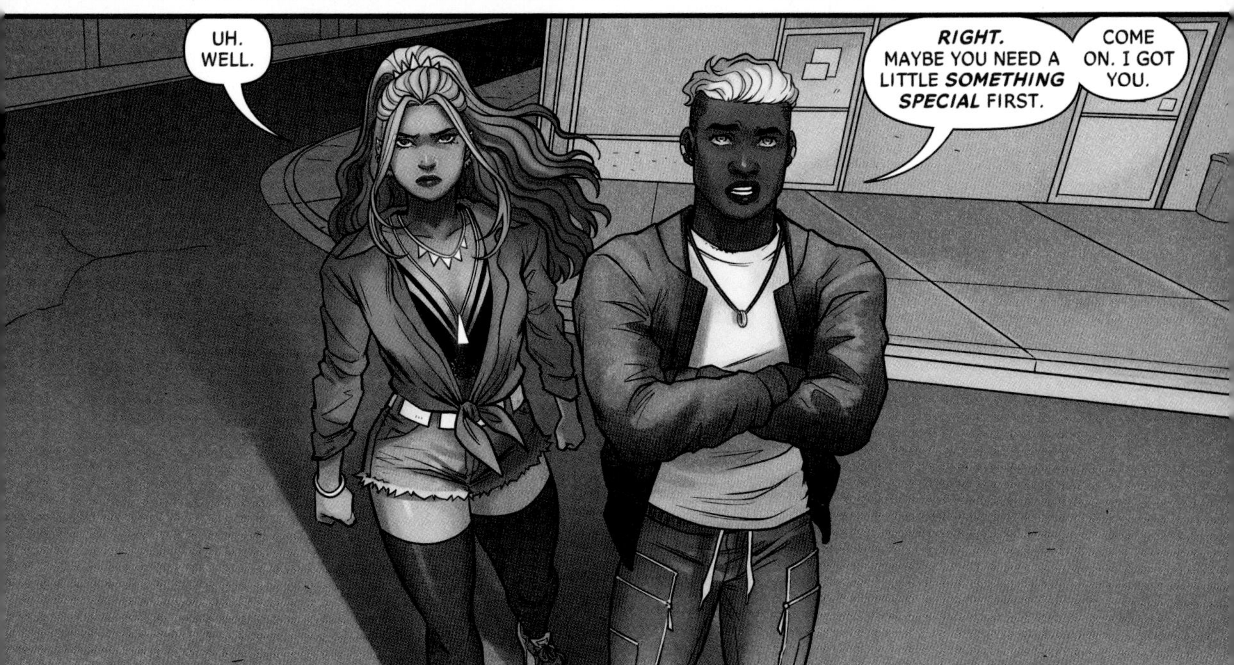
UH. WELL.
RIGHT. MAYBE YOU NEED A LITTLE SOMETHING SPECIAL FIRST.
COME ON. I GOT YOU.

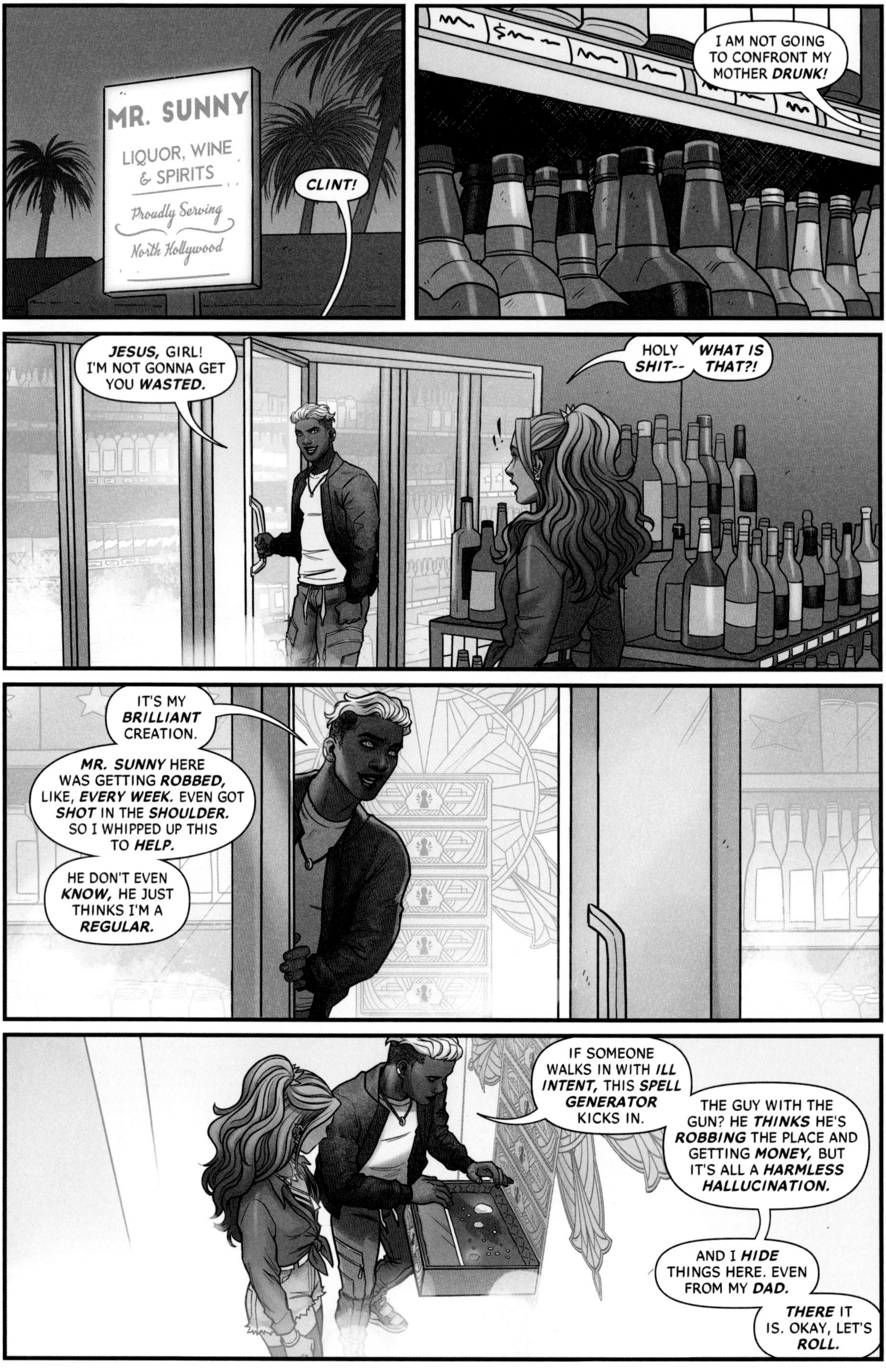
MR. SUNNY
LIQUOR, WINE & SPIRITS
Proudly Serving
North Hollywood
CLINT!
I AM NOT GOING TO CONFRONT MY MOTHER DRUNK!
JESUS, GIRL! I'M NOT GONNA GET YOU WASTED.
HOLY SHIT--
WHAT IS THAT?!
IT'S MY BRILLIANT CREATION.
MR. SUNNY HERE WAS GETTING ROBBED, LIKE, EVERY WEEK. EVEN GOT SHOT IN THE SHOULDER. SO I WHIPPED UP THIS TO HELP.
HE DON'T EVEN KNOW, HE JUST THINKS I'M A REGULAR.
IF SOMEONE WALKS IN WITH ILL INTENT, THIS SPELL GENERATOR KICKS IN.
THE GUY WITH THE GUN? HE THINKS HE'S ROBBING THE PLACE AND GETTING MONEY, BUT IT'S ALL A HARMLESS HALLUCINATION.
AND I HIDE THINGS HERE. EVEN FROM MY DAD.
THERE IT IS. OKAY, LET'S ROLL.

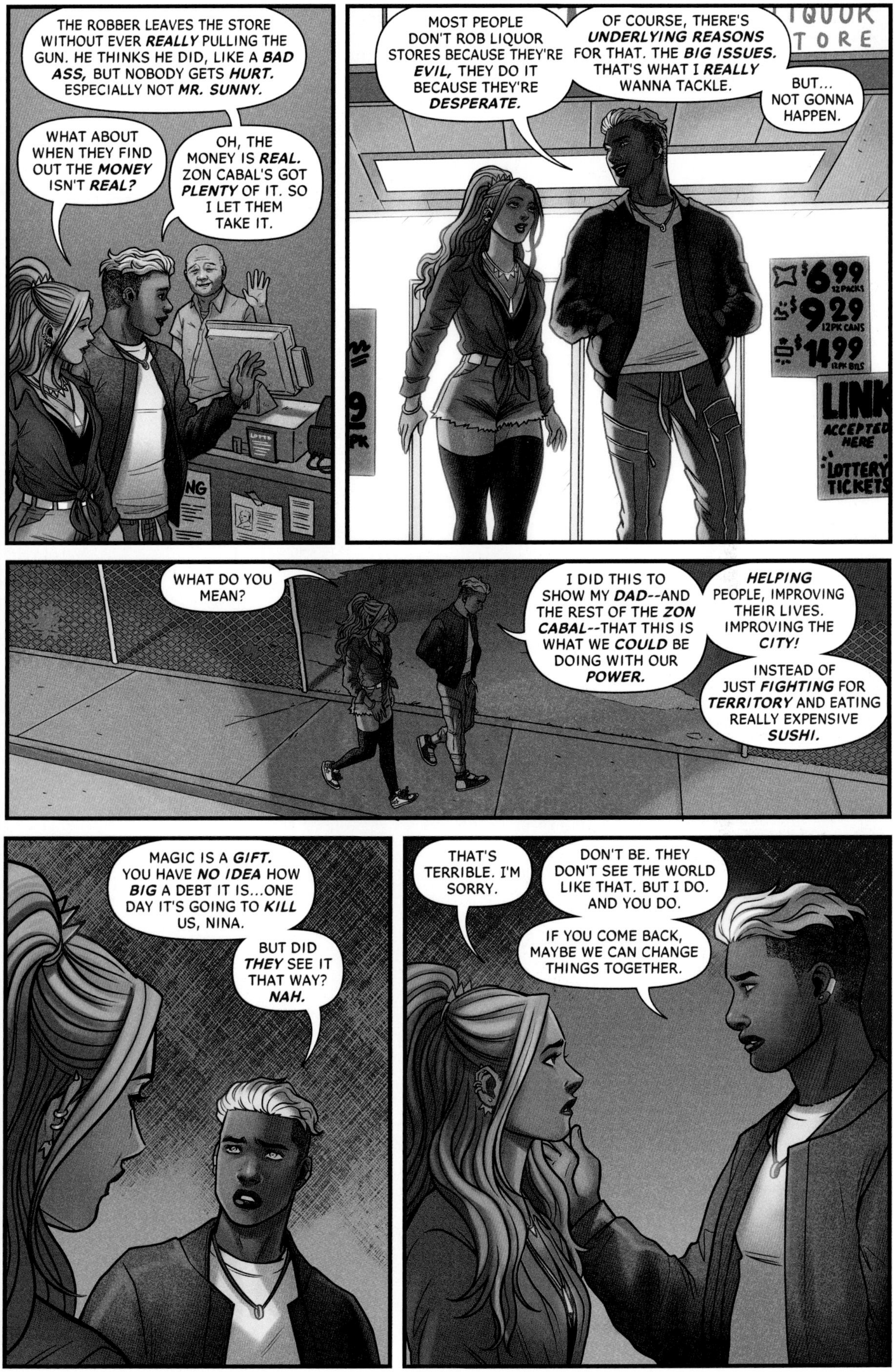
THE ROBBER LEAVES THE STORE WITHOUT EVER REALLY PULLING THE GUN. HE THINKS HE DID, LIKE A BAD ASS, BUT NOBODY GETS HURT. ESPECIALLY NOT MR. SUNNY.
WHAT ABOUT WHEN THEY FIND OUT THE MONEY ISN'T REAL?
OH, THE MONEY IS REAL. ZON CABAL'S GOT PLENTY OF IT. SO I LET THEM TAKE IT.
MOST PEOPLE DON'T ROB LIQUOR STORES BECAUSE THEY'RE EVIL, THEY DO IT BECAUSE THEY'RE DESPERATE.
OF COURSE, THERE'S UNDERLYING REASONS FOR THAT. THE BIG ISSUES. THAT'S WHAT I REALLY WANNA TACKLE.
BUT... NOT GONNA HAPPEN.
$6.99 12 PACKS
$9.29 12PK CANS
$14.99 12PK BTLS
LINK ACCEPTED HERE
LOTTERY TICKETS
WHAT DO YOU MEAN?
I DID THIS TO SHOW MY DAD--AND THE REST OF THE ZON CABAL--THAT THIS IS WHAT WE COULD BE DOING WITH OUR POWER.
HELPING PEOPLE, IMPROVING THEIR LIVES. IMPROVING THE CITY!
INSTEAD OF JUST FIGHTING FOR TERRITORY AND EATING REALLY EXPENSIVE SUSHI.
MAGIC IS A GIFT. YOU HAVE NO IDEA HOW BIG A DEBT IT IS...ONE DAY IT'S GOING TO KILL US, NINA.
BUT DID THEY SEE IT THAT WAY? NAH.
THAT'S TERRIBLE. I'M SORRY.
DON'T BE. THEY DON'T SEE THE WORLD LIKE THAT. BUT I DO. AND YOU DO.
IF YOU COME BACK, MAYBE WE CAN CHANGE THINGS TOGETHER.

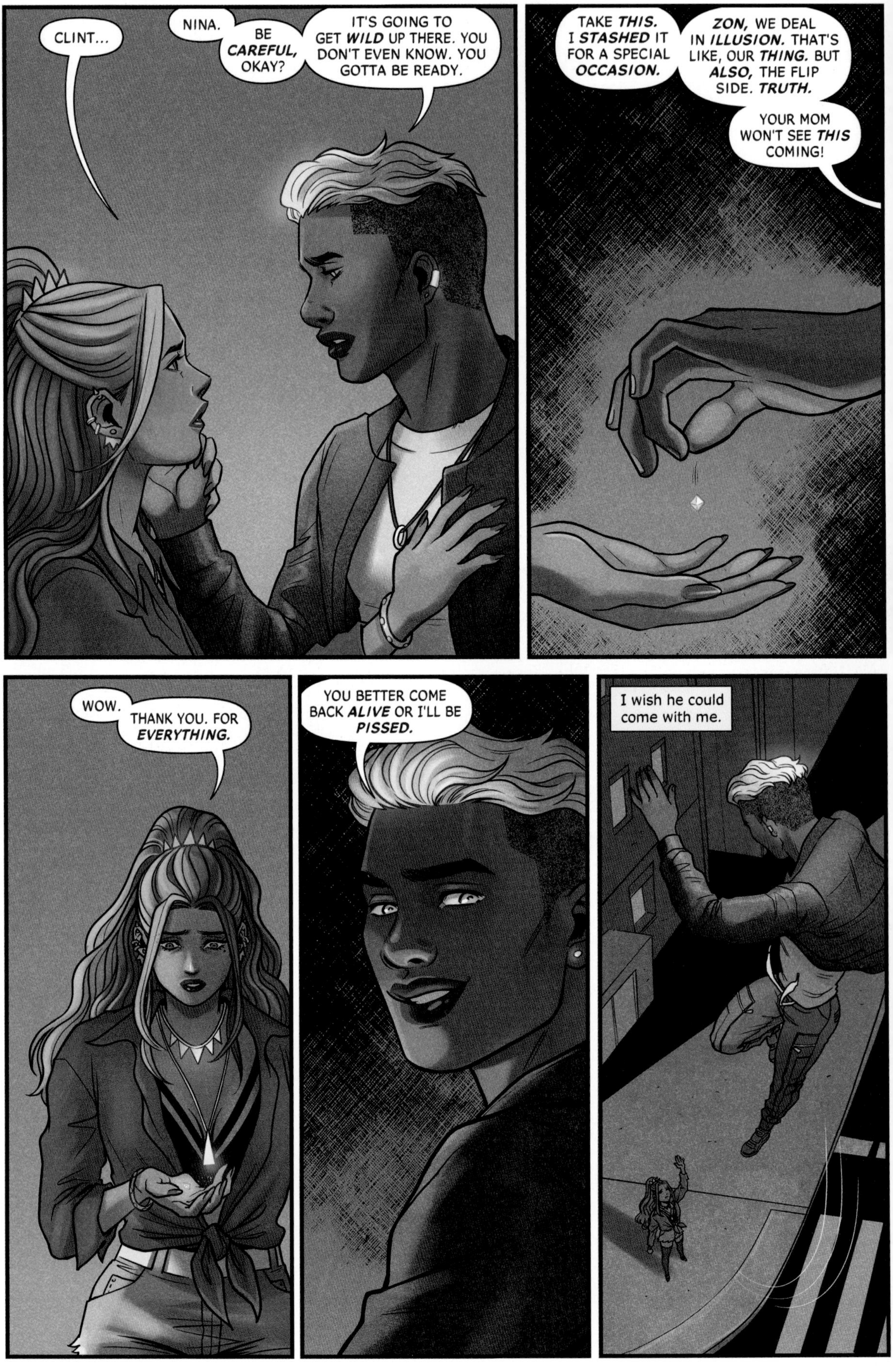
CLINT...
NINA.
BE *CAREFUL,* OKAY?
IT'S GOING TO GET *WILD* UP THERE. YOU DON'T EVEN KNOW. YOU GOTTA BE READY.
TAKE *THIS.* I *STASHED* IT FOR A SPECIAL *OCCASION.*
ZON, WE DEAL IN *ILLUSION.* THAT'S LIKE, OUR *THING.* BUT *ALSO,* THE FLIP SIDE. *TRUTH.*
YOUR MOM WON'T SEE *THIS* COMING!
WOW.
THANK YOU. FOR *EVERYTHING.*
YOU BETTER COME BACK *ALIVE* OR I'LL BE *PISSED.*
I wish he could come with me.

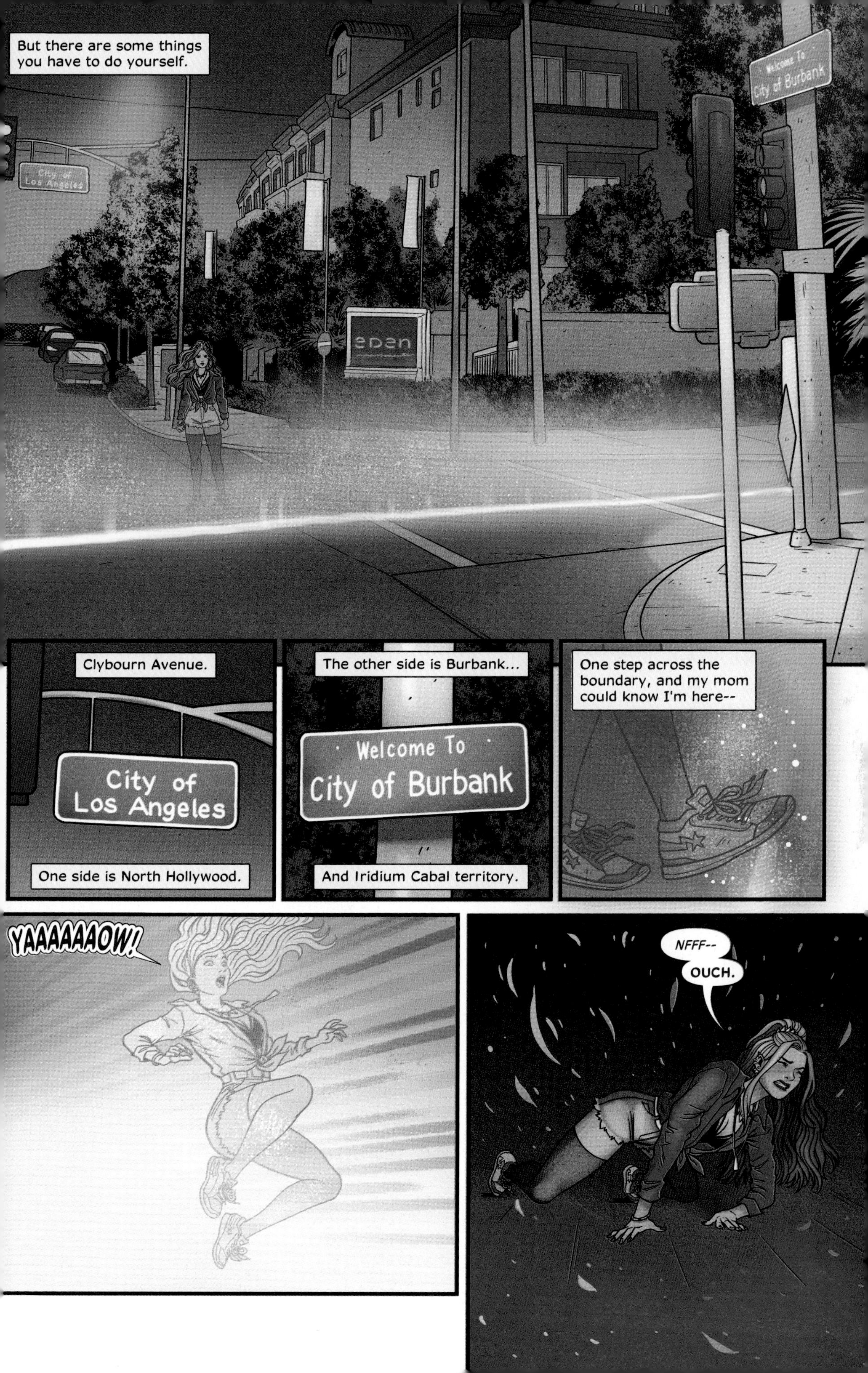
But there are some things you have to do yourself.
City of Los Angeles
Welcome To City of Burbank
eden
Clybourn Avenue.
City of Los Angeles
One side is North Hollywood.
The other side is Burbank...
Welcome To City of Burbank
And Iridium Cabal territory.
One step across the boundary, and my mom could know I'm here--
YAAAAAAOW!
NFFF--
OUCH.

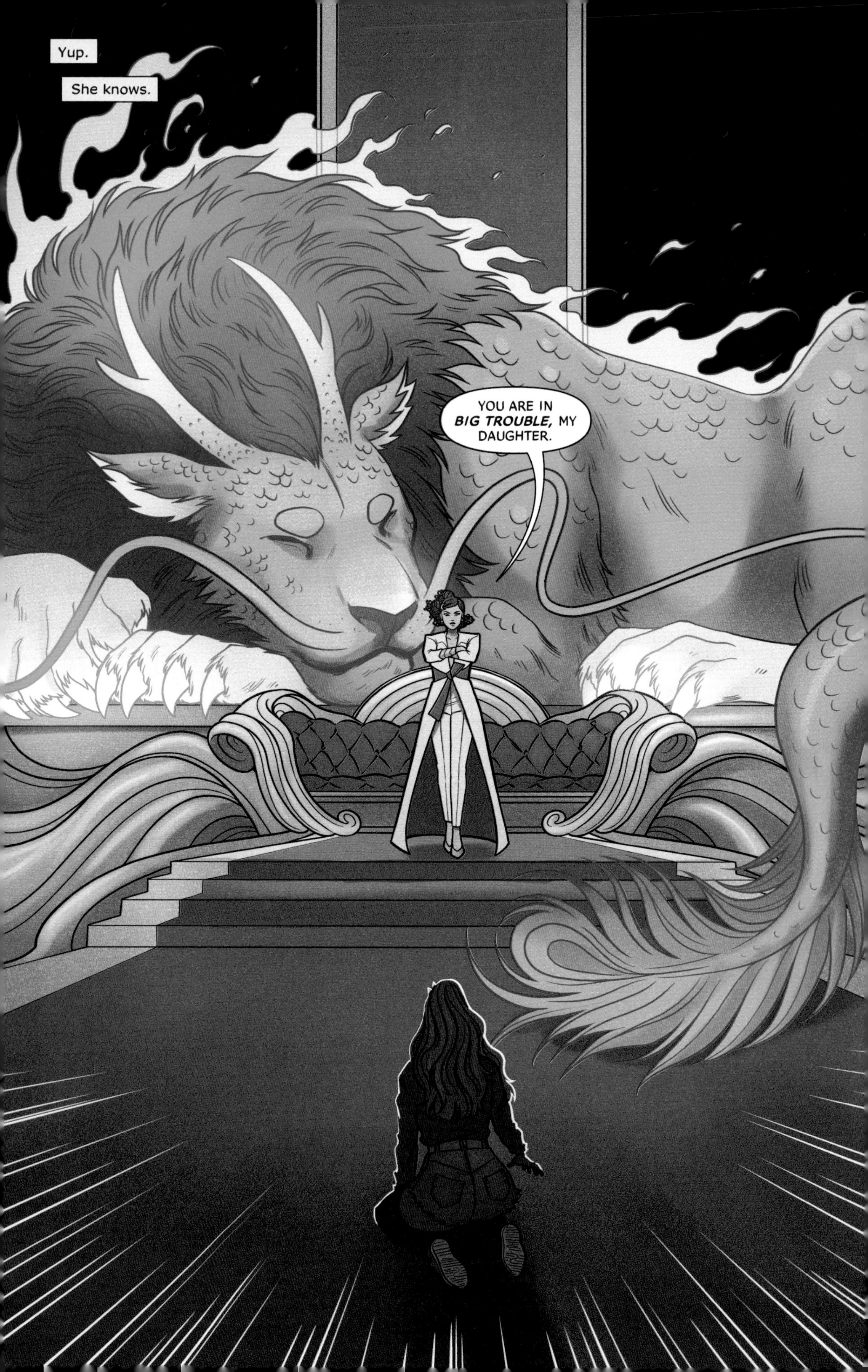
Yup.
She knows.
YOU ARE IN *BIG TROUBLE,* MY DAUGHTER.

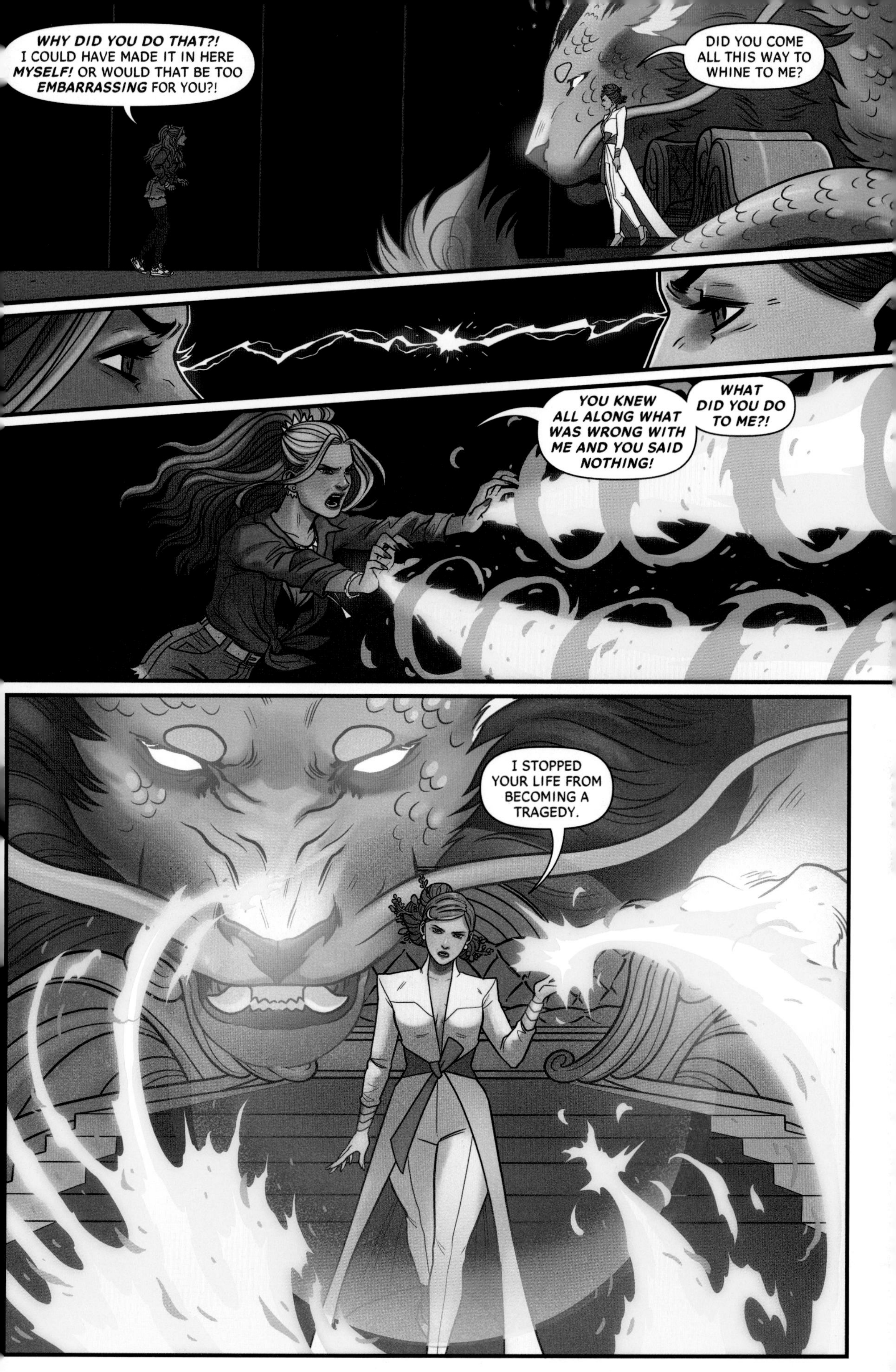

WHY DID YOU DO THAT?! I COULD HAVE MADE IT IN HERE MYSELF! OR WOULD THAT BE TOO EMBARRASSING FOR YOU?!
DID YOU COME ALL THIS WAY TO WHINE TO ME?
YOU KNEW ALL ALONG WHAT WAS WRONG WITH ME AND YOU SAID NOTHING!
WHAT DID YOU DO TO ME?!
I STOPPED YOUR LIFE FROM BECOMING A TRAGEDY.

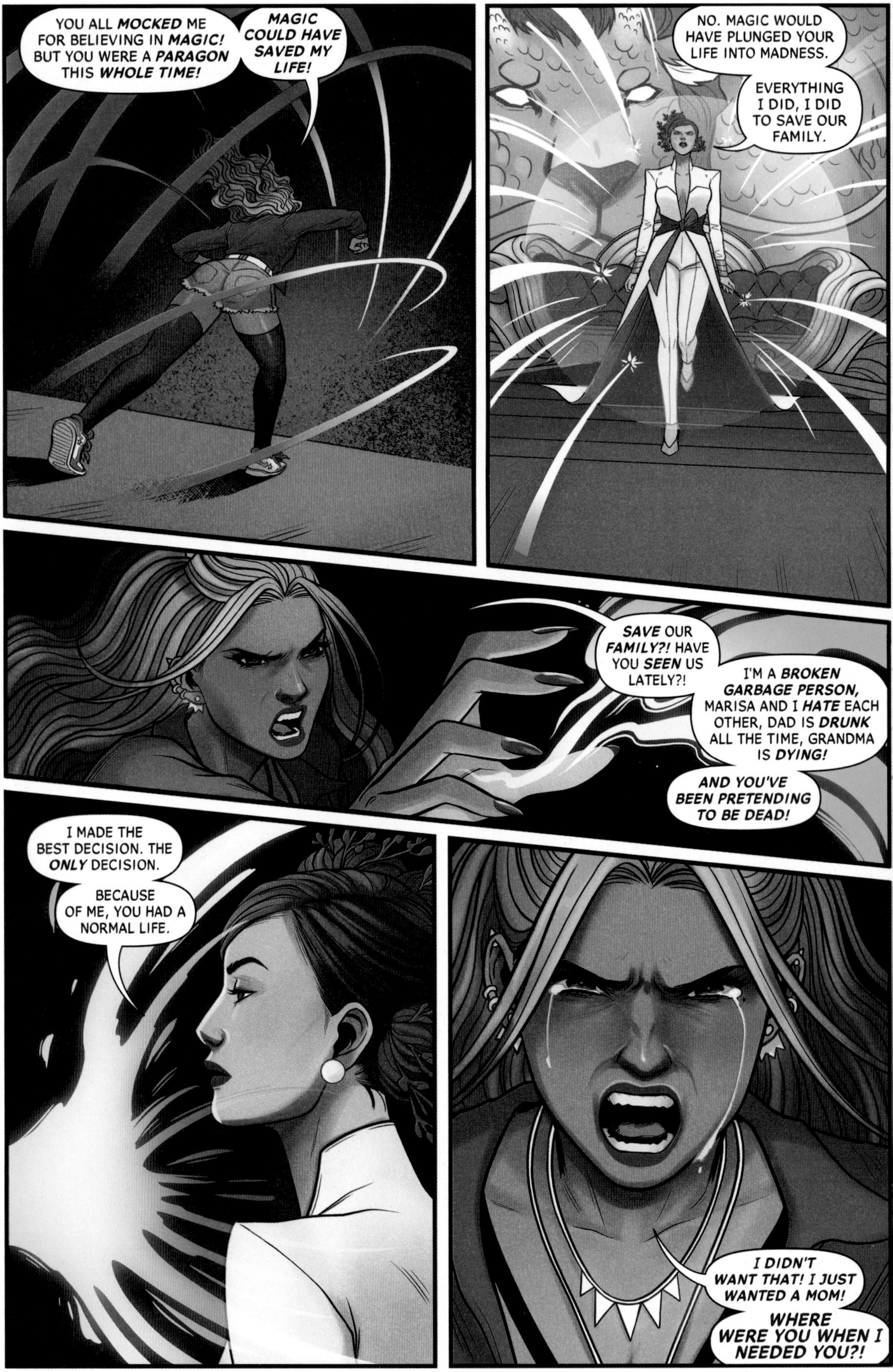
YOU ALL MOCKED ME FOR BELIEVING IN MAGIC! BUT YOU WERE A PARAGON THIS WHOLE TIME!
MAGIC COULD HAVE SAVED MY LIFE!
NO. MAGIC WOULD HAVE PLUNGED YOUR LIFE INTO MADNESS.
EVERYTHING I DID, I DID TO SAVE OUR FAMILY.
SAVE OUR FAMILY?! HAVE YOU SEEN US LATELY?!
I'M A BROKEN GARBAGE PERSON, MARISA AND I HATE EACH OTHER, DAD IS DRUNK ALL THE TIME, GRANDMA IS DYING!
AND YOU'VE BEEN PRETENDING TO BE DEAD!
I MADE THE BEST DECISION. THE ONLY DECISION.
BECAUSE OF ME, YOU HAD A NORMAL LIFE.
I DIDN'T WANT THAT! I JUST WANTED A MOM!
WHERE WERE YOU WHEN I NEEDED YOU?!

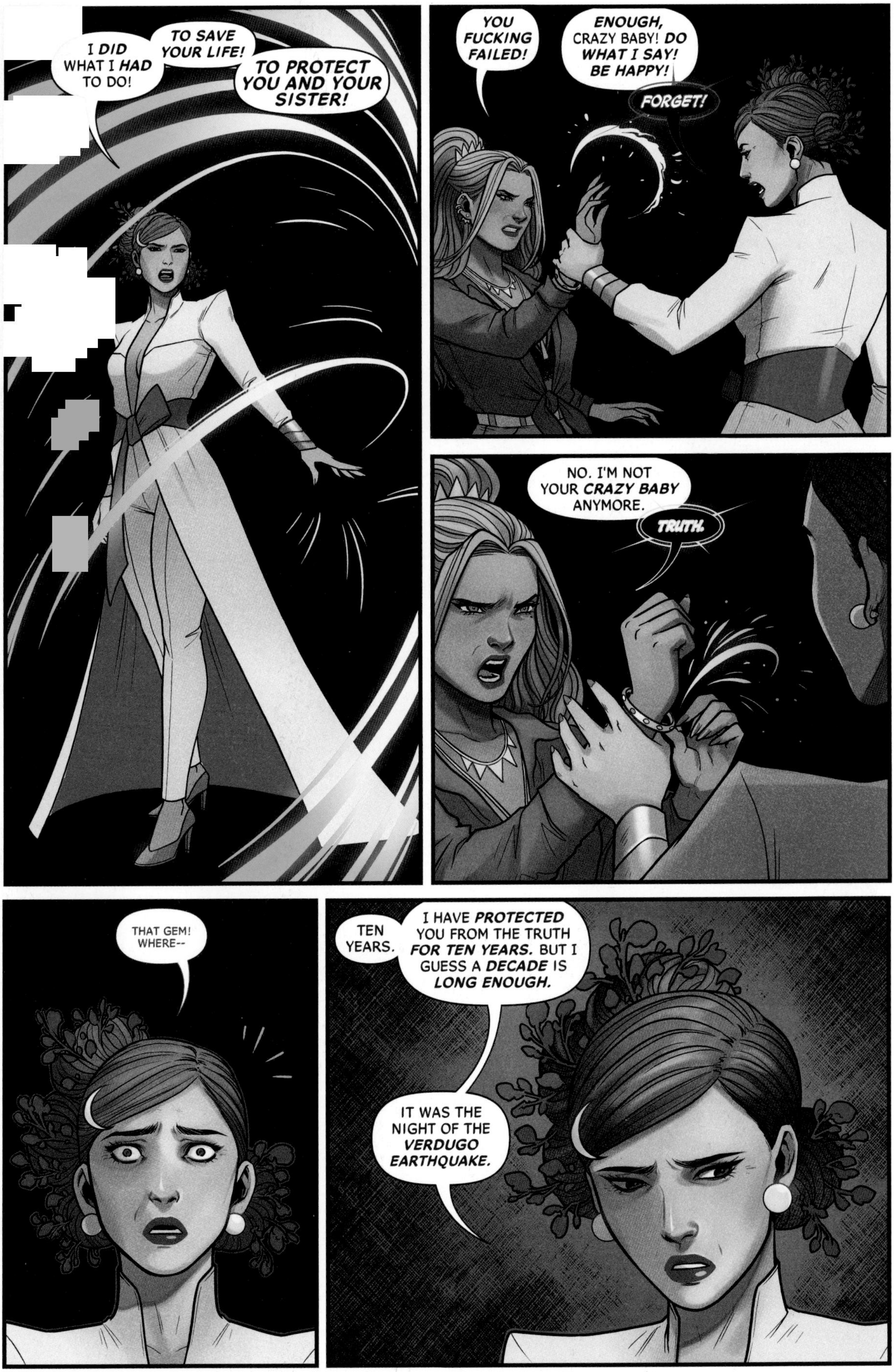
I DID WHAT I HAD TO DO!
TO SAVE YOUR LIFE!
TO PROTECT YOU AND YOUR SISTER!
YOU FUCKING FAILED!
ENOUGH, CRAZY BABY! DO WHAT I SAY! BE HAPPY!
FORGET!
NO. I'M NOT YOUR CRAZY BABY ANYMORE.
TRUTH.
THAT GEM! WHERE--
TEN YEARS.
I HAVE PROTECTED YOU FROM THE TRUTH FOR TEN YEARS. BUT I GUESS A DECADE IS LONG ENOUGH.
IT WAS THE NIGHT OF THE VERDUGO EARTHQUAKE.

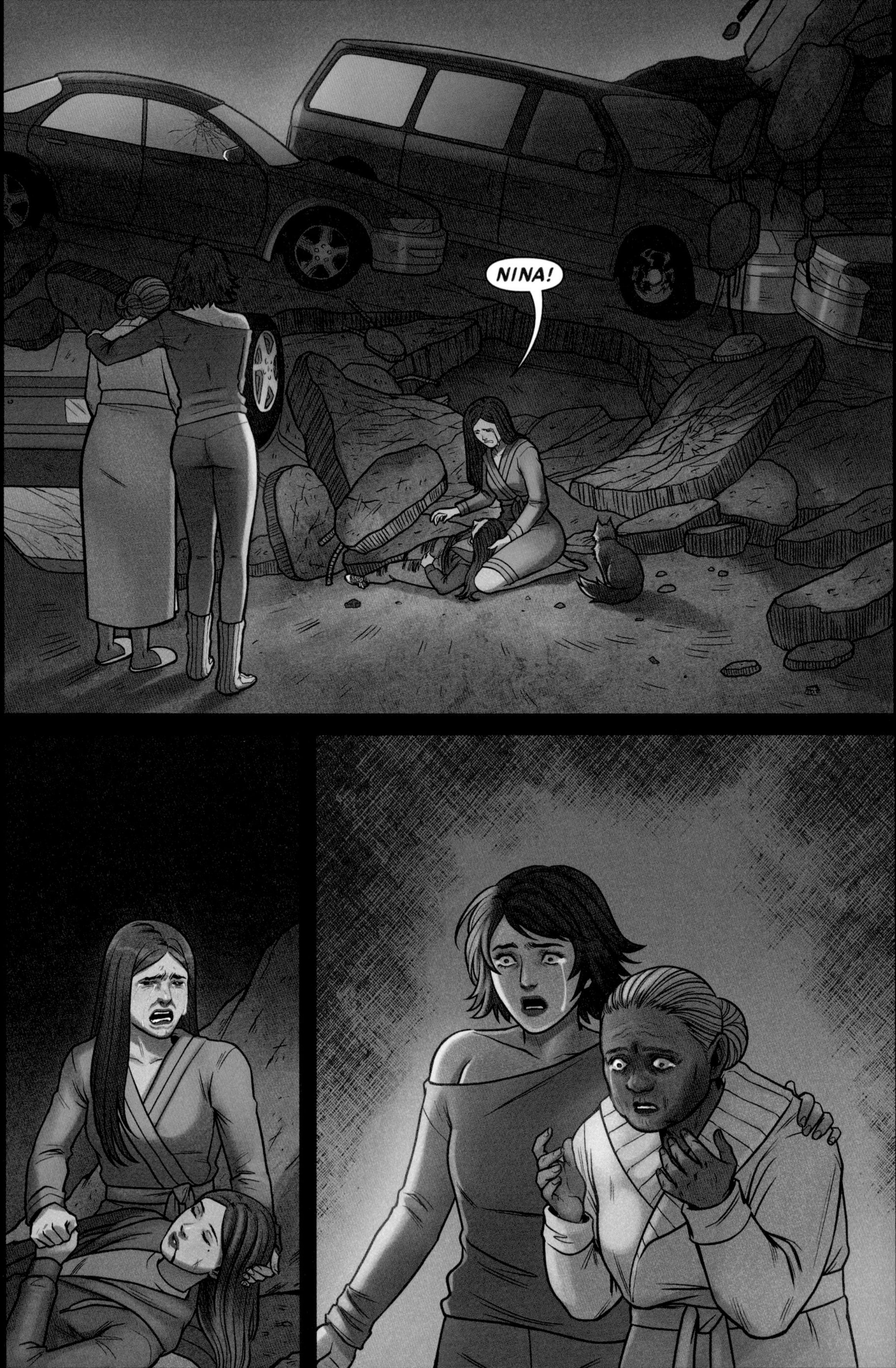
NINA!

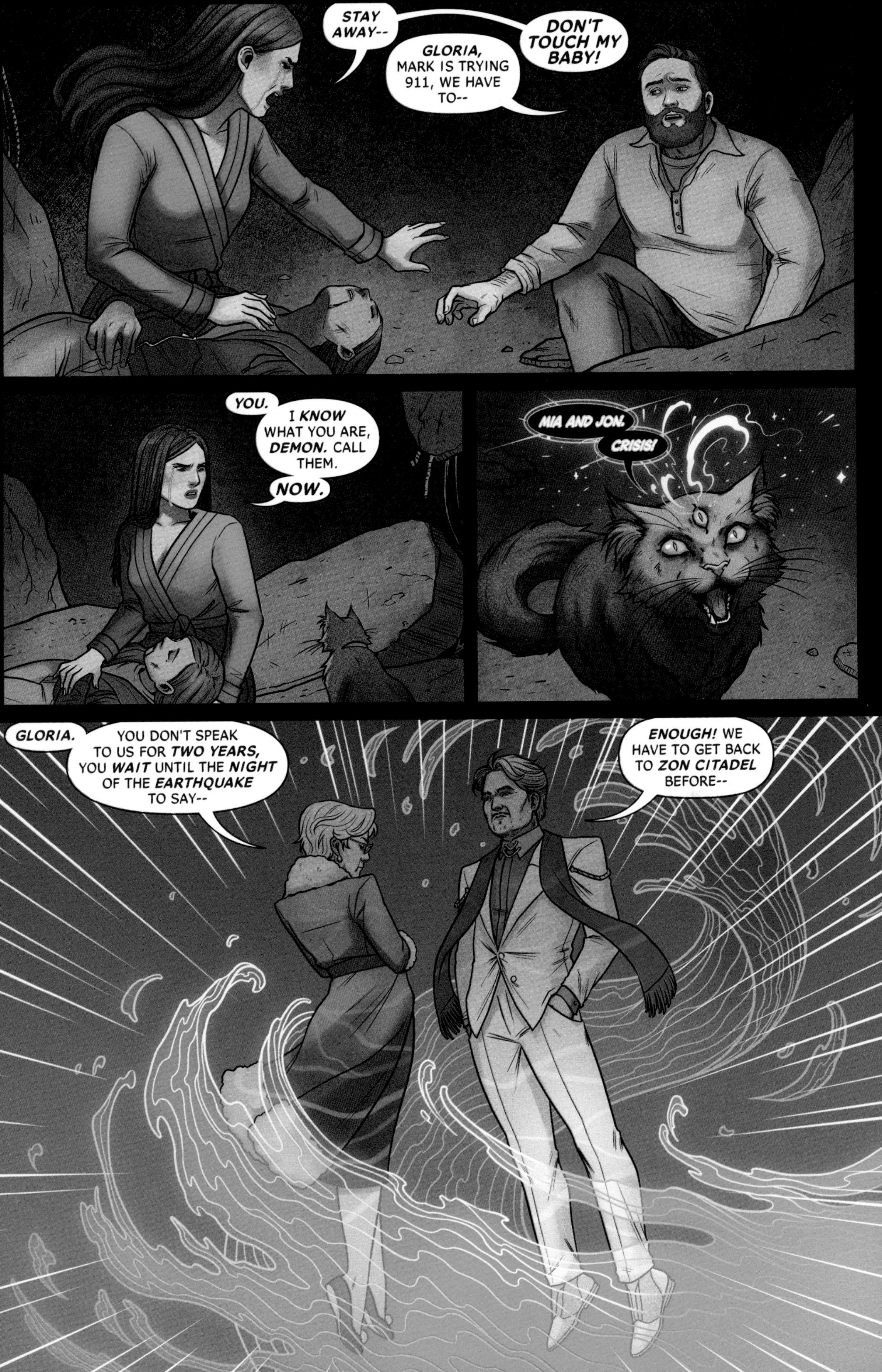
STAY AWAY--
GLORIA, MARK IS TRYING 911, WE HAVE TO--
DON'T TOUCH MY BABY!
YOU.
I KNOW WHAT YOU ARE, DEMON. CALL THEM.
NOW.
MIA AND JON.
CRISIS!
GLORIA.
YOU DON'T SPEAK TO US FOR TWO YEARS, YOU WAIT UNTIL THE NIGHT OF THE EARTHQUAKE TO SAY--
ENOUGH! WE HAVE TO GET BACK TO ZON CITADEL BEFORE--

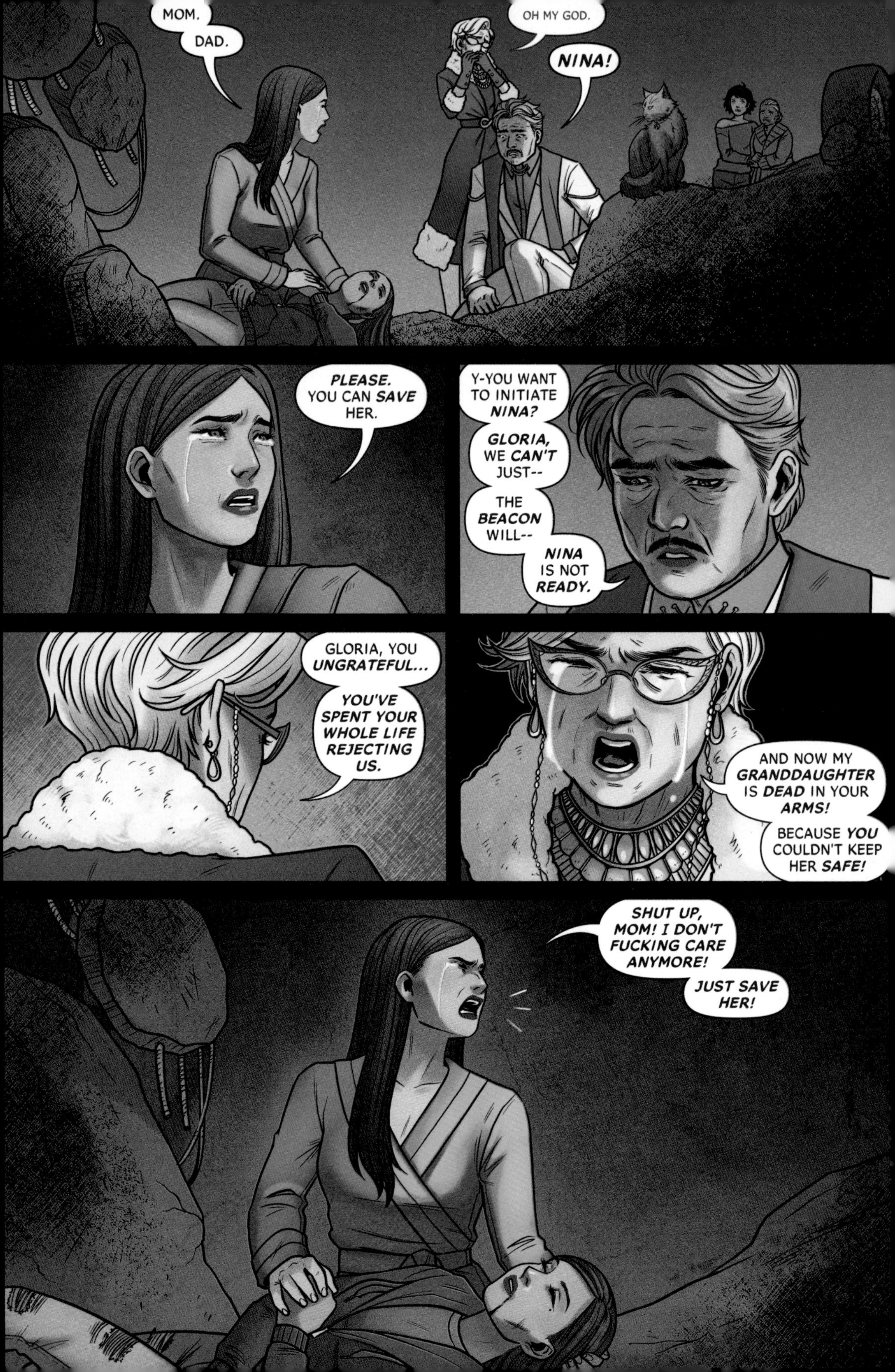
MOM.
DAD.
OH MY GOD.
NINA!
PLEASE. YOU CAN SAVE HER.
Y-YOU WANT TO INITIATE NINA?
GLORIA, WE CAN'T JUST--
THE BEACON WILL--
NINA IS NOT READY.
GLORIA, YOU UNGRATEFUL...
YOU'VE SPENT YOUR WHOLE LIFE REJECTING US.
AND NOW MY GRANDDAUGHTER IS DEAD IN YOUR ARMS!
BECAUSE YOU COULDN'T KEEP HER SAFE!
SHUT UP, MOM! I DON'T FUCKING CARE ANYMORE!
JUST SAVE HER!

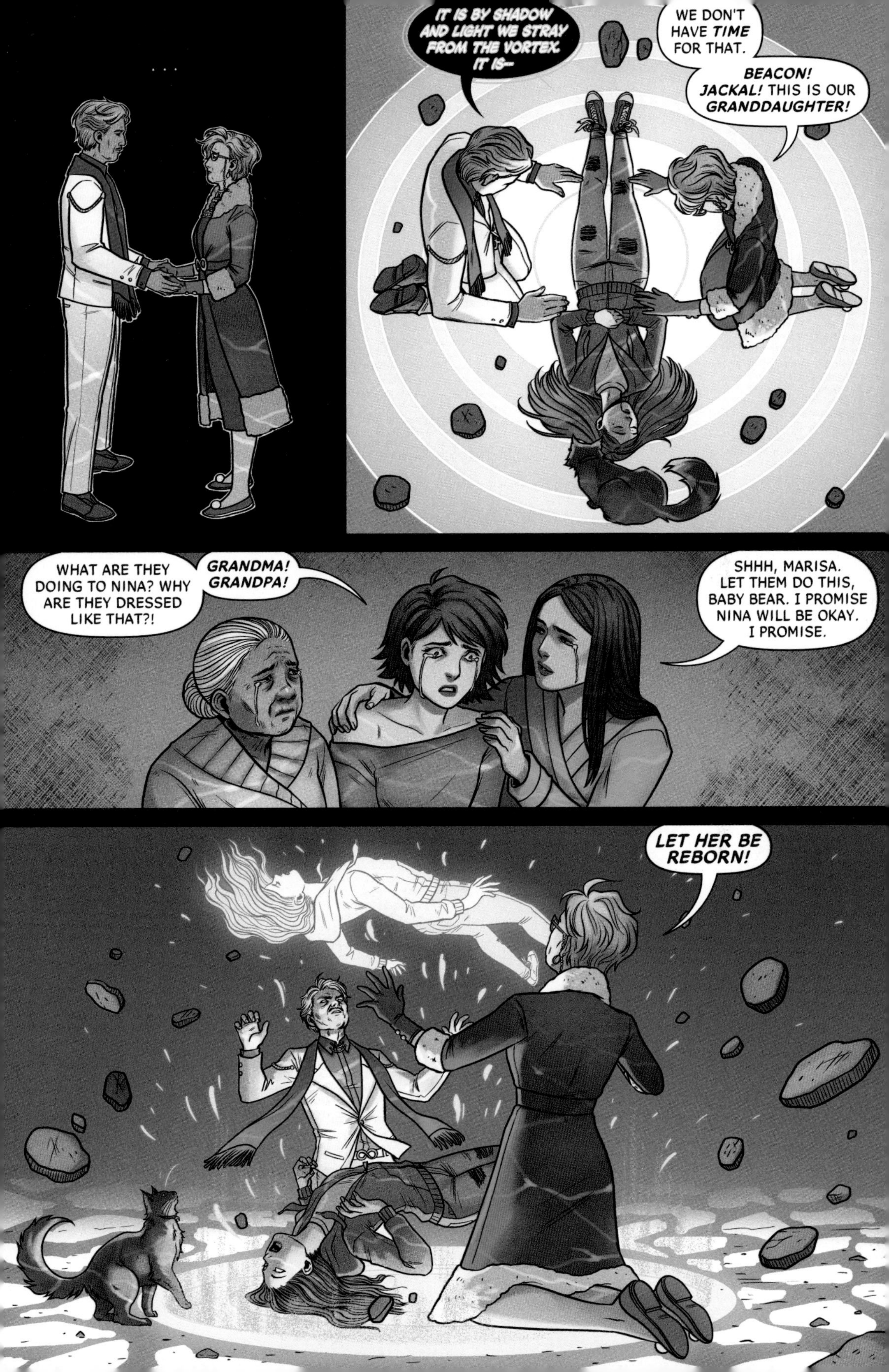
...
IT IS BY SHADOW AND LIGHT WE STRAY FROM THE VORTEX. IT IS--
WE DON'T HAVE *TIME* FOR THAT.
BEACON! JACKAL! THIS IS OUR ***GRANDDAUGHTER!***
WHAT ARE THEY DOING TO NINA? WHY ARE THEY DRESSED LIKE THAT?!
GRANDMA! GRANDPA!
SHHH, MARISA. LET THEM DO THIS, BABY BEAR. I PROMISE NINA WILL BE OKAY. I PROMISE.
LET HER BE REBORN!

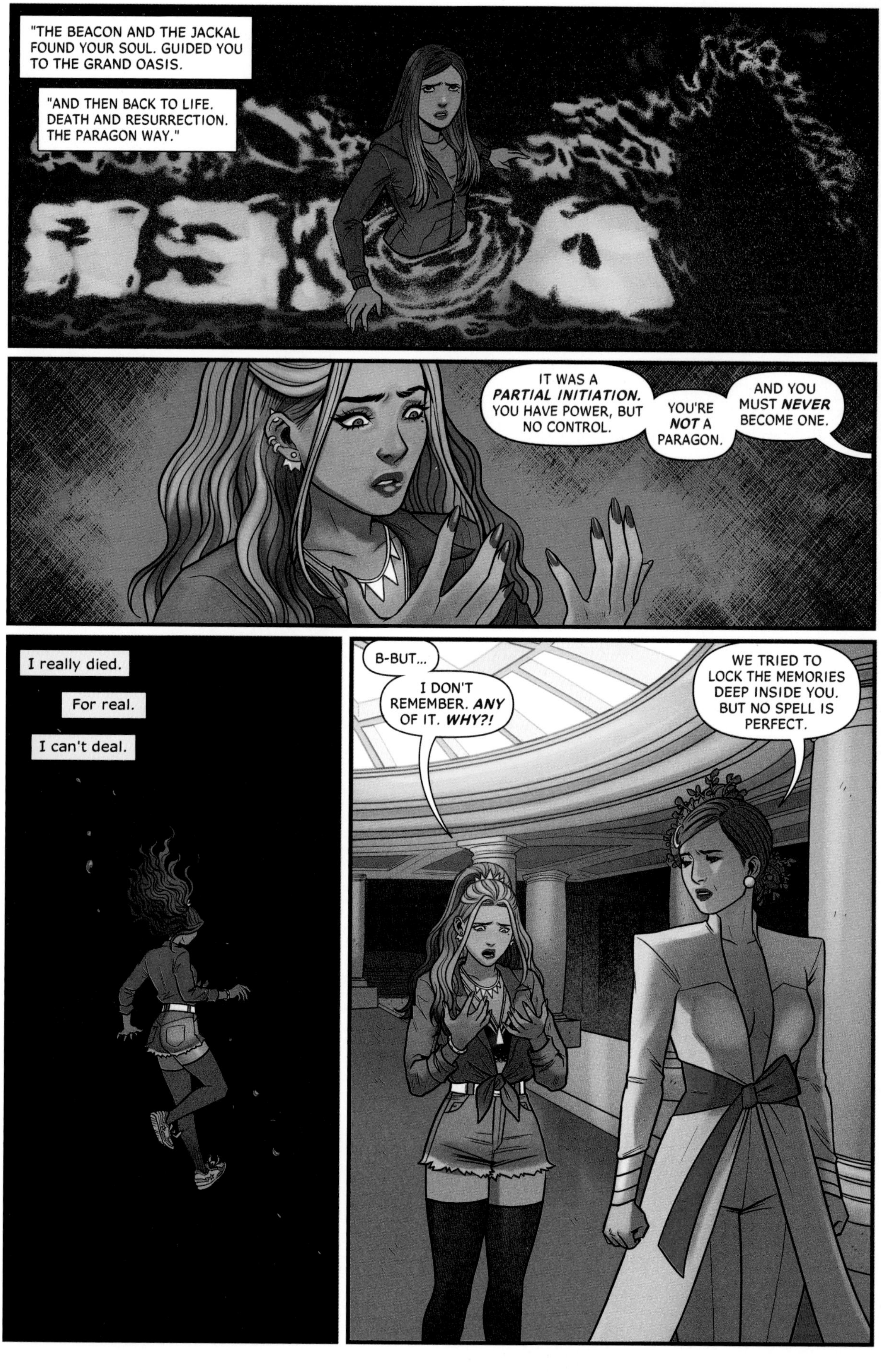
"THE BEACON AND THE JACKAL FOUND YOUR SOUL. GUIDED YOU TO THE GRAND OASIS.
"AND THEN BACK TO LIFE. DEATH AND RESURRECTION. THE PARAGON WAY."
IT WAS A PARTIAL INITIATION. YOU HAVE POWER, BUT NO CONTROL.
YOU'RE NOT A PARAGON.
AND YOU MUST NEVER BECOME ONE.
I really died.
For real.
I can't deal.
B-BUT...
I DON'T REMEMBER. ANY OF IT. WHY?!
WE TRIED TO LOCK THE MEMORIES DEEP INSIDE YOU. BUT NO SPELL IS PERFECT.

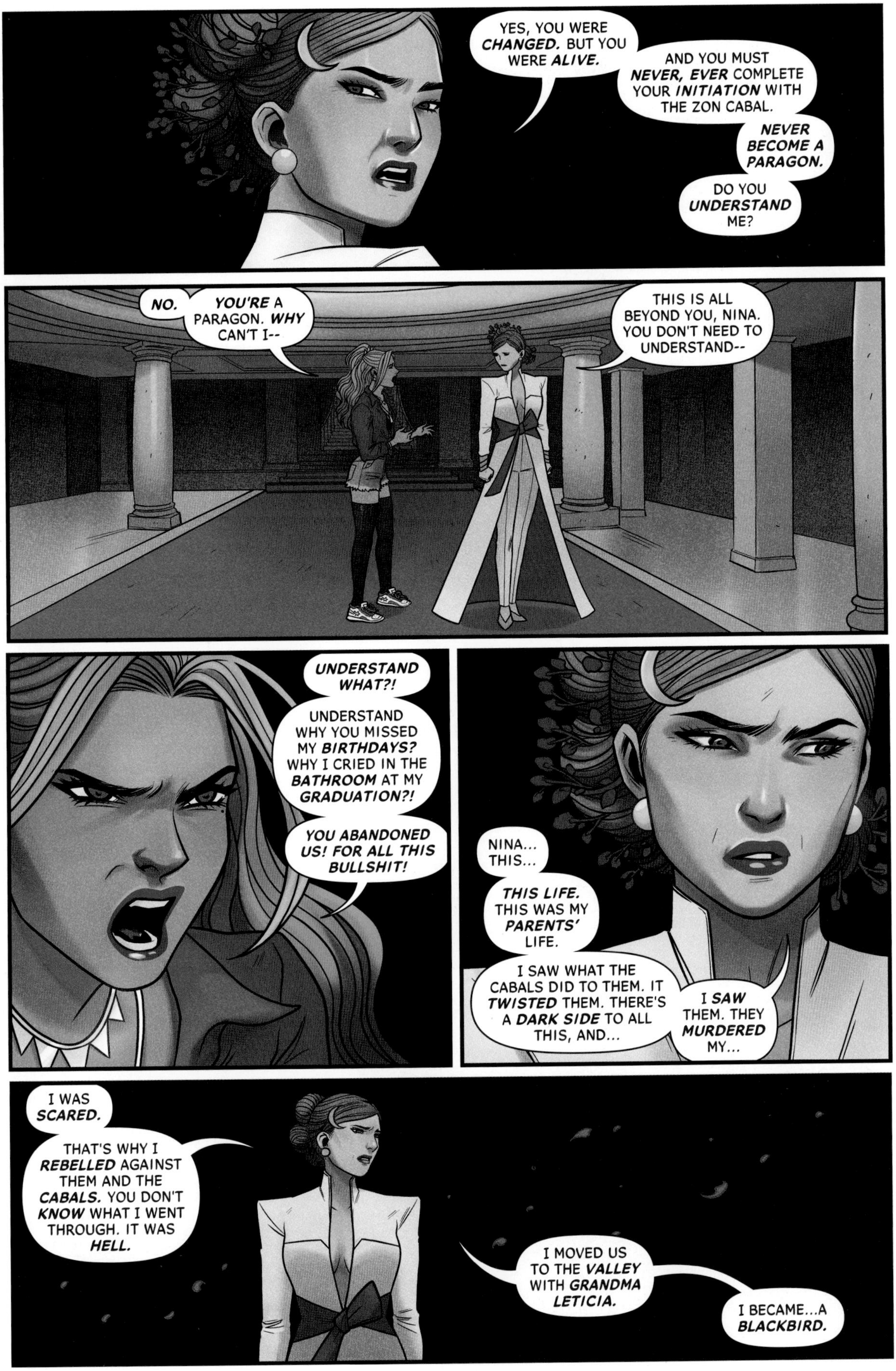
YES, YOU WERE CHANGED. BUT YOU WERE ALIVE.
AND YOU MUST NEVER, EVER COMPLETE YOUR INITIATION WITH THE ZON CABAL.
NEVER BECOME A PARAGON.
DO YOU UNDERSTAND ME?
NO.
YOU'RE A PARAGON. WHY CAN'T I--
THIS IS ALL BEYOND YOU, NINA. YOU DON'T NEED TO UNDERSTAND--
UNDERSTAND WHAT?!
UNDERSTAND WHY YOU MISSED MY BIRTHDAYS? WHY I CRIED IN THE BATHROOM AT MY GRADUATION?!
YOU ABANDONED US! FOR ALL THIS BULLSHIT!
NINA... THIS...
THIS LIFE. THIS WAS MY PARENTS' LIFE.
I SAW WHAT THE CABALS DID TO THEM. IT TWISTED THEM. THERE'S A DARK SIDE TO ALL THIS, AND...
I SAW THEM. THEY MURDERED MY...
I WAS SCARED.
THAT'S WHY I REBELLED AGAINST THEM AND THE CABALS. YOU DON'T KNOW WHAT I WENT THROUGH. IT WAS HELL.
I MOVED US TO THE VALLEY WITH GRANDMA LETICIA.
I BECAME...A BLACKBIRD.

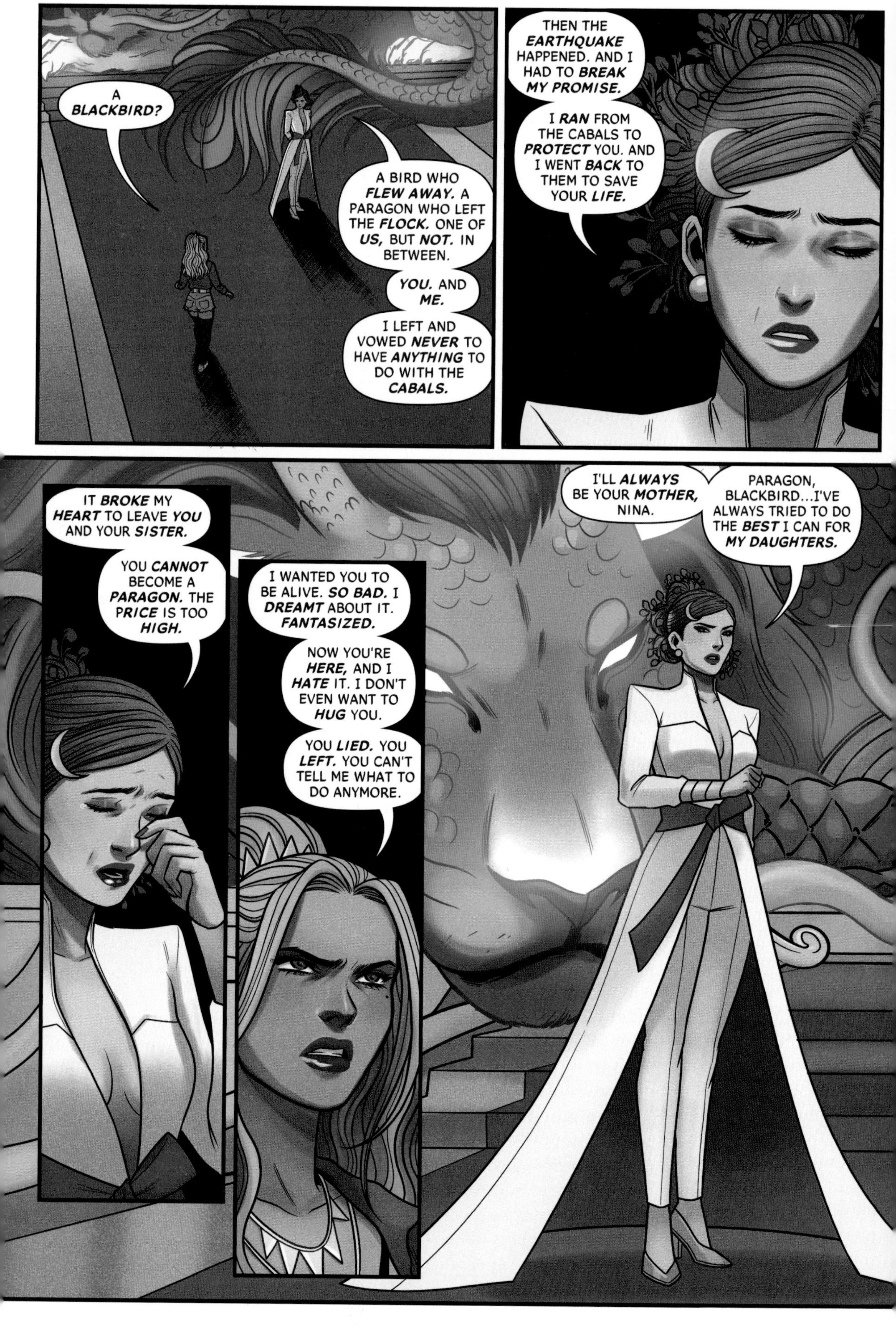
A *BLACKBIRD?*
A BIRD WHO *FLEW AWAY.* A PARAGON WHO LEFT THE *FLOCK.* ONE OF *US,* BUT *NOT.* IN BETWEEN.
YOU. AND *ME.*
I LEFT AND VOWED *NEVER* TO HAVE *ANYTHING* TO DO WITH THE *CABALS.*
THEN THE *EARTHQUAKE* HAPPENED. AND I HAD TO *BREAK MY PROMISE.*
I *RAN* FROM THE CABALS TO *PROTECT* YOU. AND I WENT *BACK* TO THEM TO SAVE YOUR *LIFE.*
IT *BROKE* MY *HEART* TO LEAVE *YOU* AND YOUR *SISTER.*
YOU *CANNOT* BECOME A *PARAGON.* THE *PRICE* IS TOO *HIGH.*
I WANTED YOU TO BE ALIVE. *SO BAD.* I *DREAMT* ABOUT IT. *FANTASIZED.*
NOW YOU'RE *HERE,* AND I *HATE* IT. I DON'T EVEN WANT TO *HUG* YOU.
YOU *LIED.* YOU *LEFT.* YOU CAN'T TELL ME WHAT TO DO ANYMORE.
I'LL *ALWAYS* BE YOUR *MOTHER,* NINA.
PARAGON, BLACKBIRD...I'VE ALWAYS TRIED TO DO THE *BEST* I CAN FOR *MY DAUGHTERS.*

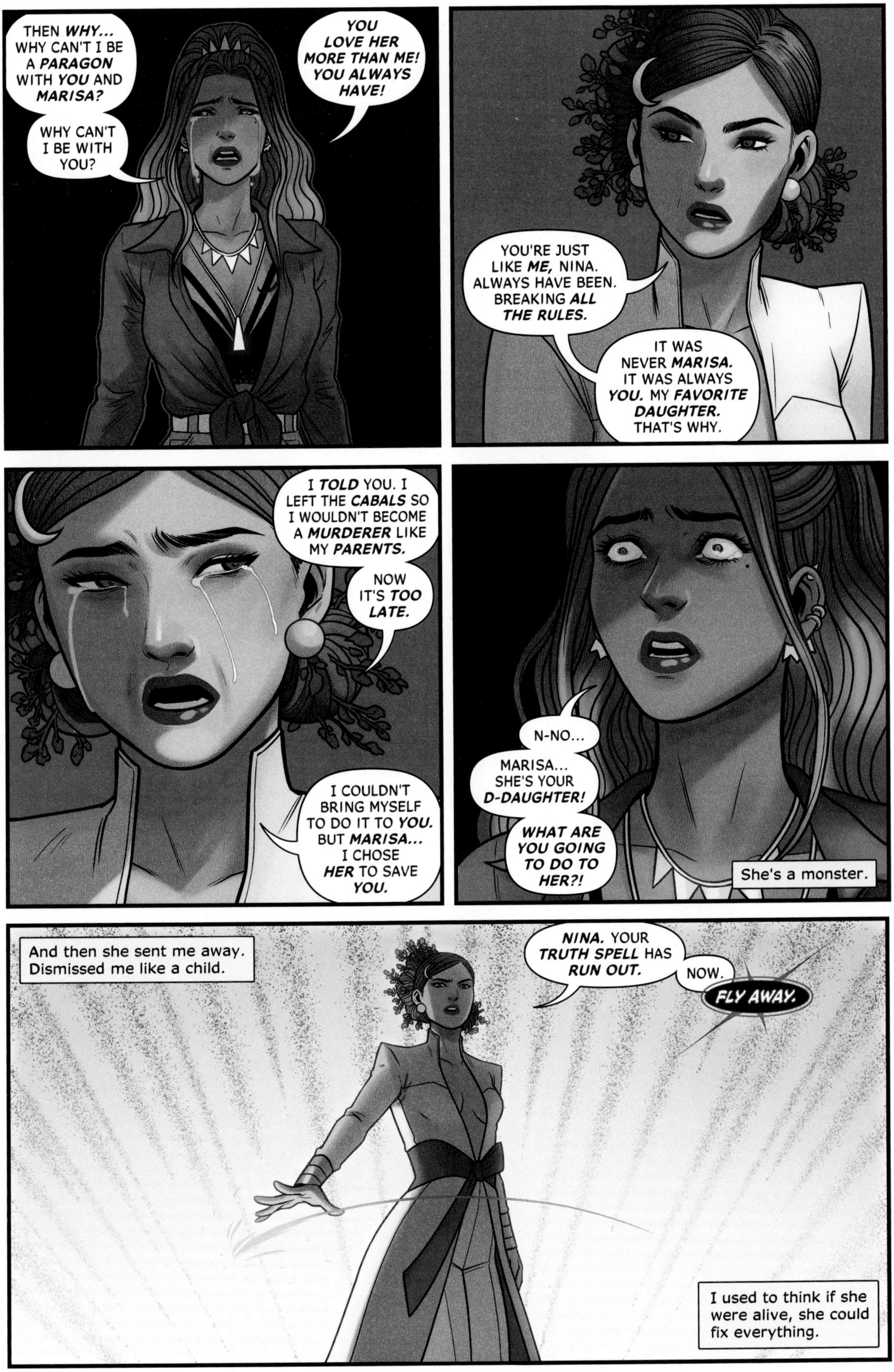
THEN *WHY...* WHY CAN'T I BE A *PARAGON* WITH *YOU* AND *MARISA?*
WHY CAN'T I BE WITH YOU?
YOU LOVE HER MORE THAN ME! YOU ALWAYS HAVE!
YOU'RE JUST LIKE *ME,* NINA. ALWAYS HAVE BEEN. BREAKING *ALL THE RULES.*
IT WAS NEVER *MARISA.* IT WAS ALWAYS *YOU.* MY *FAVORITE DAUGHTER.* THAT'S WHY.
I *TOLD* YOU. I LEFT THE *CABALS* SO I WOULDN'T BECOME A *MURDERER* LIKE MY *PARENTS.*
NOW IT'S *TOO LATE.*
I COULDN'T BRING MYSELF TO DO IT TO *YOU.* BUT *MARISA...* I CHOSE *HER* TO SAVE *YOU.*
N-NO...
MARISA... SHE'S YOUR *D-DAUGHTER!*
WHAT ARE YOU GOING TO DO TO HER?!
She's a monster.
And then she sent me away. Dismissed me like a child.
NINA. YOUR *TRUTH SPELL* HAS *RUN OUT.*
NOW.
FLY AWAY.
I used to think if she were alive, she could fix everything.

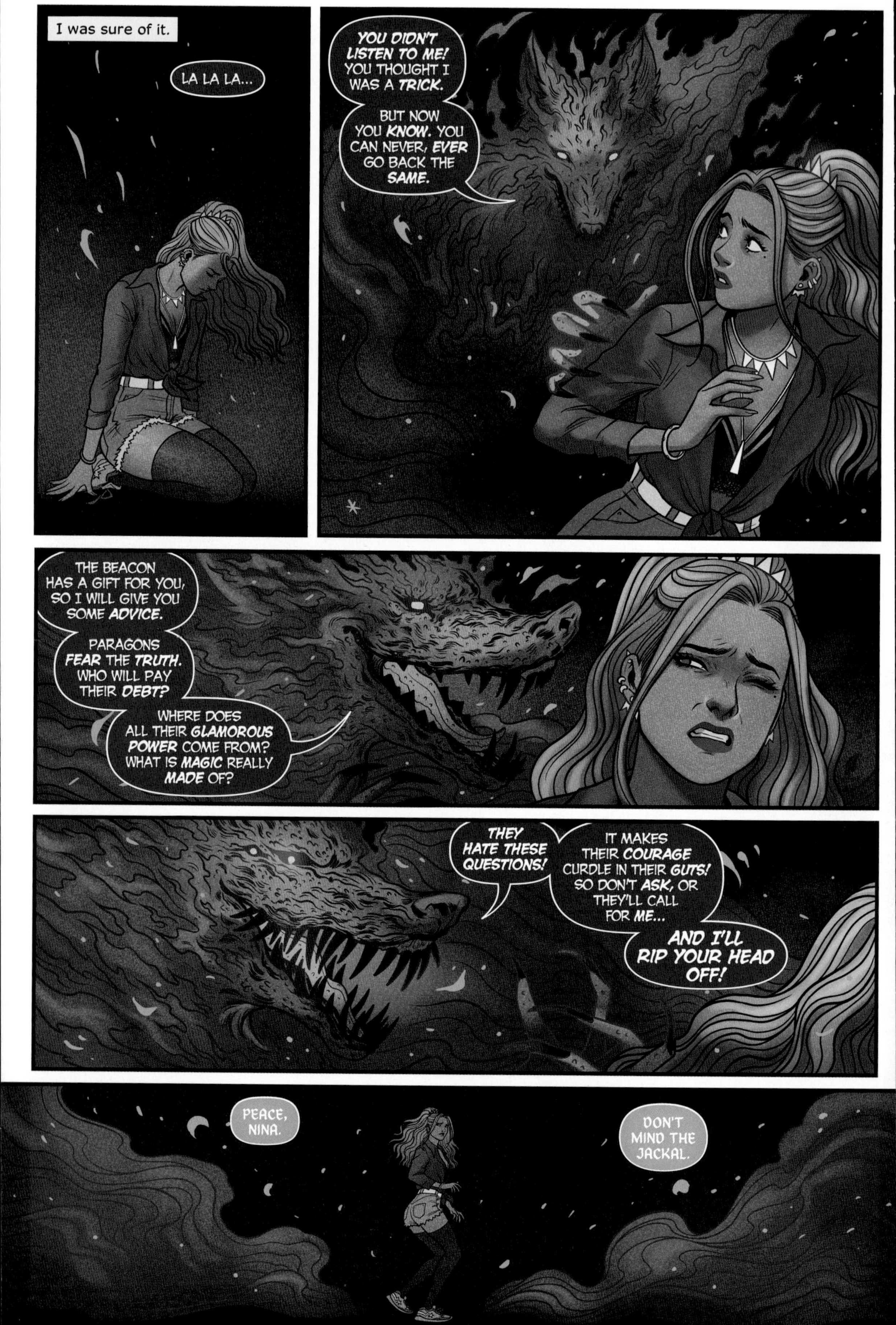
I was sure of it.
LA LA LA...
YOU DIDN'T LISTEN TO ME! YOU THOUGHT I WAS A TRICK.
BUT NOW YOU KNOW. YOU CAN NEVER, EVER GO BACK THE SAME.
THE BEACON HAS A GIFT FOR YOU, SO I WILL GIVE YOU SOME ADVICE.
PARAGONS FEAR THE TRUTH. WHO WILL PAY THEIR DEBT?
WHERE DOES ALL THEIR GLAMOROUS POWER COME FROM? WHAT IS MAGIC REALLY MADE OF?
THEY HATE THESE QUESTIONS!
IT MAKES THEIR COURAGE CURDLE IN THEIR GUTS! SO DON'T ASK, OR THEY'LL CALL FOR ME...
AND I'LL RIP YOUR HEAD OFF!
PEACE, NINA.
DON'T MIND THE JACKAL.

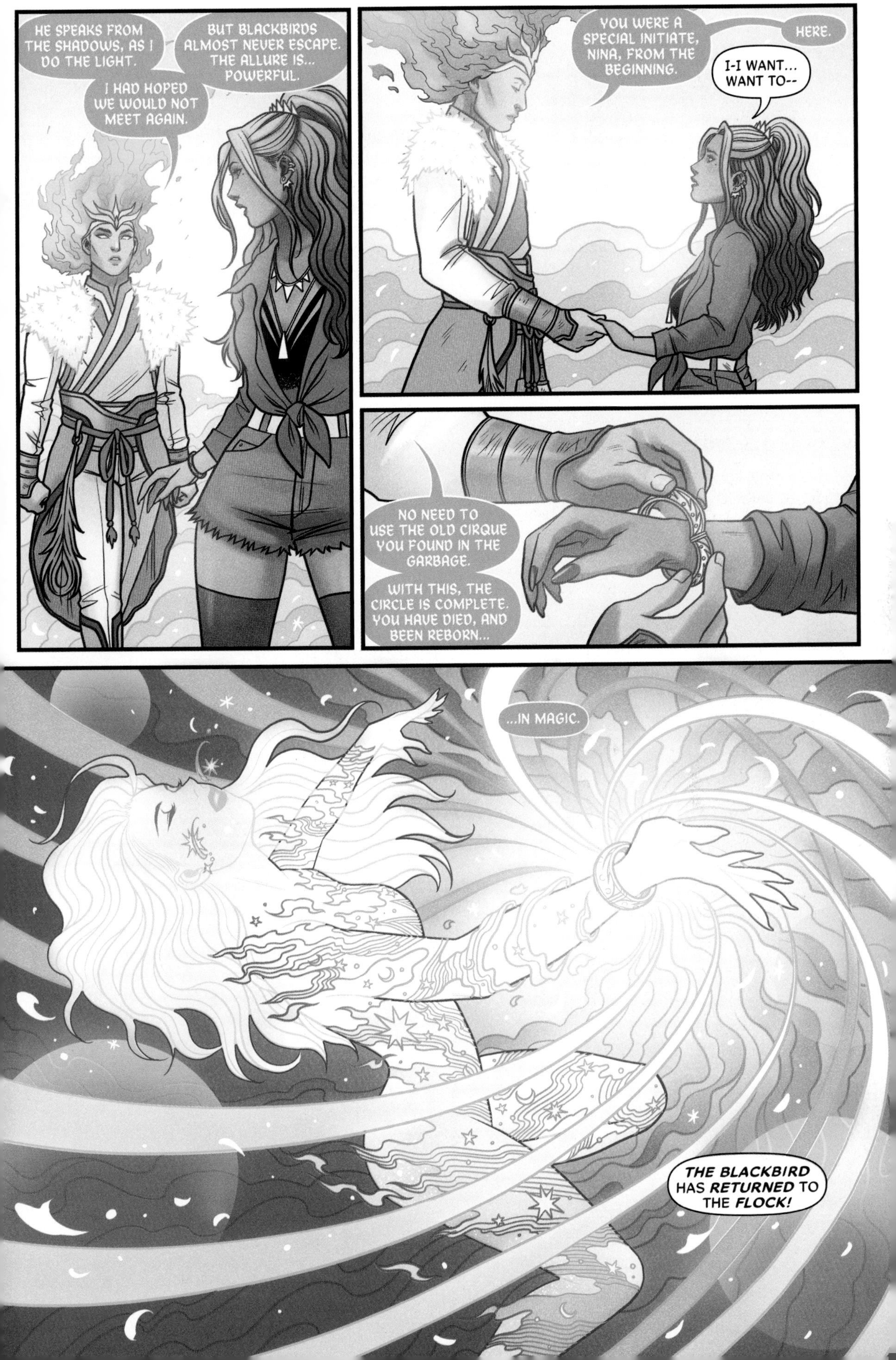
HE SPEAKS FROM THE SHADOWS, AS I DO THE LIGHT.
BUT BLACKBIRDS ALMOST NEVER ESCAPE. THE ALLURE IS... POWERFUL.
I HAD HOPED WE WOULD NOT MEET AGAIN.
YOU WERE A SPECIAL INITIATE, NINA, FROM THE BEGINNING.
HERE.
I-I WANT... WANT TO--
NO NEED TO USE THE OLD CIRQUE YOU FOUND IN THE GARBAGE.
WITH THIS, THE CIRCLE IS COMPLETE. YOU HAVE DIED, AND BEEN REBORN...
...IN MAGIC.
THE BLACKBIRD HAS RETURNED TO THE FLOCK!

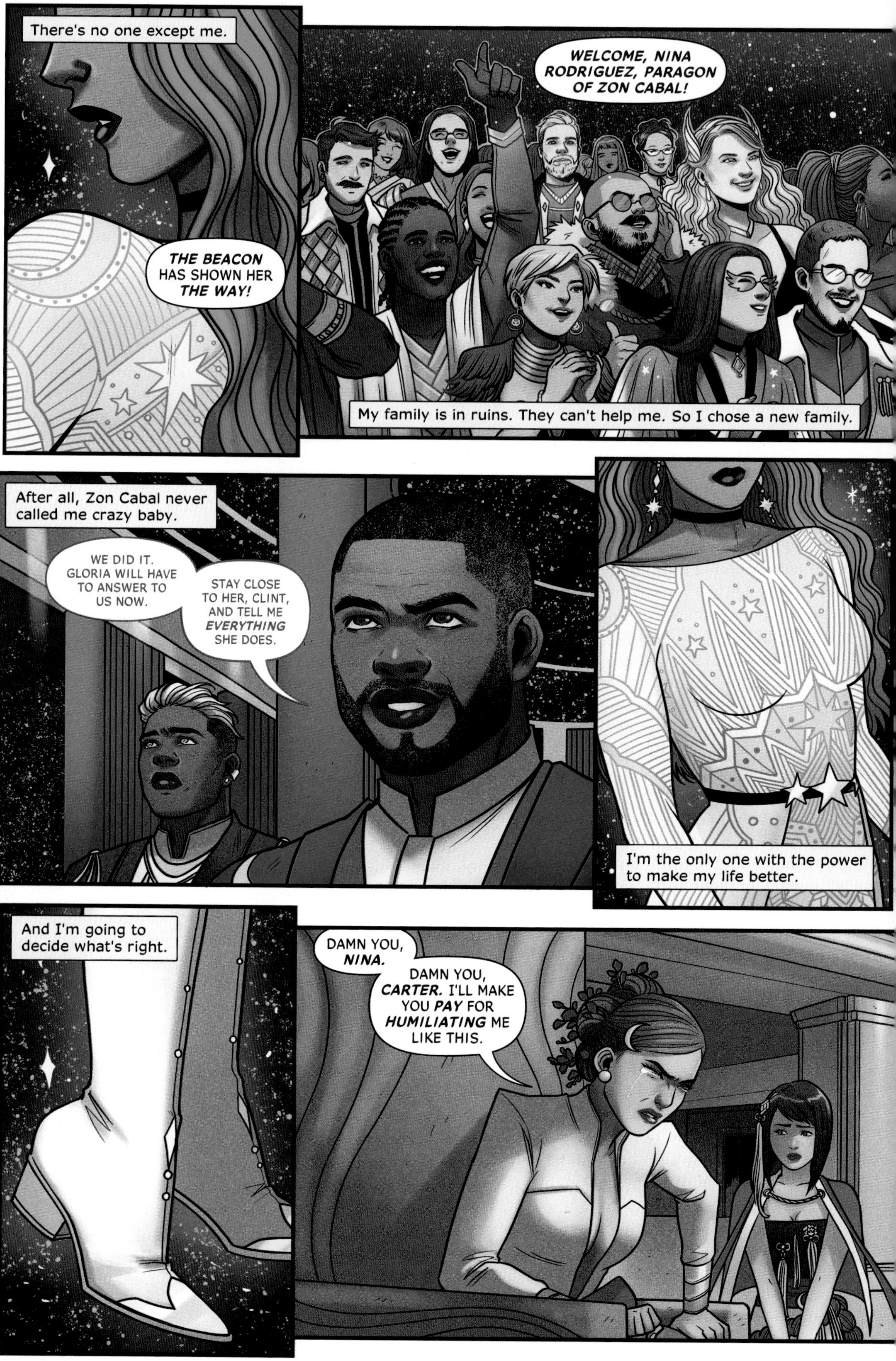

There's no one except me.
THE BEACON HAS SHOWN HER THE WAY!
WELCOME, NINA RODRIGUEZ, PARAGON OF ZON CABAL!
My family is in ruins. They can't help me. So I chose a new family.
After all, Zon Cabal never called me crazy baby.
WE DID IT. GLORIA WILL HAVE TO ANSWER TO US NOW.
STAY CLOSE TO HER, CLINT, AND TELL ME EVERYTHING SHE DOES.
I'm the only one with the power to make my life better.
And I'm going to decide what's right.
DAMN YOU, NINA.
DAMN YOU, CARTER. I'LL MAKE YOU PAY FOR HUMILIATING ME LIKE THIS.

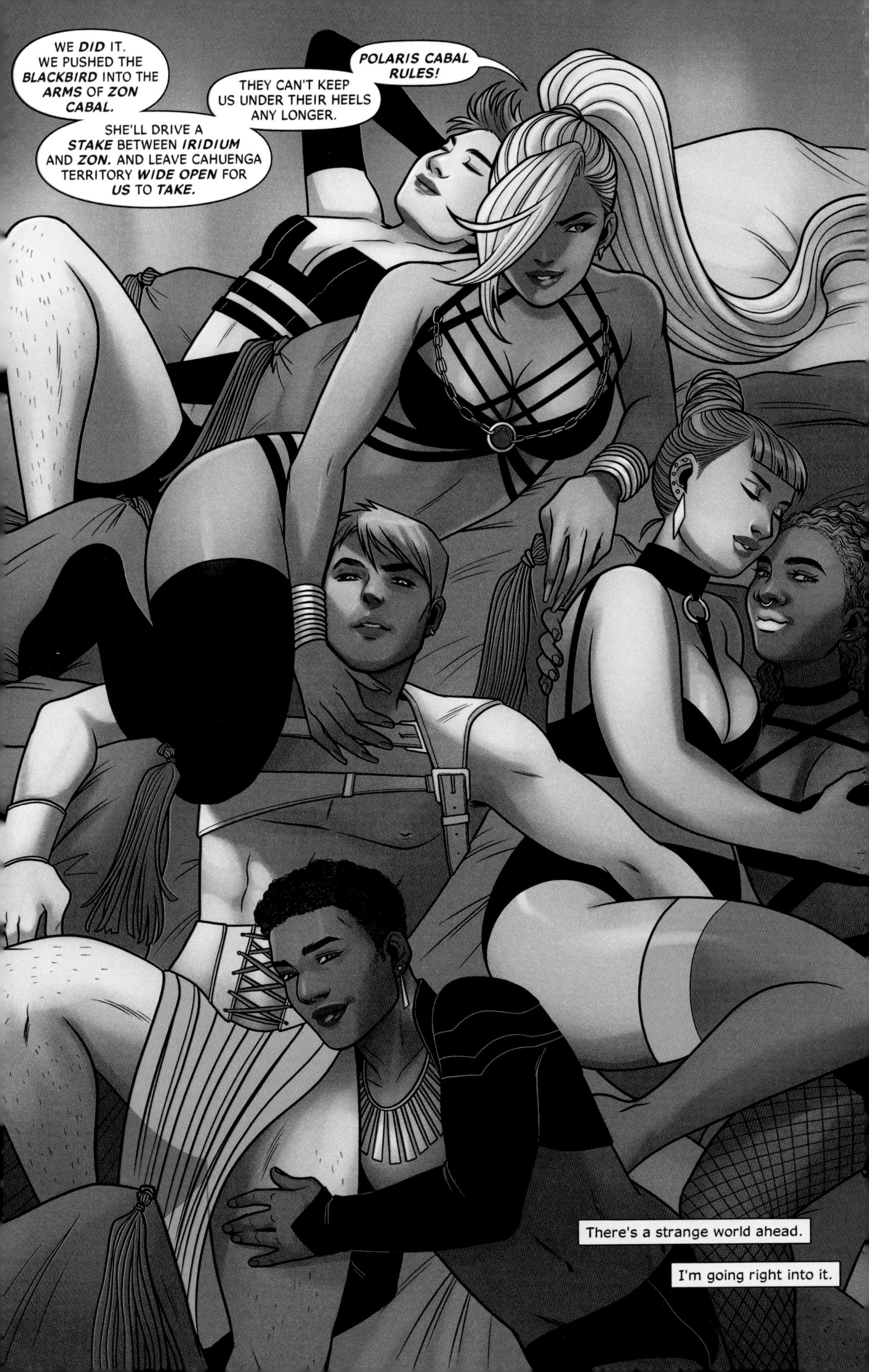

WE DID IT. WE PUSHED THE BLACKBIRD INTO THE ARMS OF ZON CABAL.
SHE'LL DRIVE A STAKE BETWEEN IRIDIUM AND ZON. AND LEAVE CAHUENGA TERRITORY WIDE OPEN FOR US TO TAKE.
THEY CAN'T KEEP US UNDER THEIR HEELS ANY LONGER.
POLARIS CABAL RULES!
There's a strange world ahead.
I'm going right into it.

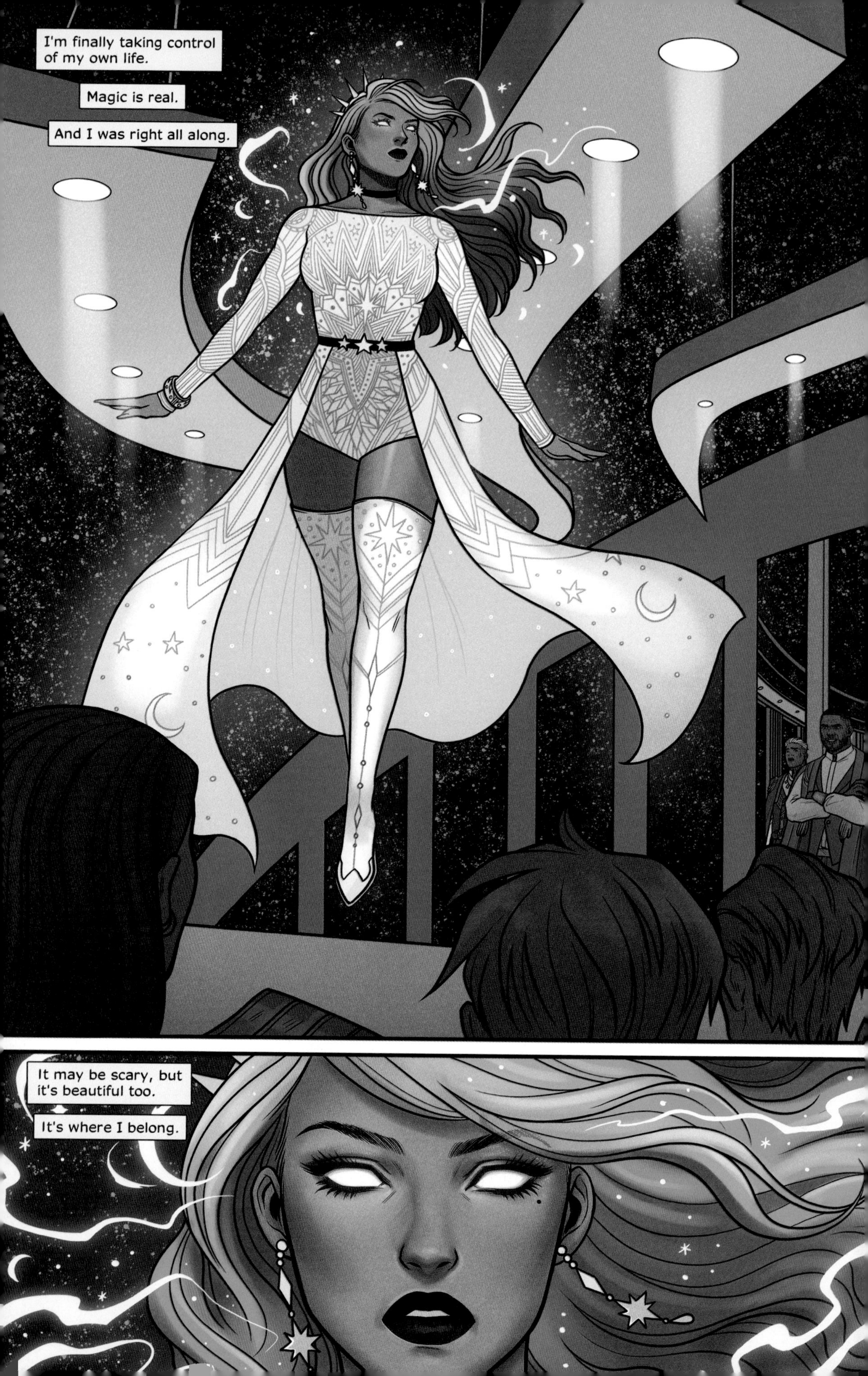
I'm finally taking control of my own life.
Magic is real.
And I was right all along.
It may be scary, but it's beautiful too.
It's where I belong.

VARIANT
COVER
GALLERY

FEATURING

FIONA STAPLES

MINGJUE HELEN CHEN

LOISH

MANDA SCHANK

SANA TAKEDA

JENNY FRISON

TULA LOTAY

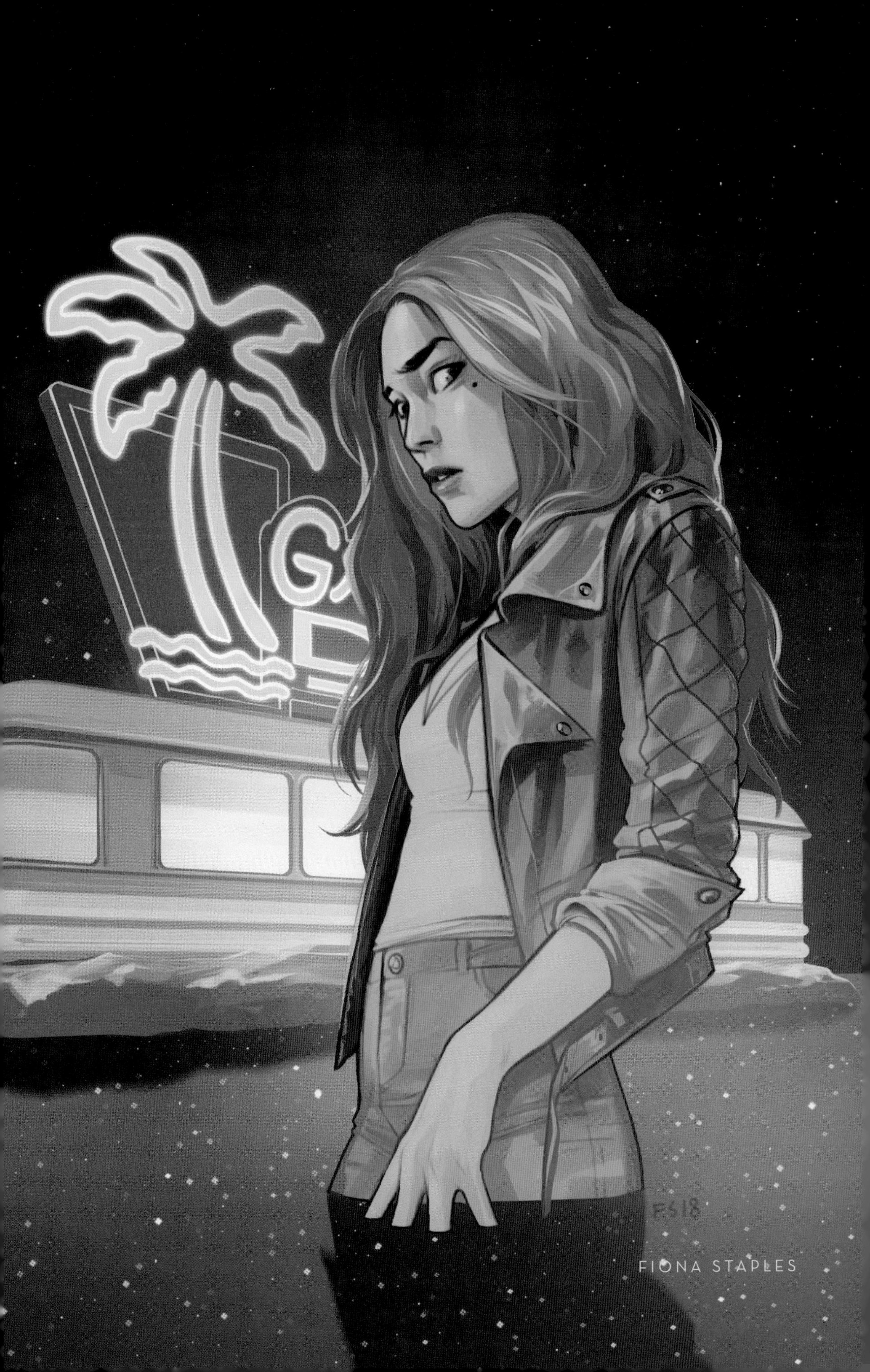

FIONA STAPLES

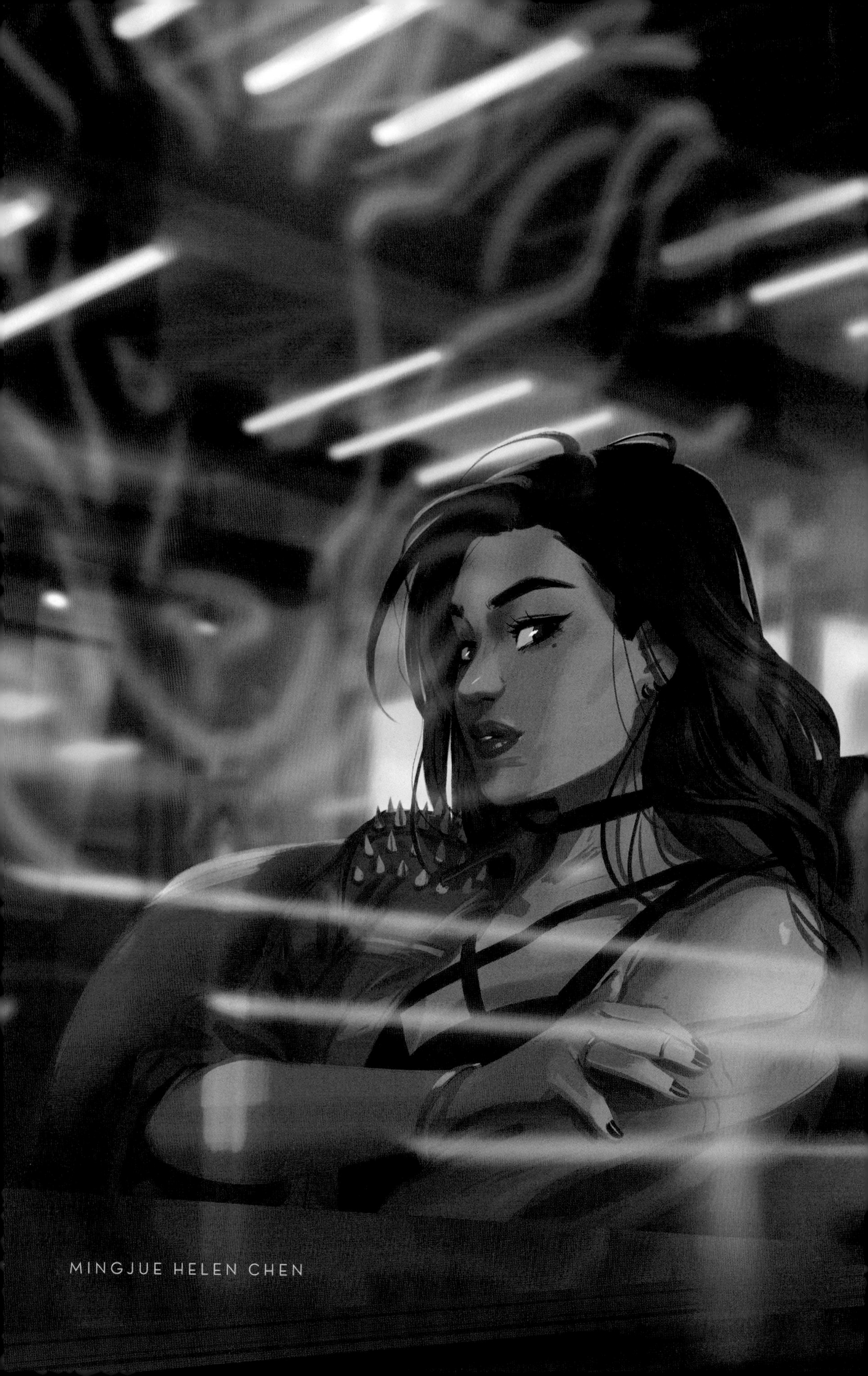

MINGJUE HELEN CHEN

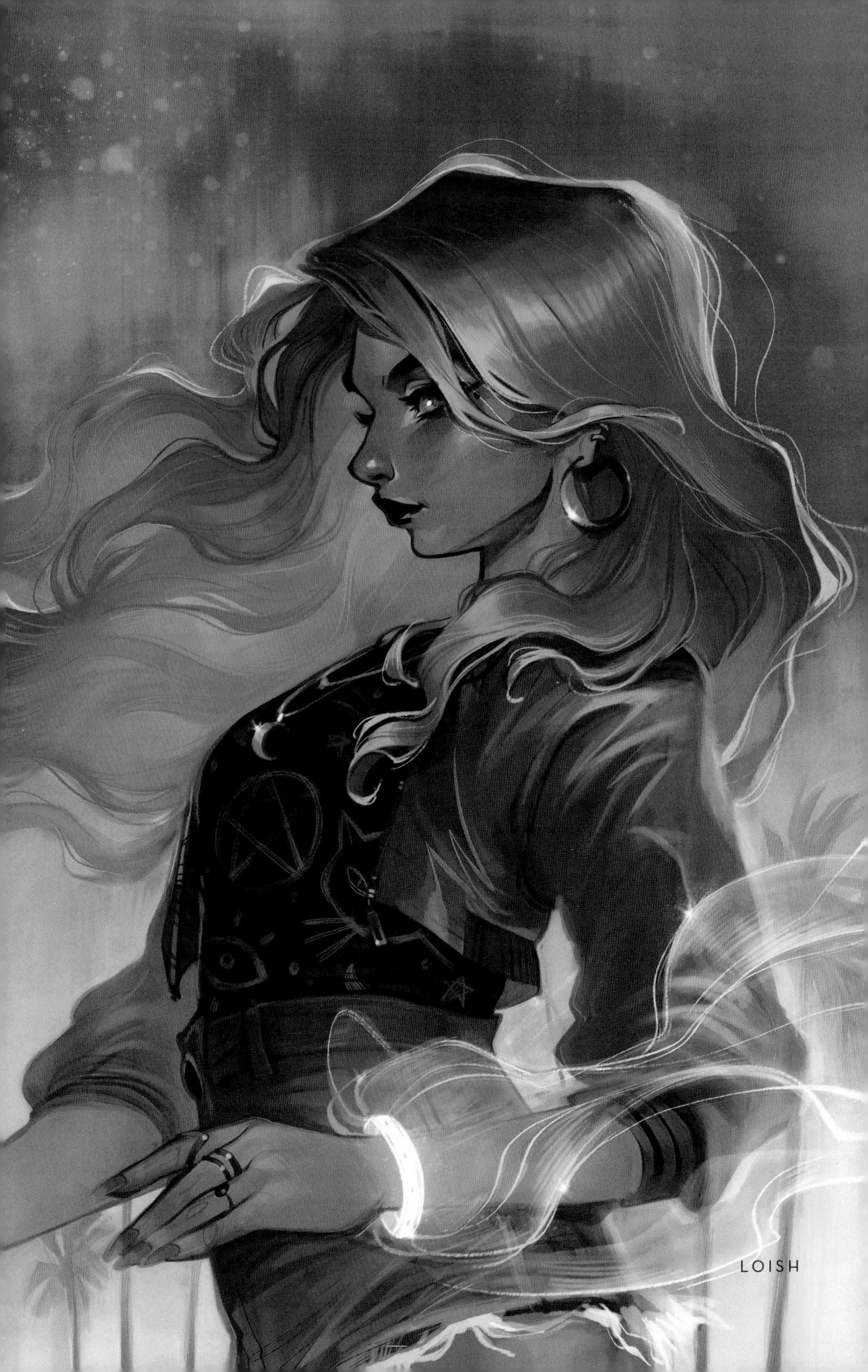
LOISH

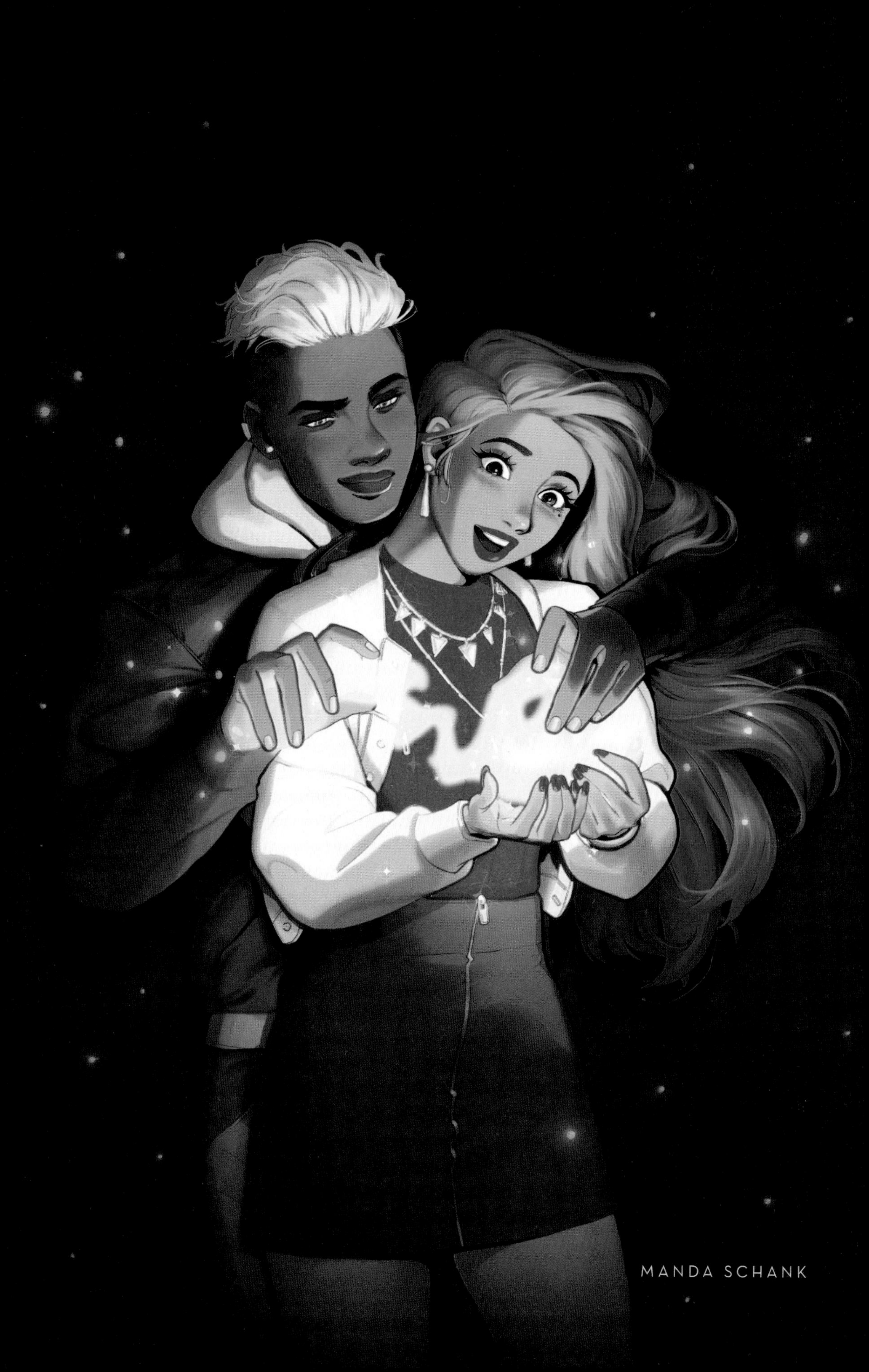
MANDA SCHANK

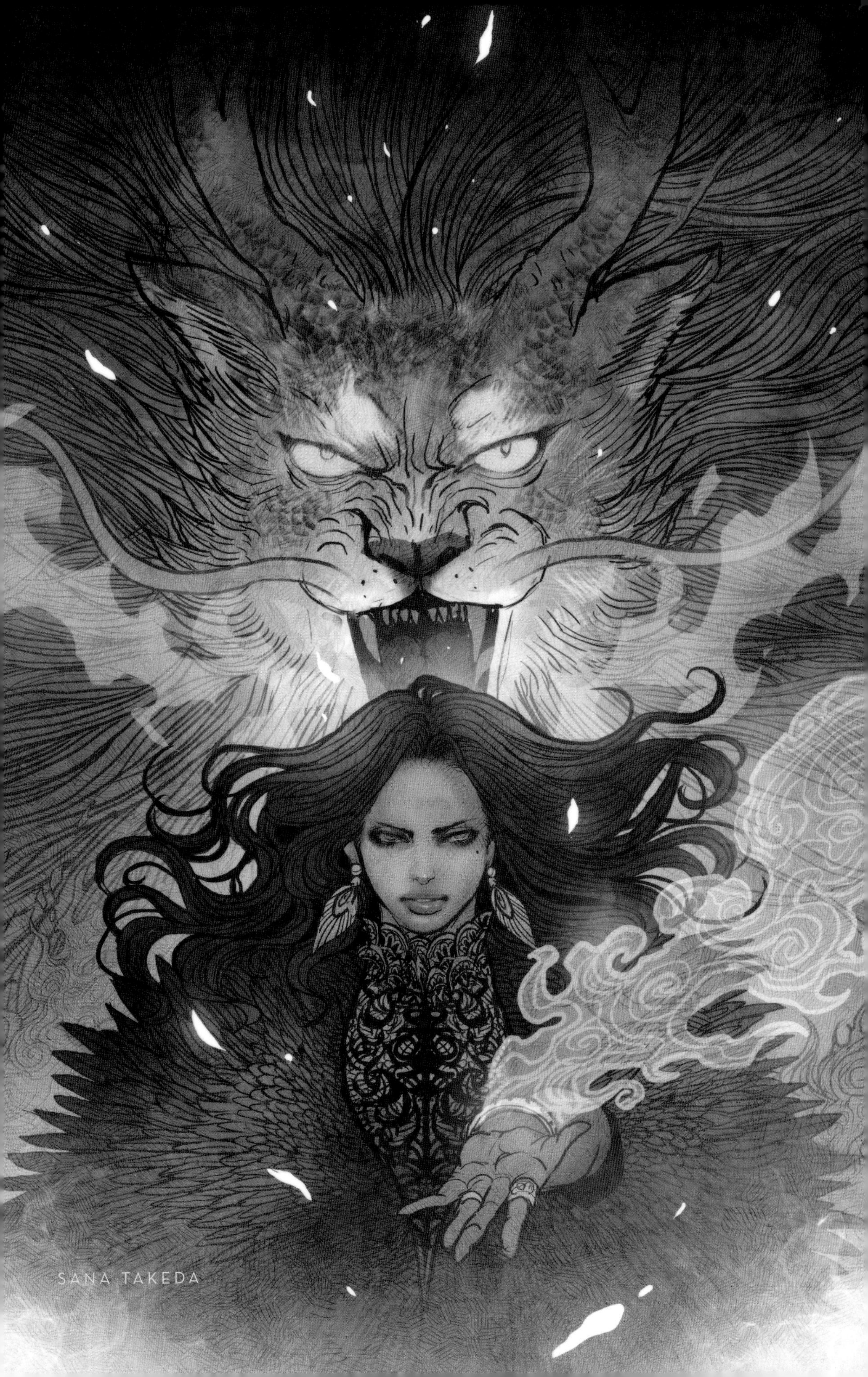
SANA TAKEDA

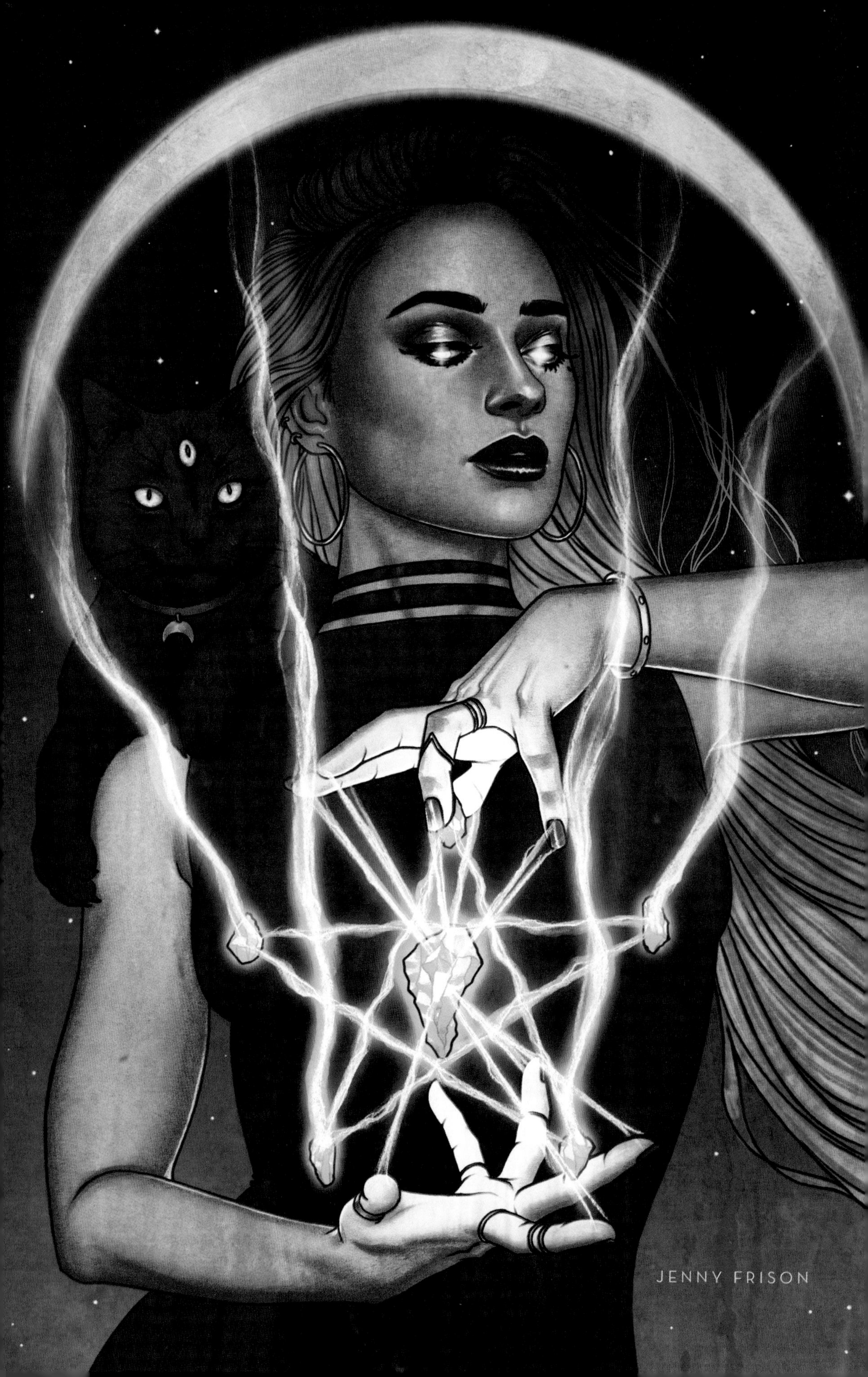
JENNY FRISON

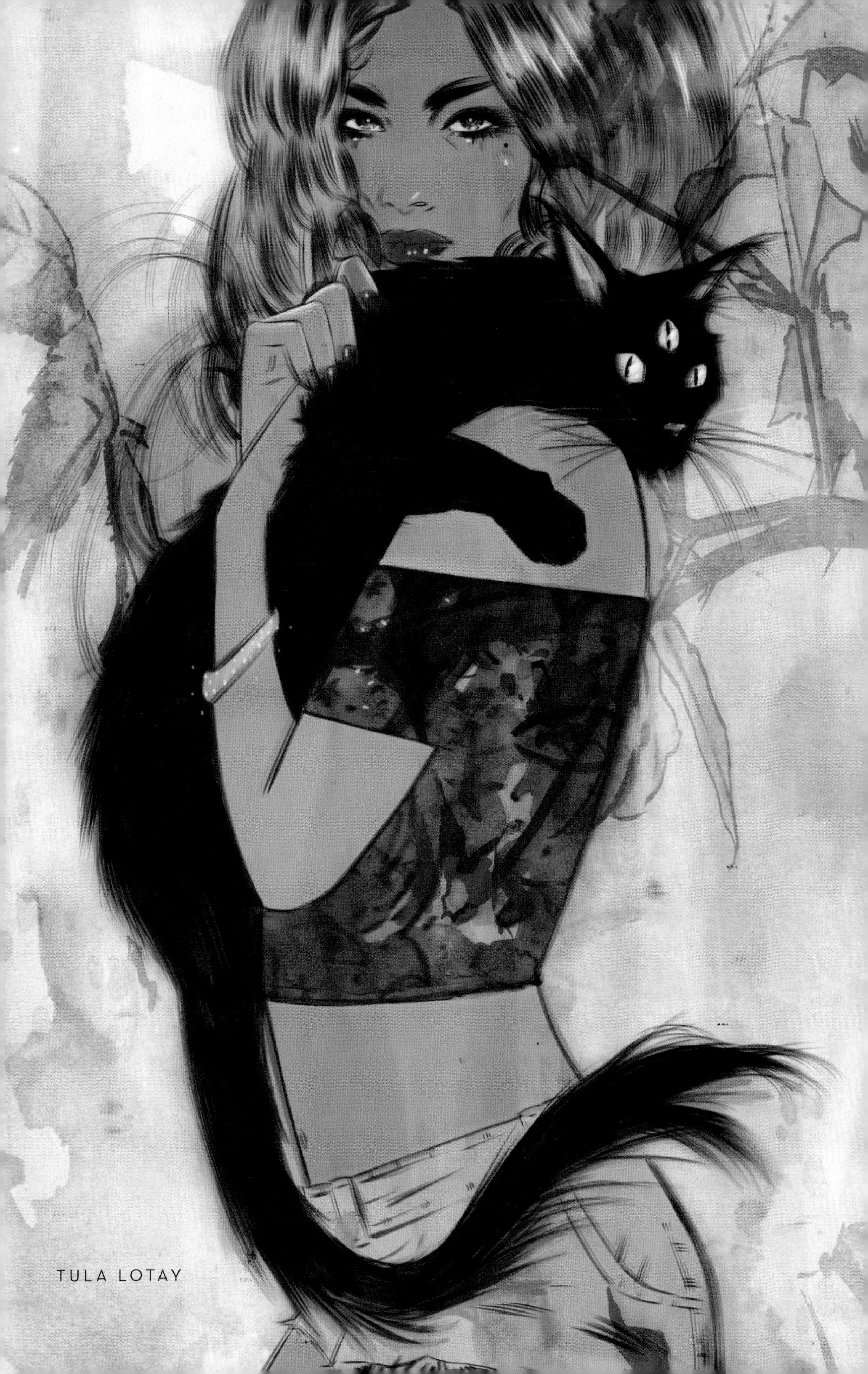

TULA LOTAY

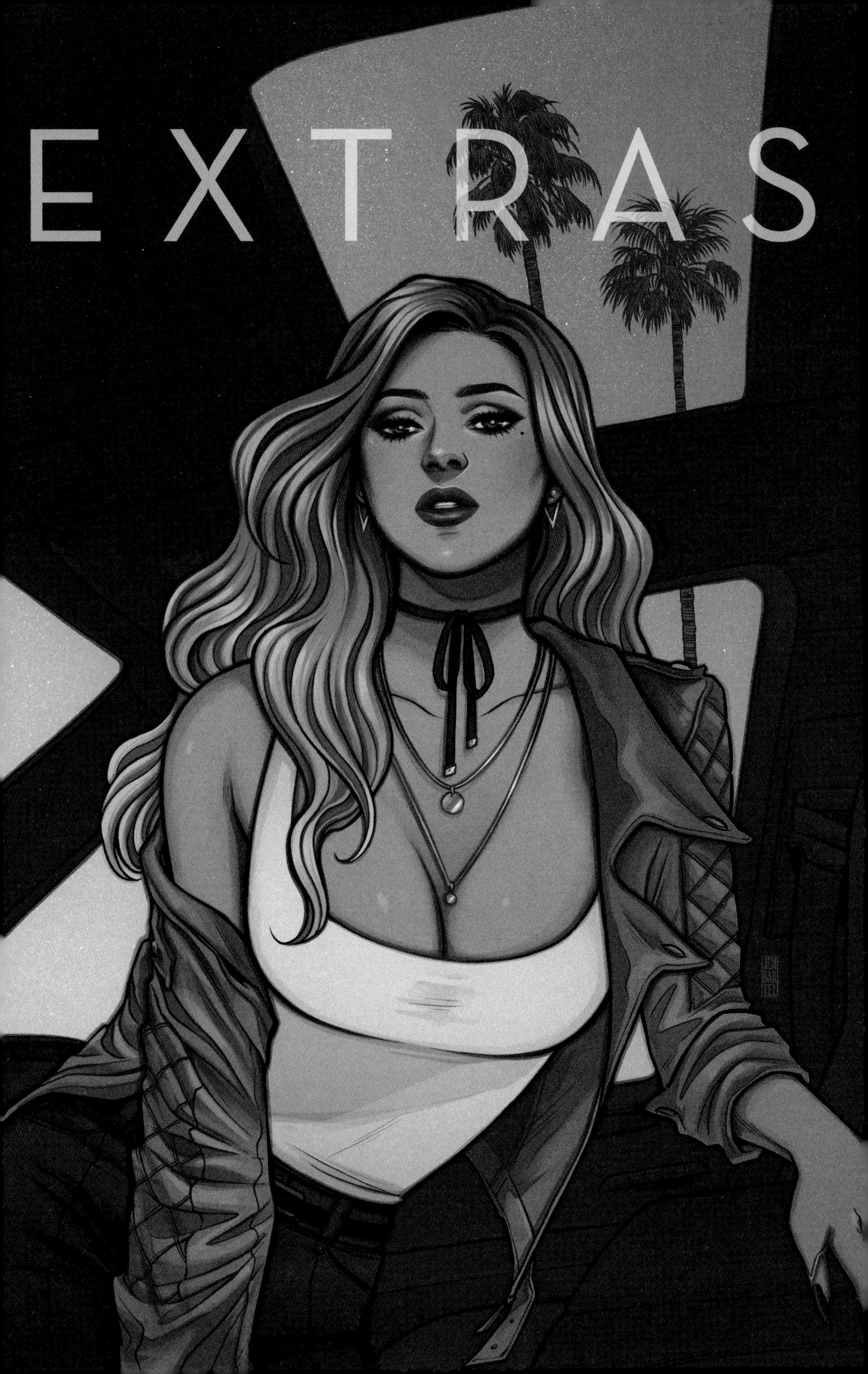
EXTRAS

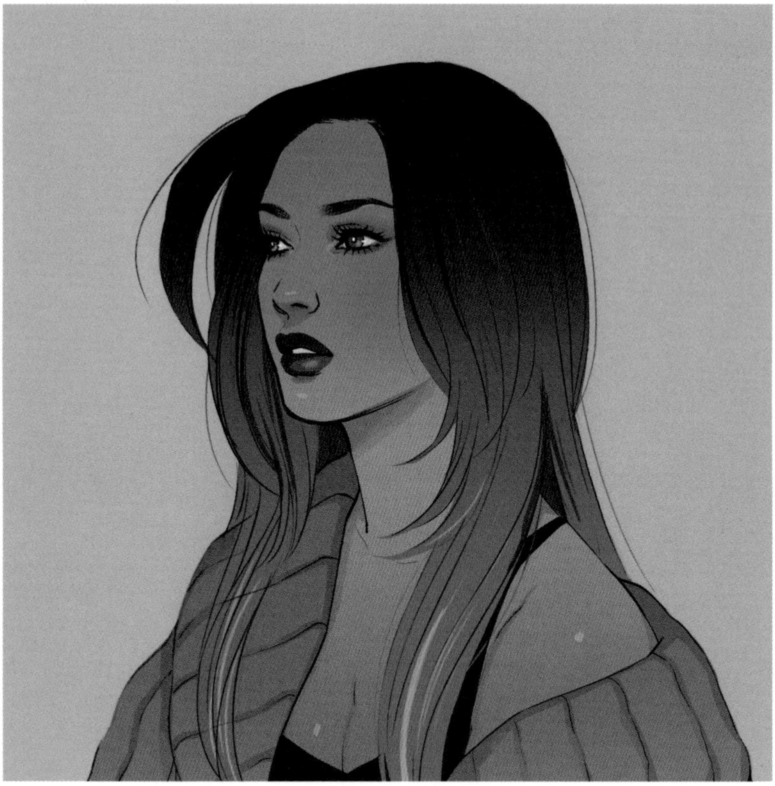

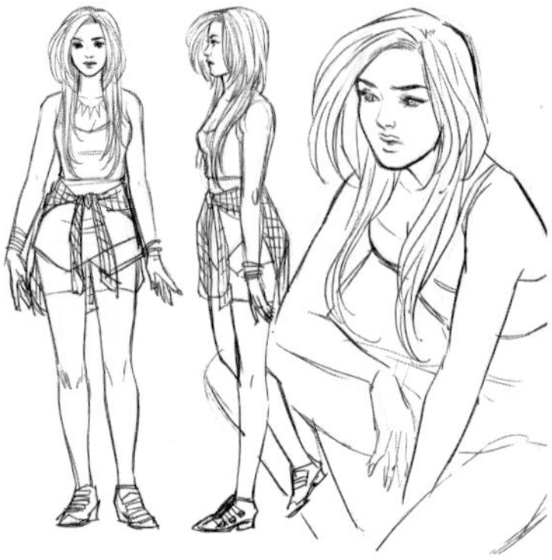

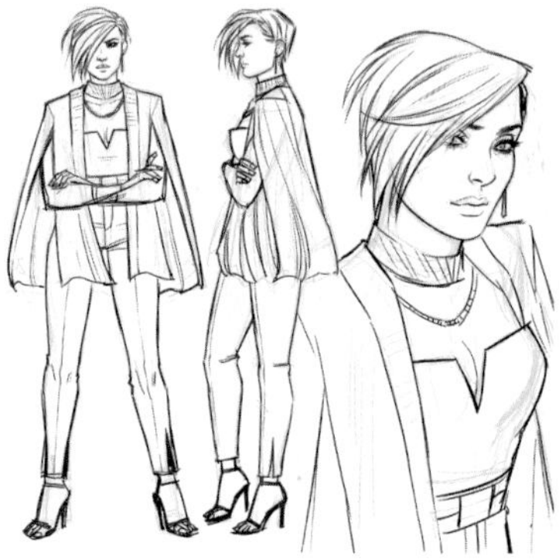

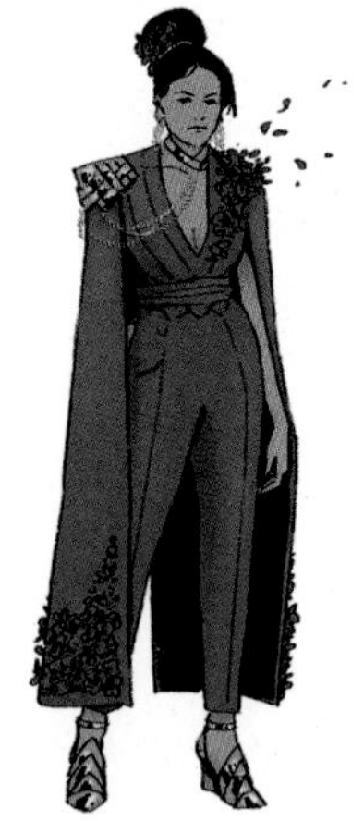

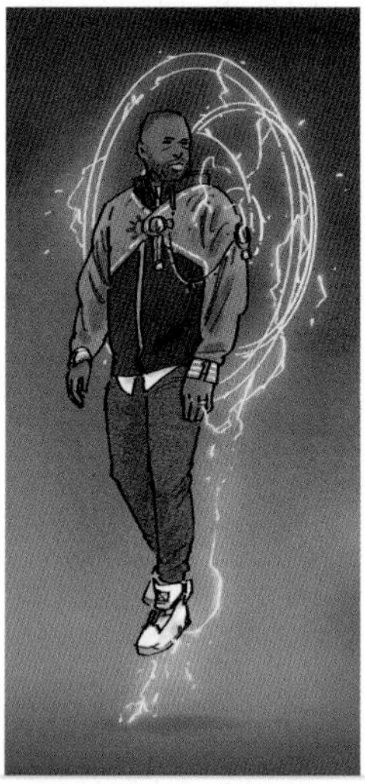

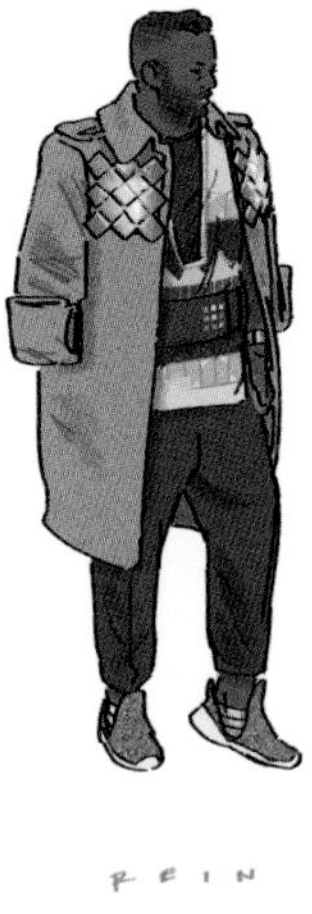
REIN

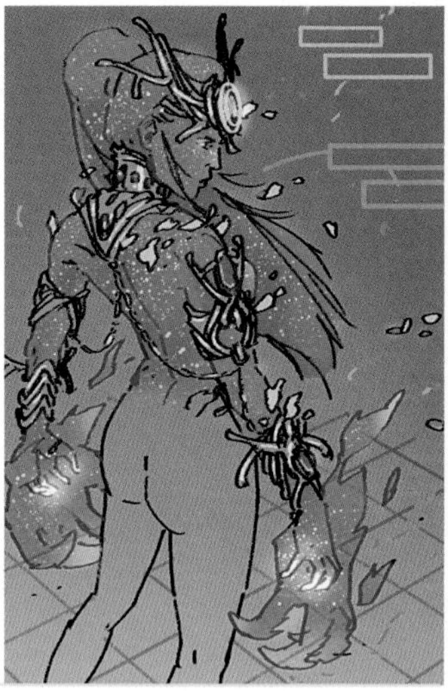

INITIAL CONCEPT ART - CARTER, GLORIA, NINA
BY PAUL REINWAND

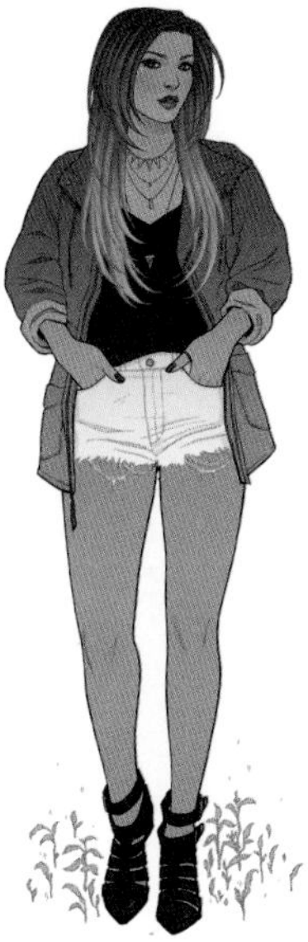
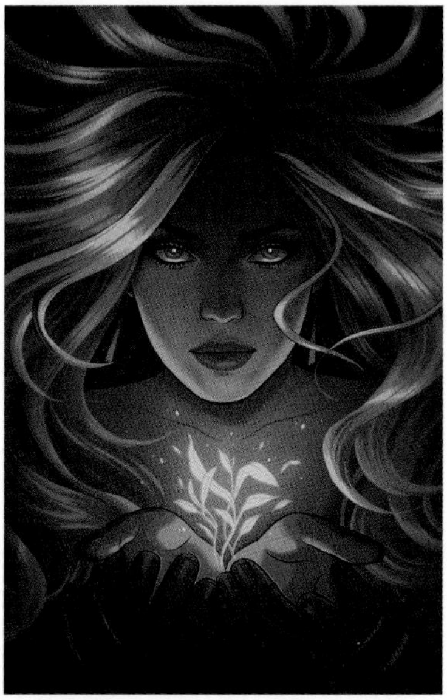
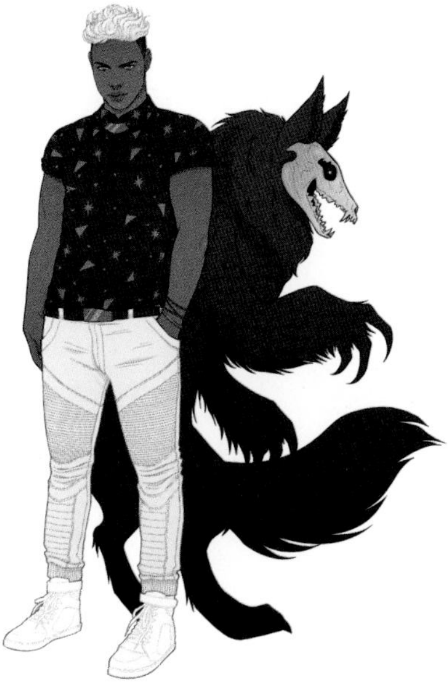
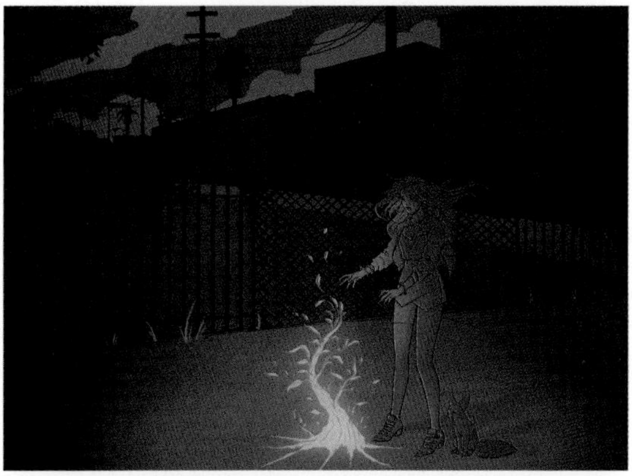
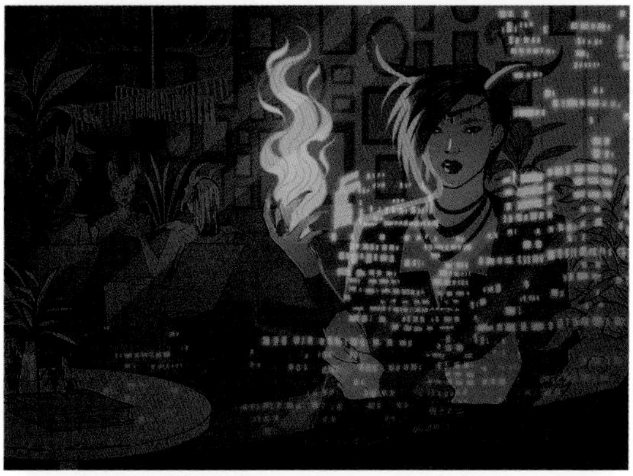
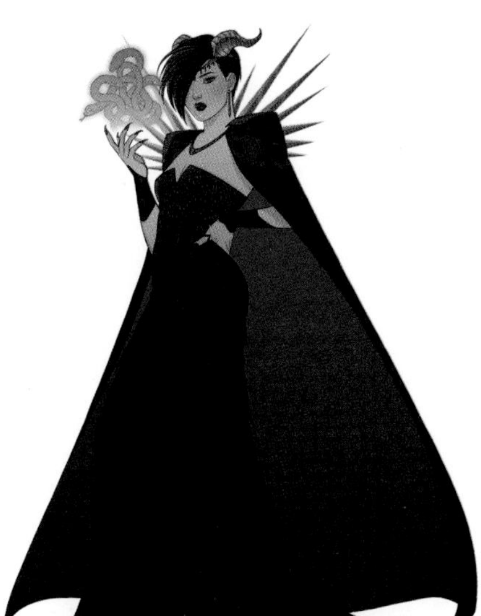
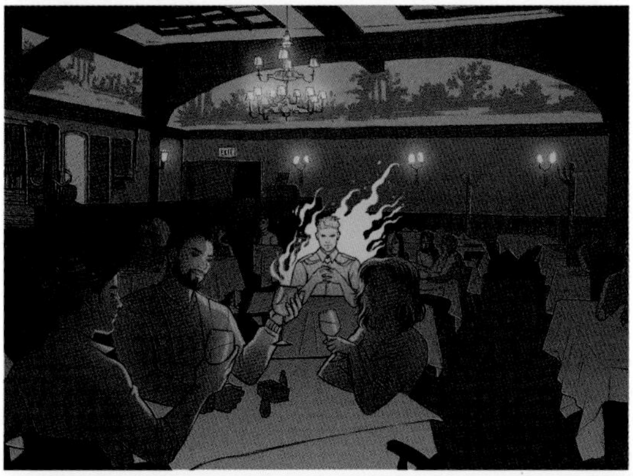

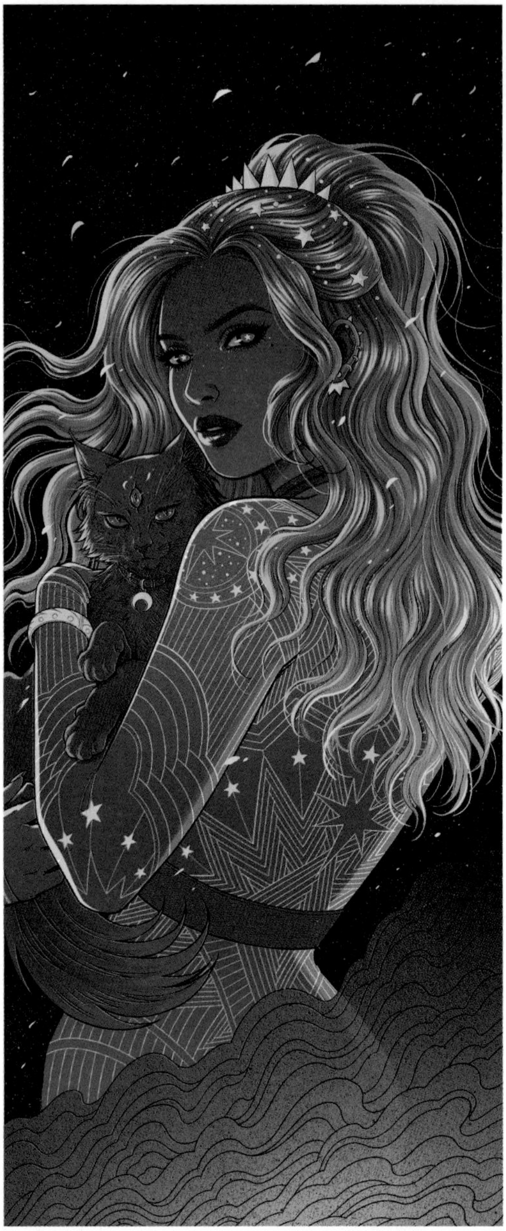

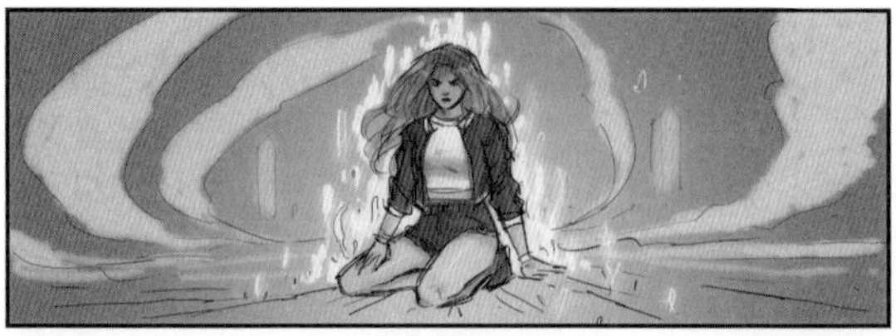

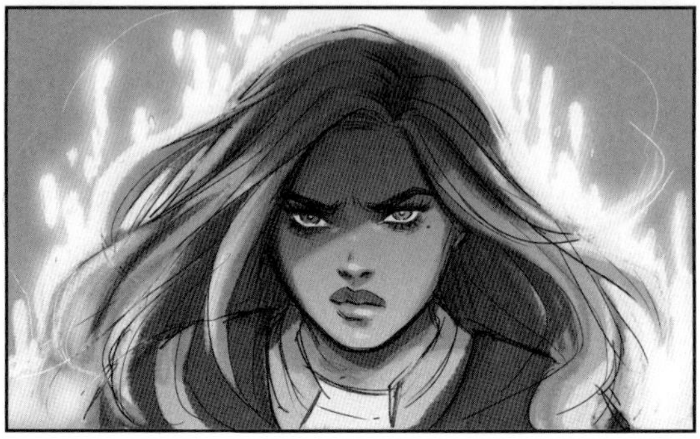

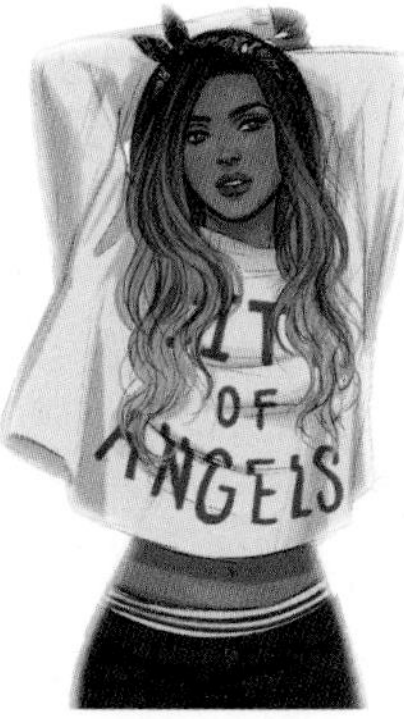

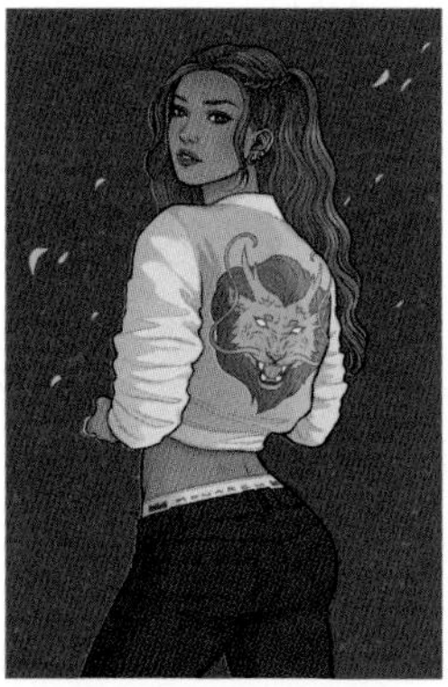

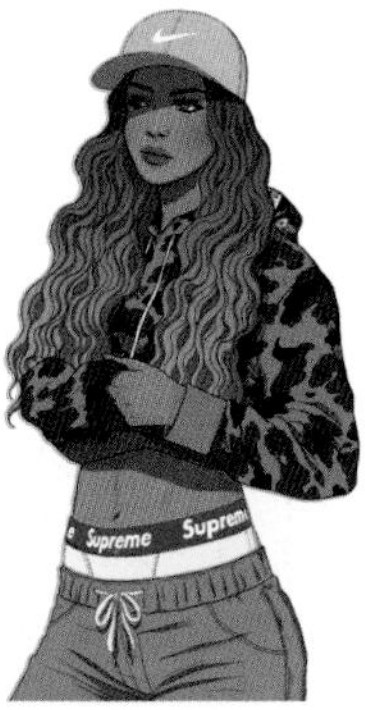
Supreme

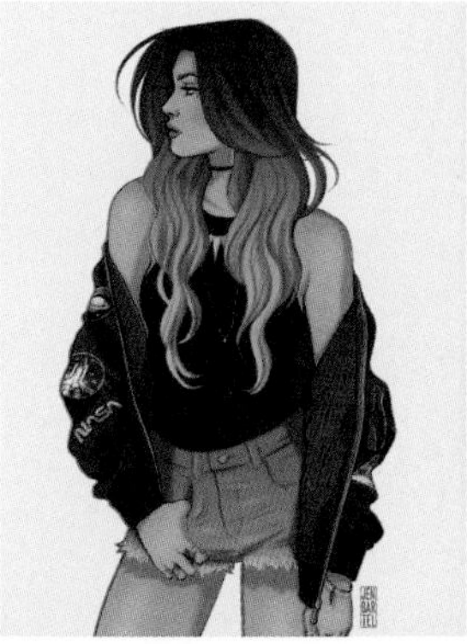

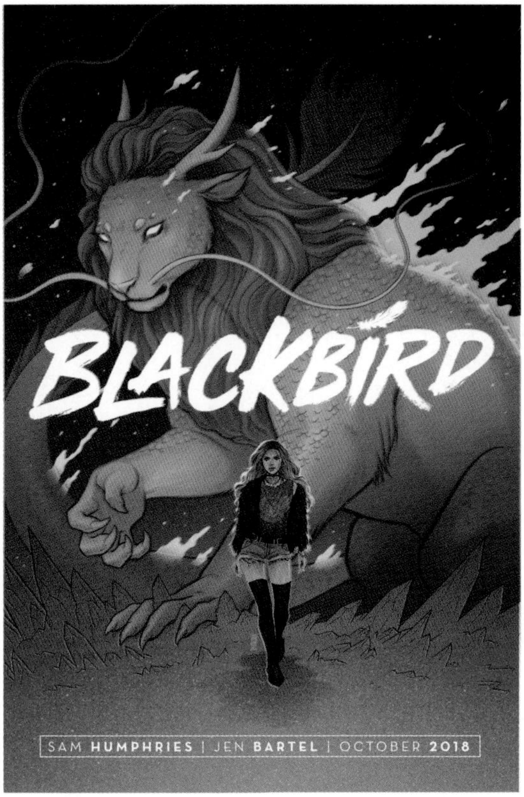
BLACKBIRD
SAM HUMPHRIES | JEN BARTEL | OCTOBER 2018

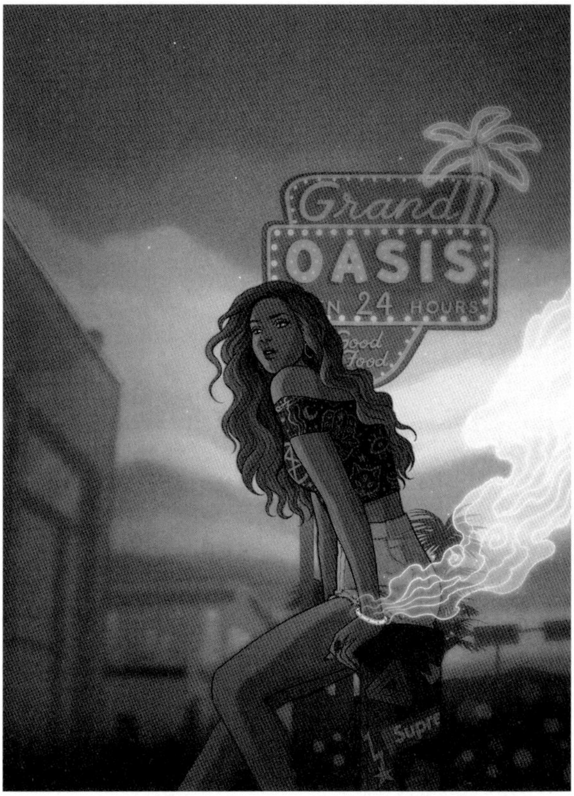
Grand
OASIS
24 HOURS

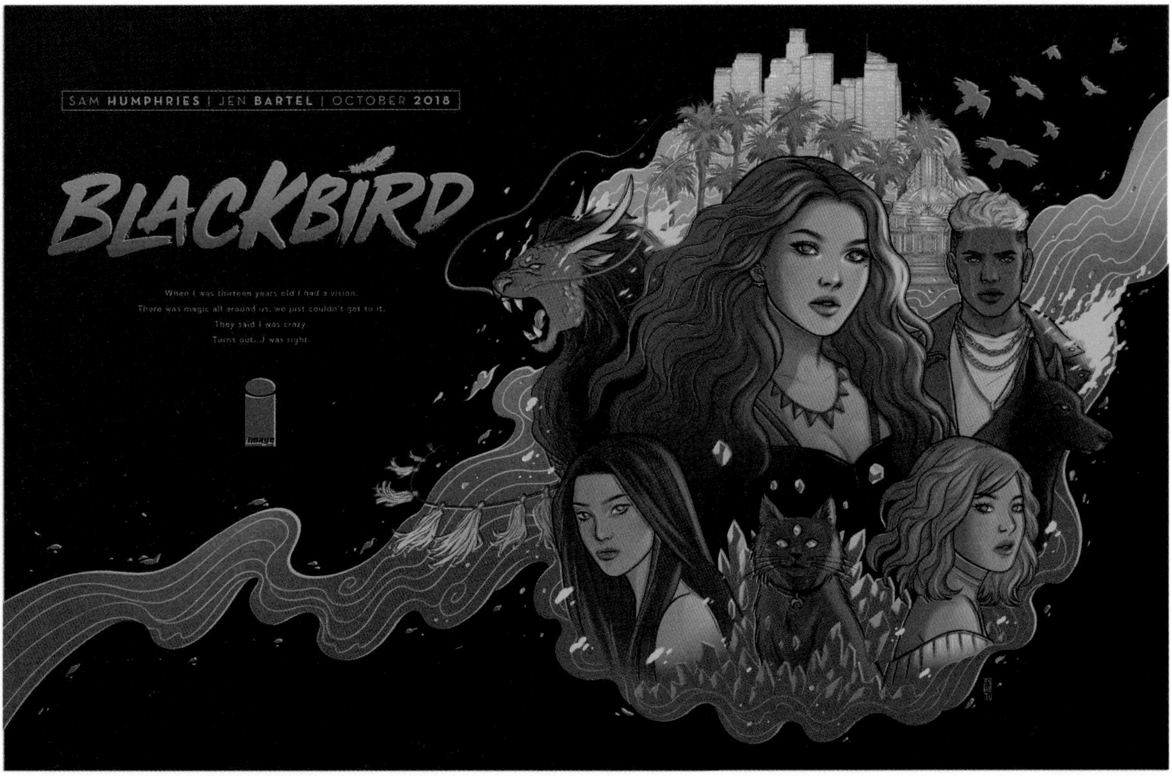
SAM HUMPHRIES | JEN BARTEL | OCTOBER 2018
BLACKBIRD
When I was thirteen years old I had a vision.
There was magic all around us, we just couldn't get to it.
They said I was crazy.
Turns out...I was right.

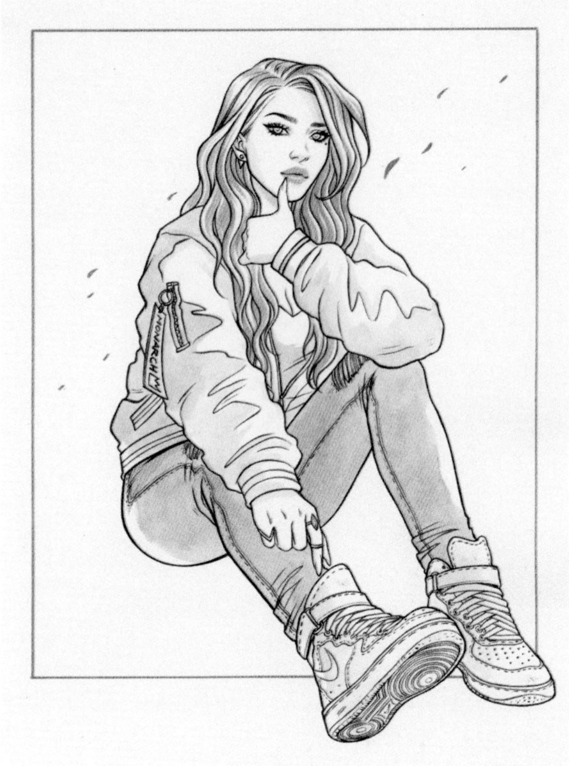

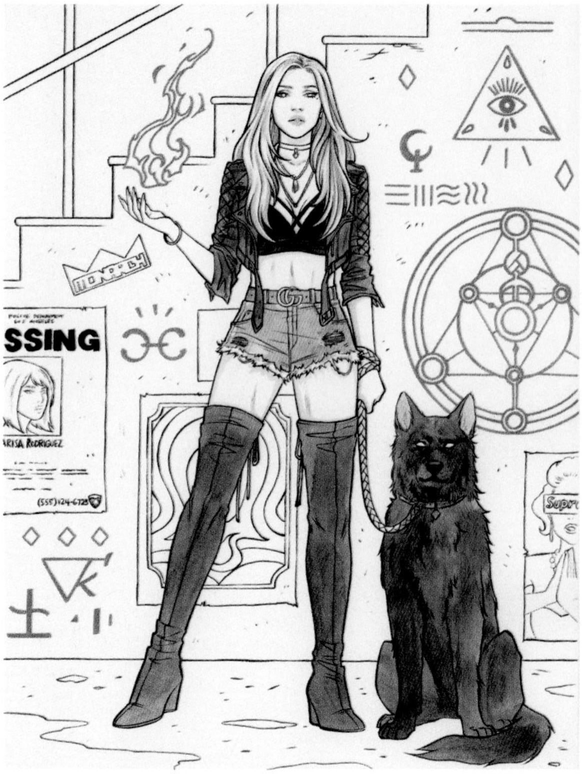
SSING

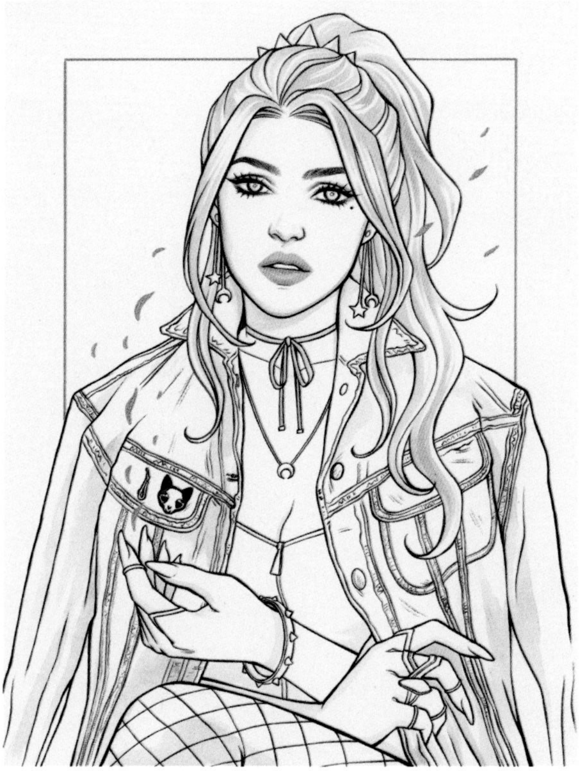

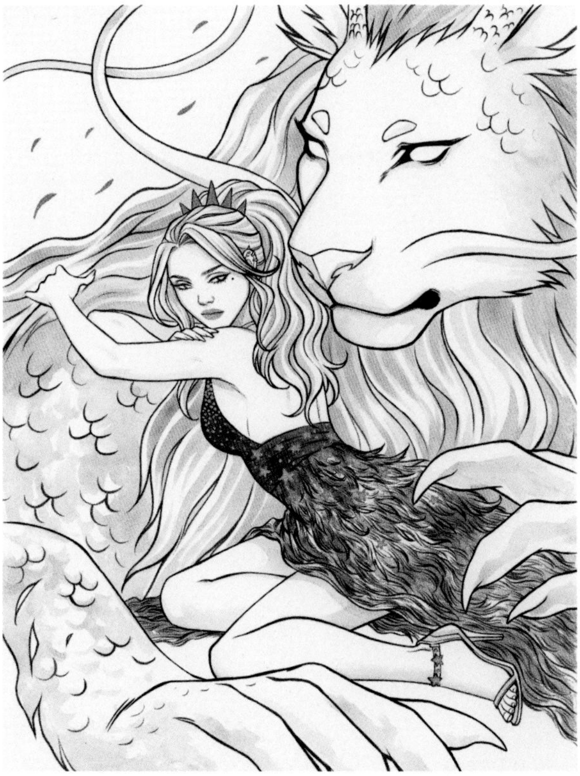

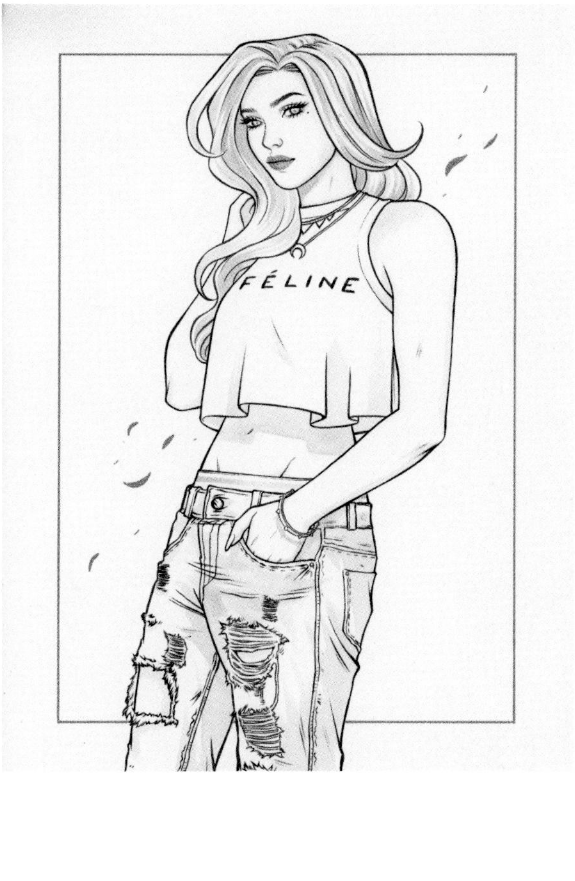
FÉLINE

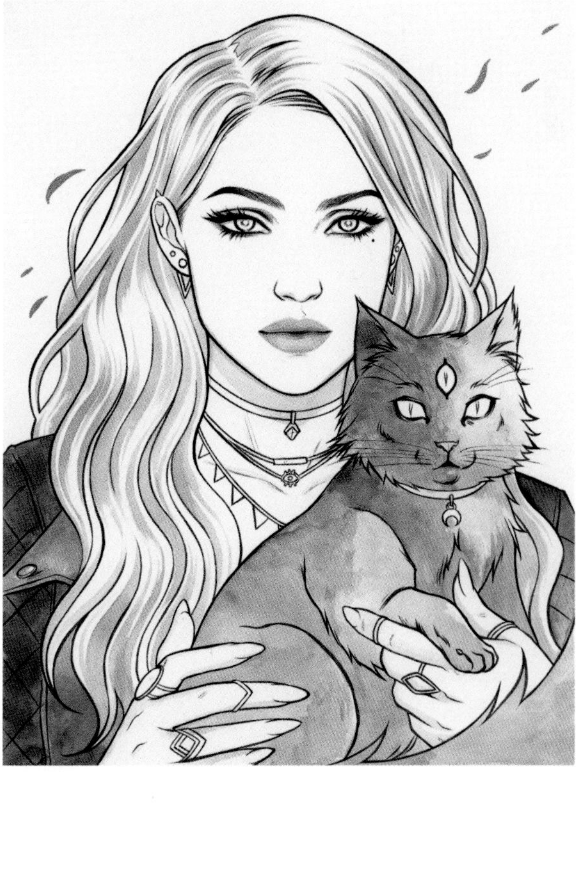

TEAM BLACKBIRD

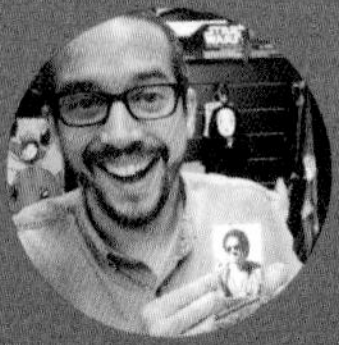

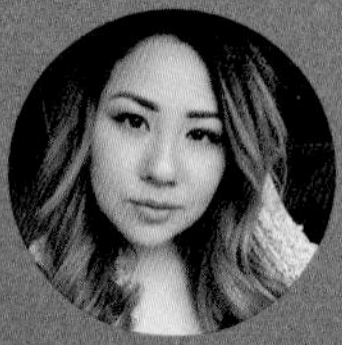

WRITER AND CO-CREATOR
Sam Humphries is the writer of *Harley Quinn*, *Nightwing*, and *Green Lanterns* for DC Comics' blockbuster Rebirth initiative, and co-host of DC Daily, the daily news show of the DC Universe streaming platform. He is also co-creator of *Goliath Girls* with Alti Firmansyah, the first English-language comic to be published simultaneously in Japan. His other comics work includes *Legendary Star-Lord* and *Avengers AI* for Marvel, as well as the original critically acclaimed books *Jonesy* and *CITIZEN JACK*. He lives in Los Angeles with his cat El Niño.

ARTIST, COVER ARTIST, CO-CREATOR
Jen Bartel is an illustrator and comic artist who is best known for her ongoing cover work for clients like Marvel, Disney, and Chronicle Books. She also has worked as an interior artist for many publishers, but *BLACKBIRD* is her first creator-owned book.

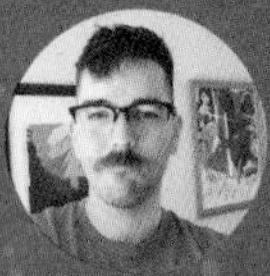

LAYOUT ARTIST
Paul Reinwand draws stuff behind the scenes for comics and games. His clients include Image Comics, Dark Horse Comics, Marvel, Bungie, and 21st Century Fox. He lives in a house made of sweets in the Pacific Northwest with his two plus-sized corgis and bear of a husband.

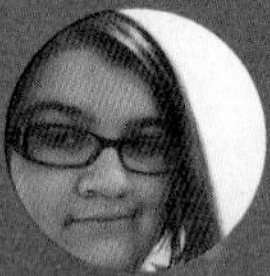

COLORIST
Triona Farrell is a colorist based in Dublin, Ireland. She works with many companies, including Image Comics, Marvel, and Dark Horse Comics. Her credits include *West Coast Avengers*, *Age of X-Men*, *Alpha*, *Crowded*, and *Terminator: Sector War*, as well as *Mech Cadet Yu* which won a Ringo Spirit Award in 2018. She is far too nerdy for her own good and when she's not coloring, she can probably be found gaming in one form or the other.

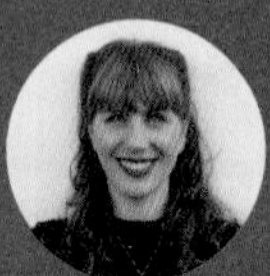

LETTERER
Jodi Wynne is an American letterer who has worked in comics since 2008. Titles include *LAZARUS*, *Wonder Woman*, *BLACK MAGICK*, *THE OLD GUARD*, and *The Ghost In The Shell*. She lives in Southern California with her husband and two children. She can be found online at jodiwynne.com.

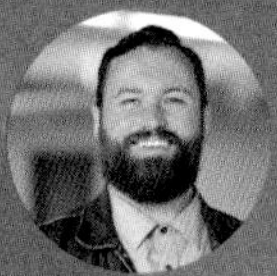

EDITOR
Jim Gibbons is a multiple Eisner and Harvey Award-winning editor for his work on *Dark Horse Presents*. He also edited the Eisner-nominated comics *The Black Beetle*, *Nanjing: The Burning City*, *Deja Brew*, and *Jaeger*, as well as the Harvey Award-nominated *Polar: Came from the Cold*, now a Netflix original film. His writing credits include *Legend of Ninkasi: Rise of Craft*, *Birch Squatch: The Last Bigfoot*, and *Mars: Space Barbarian*. His work has been featured in *Corpus: A Comic Anthology of Bodily Ailments* and *Planetside: A Sci-Fi Slice of Life Comic Anthology*.

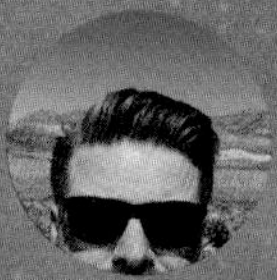

DESIGNER
Dylan Todd is a writer, art director, and graphic designer. You can find his pop culture and comics design portfolio at bigredrobot.net.